THE MEMOIRS OF A RELUCTANT BATSMAN

MEMOIRS OF A RELUCTANT BATSMAN

New Zealand Servicemen in the Fleet Air Arm 1940-45

A O 'Cappy' Masters

JANUS PUBLISHING COMPANY
London, England

First published in Great Britain 1995
by Janus Publishing Company,
Edinburgh House, 19 Nassau Street,
London W1N 7RE

British Library Cataloguing-in-Publication Data
A catalogue record for this book is available from the British Library

ISBN 1 85756 148 1

Cover design Harold King

Printed & bound in England by
Watkiss Studios Ltd,
Biggleswade, Beds

Dedication

This book is dedicated to the memory of three New Zealand Fleet Air Arm pilots who lost their lives during the Second World War.

They are:

Sub-Lieutenant (A) Joseph John Urlich RNZNVR who was killed on 9th September 1943 while returning from the dawn patrol over the Salerno beachhead, Italy.

Sub-Lieutenant Urlich endeavoured to bale out of his Seafire when returning to his carrier HMS *Unicorn* but he had difficulty in abandoning the aircraft and his parachute failed to arrest his fall into the sea;

Lieutenant (A) John Kerle Tipaho Haberfield RNZNVR
and
Lieutenant (A) Evan John Baxter RNZNVR

Both the above officers were shot down while flying as fighter escorts during a bombing and strafing attack on Palembang oil refineries, Sumatra 28th January 1945.

They both successfully abandoned or force landed their aircraft but were later taken prisoners of war by the Japanese.

They were apparently taken to the infamous Changi prison at Singapore, where they were held while the Japanese military authorities deliberated over their fate.

As in the case of the Australian servicemen captured during the 'Krait' expedition to Singapore, these two airmen were apparently accorded the status of enemy heroes.

Under the mystical feudal Samurai warrior code it was considered dishonourable for warriors to be captured and held prisoners of war. Only by death was the warrior eligible to join his ancestors.

A little more than two weeks before Emperor Hirohito ordered his forces to surrender on 17th August 1945, these two New Zealanders were ceremoniously executed in Changi Prison.

The two Japanese officers who were responsible for this ghastly atrocity committed Harakiri (suicide) to escape punishment by the Allied War Crimes Tribunal.

Joe Urlich served in 897 Seafire Squadron with the author. John Haberfield and Evan Baxter were on courses shortly after the author and they had met on several occasions during the war.

It is particularly sad to recall that both Joe Urlich and John

Haberfield were part Maori. Quite possibly they were the only two airmen of Maori descent in the Fleet Air Arm.

Foreword

When I was invited by Cappy Masters to furnish a foreword for his book about New Zealanders who had served in the Fleet Air Arm during the Second World War, my pleas of literary inadequacy and lack of naval background were to no avail.

His persuasive entreaty finally prevailed, and as a fellow New Zealander I concluded that this was a saga of naval aviation that should be recorded for posterity.

My association with the Fleet Air Arm was very temporary. In naval parlance one might describe it as little more than 'a dog watch'. Brief though it was, it certainly had its moments – some quite perilous.

On 9th April 1940 Germany invaded the neutral countries, Denmark and Norway. France and Britain responded spontaneously and despatched an Allied expeditionary force to land at several small ports along the Norwegian coast.

At this time I was serving as a Flight Commander in No 46 Fighter Squadron under the command of Squadron Leader KBB (Bing) Cross (later Air Chief Marshal Sir Kenneth Cross KCB, CBE, DSO, DFC). Our squadron was equipped with Hurricane Mk1 fighters and we were ordered to embark on the aircraft carrier HMS *Glorious* from which we were to fly off to a hastily constructed landing-strip near Tromsö on the northern coast of Norway.

Our first attempt to fly off was aborted because the field was unsafe due to melting ice. The carrier, perforce, had to return to Scapa Flow in the Orkneys where it refuelled and sailed again shortly after. This time, our CO took off, landed, but reported the steel mesh runway was still unsafe for operations. I was ordered to take the remaining aircraft to Bardufoss about 25 miles further north.

This field was very short but it was constructed on a solid foundation.

Our role was provision of fighter cover for the Allied headquarters, and the ships which were disembarking ground troops for the assault on Narvik, then held by the Germans.

One of our sorties was to provide fighter escort for five Walrus amphibians of No 701 Naval Squadron whose task was to bomb a large German munitions dump. The target was situated in a narrow fiord surrounded by near perpendicular cliffs. To drop their bombs the naval pilots would have to virtually dive bomb the target. I couldn't imagine anything more hair-raising than this! However, while we stooged around to intercept any enemy aircraft they hit the target which went up in an enormous explosion.

At about this time the Italians entered the war with their formidable speedy ships, altering the balance of power in the Mediterranean. Also, the Germans were advancing towards the coast of the English Channel and it seemed that nothing could stop them. This would add to the tremendous responsibilities of the Royal Navy and the Royal Air Force at home.

Although we had recaptured Narvik from the Germans and were in control of that northern part of Norway, it was decided, in London, that the Naval and Air resources were not available to keep the supply route open on a long term basis, so we were ordered to disengage the forces at Narvik. With this came the instructions that all military equipment, including aircraft and spares, would have to be destroyed to prevent it from falling into the hands of the enemy.

Our CO 'Bing Cross' was loath to destroy our precious Hurricanes which were so badly needed for home defence. Rather than setting fire to them he suggested that we might take the risk of attempting to land them without a hook on one of the aircraft carriers. The *Ark Royal* having the longer flight deck was the obvious choice, but regrettably her lifts were too narrow to accommodate the wingspan of the Hurricane. So it would have to be the *Glorious.*

Shortly before this expedition took place the Navy had conducted some trials by RAF and FAA pilots to ascertain whether the Hurricane fighter could be operated from a carrier. Presumably there were a number of 'prangs', so it was decided at that stage that the Hurricane was not suitable for carrier operation. Later however, the FAA carried out modifications to this fighter, which was to be used quite extensively in carrier operations even from the small auxiliary carriers.

'Bing' Cross was picked up by a Swordfish torpedo bomber and flown out to the *Glorious* for a discussion with her Captain D'Oyley-Hughes. He wanted to know what was the maximum speed the carrier could produce for landing on. The Captain assured him that he would drive it to the limit so that with a light head wind he could probably muster up to 35 knots over the deck. This would reduce the touch speed of the Hurricane to about 45 knots. 'Bing' decided it was an acceptable risk, so I was ordered to take the first group out. If we could not get in the *Glorious* we were to take our chance either to land on the *Ark Royal* or 'ditch' in the sea alongside one of the destroyers. Not exactly an enviable choice in heavy seas in the Arctic Ocean!

On 6th June a Swordfish was despatched from the *Glorious* to navigate us to the rendezvous.

My first impression when we saw the *Glorious* and her escorts was what any FAA pilot must have felt when confronted with his first deck landing. How on earth am I going to put this aircraft down on the matchbox?

I was preparing for my first approach when I was informed by a member of my flight that his engine was giving trouble. Could he land on first, otherwise he may have to 'ditch'. I could appreciate his concern so let him go first while the rest of us circled around and watched. This pilot was so anxious to get down that he commenced his approach while *Glorious* was still slowly turning in wind. Thankfully he made it. I was next. As I approached, the word Lilliputian came to mind. My view of the *Glorious* as I lined up to approach revealed a 'round down' at the stern which was pitching up and down like a cantering elephant's backside! We had all decided that we had to touch down as near this heaving rump as possible to minimise the chance of overshooting and crashing on the forecastle (the flight deck did not extend right up the bow of the ship).

Prior to leaving Bardufoss I had carried out some urgent tests to reduce the nose heaviness of the Hurricane so that we could use full brake power when we landed on the carrier. I found that a 14lb bag of sand strapped onto the rear fuselage did the trick. This meant that he aircraft was less likely to go over and damage the propellor when we slammed the brakes on. The experiment was a success – all pilots landed on without incident.

Despite this I was to receive a sharp reprimand from Captain D'Oyley-Hughes because one of my pilots had ignored the ship's flags and had landed on before the ship had completely turned into wind! As a sailor he apparently presumed all pilots, RAF and FAA, knew the naval procedure of not attempting to land on until he had hoisted the affirmative flag!

The following day 'Bing' Cross brought out the remaining 7 serviceable Hurricanes, all of which safely landed on the *Glorious* which then shaped course for Scapa Flow.

On 8th June an enemy naval force comprising two battle cruisers, *Scharnhorst* and *Gneisenau*, had suddenly appeared in this area. Their presence had not been detected by aerial reconnaissance and was unknown to the RN Flag Officer at Narvik and to the C-in-C Home Fleet. Our first intimation of their presence was black funnel smoke as they loomed up over the horizon.

Scharnhorst and *Gneisenau* took positions on either quarter and at about 10,000 yards opened fire. The first salvo fell short by about 20 yards but the second penetrated the flight deck setting fire to the several bombed up Swordfish on the flight deck and destroying our Hurricanes in the top hangar. The small calibre guns of the *Glorious* were completely useless against the much heavier German turrets. Shells came in rapid succession and *Glorious*, seriously damaged and ablaze from bow to stern, began to list to starboard. The order 'Prepare to abandon ship' was given followed by the launching of any undamaged boats and Carley floats. I shall never forget the calm, business-like manner in which the officers and men set about this task. The discipline was absolutely superb, there was not the slightest sign of panic. They could have been getting ready for a picnic or a boat race!

The 'abandon ship' had been given while I was below looking for my greatcoat. When I returned all the Carley floats and nearly all the personnel had gone overboard. The Captain and most senior officers had been killed on the bridge so I must have been one of the last to leave the ship. I had no option but to swim, which I did without my lifejacket which I had left hanging over the tail of my Hurricane, then being incinerated in the top hangar. After swimming for some time in the icy water I reached a Carley float and was delighted to find that one of the occupants was my CO 'Bing' Cross. I scrambled on, but soon after dived in to rescue a Royal Marine who I had come to know as 'Geordie'. He had been wounded and was drifting aimlessly past. The time was about 6pm and we now had 29 survivors tightly packed on to our Carley float. All the boats which had been launched had been damaged by shellfire and quickly filled with water.

In the distance we could see one of our own destroyers still firing at her heavier opponents. She finally sank with guns still firing defiantly. What a gallant crew!

After about 4 hours in freezing conditions we had our first death from exposure. At 6 a.m. the following morning only 10 of the original 29 were still alive.

With no food, water or warm clothing the conditions were unbearable. Finally after three nights, we survivors then numbering seven were rescued by a Norwegian fishing boat which took us to the Faroe Islands. One of our number succumbed in the boat and another died after arrival at the Faroes, so only five out of the 29 men on the raft survived the ordeal.

We were eventually taken to Scotland where we spent six weeks in Gleneagles Hospital recovering from the shock, hypothermia and salt water lesions. On being discharged from hospital I was granted six weeks sick leave and then posted to the command of No 266 Spitfire Squadron based at Wittering, near Stamford, where I was to serve during the Battle of Britain.

Although my association with the Fleet Air Arm was of short duration, I guess I could claim to have acquired a practical knowledge of some of the requirements and the risks that are associated with naval aviation. Given a choice, however, I would prefer to land on *terra firma*.

Air Commodore P. G. ('Jamie') Jameson CB, DSO, DFC and bar.

Wellington
New Zealand

Acknowledgements

The author desires to acknowledge the assistance given by numerous people in providing information, photographs and encouragement. Without their generous help it would not have been possible to put together this record of New Zealanders who served in the Air Branch of the Royal Navy during the period 1940–1945.

Firstly, to my contributors:
Don Cameron
Ralph Cocklin
Jack Cramp
The late Arch Foley
Dick Mackie
Alister MacLeod
Gordon Reece
Bill Ryan
Ian Stirling

Secondly, to those former Fleet Air Arm pilots and friends who appraised the manuscript during its various stages and made suggestions, furnished details and corrected copy:

Dr Chum Allen ex NZ Army Medical Corps.
Mr John Bell ex FAA
Mrs Jan Blong
Mr Geoff Bourke ex FAA
Mr Ivor Ellis ex RN
Mr Donald V Fitzpatrick ex FAA
Mr Michael Ffolliott-Foster ex RAF
Mrs Barbara Heslop

Mr Douglas Hill ex FAA
Mr Graham Finlayson ex FAA
Mr John Jellie ex FAA
Mr John Schofield ex NZ Army
Mrs Christine Somerton
Dr Roger Wallis ex FAA
Mr Walter A Ware ex RNZNVR
Mr Jack West
Mr Don Whitwell ex RNZAF
Mrs Nola Whitwell
Mr Haruo Sugita Mayor, City of Owase, Japan
Mrs Sandy Peters
Mrs Ann Evans

who gave unsparingly of their time in typing the manuscript. And finally to my wife Joan for her infinite patience and her remarkable memory for detail and events which took place over 50 years ago.

Introduction

A few months ago, I had the privilege of reading a book recently written by Major Hajo Herman, a much decorated German night fighter leader. At the age of 75 he had decided to record his impressions of stalking British bombers during the night raids on German cities during the Second World War.

It was an enthralling story, but as I read it, the thought occurred to me that perhaps it was not too late for someone to record the experiences of New Zealanders who served in the Air Branch of the Royal Navy – the Fleet Air Arm. To the best of my knowledge no one has previously compiled a book on this subject.

Early in 1940 the Admiralty in London sought the assistance of the New Zealand Government in the recruitment of volunteers for this service. The Royal New Zealand Air Force indicated its willingness to undertake the selection and medical examination of the candidates. The Admiralty was then offered 20 candidates per month for a period of 12 months, subject to all training being provided by the Royal Navy. A short time later the New Zealand Government offered to send up to 250 volunteers in one or more drafts as and when required.

In the interim, the Admiralty had accepted the offer of 20 for the first draft, but requested that the second and subsequent drafts be increased to 40.

On 24th June 1940 a recruiting circular for what was later designated Scheme 'F' was drafted. On entry, recruits would be rated Naval Airmen, 2nd class, and go to England to join HMS *St Vincent*, a training establishment at Gosport, Portsmouth. After initial naval training there they would be advanced to acting Leading Airmen and selected to undergo training as pilots or observers. All who successfully passed these courses would be granted temporary commissions in the Air Branch of the Royal Naval Volunteer Reserve. Those not qualifying either as pilots or observers would be offered transfer to gunner or some other technical rating and be eligible to gain commissioned rank under the conditions applicable to the Navy generally.

The New Zealand Air Board had a long waiting list for entry for the Royal Air Force. As the qualifications for the Fleet Air Arm were in most respects identical, it was decided to select air entries for the Navy from those RAF candidates who wished to be considered. Pay and allowances would be at Royal Navy rates, but the Government would supplement them by payment in New Zealand of the difference between them and the higher New Zealand rates. The first draft of 20 sailed on 9th July 1940, and was followed by a draft 38 strong in August, a third of 37 in September, and a fourth in October.

On 25th November 1940 a draft of 18 Fleet Air Arm recruits sailed from Auckland in the MV *Rangitane*. Two days later, it was intercepted by the German armed raiders *Orion* and *Komet*. The passengers and crew were taken prisoner and the *Rangitane* sunk by gunfire. The Fleet Air Arm recruits were, as usual, travelling in civilian clothes but were shown on the passenger list as naval ratings.

On reaching Emirau Island in the Bismarck Archipelago the raiders, which had by that time become embarrassed by the large number of several hundred prisoners, decided to put them ashore on this island.

Among the prisoners were 12 Royal Air Force personnel in uniform. They were transferred to the *Orion* still in captivity. The Fleet Air Arm volunteers were then invited by the German commander of the raiding force, to give their parole not to bear arms against Germany for the duration of the war. Five of the Fleet Air Arm draft refused to comply, so they too were transferred to *Orion*, taken to Germany where they spent four and a half years as prisoners of war.

The other 13 ratings were put ashore and later returned to New Zealand.

By the end of May 1941 five more drafts totalling 234 recruits had sailed for the United Kingdom. The largest draft of 65 sailed in the *Dominion Monarch* from Auckland on 21st July.

On arrival in the United Kingdom most drafts were met at the port of disembarkation by the New Zealand High Commissioner Hon. (later Sir) William Jordan.

The training for pilots took place in four stages:

(1) Naval indoctrination at HMS *St Vincent*, Portsmouth, England.
(2) Elementary flying training at either Elmdon, near Birmingham or Luton which was later superceded by Sealand in Cheshire. A smaller group were transferred to the United States Naval Air Station at Pensacola, Florida where they did two stages of flying training.
(3) Service flying training at Netheravon, Wiltshire. This course was terminated mid-1941 and transferred to Kingston, on the shore of Lake Ontario, Canada.
(4) Operational training – Fighter pilots at Yeovilton or Henstridge in Somerset, torpedo bomber pilots at Crail and Arbroath, Scotland and amphibian pilots at Poole near Bournemouth.

The percentage of rejection at each stage of training gradually depleted the numbers that qualified. Those who 'dipped' at flying schools were given the opportunity to 'rescrub' as observers.

Of the 65 recruits on 31 Course at HMS *St Vincent*, six elected to become observers, eight went to Pensacola, 21 went to Luton and later Sealand, 20 went to Elmdon with ten failing the indoctrination course. Some of these subsequently qualified for commissions in the seaman branch.

Further rejections at EFTS and SFTS reduced the number of pilots who graduated to 42.

Following the operational training unit, pilots were then posted to either the first line operational fighter or bomber squadrons or to fleet requirements squadrons which specialised in transport, communications, target towing, some coastal patrol work, anti-aircraft gun calibration, air sea rescue etc.

Having completed their EFTS and SFTS training under the Royal Air Force instruction the trainee pilots would then be given operational instruction from experienced naval pilots. Because the operation of aircraft from carriers required special skills and techniques, a lot of what was learnt under RAF instructors had to be supplanted by the requirements of naval aviation.

One aspect, in particular, where a specialised skill had to be developed was in deck landings. Under RAF instructors, Fleet Air

Arm cadets had been taught to fly their circuits when preparing to land at 1000 feet. This was drastically reduced to no more than 200 feet at the Naval Operational Training School. Also, no longer would pilots tend to glide down with plenty of safety speed to land on the runway. At the Naval OTU the approach speed and margin of safety was reduced to no more than five knots above stalling speed. The aircraft also had to approach in a 'tail down' attitude with plenty of power on the engine. The difference was, that to be successful at carrier landings, the pilot was required to virtually lower his aircraft on to a pitching or rolling deck at a few knots above the stalling speed. This would enhance his prospects of the tail hook catching an arrester wire and prevent the possibility of crashing into the barrier or worse still going over the side into the 'drink'.

Inevitably, with these demands, the accident rate was very high. A naval pilot would be authorised to carry out his first deck landing only after completing 100 or more ADDLS (assisted dummy deck landings) on an aerodrome. Despite all precautions the crash rate was fearful. The Firth of Forth where most initial deck landings were carried out must be a veritable graveyard for naval aircraft and unfortunately for many young airmen.

Specific details recently obtained from New Zealand National Archives:

(1) The total number of volunteers from 12/7/1940 to 6/6/1945 was 1066.
(2) 260 volunteers who left New Zealand after January 1944 had not completed their training and were unavailable for operations.
(3) 152 were killed.
(4) As at 1/9/1944 – 145 had failed to meet the minimum standard for pilots and navigators.

The fatalities on 31 Course totalled nine, six pilots and three observers.

New Zealanders were prominent in the list of awards with one DSO, 39 DSC (two with bars), one DFC, three MBE, 48 Mentions in Despatches and two letters of commendations.

Lieutenant Commander (A) A. R. Richardson was recommended for a posthumous Victoria Cross for exceptional courage during an attack on the German Battleship *Tirpitz* while it was sheltering in Alten Fiord, Norway 1944.

The recommendation was endorsed by no less a person than Admiral Sir Bruce Fraser, Commander in Chief of Home Fleet, but regrettably it was disallowed by the Awards Authority. Instead a posthumous mention in despatch was then awarded.

31 Course may have been slightly below average with one DSC and four mentions in despatches. But with all service awards it is usually a case of being in the right place, doing the right thing, at the right time.

Fleet Air Arm operations took place in many parts of the world during the 1939–1945 period.

Early operations, such as the Norwegian campaign, the Battle of Britain, the sinking of the Bismarck etc, were supported by permanent naval officers, of whom 55 served in fighter squadrons during the Battle of Britain, some being temporarily seconded to RAF squadrons.

The other theatres of war included the Atlantic, the Mediterranean, Russian convoys, Malta convoys and Malta island defence, the second Front invasion of France, the Western Desert in support of the Eighth Army, Madagascar, the invasion of French North Africa, Sicily, Italy, South France, the Aegean Sea, Indian Ocean, the Andaman Islands, Palembang and Sourabaya in Sumatra and finally the Okinawa campaign and the final assault on the Japanese mainland.

The representation of aircrew was predominantly British and New Zealand, with a few personnel from Canada, South Africa and Southern Ireland. There were at least two fighter squadrons comprising Free French and Dutch naval airmen. A small number of Australians were recruited from the Royal Australian Air Force just prior to the cessation of hostilities.

During the period of war the Royal Navy had in service 14 Fleet carriers, five light fleet carriers, 44 escort carriers, three seaplane carriers, two maintenance carriers, 1 trials carrier and 19 merchant aircraft carriers.

This is the story of a typical group of young New Zealanders who joined this unique service.

11.25 a.m. 8th May 1945

I was controlling the landing of a Seafire aircraft of 887 Fighter Squadron returning from a combat patrol to HMS *Indefatigable*.

My 'looker' (a leading naval airman who is appointed to assist the Batsman) has just reported in sequence, 'undercarriage down – flaps down hook down – no damage.' The looker examines each aircraft through his binoculars and assesses the condition and assures the batsman that the pilot has completed his pre-landing routine.

A moment later he screamed: 'Look out sir – there's a bloody Jap diving at us – get off the deck!'

We had previously been alerted over the carrier's internal communication system 'Tannoy' that the fleet's radar had detected a large force of enemy aircraft approaching from Formosa (now Taiwan).

A second progress report indicated that this raid was still heading in our direction.

Its ETA (estimated time of arrival) would closely coincide with the flying off and landing on of our next strike of bombers and CAP fighters.

On hearing this urgent call from my 'looker', I momentarily looked away from the approaching Seafire and there to my horror I saw an aircraft at about 8000 ft diving directly towards our deck.

Although this was my first experience of a kamikaze (suicide) attack I knew that the Japanese pilot would aim his aircraft to strike the most vulnerable part of the carrier. This would be either the 'island' (the bridge from where the ship is commanded) or the 'round down' (the area of the flight deck where aircraft take off and land on). A kamikaze strike on the 'round down' could also damage the ship's steering control.

Prior to my 'looker's' warning there had been no announcement that an element of the kamikaze force was overhead. I quickly returned attention to the approaching Seafire and moved to the centre of the deck to give him an urgent wave off.

The pilot himself was obviously unaware of the menacing situation but happily he reacted promptly to my signal and veered off to starboard and raised his undercarriage.

As I dived towards the batsman's shelter, I realised that the flight deck behind me was completely deserted. Everyone had gone for cover. I was the last to leave. I guess that is an occupational hazard of a batsman.

Once under the protection of the armour plated section of the flight deck which had resisted earlier kamikaze attacks, I could not ignore the opportunity of a grandstand view of proceedings.

Coinciding with my departure from the flight deck the four stern turrets, each two 4.5 inch multi purpose guns (two turrets port, two starboard), opened fire on the enemy aircraft.

I have since been informed that each of these guns could discharge about ten shells a minute, making a total fusillade of 80 per minute from the four turrets.

From our position only about 20 feet behind the rear port turret the noise of the guns was excruciating.

Although I did not realise it at the time, the reverberation from this incredible rate of fire burst both my eardrums – an injury which I have suffered from ever since.

What followed however, was the most spectacular incident that I had ever witnessed during my naval career.

One of the guns scored a direct hit on the Jap aircraft and removed a large section of his port main plane. The aircraft staggered and looked as if it was going to dive into the sea behind us, but miraculously the Japanese pilot recovered control and regained some height.

By this time, he had to abort his attack on our carrier as his diving angle was obviously now too flat. Undeterred, however, he quickly changed direction and headed to starboard and launched an alternative attack on HMS *Formidable.*

This carrier had just recently joined the British Pacific Fleet – Force 57, and was not fully worked up. *Formidable* was somewhat slower in flying off strikes and recovering aircraft than the other fleet carriers, *Indomitable, Victorious* and *Indefatigable.*

While we had completed our flying off operations, *Formidable* still had a sizeable range of Avengers and Corsairs ready to take the air.

This was now the target for the Japanese kamikaze pilot and he obviously relished the opportunity to join his ancestors.

He hit *Formidable* in its most vulnerable part – right in the middle of the deck park of Corsairs.

The explosion was enormous. A monstrous cloud of flame and dense black smoke erupted from *Formidable*'s round down. It had obviously been severely damaged because it immediately lost steerage and turned to starboard away from the fleet's line of advance.

Eventually *Formidable* accompanied by several protective

destroyers disappeared over the horizon. It subsequently transpired that the kamikaze explosion had severely damaged her flight deck and arrester gear.

In his book *Action This Day* the late Admiral Sir Philip Vian GCB, KBE, DSO, reports this incident as follows: 'the 20 millimetre shell with which it (the kamikaze) was hit failed to divert it. It plunged down to crash on the flight deck where its bomb exploded. Fifty men were killed or wounded in the explosion, a large fire was started amongst the aircraft parked on the deck, eleven of them being destroyed. The flight deck was holed and dented to a depth of two feet. Out of the smoke and flames rising from his ship came a short signal from Captain Ruck-Keene of the *Formidable*, flashed by Aldis lamp, 'Little yellow bastard.'

Vian's reply was typical: 'Are you addressing me?'

I would not presume to question our highly respected Admiral's version of the incident. It is possible that this aircraft was hit by some gunfire from the *Formidable*, but undoubtedly the damage inflicted by our rear turrets caused it to change direction from the *Indefatigable* and concentrate on the *Formidable*.

It is perhaps interesting to recall that this was the second occasion during the war that I had served under the command of Admiral Philip Vian and likewise in a carrier commanded by Capt. Q. D. Graham of the *Indefatigable*. The previous episode was operation 'Avalanche', code name for the seaborne invasion of Italy at Salerno on 9th September 1943.

Admiral Vian had established a reputation early in the war when in command of the destroyer HMS *Cossack*. On 16th February 1940 he led a small flotilla of destroyers into a very narrow Joessing Fiord in northern Norway to release some 300 British seamen who were held in the German prison ship *Altmark*.

Following the *Altmark* affair, which in German eyes had all the elements of piracy at sea, Admiral Vian was singled out for rapid promotion.

Having had no prior experience with aircraft carriers it was a stupendous challenge and a calculated risk to give him command of the carrier force of one light fleet carrier HMS *Unicorn* and four Woolworth carriers *Hunter, Stalker, Battler* and *Attacker* for the Salerno operation.

The secret of his success was his ability to communicate. His personal briefing in Malta Harbour to all aircrew involved in the Salerno operation was a real masterpiece. Every pilot from Wing Leaders, to junior sub-lieutenants knew precisely what was expected of them. It was the real Nelson touch.

Although he flew his flag in HMS *Indomitable* during operation 'Iceberg' against the Sakashima Gunto attacks, he was always in close touch with the activities of flying personnel in the other four carriers *Illustrious, Victorious, Formidable, Indefatigable* and later the *Implacable*. He made it his job to know many airmen of junior rank and was spontaneous in dispatching signals to acknowledge outstanding performances in the air.

One particularly memorable incident in May 1945 was his recommendation of the immediate award of the DSO to a very modest New Zealand fighter pilot, Lieut (A) Alex McCrae RNZNVR.

This was a very high decoration for a junior officer. It was a typical spontaneous Vian gesture.

Capt Q. D. Graham of the *Indefatigable* was a big raw-boned Irishman who appeared to be somewhat taciturn by nature. Although undoubtedly an accomplished seaman, he gave the impression that under desperate circumstances, he might be inclined to use his carrier as he would a cruiser. One of his compatriots was Capt. G. D'Oyly-Hughes (a former submariner from World War I who had been awarded the DSO as a lieutenant for a particularly meritorious exploit in the Sea of Marmora). Captain D'Oyly-Hughes was in command of the aircraft carrier *Glorious* when it was intercepted on 8th June 1940 and sunk by a superior German force comprising the battle cruisers *Scharnhorst, Gneisenau* and the cruiser *Hipper*. Following this disaster rumours spread that D'Oyly-Hughes consistently rejected the advice of his commander (Flying) and seemed to be obsessed with the prospect of adding a VC to his DSO and DSC.

School Days

I was born at Stratford, New Zealand on 7th November 1920. I attended Stratford Primary School and for two years (1933–34) Stratford High School. I was generally a year younger and consequently smaller in stature than my classmates, but despite this, I had an enthusiastic interest in all sports, rugby, cricket, tennis and swimming. These were the days of the Depression and although I was unable to comprehend the reasons for the economic débâcle, I was conscious of some of my schoolmates who were living in appalling poverty. A lot of children in those days were poorly clothed, went barefooted and had only a minimal diet. I can recall many children from impoverished families being sent to school wearing parts of sugar bags, no footwear and if they were lucky a piece of flour bag for a handkerchief. There were many snotty noses and smelly children around in those sad days.

Many years later at a school reunion one former pupil whose family were in very poor circumstances confessed that her days at primary school were most unpleasant. She had been subjected to ridicule by fellow pupils and a certain prejudice by some teachers. Human beings can be quite callous and uncaring. I was one of the fortunate ones, my father owned a fairly large department store which traded in groceries, farm supplies, bread, hardware etc. There was always a plentiful supply of wholesome food on our table. A family who lived over the road from us were not so lucky. The father, an ex-serviceman from the First World War was unemployed and on relief work. What money he did earn seemed to be spent in the hotel and his poor wife and children were left to survive in the worst conditions imaginable. This did leave an impression on me because I knew that I was one of the privileged. My sister and I frequently sneaked apples and other titbits to give to our poor friends over the road.

It was during this period that I developed an intense interest in rugby football. This was inevitable considering that my father had represented Wanganui and his two brothers Taranki. Harold the youngest became an All Black in 1923.

Probably because I had a propensity to organise unofficial rugby games with the local boys, someone coined the nickname 'Cappy'. This nickname has remained with me ever since. Through primary school, Stratford High, New Plymouth Boys High, Victoria University, the NZ Territorial Army and finally the Fleet Air Arm there was always a group of acquaintances who only knew me as 'Cappy' Masters. At times nicknames can be an embarrassment because there are people who know you only by your given christian name and others only by your nickname. So occasionally I would have some school headmasters and senior naval officers referring to me by my nickname while with others it would be the christian name.

It was about this time that I became intensely interested in the history of World War I. My father joined the elite brigade of the NZ Army – the NZ Rifle Brigade. His first day in action was Christmas Day 1915 at Mersa Matruh in Egypt when the Brigade was fighting against the Senussi Arabs who were led by German and Turkish officers. They defeated the Arabs and withdrew to a camp at Cairo. My father was then seconded to an Officers Training Unit near Alexandria. By then his brother Harold arrived in Egypt. Harold had enlisted in the Divisional Signallers, and somehow persuaded my father to withdraw from the OTU and join his unit.

They sailed to France together and some time later joined forces with the British and Australian Armies on the Somme.

The two brothers entered the front line trenches on the Somme front on about 14th September 1916. Their position was just a few hundred yards east of the village of Longueval.

Before dawn on 16th September my father was detailed as a member of a party of eight signallers to go out into No Man's Land behind the front line trench to restore breaks in the telephone wires caused by shell bursts.

They stayed out in No Man's Land until about 2 p.m. when a German or a short British shrapnel shell burst immediately overhead. My father was the only one of the eight who survived.

When the wiring party failed to return to the front line trench, his brother Harold, at that time a sergeant, mustered a team of volunteers to crawl out in broad daylight, through the mud and slush of shell craters full of water, to ascertain what had happened.

Harold and his team found the wiring party. Only my father seemed to be alive but desperately wounded in the head.

The party then crawled back to the front line dragging my father behind them.

A doctor at the regimental aid post pronounced my father to be beyond medical assistance. Head wounds such as he had suffered were beyond the normal medical skills of the time.

Undeterred, Harold pleaded with the doctor to send him back to a field ambulance post. The outcome was that after five days unconsciousness he finally arrived at Balmer Lawn Hotel, Brockenhurst, Hampshire. This gracious old hotel had been converted into a military hospital for very seriously wounded NZ and Canadian Servicemen.

In the intervening period, he had survived what was in those times a miraculous cranial operation to remove fragments of bone which had been crushed into his skull by the shrapnel blast. Thence by hospital train to Calais or Boulogne, hospital ship to Southampton and another hospital train to Brockenhurst.

After a lengthy convalescence he returned to NZ, married in 1920, pursued an active career in business and died at the ripe old age of 73 years.

My father had acquired an excellent set of nine volumes on the war history. I was enthralled with the exploits of soldiers, sailors and airmen. I revelled in the stories of the fighter pilots Mannock, Ball, McCudden, Bishop, Harker, von Richtofen, Boelke, Immelman and sailors like Evans of the *Broke*, Jellicoe and Beattie.

It was also about this time that two memorable movie films were produced in Hollywood. One was entitled *Hell's Angels*, starring Richard Arlen. The fact that it may have been a silent film did not detract from the glamorous exploits of Allied and German fighter pilots.

Another was *The Last Days of the Emden*.

The *Emden* was a German light cruiser commanded by Kapitan Karl von Muller. It had been despatched from Germany to intercept and destroy British merchant ships in the Indian Ocean. It was finally brought to battle and sunk by HMAS *Sydney* under the command of Capt J. C. T. Glossop off Cocos Island on 9th November 1914.

On 1st July 1989, seventy three years after the first Battle of the Somme, my wife and I joined a small tour party led by a well known war historian, Martin Middlebrook, and spent four enthralling days visiting battle sites and cemeteries in the Somme area. Our party stayed in a modest hotel in Albert which was the focal point of the battle which raged from 1st July 1916 until November 1918.

Martin Middlebrook knew precisely the sector of the front that was held by the NZ Rifle Brigade near the village of Longueval and flanked on the right by Deville Wood which was heroically defended by South African troops.

Today it is difficult to believe that in the first hour of this long drawn out battle over 30,000 British and Empire troops were killed or wounded!

The total casualties on the Somme front were over 1,300,000, fairly equally divided between the German and Allied Armies. Conceived by the British and French General Staff and led by Field Marshal Sir Douglas Haig as the big push to end the war, it turned into a ghastly battle of attrition that finally ended on 11th November 1918.

The 3rd of February 1931 is a day that will for ever be remembered by New Zealanders of my age.

At precisely 1046 hours 23 seconds the twin cities of Napier and Hastings were devastated by an earthquake of magnitude 7.9 on the Richter scale.

The epicentre was at Bay View about five miles north of Napier. The damage was extensive. From Wairoa in the north to Dannervirke in the south buildings, schools, hospitals, bridges, railways, roads and private homes were destroyed.

With 258 people killed it was the biggest natural disaster in NZ history.

The time of the earthquake coincided with morning interval in most schools. At Stratford Primary we had, in fact, completed the interval and a teacher was taking us for physical training on the tennis court. We were facing north when suddenly I felt rather giddy as if I were going into a faint.

Now this was about the worst period of the Depression so it was not uncommon to see children fainting. This was due to malnutrition and consequent lack of stamina. As I looked ahead the telephone wires seemed to be heaving up and down and the posts swaying from left to right. This was a faint all right but somehow I had still managed to stay on my feet! The teacher then appealed for calm, stating that what was happening was a much larger than usual earthquake.

At Taradale about four miles west of Napier, a ten year old girl Joan Rees, with 40 other children, was fighting to get through the door of the standard 4 classroom. In fear and panic one of the boys pushing behind her screamed, 'it's the end of the world.'

The quake hit Taradale with a devastating force. Part of the school collapsed and some of the children were trapped inside and killed.

Joan's father, then the secretary of the Napier Hospital Board also had a very narrow escape. The hospital was somewhat closer to the epicentre and the loss of life here was quite heavy.

Even at that young age I guess I displayed the characteristics of a rebel. I can recall two incidents in particular.

When I went off to school each day my mother would frequently admonish me not to get my feet wet. When these warnings were given in the presence of friends I was naturally inclined to resentment. On one such occasion my friend Neville Turnbull and I were struggling home from school, and contrary to instructions we were wading along the gutter which was full of mud and water. I was obviously going to be in trouble when I arrived home. Just at that time two young girls about the same age were casually wending their way home on the footpath. Turnbull said something rather provocative to them, whereupon a precocious little girl Jean 'A' retorted quite sharply – 'I wouldn't turn the bull in your trousers, Turnbull, for all the tea in China.'

I was speechless – how on earth did a young girl of seven know about the 'apparatus' that Turnbull had concealed in his trousers! This was one of my first encounters with the opposite sex and obviously I was on the side of innocence.

The second incident I recall was a settlement of a dispute by fisticuffs. In those days it was quite common for boys of my age to settle their differences by primitive jungle law. Something had erupted between me and a boy named Terry Tocker. Terry was the one offended so he challenged me to a duel. It was accordingly arranged that we should meet after school at Victoria Park which was just over the road from school. The news of the impending bout spread like wildfire. When school adjourned in the afternoon dozens of youths were seen making a beeline for a bushy place in the park. The two contenders appeared – adrenalin flowing and mouthing suitable insults. Despite the usual nervousness I knew how to defend myself because we had been having boxing lessons in our Boy Scout troop. I knew that the rules barred any 'underhand' tactics, kicking, biting etc. We set to and hammered away at each other, Terry scored a few and I planted him in the appropriate places. To be hit by a bare fist can be quite painful but neither of us was tempted to give in. Anyway somehow the scrap came to an end and after shaking hands we withdrew to take stock of the wounds. I knew Terry had hit me a beauty in the eye because it was already puffy. By the time I arrived home it was closed and rather black, so this called for some explanation. What does one do with a son who persistently gets into trouble?

An incident which further crystallised my interest in aeroplanes was the second flight across the Tasman by the late Sir Charles Kingsford-Smith. On his first crossing on 11th September 1928 he and his crew landed at Wigram aerodrome Christchurch but on this occasion, the large tri-motor Fokker monoplane *Southern Cross* landed in the grass aerodrome at New Plymouth.

In his book *My Flying Life*, Sir Charles described the arrival at New Plymouth in the following passage:

> We were never off our course; in fact, we were dead on it, as appeared when, a few minutes after Taylor had said something about 'seeing Mt. Egmont soon,' we saw it. Mt. Egmont is a magnificent landmark on the west coast of New Zealand, over 8000 feet high, snow-capped, bold and conspicuous, and altogether a wonderful sight for airmen coming from the west.
>
> When the trans-Tasman airman sees Mt. Egmont, he knows that all his troubles are over, and so were ours, as we circled round over the New Plymouth aerodrome, where a crowd of 15,000 had gathered to watch our landing.
>
> The next day we began our 'joy-riding' programme.
>
> We were as successful in this venture as on our tour in Australian States. Everybody wanted a flight in the famous old plane, and we were all kept busy supplying the demand. In the North Island of New

> Zealand alone we carried 2000 passengers, and we had similar good business in the South Island. This was the first venture of its kind in Australia or New Zealand.

If his estimate of 15,000 people was even approximately correct, it would have been equivalent to the total population of the town of New Plymouth.

The following day, 13th January 1933, even greater numbers wended their way, by train, car, bus, horse and cart to the New Plymouth aerodrome which was about 26 miles from my home in Stratford. My father packed the family in his *Essex* car and joined the pilgrimage.

Shortly after our arrival it was announced over the public address system that Kingsford-Smith would be giving flights to groups of about 24 people at a time, over the town and harbour area at ten shillings per trip, which in those days was quite a lot of money.

It was the opportunity of a lifetime and my father took me aside and posed the question. 'Would I like to fly in the *Southern Cross*?'

Well how many lads of 12 years could decline?

This really made my day – it was a very proud moment.

At Stratford High School I was in the classical form taking three languages – English, French and Latin, Maths, General Science, History, Agriculture and Dairy Science. The school was a technical high school and specialised in a farm training curriculum. The Principal Mr A. H. R. Amess and his assistant Mr H. C. Johnson were both recognised as authorities in this sphere. Although I was a year younger than the average I performed reasonably well in all subjects and was usually in the top three of the class. I particularly liked the practical aspect of the agricultural and farm subjects: I was in fact so keen on the farming studies that for two years in succession I won the Friesian cow judging contest for secondary school pupils at the Stratford A & P show. To beat the sons of farmers was rather an achievement.

At the end of my second year my family moved to New Plymouth where I was enrolled as a day boy at New Plymouth Boy's High School. I will never forget that day in January 1935 when I was taken by my parents for an interview with the Headmaster, Mr W. H. (Bill) Moyes. Mr Moyes was a man of commanding presence and had earned an outstanding reputation in academic and sporting spheres. 'Bill' was given my reports from Stratford and then enquired what course I wished to take at NPBHS. On being told by my father that I had developed an interest in farming subjects, 'Bill' removed his glasses and in a Churchillian gruff voice announced: 'Well, Mr Masters, this lad won't be taking an agricultural course at my school. On his reports from Stratford there is only one place for him – 5A English, French, Latin, Maths, History, Science and Physics.' With that the interview concluded – the die had been cast.

My introduction to 5A was quite awesome. I was the youngest and the smallest in a form of about 35 pupils. Many of my new class mates were really men dressed in short trousers. Many shaved and more than a few were addicted to tobacco leaf. My desk mate Jack 'C' must have consumed several packets of fags each week. The fingers of his right hand were deeply stained from tobacco smoke and his clothing stank of tobacco fumes. The masters who passed our desk could not help but be aware of the fact that Jack was an addict but it was another thing to catch him in the act. In that event retribution would have been swift and severe. 'Bill' had established a policy that any boy caught smoking would receive a public whacking in the assembly in front of the entire complement of staff and around 600 pupils. I can recall several such public whackings during my years at NPBHS.

The school was conducted on spartan lines rather like a military academy. While scholastic achievements was always No 1 priority, all boys were encouraged to participate in winter and summer sports. In winter there was only one sport – rugby football. Unless a boy possessed a doctor's certificate exempting him from this robust sport, everyone had to play – like it or not.

The masters who took 5A were a really select group of teachers – the cream of the staff. Our form Master was 'Hori' Diprose (Mathematics) supported by 'Yank' Kerr (French), 'Podgy' Papps (Latin), 'Jazz' Leggatt and later 'Wit' Alexander (English), George Bottrill (History), and A. G. Johnston (Chemistry & Physics), plus W. R. (Bill) Shrimpton. By any standards this was an outstanding group of men who were committed to Bill Moyes in turning out well rounded citizens.

In April of that year the senior rugby master 'Podgy' Papps ordered a parade of all pupils for the selection of rugby groups. The first Group comprised the 1st and 2nd XVs, 2nd Group played 4th grade rugby and 3rd Group 5th grade. Altogether the school must have fielded about 20 or more teams, many of which competed in Saturday competitions against outside clubs. When the selection took place, I recall Podgy announcing to the assembly that anyone with the name of Masters must be a potentially good rugby player. With that I was drafted into the 3rd group to play 5th grade which was really well above my expectations.

Well, 'Podgy' had issued a challenge – I had no option but to prove that his selection was not in vain. That year I held my place in the 5th grade team, progressed the following year to 4th grade and captained the school under-16 team in a fixture with my old school mates from Stratford High School. We defeated them by a handsome margin of about 20 points. I became a permanent member of 1st XV in 1937 and '38.

My summer sport was cricket to which I was somewhat more dedicated than rugby. Cricket is a game, however, that calls for rather special skills. While I was an above average batsman I could not win a place in the 1st eleven, I had to be content with the 2nd eleven which I captained in 1938. One of the highlights of my cricketing days at NPBHS was being chosen to play in a testimonial match to honour the return of Martin Donnelly from the NZ Tour of England. Donnelly was the idol of all the younger boys – he was an outstanding all rounder, Head Boy of the school, captain of 1st XV and a first class student. He set a marvellous standard of achievement and, despite his high profile, he always retained a sense of modesty. Because rugby did not require such technical skill I was able to enjoy a higher profile in this sport. The team was coached by 'Yank' Kerr. We practiced on the racecourse, rain, hail or snow two nights a week during the winter. The boarders in the team could then return to their dormitories for hot showers, but we day boys had the most spartan of facilities – ice cold showers. They certainly bred them tough in those days. 'Yank' Kerr was an outstanding coach – a real student of the game. One session each week was held in a classroom where he would demonstrate the moves on the blackboard until every member of the team understood our tactical plan to a nicety. His dedication paid dividends. In August 1938, he took the 1st XV to a quadrangular tournament to Dunedin to take part in the 50th anniversary of the Otago Rugby Union. We played two games defeating Southland Boys's high School 35–nil and Otago

Boys' High School 41–3. This was the wind up of a highly successful season in which we had won six matches against other leading boys schools, 136 points for 28 against. 'Yank' Kerr's association with the team never waned.

During the four years that I later spent in the Fleet Air Arm, Yank was writing to me two or three letters a year. I felt very privileged to have been on his mailing list. Possibly there were others in the Army or the Air Force that he and other masters corresponded with, but gestures such as these typified the unique school spirit that Bill Moyes had cultivated in his school.

Academically, my first year at NPBHS was very difficult. While I could hold my own in languages and history, I discovered that Stratford had been woefully behind in subjects like mathematics, science and physics. Expressions like quadratic equations, sines and cosines were completely beyond me, nor could I understand the chemical formulas which they had obviously studied in the 4th form at NPBHS. It was one hell of a struggle that year to catch up on my classmates. I had no one to help me – these subjects were completely foreign to both my parents. Remarkably, however, my desk mate Jack 'C' had somehow formed the opinion that I was pretty bright, so he would lean over in maths and chemistry and 'duck shove' (copy) my answers. No matter what I did to let him know that I was not *au fait* with the subject, Jack would still continue to record my answers. Just what the masters thought when they checked these two pupils' papers goodness only knows. Nothing was ever said.

At the end of the year we sat our Matriculation examination, which in those days one had to pass for entrance into university. I passed quite respectably in all subjects but to my horror I failed by just two marks in English. This was the one subject that I did not worry too much about – I thought it was a 'piece of cake'.

That result was a real blow to my pride. It was the first time in my life that I had failed to achieve. It really rocked me.

In retrospect, however, a second year in 5th did me no harm. I was then associated with boys more of my own age but I was still below the class average age. That year I passed with flying colours.

The decision then had to be made regarding my 6th form studies. I considered the various professions – medicine, dentistry, law, teaching, but none of these held any appeal for me.

I settled for accountancy, no doubt influenced by the fact that several of my friends in the rugby and cricket world were choosing this course.

Our form master was another well known personality, Mr E. R. (Crackety) McKeon. 'Crackety' had established a national reputation through New Zealand for producing budding accountants who were eagerly snapped up by public companies. In 6B (accountancy) we were treated like university students. The masters assumed the role of lecturers rather than teachers, so in a form of about 14 students we developed a very close rapport with the staff. The curriculum was based on extra-mural studies with the University of New Zealand. We studied Accountancy & Mercantile Laws (Mr McKeon), Economics Stage I (Mr Bottrill) and Commercial French, Mr V. E. Kerr. At the end of the school year we sat University Examinations for entry to the New Zealand Society of Accountants, and a few of us tendered economics for the Bachelor of Commerce Degree.

When the results were published I had been credited with three passes – two for Accountants Professional and one for B. Comm.

At the end of 1937 my parents moved back to Stratford, so I had to make a decision whether to go to University or to have one more year at NPBHS. The decision was mine to make. I opted for another year at NPBHS – another year in the 1st XV and with a little bit of luck the first XI.

That year was undoubtedly the most satisfying year of my secondary school career. At the end of the year University examinations I gained four more subjects three for the professional and another for the B. Comm.

If I may digress here, I would like to go back to Monday 5th July 1937. On a previous Saturday the school's 1st XV played its annual fixture against St Patrick's, Silverstream at Hawera. I have previously mentioned that every student had to play rugby unless they had an exemption by medical certificate. Likewise every student not in the 1st XV was morally expected to travel to Hawera to cheer for the school team. Transport was provided by New Zealand Railways which laid on a steam locomotive and about 15 carriages to accommodate the staff and pupils. This was an annual event that was looked forward to with keen anticipation. Each pupil would have been given sufficient money for the train fare, plus any incidentals in Hawera. A high priority on the list of incidentals was for many, a packet of fags. Once the train arrived in Hawera the nearest store was invaded by an avalanche of NPBHS supporters wearing yellow and white scarves, and ribbons, and who rapidly denuded the store of cigarettes. Although masters had been appointed to supervise each carriage, they were generally inclined to turn a blind eye to the exuberant behaviour on the return journey. Invariably someone would pull the communication cord and the train would be brought to a halt at a remote section of the line. Rolls of toilet paper would trail behind and the cigarettes were being consumed as if they were going out of fashion.

The first XV and school prefects enjoyed the privilege of VIP treatment having a carriage to themselves. The behaviour here was impeccable – there was too much at stake to risk the headmaster's wrath.

In the assembly hall on Monday morning, Bill Moyes, as was his wont, reviewed the game against St Pats. We had been defeated 17–6, and one of the faults was the lack of possession. One particular member of the team attracted some criticism. This was the hooker, one named Masters, who came on as a replacement player, just after half time. Masters was not a specialist hooker – he was a front row prop, but Bill Moyes obviously thought he should have done better. For a lad of 16 and the smallest in the forwards, I was stunned, but on reflection I guess Bill knew his comments would inspire me to greater efforts. They certainly did.

Having reviewed the game, Bill then launched into a general commentary on pupil behaviour. He and his wife had travelled to Hawera by car and on the return journey they had stopped at the Stratford railway station.

Bill went on to say that he could see a train in the distance as it entered the Stratford straight. A considerable amount of smoke heralded its approach, not all of which was emission from the engines. This was received with a rollicking roll of mirth from junior to senior boys. Bill was irate, 'So you think that's funny, do you? I've a damned good mind to whack the lot of you!' That provoked an even more raucous response. Bill was livid. 'All those boys who were smoking on the train take a pace forward.' From where I stood with the senior boys at the back it seemed as if the entire school surged forward with 4th and 5th forms impinging on the 3rd forms and preparatory class.

Bill turned to his masters – 'Gentlemen please remove your gowns and jackets – we have work to do.' Someone was despatched to his office for the cane and the first master to administer three strokes was 'Yank' Kerr, a tall well proportioned man. Any whacks from him, if delivered with force, could be quite severe. After 'Yank' had done his dash the cane was passed to the next master until all 16 had taken their turn. When the orgy was over, more than 300 boys had received three of the best on their *derrières*.

While all this was going on the Head Boy, Athol G. McIntyre, came around the prefects and the members of the 1st XV and told them to stand fast. He did not ask whether any had been smoking, but exercising his discretion as Head Boy of the school he possibly reasoned that it would have been an embarrassment for a prefect or a member of the team to be whacked in the presence of the junior boys. He therefore said he would take us all up to Mr Moyes when the onslaught was over.

Well the visit to Bill Moyes, well intentioned though it may have been, was more of an ordeal than the corporal punishment we had just witnessed. Again without inviting any culprits to step forward Bill dished out the toughest reprimand that it has ever been my experience to listen to. He inferred that his senior school had let him down. He would have admired us more if we had come forward and taken our medicine like the others. As a member of the 1st XV I can say quite truthfully that I never saw anyone in our carriage smoking but it would have been futile to try and convince our headmaster given the intensity of his fury.

The remarkable thing is that not a word of this incident was reported in the media. How differently it would have been received in this day and age.

Towards the end of the 1938 year our form master Mr McKeon had been contacted by a firm of Wellington-based chartered accountants, Messrs Wilberfoss Harden & Co. One of the junior partners Robert Bradshaw was an old boy of the school and had previously been one of Mr McKeon's pupils. This firm was seeking to expand and wanted two accounting students to commence duties immediately.

Philip Taylor and I were already enrolled for Victoria University in Wellington so Mr McKeon put the proposition to us. As we were both intending to be part-time students we accepted with alacrity.

Bob Bradshaw was also the warden of Weir House, the mens' University boarding hostel. He was therefore able to support our application for accommodation. We commenced duties early in December that year.

The university vacation lasted until March, so we had a few months to find our feet before lectures commenced in earnest.

I immediately signed on for two Summer sports in the Varsity cricket and swimming clubs.

Weir House comprised 80 resident students apart from the Warden and Matron. These students originated from secondary schools in the lower North island and the northern districts of the South Island.

The following former students of New Plymouth Boys' High School resident in Weir House 1939–1941.

Robert C. Bradshaw – Warden – prisoner of war
Ron J. Corkill – New Zealand Army – killed Italy
Tom Larkin – Royal Navy
Lynn M. Papps – RNZAF
Jim Halpin – New Zealand Army – killed Western Desert
Phil Taylor
Don Whitwell – RNZAF
Alister MacLeod – Fleet Air Arm
Ian Morton
Owen Masters – Fleet Air Arm
Jim Annand – RNZAF – killed in Italy
Bill Annand – RNZAF
John Woodward
Miles Ekdahl
Alister MacLennan

By far the largest contingent over 15 per cent came from New Plymouth Boys' High School. With our sporting background we were particularly dominant in the Varsity rugby and cricket clubs.

When lectures commenced we soon discovered that the carefree days were over. During the day Phil and I worked in the firm from 8 a.m. to 5 p.m., for which we were paid the magnificent starting wage of £1/0/0 per week. Following the old English custom of articled clerks in the law and accounting profession, the employers considered that we should accept a lower than normal wage scale in return for the privilege of 'learning the ropes'. Those of our contemporaries at Weir House who worked in Government Departments were paid a starting wage of £2/5/0 per week. Our board was 30 shilling per week, so obviously one's parents had to assist in this respect.

Wilberfoss Harden & Co. was an accounting practice comprising three partners, the senior of whom, Mr George Samuel Thorpe Harden, was a former naval officer serving in North Sea minesweepers during the First World War. Mr Harden commanded the practice as he would a ship. He exuded a quiet sense of confidence and integrity that instinctively commanded respect in the profession. The intermediate clerk to whom I was assigned was Stuart Wilson, several years senior to me. Stuart was further advanced in his accountancy studies so he was put in charge of a section of audit clients, of which a substantial number were hotels. The practice had acquired a strong reputation for hotel audits, holding appointments for 17 of the then 51 hotels in Wellington and Petone.

These audits took us to an interesting variety of jobs, some top grade and some in the slum areas of inner Wellington. Two in particular I recall. Stuart and I would be entrusted with Mr Harden's Lincoln Zephyr sedan which was for those days a luxurious vehicle. We would commence at 8.30 a.m. Our first call would be the Victoria Hotel in Abel Smith Street, at that time one of the most depressing slum areas. The manager of this hotel was an old Irishman, Jimmy O'Hanlon. After taking stock in the bars and cellars, Jimmy would always turn on morning tea which comprised delicious hot buttered scones and some of the strongest tea it has ever been my experience to taste. This job was done by 10 a.m. by which time the pub was due to open. There was always a lengthy queue of 'down and outs', alcoholics, drones and misfits waiting outside. Many carried 'riggers', a square type of bottle which was supplied for JDKZ gin. The clients would pay perhaps one shilling to have their rigger filled with draught ale. They would then disappear to their hovel and consume the contents as a 'pick me up'. This went on all day as long as the dole money held out.

One task which was associated with the audit of the Victoria Hotel was the collection of rents for a large landlord, the E. C. Gibbons estate. This required me to visit a number of derelict dwellings in the Abel Smith and Tory Streets. Although I was quite capable of defending myself, I must admit to being a little apprehensive about collecting rents from some of these mysterious tenants.

The other hotel audit that comes to mind was that of the Empire Hotel in Willis Street. This was a luxury grade hotel owned by NZ Breweries Ltd and managed by Mr Matt Carr. Stuart and I would muster there at 8.30 a.m. and proceed to take stock in the three public bars. This would be completed by about 10 a.m. when we would adjourn to the House Bar. There we were served with the traditional scones and morning tea. Having taken stock in the House Bar, Stuart would then lock the door and say, 'Well Masters what type of cocktail shall we have today?' At that time I knew nothing about the ingredients of these sophisticated drinks, but under Stuart's tuition I soon learned the standard recipes.

There was usually a base of gin, vermouth, a dash of angostura bitters, topped up with lemonade and flashed off with cherries etc.

These were a magnificent finale to a hard morning's work. We returned to the office rather light headed and then attempted to work out the hotel percentage statements.

Meanwhile life at University and in particular at Weir House continued at a frenetic pace. There was never a moment to spare, what with sporting and cultural activities. Along with several other Weir House residents I became involved in a stage production in the Wellington Opera House which was featured to coincide with the University annual capping ceremony. Although my part in the production of Ron Meeks *Vikings* was that of a chorus member, we were nevertheless involved in practices and rehearsals. The Varsity extravaganza ran for three nights, each with full houses. Each night's production would be followed by a dance or cabaret at either the Star Boating club or Margaret O'Connor's dance studio. The revelry continued well into the early hours of the following morning. An alarm clock was essential if one was to surface in time for breakfast and report for work by 8.30 a.m.

My involvement in rugby at Victoria University commenced with the Clubs' 3rd (1st grade) team. This was a team comprising students from secondary schools in the lower North Island and Nelson and Marlborough in the South Island. In the 1939 team we had players from Wanganui Collegiate, Palmerston North Boys' High, Fielding Agricultural College, Wellington College, Nelson College, Hawera High School and New Plymouth Boys' High School.

All had played in the 1st XV at their respective schools. This university team was treated as a source of replacements for the University 1st XV.

In the following year a vacancy did occur in the front row of the 1st XV and I was the first 3rd grade player to win a promotion. My old school mate Alister MacLeod followed me shortly afterwards as centre threequarter.

It was about this time that the international tension that had been gradually increasing since 1930 suddenly became ominous.

Hitler in Germany and Mussolini in Italy were forming an axis of power in Europe and across the North African coast. Hitler's army had marched in and reclaimed the Saar basin on the border with France, and Mussolini launched his invasion of Abyssinia. Hitler following this with a plebiscite in Austria, then marched in and annexed Czechoslovakia. Following an international conference at Munich, Hitler and Mussolini both gave undertakings that they had no further territorial ambitions.

Scarcely a few months had passed, however, when Hitler was chancing his arm again. This time it was over the 'Danzig corridor', a part of Poland which Hitler claimed as former German territory. The Poles resisted his claim, so Hitler invaded Poland and this resulted in a declaration of war by France and Britain on 3rd September 1939.

While this tension was building up in Europe many young men of my age volunteered to join the New Zealand Territorial Army. The unit which I and several of my University friends joined was the 1st Battalion of the Wellington Regiment. We were issued with uniforms and rifles and paraded one night each week at the Winter Show buildings. Fortunately these parades did not clash with lectures at the University so there was no problem over attendance.

Whilst about six Weir House students joined the Wellington Battalion several more had joined the Artillery unit that was based at Fort Dorset, the entrance to Wellington Harbour.

When war was declared these Fort Dorset students were immediately called up for permanent service and became the envy of those who had enlisted in the Wellington Infantry Battalion.

Shortly after the declaration of war my mother accompanied by my sister visited Wellington for a short holiday. I saw them on several occasions and on one such visit I plucked up courage to mention that I was interested in joining the Air Force and asked my mother whether she would give her approval on an enlistment form. To my great surprise she agreed, but in retrospect I doubt very much whether she realised that by doing so I would be immediately qualified for overseas service.

Emboldened by this unexpected approval I then despatched the papers by mail to my father for his signature. Not unexpectedly I received a very firm but none the less respectful refusal. The gist of his reply was that as a returned serviceman of World War I he knew better than I the horrors of warfare and, while he admired my gesture, I would just have to remain patient until I reached 21 years of age, when the decision would be mine alone.

In March 1940 an incident occurred which had a profound and exceptionally happy influence on my life. Philip Taylor my room mate at Weir House had received an invitation from a Mrs Holmwood who lived at Glen Road, Kelburn to have an evening meal at her residence and provide male company for two trainee school dental nurses. Phil asked me to join him. The prospect of a change of diet was most attractive because the Weir House fare had become rather frugal and unappetising. On arrival we were introduced to the two ladies, Josie Barber and Joan Rees. Conversation centred around the School Dental Clinic Hostel and Weir House with the inevitable comparison of menus etc. Of the two Joan seemed to be the better conversationalist and kept us all amused with her impressions of hostel life etc. When it was time to leave Phil and I offered to escort the two girls back to their hostel which was about two-three miles away from the Holmwood's residence. Physical differences seemed to determine who escorted who. Both Phil and Josie wore glasses so they seemed to be obvious partners. I was privileged to be Joan's escort. This 'blind date' was followed by numerous later meetings and survived the rigours of four and a half years overseas service. Joan and I became partners for life on 20th March 1945.

Army Service

About May 1940 our battalion was finally called up for three months full time training. We continued to use the Winter Show buildings as our base and trained on the various parks and reserves in that vicinity. Our battalion comprised three infantry companies each of which had Lewis machine guns, a composite company comprising signallers, despatch riders, heavy Vickers machine guns and headquarters administration.

Towards the end of our training period we moved into a tented camp for one month on Wanganui racecourse when we were able to carry out more advanced manoeuvres at day and night along the coastline.

While in Wanganui we had several sporting fixtures with local clubs, the highlight being a rugby match between the battalion teams against the Wanganui A & B representative sides.

During that season I had the misfortune to develop water on both my knee and elbow. This latter affliction had not been caused by leaning on a hotel bar – I couldn't afford that luxury. However, I was determined to get into one or other of those teams despite this disability.

I kept the problem strictly to myself and played in the trial matches with heavy elastic bandages on both knee and elbow. Understandably both swelled like balloons when the bandages were removed after the trial game. The teams were announced and I was somewhat disgusted to have only made the B team when my two close friends Alister MacLeod and Arch Foley had been selected for the A team. Under normal circumstances I knew that I was good enough to be with them.

Both matches were played on Spriggens Park. The A team won their match and we drew nil all with the Wanganui B team.

At the conclusion of the three months training period a number of us were invited to extend our service by entry to an officers and NCOs course which was scheduled to commence immediately at Foxton racecourse. From our platoon Alister MacLeod and I had been invited along with others from other platoons and companies. It was pleasing to see that Arch Foley with whom I had become friendly was one of those invited from another company.

When we reported at Foxton racecourse we found ourselves in company with personnel from several other regiments, all of whom had aspirations to higher army ranks. These regiments were Taranaki-West Coast, Wellington Scottish, Hawkes Bay East Coast and Queen Alexandra's Mounted Rifles.

At Foxton we were under the supervision of no-nonsense permanent force officers and NCO instructors. Our training was vastly different, because at the end of the course we would either qualify as second lieutenants and sergeant instructors, or be returned to our regiments as drop outs.

Our training at Foxton lasted about six weeks. It was pretty rigorous and the discipline strict. The basic purpose was to sort out those who had potential to command so each recruit had to take his turn in instructing his mates.

At the end of this course I was one of several who were ordered to appear before a selection committee. I had received no warning so I had no inkling of what the call might be about. I was, however, rather concerned that my two close friends Arch and Mac had not received the call. I duly appeared before three permanent force officers and without any preliminary briefing I was asked quite bluntly 'Masters, you have been considered for a commission – do you think you can handle it?' My mind was in a whirl. There were so many things to consider and they expected an answer on the spot. The first thing that came to mind was that to accept a commission would obviously damage my friendship with Arch and Mac. Secondly at the tender age of 19 – was it right to accept? Thirdly, I suddenly realised that there might have been some undue influence involved, because I had an uncle who held the rank of colonel and he knew I was on this course. In fact his own son was also on the course with me and he was obviously being groomed for a commission. Rather hesitantly and not very enthusiastically I muttered, 'Yes – I suppose with a little more training I could hold a commission.'

With that I knew that I had burnt my boats – but I felt strangely relieved and in retrospect years and years later I am glad that I tactfully declined their offer.

Had I accepted I am certain that my future service career would have been vastly different and I would have lost two valuable friends, not to mention my later service in the Fleet Air Arm.

After our sojourn at Foxton we advanced to Tauherinikau racecourse near Featherston. By this time our numbers had been substantially reduced and we were all sergeants plus a few 2nd Lieutenants.

Tauherinikau was really the 'finishing school' for army instructors. If one had any rough edges this is where they were knocked off.

The course terminated just prior to Christmas 1940. We were given seven days leave and instructed to report to Waiouru Army Camp early January 1941 as instructors to the new formed 2nd Battalion Wellington Regiment, membership of which was totally conscripted.

While I had been in the Army I contrived, when I could, to attend University lectures. This was not possible at Tauherinikau, but as it was then getting close to the University examinations I decided to continue swotting and sat two subjects while in camp. More by good luck than a surfeit of knowledge I was successful in passing one (Statistical Method) while with the other (Auditing) I depended solely on my practical experience and failed in that.

This pass gave me a total of 12 passes towards my B Comm degree of 15.

On arrival at Waiouru Arch Foley and I were assigned to the same platoon in B Company. Our platoon commander was 2nd Lieut. Williams, I was the sergeant and Arch the lance sergeant. The conscripts comprised a wide variety of ages, 18 to 40, and occupations – clerks, labourers, mechanics and others not in reserved occupations, married men and single. Three of the most interesting personalities in our platoon were Ernie Willis (about 30) who owned and operated a gymnasium in Wellington, Cyril Phelps, one of Ernie's protégés who had just recently won the title 'Mr New Zealand' and a little Scotsman named Steward (40) who was an antagonistic watersider.

In the main, the trainees accepted their conscription with good grace, which made it much easier for Arch and myself. At the tender age of 19, it was a terrific challenge to be in command of many in our platoon who were in the 30–40 age groups.

The accommodation at Waiouru was all in tents. The only buildings constructed at that time were cookhouses and messing halls.

The countryside was hilly and covered in tussock. It was ideal for all forms of military training and manoeuvres.

The training of the 2nd Battalion lasted three months, at the end of which the trainees were released to return to their former civilian occupations.

Whilst in the army I had continued my enquiries re enlistment in either the air force or the navy.

Because I was under 21, I was unacceptable for the army, and if I had volunteered for overseas service the army would have been my last choice. I was able to maintain contact with an old school friend Jim Halpin who was also a resident at Weir House and who worked in the Navy Office. Jim was able to furnish me with the details of various schemes for entry into the Navy. Scheme Y was for amateur yachtsmen, which I was not. Scheme B was for passage to England and train there at HMS *King Alfred* for a deck commission.

The Paymaster Branch had vacancies and Jim suggested that with my nearly completed degree I would have a very good chance of acceptance, but who would want to fight a war sitting behind a desk? That was not for me. Then Jim came up with Scheme F. What was Scheme F?

This was entry to the Air Branch of the Royal Navy ie the Fleet Air Arm. The Royal Navy would accept volunteers for pilots and observers over the age of 18. If selected in New Zealand one travelled to England as a civilian, and if accepted there was inducted to the Royal Navy at HMS *St Vincent*, Portsmouth.

Now we were talking about something that really did appeal to me. It offered the best of two worlds – the life at sea and flying as well.

I asked Jim to secure the application papers and this time I managed to persuade both my parents to approve of my under age application.

Jim then gave me an introduction to one Jack Loftus, who looked after recruitment to the Fleet Air Arm. Little did I realise when I was pressurising Jack Loftus that he himself was in the process of joining the FAA. We actually left New Zealand together in the same draft on MV *Dominion Monarch*.

All this hasty organisation was completed when I had two days leave from Waiouru to visit Wellington.

On my return to Waiouru I was privileged to announce to my friends MacLeod and Foley that I was handing the army over to them – I was joining the Fleet Air Arm.

Now in those days the FAA was a relatively little known and rather mysterious service. The natural reaction of my two friends was 'what the hell is the FAA?'

Once informed they were both agog and wanting to know how to join me. I passed on the necessary information and Mac and Arch submitted their applications to join me.

On our return to Wellington we were obliged to resume our civilian jobs. It was not easy to adjust after the temporary service life but one had to be thankful that one had an understanding employer who was prepared to employ one.

Once back in Wellington the word spread around our friends and others wanted to join our FAA bandwagon.

Among those interested were Bill Ryan (ex New Plymouth Boys' High School) and my old room mate Jack Brown (es Wairarapa College). Sad to relate that Jim Annand and Jack Brown were rejected temporarily for medical reasons but Bill Ryan was accepted and joined us on our draft. Jack Brown joined a later draft, but regrettably was killed in an aircraft accident in the United Kingdom on 10th August 1943.

Our next hurdle was the entrance medical examination and all of those with a history of sporting activity would have considered this a 'piece of cake'.

When I was examined I seemed to have passed all the standard tests until the doctor measured my blood pressure. It was then that the alarm bells rang. The doctor was obviously a trifle disturbed. He asked me whether I smoked very much to which I replied that on my meagre earnings I could not afford to. With that he pronounced that my level was a bit higher than the maximum limit and I would have to come back in a week's time.

When I returned there was no change in the reading – this was a critical situation. The doctor, who probably knew very little about aero medicine, must have detected my extreme disappointment and then decided that his patient was mad keen to get into the fighting and once there probably wouldn't survive very long, so what the hell – let him go. He endorsed my medical report and the big adventure was about to begin. It was not until several years later that I came to realise that for one who was to become a fighter pilot a higher than normal threshold for blood pressure was an advantage rather than a disadvantage. One did not tend to 'black out' under high forces of gravity as did pilots with a normal blood pressure. I was later able to prove this theory in a dog-fight with another pilot who was wearing a water pressure suit.

From the date of our acceptance for the FAA all that remained was to await our departure date.

MV Dominion Monarch Troopship

Eventually a telegram arrived from the Navy Office 'Report – HMS *Cook Wellington* 0900 hrs Saturday 19th July 1941.'

About 40 entrants mustered that morning, comprising groups from the South Island, Wellington and Central North Island districts. There was little to be done after the roll call and making our last will and testaments. This latter task served to suggest that not all of us might be fortunate to return to New Zealand.

I had negligible assets to bequeath to my father, because only a few shillings and pence remained in my Post Office Savings Bank account after I had managed to convert about £30 sterling into United States dollars. I knew that New Zealand money was valueless overseas but anyone who had United States dollars could convert them readily.

The previous evening I had contacted my friend Joan Rees and bade her a fond farewell. We both promised to write to each other. Little did we realise that over the next four and a half years, more than a hundred letters would pass between us.

Our draft was scheduled to depart by train to Auckland at 4 p.m. that day. The only members who I knew were Alister Macleod and Bill Ryan, both ex New Plymouth Boys' High School, both of whom were in some strange way influenced by my decision to join the FAA. Another who I recognised from Victoria University was David Muir. I was formally introduced to David by Mac who had been associated with him in the university boxing team. Mac had won a blue the previous year in the heavyweight division and David a blue in one of the lighter weights.

Actually I felt entitled to claim some credit for Mac's boxing prowess because he had used me as a sparring partner in the Weir House gymnasium. Our practices were not all one sided. I did know how to defend myself in the ring and I can recall one occasion when I penetrated Mac's guard and landed a straight left on his nose. It didn't exactly improve his otherwise handsome countenance.

We were all set to enter our respective carriages when suddenly at the end of the platform we became conscious of a series of 'Yoohoos' from the entrance to the platform. In the murky distance two female figures were joyously bounding towards us. They were both attired in basketball uniforms and School Dental Nurses blazers. One was my lovely friend Joan Rees and the other was her companion Barbara Heale. They were both breathless after having defeated their arch rivals the Wellington ASPRO team. There was little time to talk because the engine whistle sounded, but to the accompaniment of a chorus of wolfish whistles and ribald remarks, we bade each other a fond and demonstrably passionate farewell. What a girl! I never expected that, but I felt confident there and then that this was not the last we would see of each other.

Our rail journey to Auckland was uneventful except when two adventurous characters dashed off the train at Taumarunui to purchase a few bottles of beer at a nearby hotel which specialised in illegal after hours trading. Luckily they got back in time.

On arrival in Auckland we were transported by bus to our troopship the large ex Shaw Savill passenger liner MV *Dominion Monarch*.

Several officers from the Auckland Naval Depot HMS *Philomel* received us on board. Two long service RN able seamen who were returning to the United Kingdom had been assigned to escort our draft which now totalled 65 (Arch Foley had by then joined the draft).

One of these was a Cockney called George Claygate. He had all the hallmarks of a real scoundrel as we were to learn to our cost some time later. The other was a nondescript inoffensive individual who had the most unusual name of Redvers Isgrove. The navy could never have chosen two more dissimilar characters.

The total complement of servicemen must have been several thousands, all of whom were Australian and New Zealand aircrew personnel plus a small draft of New Zealand radar trainees. Most of the aircrew were destined for disembarkation at Canada for further service training, but a small number who had qualified as pilots and navigators were going direct to squadrons in the United Kingdom.

The navy has always been renowned for caring for its personnel so it was hardly surprising that our FAA draft was assigned to the luxury of cabin accommodation whereas the majority of air force personnel had to sleep in hammocks.

We were generally allocated two berth cabins. My cabin mate was one Harry MacKay who hailed from Napier. Harry was a jovial, rotund, slightly balding character who enjoyed life and relaxed very easily. He had been employed in the pharmacy at Napier Hospital, the secretary of which was Mr E. T. Rees, father of my friend Joan.

The Voyage to England

The *Dominion Monarch* slipped moorings about mid-day Monday 21st July, and proceeded down the harbour into Rangitoto channel followed by our escort the armed merchant cruiser HMS *Monowai*. That afternoon we sailed north into quite heavy seas. This was my one and only experience during my four and a half years naval career that I felt a trifle squeamish. I had later sailed in some pretty turbulent seas particularly in the Bay of Biscay, so this passage out of the Hauraki Gulf must have been quite heavy going. It was comforting, however, to see the *Monowai* plunging and pitching in the distance as there had been several incidents since the declaration of war where German surface raiders had either intercepted merchant ships or sown mines in the customary shipping lanes.

In mid 1940, two German raiders the *Komet* and the *Orion* sank several coastal vessels, laid mines and unsuccessfully fired two torpedoes at a Cook Strait ferry steamer.

On 19th June 1940, the SS *Niagara* which was carrying a consignment of gold bullion, hit one of these mines in the Hauraki Gulf and sank.

On 26th November 1940, the MV *Rangitane* with a draft of FAA personnel was intercepted by a German commerce raider in the Bismarck Sea north of Papua, New Guinea. The German captain offered to put all his prisoners ashore on the island of Emirau provided they signed a parole that they would not bear arms against Germany for the duration of the war. Two old high school friends, Max Burn and Brian Huggett, were amongst the FAA entrants who were taken prisoner.

For reasons best known to themselves but probably inspired by their loyalty to King and country and abiding by the code of their former headmaster Bill Moyes, Burn and Huggett refused to give their parole and virtually told the Germans where to put it. They were therefore held prisoner while the raider made its way back to Germany via the Indian Ocean, around the Cape of Good Hope to Bordeaux, France.

Both Burn and Huggett were incarcerated in prisoner of war camps in Germany until their release mid 1945.

Early the following morning we found that the two ships had changed their north easterly course and were now heading south east on a zig-zag course to the Southern Pacific ocean. Even the overnight temperature change was noticeable. We continued on this south easterly heading for several days with the weather becoming bitterly cold and very stormy.

One of our party, Spence Wright, who we later discovered had a flair for ingenuity, had begged, borrowed or stolen some materials from which he set to work and fashioned a sextant. When it had been assembled Spence took it on deck and secretly 'shot' the sun. Apparently he also had access to some kind of chart because he was able to furnish us with a daily position in latitude and longitude as well as calculating the distance travelled in 24 hours.

The New Zealand and Australian Air Force navigators were completely mystified by the knowledge that our FAA draft travelling as mere civilian passengers could have access to such confidential navigational information.

I am sure that many of them suspected that we were part of the 5th column, or anti-war group.

Although we had no official ship's duties the days passed without tedium. Many practices were devoted to 'Abandon Ship' stations, while deck sports, card games etc. occupied other daylight hours.

Because we were privileged to have cabin accommodation many of us devoted the afternoons to siestas.

The less said about meals the better. Suffice to say that those of us who had served some time in the Army or at boarding school found them only just tolerable, but for chaps who knew nothing more than their mothers' home cooking they must have been a grave disappointment. The providors who supplied the *Dominion Monarch* must have made a whacking profit out of the low quality meat etc. which they had supplied.

At night the mess decks were opened for a beer ration and schools of crown and anchor and two-up, which of course were dominated by the Australian contingent. The chaps who ran the crown and anchor boards must have been fairly wealthy by the time they disembarked at Halifax.

After about ten days sailing the course changed to almost due north, almost parallel to the coast of Chile, but Spence Wright reported that we were well away from customary shipping lanes.

Each successive day we noticed that as we sailed north the temperature became noticeably warmer.

Eventually we arrived in Balboa, the entrance to the Panama Canal Zone. The ship moored there but for security reasons we were informed that no shore leave could be permitted.

Three members of our draft chose to ignore this warning, clambered down the stern mooring ropes and went in to paint the town red. After sampling a few local bars they returned and successfully climbed up the same mooring ropes. Luckily for them no one had noticed the escapade but it did nevertheless suggest to the RAF types that the navy boys had more initiative.

Some years later, it was rumoured that the withdrawal of shore leave privilege at Panama had been influenced by an escapade perpetrated by a member of an earlier FAA draft. The story goes that a certain naval airman who was pleasantly inebriated having spent some time in one of the sleazy watering holes, passed the German embassy. He noticed that a Nazi flag was flying above the entrance. This offensive emblem presented an unusual challenge so he climbed over the parapet, removed it and then proceeded to urinate on it in full view of the Embassy staff. The Huns did not take very kindly to this and quickly grabbed our misguided youth. This constituted a very sensitive international confrontation and only by some top level diplomacy was the miscreant released and allowed to rejoin the ship to the United Kingdom.

I cannot vouch for the truth of this story but it certainly had the hallmarks of FAA audacity. It could also explain why FAA drafts travelled to the United Kingdom in civilian clothes rather than naval uniform.

At Balboa we bade farewell to our naval escort HMS *Monowai* and proceeded through the Canal to Colon on the eastern seaboard. From there we sailed south east to the Dutch Island of Curaçao. This was quite an unexpected diversion, but apparently this was an ideal oiling station before proceeding up the North American coast to Halifax.

At last we were given a day's shore leave at the oiling station. Once ashore we telephoned through to the capital Wilhelmstad and ordered a taxi to come out and collect us. Six of us piled in and off we went to see the sights. Curaçao is a barren, treeless landscape rather like the surface of the moon. It had been colonised by the Dutch but at the declaration of war Britain had despatched a battalion of the Green Howards regiment to defend the territory against possible annexation by German forces. It therefore became strategically important to the British merchant fleet as an oiling station close to the Venezuelan oil fields.

We arrived in Wilhelmstad at about 1300 hours and because it was a siesta period there was scarcely a person to be seen. The place slowly came to life about two hours later. Bars opened and dozens of prostitutes came out on their verandahs to solicit business. To the best of my knowledge there were no such takers. Incidentally it seemed that only the FAA draft ventured into Wilhelmstad, there was no sign of any New Zealand or Australian Air Force members. Perhaps it had been ruled 'out of bounds' to them. The Dutch policemen showed obvious signs of brutality in the way they dealt with the local inhabitants who were predominantly mulatto. By comparison the soldiers of the Green Howards had a very professional bearing. They obviously were from a crack regiment and left for dead the American troops who we had seen on duty during our passage through the Canal Zone. The Yanks were just a second rate, undisciplined rabble and they also displayed a penchant for truculence to the Panamanians employed by the Canal Company. When we saw one incident of two Yankee soldiers bashing a native onto the ground with rifle butts and then kicking him, this raised the ire of all our troops who were assembled on that side of the ship.

The harbour at Wilhelmstad was reminiscent of the West Indies piracy era. The entrance, which must have been quite deep to take the large tankers and cargo vessels, was surprisingly narrow with two old forts on either side. This led into an enormous inland lake which could accommodate a very large number of ships. The *Dominion Monarch* was probably drawing too much water to enter this secluded anchorage.

We sailed that night north through the Caribbean Sea and then hugging the coast of the United States of America we were now without any armed escort. But at that stage of the war, U Boats were not deployed in that area and the *Dominion Monarch* was sufficiently fast to outrun any stalking submarine, unless by chance it was lying in wait approximately on our mean track.

Several days later we reached the Nova Scotia port of Halifax and entered a land-locked harbour that was large enough to accommodate the best part of the Royal Navy. In fact a few days after our arrival at Halifax we stood on the top deck, and over a period of about two hours or more, watched a convoy of over a hundred cargo ships large and small, sail out to be marshalled into position by their fussy naval frigates and destroyer escorts. It was a sight that suddenly emphasised the proximity of war and the dependence of Britain on its merchant fleet for supplies of food, fuel, ammunition, aircraft, tanks, guns, etc.

We were destined to spend about a week in Halifax. Most of our New Zealand and Australian trainees disembarked and headed for pilot, navigator and air gunner training stations in Ontario, Manitoba, Saskatchewan and Alberta. Their places were taken by aircrew who had completed their training and now wore the highly prized brevet indication of pilot, navigator or air gunner.

The cabins which had been allocated to us were near the after entrance to the forward hold. It so happened that one morning when several of us emerged to proceed along the passageway, we happened to notice a party of the ship's crew emerging from the cargo hold and they appeared to be carrying wooden crates. They saw us and instinctively made a move to return to the hold. But one of our party recognised the Ship's Bosun and quickly put two and two together. The Bosun and his mates, about six in all, were caught in the act of exercising an age old maritime perquisite – broaching the ship's liquor store. The crates contained bottles of Speights Ale.

With a suitably measured tone of authority our spokesman said, 'Well Bosun, I guess this is a fair catch. What are we going to do about it?' Dead silence from the gloomy end of the passage. 'Tell you what – how's this for a proposition, 50/50 on the deal we won't say a word about it. On the other hand, if you don't agree, we'll spill the beans and you chaps will end up in the brig.'

The Bosun demurred. 'Christ, that means we hand over three crates, 72 bottles. You young blokes couldn't handle that.'

'Oh, yes we would – take it or leave it, that's our final offer.'

They realised they had no option, so the three crates were passed over. The crew departed with their share, muttering threats asthey stalked down the passageway.

It was imperative that we disposed of the ill gotten gains as quickly as possible. Obviously we could not consume it there and then, an inebriated draft of naval airmen would have attracted unwanted attention. So we removed the crates to three adjacent cabins and then proceeded to dismantle the wire reinforced wooden crates and hide the bottles in dresser drawers and various cupboards. The wooden slats had to be disposed of so these were flung out the portholes into Halifax harbour.

We had only just completed this when Able Seaman George Claygate appeared. Normally we hardly ever saw the old devil but obviously he had been tipped off by the Bosun.

In his repulsive cockney accent he addressed us. 'Gentlemen – I have just heard that you have landed yourselves in a rather compromising situation. I suppose you appreciate the consequences if this matter comes before the Naval authorities. It would be the end of your careers as officer cadets. In fact, you would spend the rest of the war on the lower deck. Not a prospect I would recommend. But fortunately there is a solution. If you cut me in on half of your loot I will say no more about it.' Bloody scoundrel, but like the Bosun and his mates, we had no option.

'O.K. George – we give in – but if you breathe a word about this to anyone else we'll have your knackers for garters.' George crossed his ancient heart and gave a solemn promise. So he ended up with as much ale as we did.

It was now a very sensitive situation. We had to dispose of the grog as quickly as possible. One of the conspirators suggested that we empty our suitcases, fill them with bottles and then go ashore. We had heard of a place called Point Pleasant Park near the harbour entrance. The name sounded attractive and safe so off we went. There was only one thing to do, drink the damned stuff, which we did and had a whale of a party. The roisterers who took part in this escapade were Alister MacLeod, Bill Ryan (both ex New Plymouth Boys' High School), Arch Foley (ex Wellington regiment), Bob Howell (from Pahiatua), Harry MacKay (my cabin mate), 'Junior'

Williams, and myself. How on earth we demolished the grog remains a mystery to this day.

On returning to the *Dominion Monarch* we were pleasantly surprised to find, that in our absence a South African ship had berthed ahead of us and was discharging a cargo of oranges. One of our more astute members suggested that oranges could be readily converted into money en route from Canada to the United Kingdom.

Accordingly with Army practice we posted two sentries one at each end of the cargo shed and then proceeded to fill all our suitcases with this magnificent fruit. We then returned to *Dominion Monarch* with bags heavier than when we had gone ashore. Two days later the *Dominion Monarch* left Halifax in company with two other large passenger liners *Empress of Russia* and *Stratheden* escorted by four destroyers. This was to be a fast convoy each ship being capable of 28 to 30 knots.

Between the three ships the total complement of British, Canadian, Australian and New Zealand pilots, navigators, bomb aimers, air gunners and wireless operators must have been not far short of 8,000. Quite a rare target for a U-boat commander. Shortly after departure Mac and Arch decided to test the market with their oranges. They found many ready buyers amongst the English aircrews. Harry MacKay and I, on the other hand kept ours in reserve until we were nearer our destination when the 'Poms' would be more amenable to a higher price.

Having sold their loot and spent most of the proceeds in the evening mess sessions, Mac and Arch then made overtures for some additional sustenance from our stock. They were, of course met with a polite but quite emphatic refusal.

Mac was a little bit the worse for wear and did not take too kindly to this response. 'You're a couple of miserable old Shylocks – I've got a good mind to toss you overboard, Masters.'

By that time we had made our way to the top deck to get a bit of fresh air. The sky was clear but a tremendous sea caused the ship to roll as much as 30°. Whether joking or not Mac repeated his threat to throw me overboard. Well, the last thing I was going to do was to give in, so I challenged him to do his worst. Happily Mac desisted. Maybe it was the memory of a 'snorter' that I had once hung on him during a sparring bout in the University Hostel gymnasium. There would have been no chance of being picked up if either of us had gone over the side.

When Harry and I returned to our cabin we gave Mac and Arch one dozen oranges with explicit instructions to limit them to one each per day for the rest of the voyage.

We then decided to obviate any further dissension by offering our stock to the Brits next day.

In the meantime the convoy had been heading into sub-arctic waters. We were probably sailing in the latitude of Iceland – it was very cold and the seas very turbulent.

After a few more days we were obviously in the 'killing zone'. We passed a lot of flotsam, empty lifeboats and Carley floats etc. from sinkings on an earlier convoy. This brought home to us the real significance of the convoy system as a defence against the U-boat packs that were lying in wait.

Next day we were relieved to sight our first long range anti-submarine aircraft – a huge Sunderland flying boat which circled the convoy hour after hour until relieved by another aircraft.

We passed the northern coast of Ireland and entered the Irish Sea heading for our destination, Liverpool.

Our next sighting of aircraft were Spitfire fighters over the entrance to the Mersey River. As we were to learn some time later these were not from an operational squadron but from a fighter training establishment at Hawarden which was some time later adjacent to our Fleet Air Arm Elementary Flying School at Sealand, Cheshire.

On 1st September as we entered the Mersey estuary we encountered our first glimpse of civilian war damage. Naval boom defence vessels were followed by the masts of several vessels that had been bombed, or sunk by the mines in the channel. As we approached our berth we were appalled at the extent of destruction to the port facilities and to the adjacent railway sidings.

The arrival of such a large contingent of airmen was a very special occasion and our very popular High Commissioner Hon. Bill (later Sir William) Jordan had travelled up from London to welcome us. He gave us one of those Lord Nelson pep talks. 'New Zealand expects that every man will do his duty.'

Leaving the dockyard station our train passed through mile after mile of bomb damaged buildings – the devastation was really awesome. Before leaving New Zealand we had heard and read about large bombing raids on cities like London, Birmingham, Portsmouth, Coventry, Plymouth etc, but to see it at Liverpool was unexpected. One would have thought that Liverpool, although a prime maritime target, would have been at the extremity of the German bombers' range from their bases in Western Europe.

We arrived in London at Euston Station with no one officially in charge of us. A select council of war was convened, at which it was unanimously decided that our most senior member Cliff (Lefty) Bissett would assume the role of our spokesman and we would respect his decisions. To this day I don't know how Cliff acquired the nickname Lefty, perhaps he was left handed or left footed. Anyway he was an admirable choice. At 28 or 29 years he had that air of maturity that one acquires with old age. In civilian life Cliff had been a school teacher and a prominent sportsman having played rugby for his province Otago on the wing. Under Lefty's command we spent several hours mooching around London and making our way to Victoria Station to connect with another train to Portsmouth.

En route to Portsmouth we discovered by casual conversation with some other passengers that our destination HMS *St Vincent* was on the opposite side of the harbour from Portsmouth or 'Pompey' as all naval personnel referred to it. This meant that we would have to detrain at the nearest station which was Fareham. By this time we came to realise that each major station had an RTO office (Rail Transport Officer). Fareham was happily one such station. Once again no one knew of our impending arrival so we were by this time becoming a trifle disillusioned with the incredible vagueness of the English people. It is in fact a national characteristic. Anyway, someone suggested that we should telephone HMS *St Vincent* (a shore based barracks), and if they wanted us they would surely despatch some trucks to collect us. Sure enough about four large naval trucks duly appeared and were off on the final leg of our journey.

HMS *St Vincent*

It was dark by the time we passed through the gates of the barracks which only a year or so earlier had been the chief naval indoctrination centre for seamen boy recruits. Apparently shortly after the outbreak of war it was allocated to the Air Branch of the Navy as an initial training school for RNVR fleet air arm cadets.

We were met on the parade ground quite informally by a Chief Petty Officer who was to be our martinet for the next three months. Chief PO Wilmot was one of the most senior masters at Arms in the Navy. He was well chosen for the job of instilling navy discipline and creating officers out of raw cadets.

Before passing us over to some junior petty officers for accommodation etc., Wilmot enquired whether we had had supper. Some character in the rear piped up, 'Supper? For Christ's sake man we've only had a cup of tea and a sawdust bun since we left the ship. Anyway it's only 7 p.m. that's too bloody early for supper.'

Wilmot was undeterred. 'Perhaps I should explain that we're not like Noo Ziland. We have four meals a day – breakfast, lunch, high tea and supper. I will arrange for a meal to be prepared for you now.'

After being shown to our quarters and issued with a palliasse and a blanket we received a call over the loudspeaker to muster for a meal in the mess hall. The chaps were ravenous by this time, so we answered the call with alacrity.

The meal was fish and chips. Those who had been used to boarding school fare or army menus took to the meal with great gusto.

No one could have given it high marks for culinary art, the fish was stale and the whole meal lukewarm. The top blew off when two of our chaps claimed that monstrous cockroaches had walked over their plates. This was too much. Most of our draft left the mess en masse leaving just the few ex Army types to polish off their meal.

That night we were escorted to subterranean air raid shelters which we were told would be our sleeping quarters for the rest of our stay at *St Vincent*.

The stench of these shelters was enough to turn anyone off. The stale air combined with oppressive body odours and urine were just too much to bear. One night was enough. Anyone who slept there every night during our stay at *St Vincent* would surely have contracted tuberculosis. From that time on we decided to take the risk and sleep on the messdecks. We laid our palliasses on the top of the mess tables. At least the air was fresher and we woke up clear headed in the morning.

Reveille as we knew it in the army took quite a different form. Instead of a bugle call, it would be a bosun's pipe followed by the raucous voice of a petty officer chanting 'Wakey! Wakey! Wakey – show a leg – show a leg – Rise and shine the sun's scorching your bleeding eyeballs.' Later we were to hear more imaginative calls such as a 'Wakey! Wakey! Rise and shine – 'Ands off your cocks – on with yer socks – hit the deck there – hit the deck'. The naval petty officers certainly had a sense of humour.

Next day was fully occupied with our indoctrination process at 'Pussers Store' (probably a naval distortion of pursers store). We were issued with two complete uniforms, one for work and the other for shore leave; any rank badges and other emblems on the work uniform were in red and on the No 1 uniform, gold. The bell bottomed trousers were unusual in that they had no side pockets or conventional fly. There were two deep pockets in the front and a button up flap instead of the fly. To complete the uniform there was a white chemise with a navy blue band around the throat, a Jean with collar attached which tied around the waist, a black tie (in memory of Nelson's death). To complete the ensemble we had a white lanyard and whistle, attached plus the traditional sailor's cap on which we wore a white band which signified we were officer cadets in training. Finally underwear, boots, gas mask and steel helmet, the latter two of which we were required to carry at all times. There was also the naval great coat which was an obvious necessity in the English winter to come.

All this was followed by yet another medical examination, the announcement of which left me with grave trepidation. If I only just managed to pass the New Zealand medical, how would I fare in the probably more demanding Royal Navy examination? Well, surprisingly enough, the doctor expressed not the slightest concern – I passed with flying colours.

Having struggled into the 'rig of the day' which for general duties was our No 2 or working uniform. We were called by bosun's pipe. 'Did ya hear there! Did ya hear there! All New Zealand naval airmen who joined ship last night are to muster on the parade ground.' We sauntered down, preening ourselves and making critical and derisive comments about others' uniforms.

A little sparrow of a PO was in charge. In a ridiculous cockney accent we were to receive our first naval command which went like this: 'Righty oh youse Colonials – get fell in 'ere three thick.'

Most of us had had some form of military training either in the school cadets or others like Mac, Arch, Bill Ryan and myself in the Territorials. We couldn't believe it! Was it some sort of comedy? No – it was real. This PO wanted us to fall in in front of him in three ranks. We shuffled and complied but there was some resentment over the reference to our status as second class subjects. Next came one word which sounded like 'Chow' but was meant to be the equivalent of the Army command 'atten-shun.' This was becoming too farcical for words with one of our chaps suggesting that 'Chow' meant morning tea time.

We were to learn, however, that in the Navy there is no such command as 'atten-shun' but various versions such as SHUN – HUN – CHAR and like this PO CHOW!!

We were then addressed by a Captain Bach (Royal Marines) who bore a striking resemblance to Lord Gort who was field Commander of the British Army before the retreat from Dunkirk. Henceforth Captain Bach was always referred to as Lord Gort. We also had our official introduction to Chief Petty Officer Wilmot, the Master at Arms who was to virtually rule our lives day and night for the next three months.

It was explained to us that we had arrived at *St Vincent* at an inconvenient time. This was most inconsiderate of us – we should have planned our arrival from 12,000 miles away to coincide with the date when the next course was scheduled to commence. The instructional staff did not want us around so much to our delight we were given seven days leave and told to get the hell out of it. Money would be made available and travel documents processed. Most of our chaps elected to go off in pairs on the well known Lady Ryder scheme which had been introduced to provide hospitality for overseas servicemen.

Accommodation was provided over a wide area of England, Scotland and North Wales. Most of our chaps chose baronial type residences in the farthest places such as in the Lake District in Cumbria and Scotland.

I decided to go it alone and visit some relations in Merthyr Tydfil north of Cardiff. This was quite a challenge as I had to travel by train via the southern counties to Bristol. At each stage of this journey it seemed that I was destined to arrive in the blackout. Bristol had been severely damaged in an air raid a short time previously, but I managed to locate a modest hotel near the railway station.

Next day I proceeded to Cardiff via the Severn tunnel and eventually arrived at Merthyr Tydfil at midnight.

The Welsh people are renowned for their Celtic characteristics and taciturnity. They are not generally at ease with foreigners and that means other inhabitants of the British Isles, let alone Kiwis. Nevertheless, I received a very warm welcome from my aunt and uncle and other members of their family.

My aunt had always been active in civic affairs and was at that time the Mayor (not the Mayoress) of the city of Merthyr, the population of which was in excess of 80,000 people. My uncle was manager of a large coal mine at Aberfan, the village which many years later was to suffer a major tragedy when an avalanche of slag heap descended on the public school.

The ration cards which had been issued to me for this leave were much appreciated by the family. Everything was subject to a very stringent coupon system – meat, fish butter, sugar, petrol, clothing etc. It was a very harsh and austere existence.

On my return journey via London I had arranged to meet up with Bill Ryan and Bob Howell who had both gone to Scotland on the Lady Ryder scheme. At Paddington station I made my way to the Underground but one look at the Underground map was enough. I emerged and decided to travel by taxi which I could ill afford to Trafalgar Square. This was the nearest focal point to the New Zealand Forces Club in Charing Cross Road. There I met my two very thirsty compatriots so we adjourned to the renowned New Zealand watering hole called the Sussex Hotel which was to become a Mecca on all future leaves in London.

On our return to *St Vincent* we were informed that our course was not yet ready for us, so we were assigned to the pool of pilots and observers for the next three weeks.

The waiting period, however, was not entirely wasted. A variety of activity was organised to keep us out of mischief and every opportunity was taken to impress on us in no uncertain manner, that while we had joined the Navy to fly, we were sailors first and foremost. Woe betide the man who thinks he's a 'Brylcream Boy' –

your allegiance is to the Navy always and at all times NOT the Air Force.

Our 31st pilots course finally got under way on 6th October and extended over eight weeks. It was a very extensive training period during which many would-be aviators were sorted out either to 'rescrub' as observers or be relegated to the seaman branch.

By this time we had become associated with our English, Welsh, Scottish and Irish counterparts. We were divided into two watches, Port and Starboard, which were on duty or leave 'ashore' alternatively.

New terms and expressions came into common usage. The navy has a language all of its own.

Some of the interesting expressions are:

The Navy – the 'Andrew'
The sea – the 'oggin'
In a ship – not on a ship
On a boat (submarine) – not in a boat
Latrines/Toilets – the 'heads'
Captain of the Heads – cleaning the heads for punishment
Cookhouse – the galley
Leading Hand badge – a Killick
Libertymen – men going on leave
Liberty boat – the boat for the above
Sailor – matelot
A well turned out sailor – a Tiddly matelot
To have a zizz – to have a sleep
The clothing store – Pussers store
Issue from clothing store – slops
Make and Mend – a half day given off duty often in bad weather
A midshipman – a 'snottie'
The ship's 1st Lieutenant – Jimmy the one
A ship's rumour – souttlebutt
In line for punishment – in the rattle
To be up and put away – lash up and stow one's hammock

And so it goes on. There are many many more quaint expressions dating back to the days of Nelson and beyond. Our instructors seldom lost an opportunity to remind us of the Nelson mystique. It was even suggested that space had been provided in every naval aircraft to accommodate Lord Nelson. When one considered the antiquated aircraft that the Navy was then operating – Swordfish, Albacores, Blackburn Skuas and Rocs, Gladiators and Fulmars – this story seemed to have some credence.

Our United Kingdom course mates were a very mixed bag. The majority were around 18 to 22 years, of public school or grammar school origin. There were a few Royal Navy seamen who had been transferred, plus three former policemen, each from the London Metropolitan Police Force.

Following the earlier reference to our status as colonials, some of us were determined to dominate the Brits at every opportunity. This we did in no small measure.

The average Kiwi has had the advantage of living in an outdoor environment, so it was not difficult for us to excel at all sport – rugby, swimming, physical training etc. One activity where Kiwis really excelled was in swimming. Very few of the British lads were good swimmers and a large number were unable to swim at all. There were weekly sessions conducted by Petty Officer physical training instructors in the barracks swimming pool. It was essential that trainee aircrews should acquire some swimming skills, if only to clamber into an inflatable raft in the event of ditching an aircraft in the sea. The Petty Officers readily acknowledged that all our New Zealand members were more competent than they were, so they handed some of the instructional work over to us. Also, from an intellectual aspect the Kiwis were above average, many being university students, teachers, civil servants etc. We more than held our own in classroom subjects. In fact there was only one English cadet who performed better in ground school, and he was an aeronautical apprentice from the Fairey Aviation Company.

A wide range of subjects and technical skills were included in our curriculum, ship and aircraft recognition, morse code, semaphore, Aldis lamp signalling, weapons training, ropes and splicing, boating in Portsmouth Harbour etc.

Immediately after our course commenced there was a call for anyone who had a knowledge of Lewis machine guns.

Arch, Mac, Bill and I had been trained on Lewis guns in the New Zealand Army, so we proudly stepped forward. There were no takers from the English contingent, so once again we had a chance to show our versatility. We were given our ‘action stations’ in the event of an air raid, but surprisingly no one gave a thought to testing our qualifications to fire this gun let alone clear the complicated stoppages to which it was prone.

Two nights later the air raid sirens went off. Mac, Bill and I had been assigned to a gun emplacement on the roof of a three storied barracks block. We raced to our post, slammed a pannier of 303 ammunition on the gun and stood by for something to happen. We did not have long to wait. A steady drone of aircraft engines grew louder and louder and suddenly the sky was lit up by dozens of searchlights followed immediately by anti-aircraft gunfire.

Hunks of shrapnel were landing on the roof, so we dived to get the steel helmets out of the cabinet. Just my luck – there were only two helmets – Mac and Bill had got to them first.

For the next half hour I felt quite naked as I ducked beneath the parapet and listened to the explosions and bits of metal screaming through the night sky.

It was very nearly *coup de grâce* for us when one German bomber came overhead and dropped a large bomb about 500 yards north of the barracks. There was one hell of an explosion. I could not resist the chance to look over the parapet and see the debris falling and the smoke curling skywards.

On reflection, however, our Lewis gun emplacement was absolutely futile. The only circumstances when we could have provided any effective resistance would have been a very low flying aircraft in broad daylight. That and other evaluations of defence installations along the south coast led me to believe that had Hitler proceeded with his original plan for a seaborne invasion, his armies would have encountered very weak defences. Part of one afternoon per week was given to sports and we found that there were plenty of local rugby clubs vying for matches against the Kiwis. Our 31st course team comprised 14 Kiwis and one Dubliner, Bill Wallace. Our manager was a RN Warrant Officer and our selector David (Butch) Muir. To win a place in the team was quite an honour. 'Butch' would announce each selection by climbing on top of a messroom table, calling for silence from Poms and Kiwis. 'The team to play Portsmouth Police this afternoon is as follows.' Then he would with suitable emphasis read out the names.

Our team would have graced any senior competition in New Zealand. We had four provincial representatives Cliff Bissett (Otago),

Colin Davidson (Wellington), Murray Heath and Buck Ryder (Nelson Bays). In addition we had several university 1st grade players, plus many from other senior clubs around New Zealand. In all we played eight games during which we scored 180 points and had only 20 scored against us.

I shall never forget a comment which I received from an opponent after one of our first games. It came from Joe Brough, a well built 6′ 2″, former pupil of the famous Mill Hill Public School in London. Joe came up to me after the game and in his cultured Mill Hillian voice said: 'Masters old chap, could we have a word?'

'Yes Joe, what's the problem?'

'Well, Masters, I just wanted to tell you that you are the roughest man I have ever encountered in a rugby match.'

'Thanks Joe – I am pleased to hear I'm the roughest, but I wouldn't have been happy to have been the dirtiest.'

From that moment a great bond of friendship had been created. Our paths crossed on many occasions over the next four years. Joe and his course mate Martin Turner (Wye Public School) who played wing threequarter for England in 1946–47 have remained my close friends ever since. Our last meeting was in 1989 when my wife and I visited the United Kingdom.

As we settled down to our naval routine we were all conscious of the fact that we were 'new look' matelots. The new look did not command respect from the old salts so something had to be done about improving our image. Several methods were employed to give the uniform an aged appearance. If the Jean was washed many times it acquired a lighter colour; if you slept in your cap as Mac discovered it would give it a decidedly crushed appearance. The prospect of growing a bear appealed to some of us. This entailed putting a request in to the Ship's Captain. Having done so the applicant would muster at Captain's Requestmen's parade, be marched in before God and say, 'Permission to grow sir.' God would then have a good look at your visage and warn that if he consented you would have to keep the beard for three months and could only shave it off subject to his subsequent permission.

As a joke several of us tried it. Some produced some excellent 'sets' but others were pretty straggly.

All sailors over the age of 21 were entitled to a daily tot of pussers rum. Unfortunately, many of us were classified as U/S (underage) and in any case Naval Airman cadets were prohibited from receiving the tot. Instead we received an additional three pence per day to compensate for the loss of this age old privilege. Tobacco was also a free issue. You could place an order for the cut leaf to be made into cigarettes or the full leaf which some sailors rolled inside sacking, dipped it in their rum issue and later cut it into blocks for chewing. Immediately following the tobacco issue, a van would appear at the barracks offering a cigarette rolling service at a small price per pound by weight.

Quite a few of our more gallant lads saw themselves as 'jack tars' of the old windjammer days and couldn't resist the thrill of climbing the 150ft mast in the parade ground. One had to have an unusual liking for heights to pursue this activity.

'Shore leave' was available on alternate days and overnight shore leave once per week. When we were rostered for overnight leave we invariably crossed the harbour from Gosport to spend the night at an overseas sailors hostel, the *Empire Rendezvous* at Southsea, which was run by Molly Cowell, a South African lady.

The extent of air raid damage at Southsea had to be seen to be believed. While there was some damage on the Gosport side, a large area of Southsea approximately one square mile had been pulverised.

Hardly a building was left standing. Surprisingly, however, the naval establishments such as HMS *Nelson* and HMS *Vernon* which would have been prime military targets were quite untouched. Likewise the shoreline of Southsea on which were located dozens of luxury holiday hotels.

Our seamanship training included whaler boat rowing on Pompey harbour. A Whaler would provide for 10–12 rowers. We got good exercise rowing around a variety of naval ships in the harbour, destroyers, frigates, mine sweepers etc., but by far the most interesting was the old French battleship *Courbet* which had joined the Free French navy after the French surrender in 1940.

The *Courbet* was then permanently anchored in Portsmouth harbour and acted as a heavy anti-aircraft gun platform. A great deal of metal was thrown up from the *Courbet* during the German air raids.

It is interesting to note that a few months earlier the *Courbet* had been commanded by a high ranking French Naval Airman Corvette

Capitaine André Jubelin who was later to transfer to the RAF and flew in both day and night squadrons.

As I had mentioned earlier we Kiwis never lost an opportunity to exercise our dominance over our Pommie course mates, many of whom were still incredibly immature and naive.

One occasion will always remain in my memory. An essential feature of our training was the development of confidence and the ability to command. The cadets were in three divisions, each named after famous admirals, Nelson, Collingwood and Rodney. Our 31 Course was Rodney division which was divided into four squads comprising about 30 cadets each.

On this particular day the cadet who was on duty as the squad commander was a young Englishman, probably about 18 years who looked pretty wet behind the ears. He was one who hadn't yet cultivated the 'worn image'. He still wore his lanyard and whistle which most Kiwis had consigned to the dump and his cap was precisely square on his head whereas most 'tiddly matelots' preferred a jaunty angle.

He called the squad to attention and asked if we were all present. 'Butch' Muir was standing alongside me and just for a lark I said, 'I wonder what would happen if someone told him Cunthooks was "adrift".'

Now 'Butch' was renowned for his acting and practical joking – he rose to the challenge and told our leader 'Oh no! I think Cunthooks is not back yet.'

'Who did you say?'

'Cunthooks.'

'Cunthooks – I don't know anyone by that name.'

'Yes, you do – he's that red haired Irish bloke – he dashed off for a quick one at the Heads – he must have the gripes because he's not back yet.'

The young Englishman looked bewildered, but 'Butch' seemed so genuine and everyone maintained a straight face so he had no option but to call us to attention again.

He did a smart about turn and marched up to report to the Chief Petty Officer Wilmot.

'No. 2 squad Rodney division present and correct, Chief except that Cunthooks appears to be adrift.'

Wilmot tilted his cap back on his head, lowered his glasses to the end of his nose, leaned down to this unfortunate cadet and enquired, 'Oo did yer say was adrift?'

At this point the cadet must have realised that something was not quite right but he had no option but to repeat the name of the sinner in a somewhat more subdued tone.

'Cunthooks, Chief.'

Wilmot said: 'I think someone has been pulling your leg sonny. Get back to yer squad and don't come to me again with any more nonsense like that.'

Wilmot then looked over to our squad where all the 'pig islanders' as he was then wont to call us were rolling around in paroxysms of mirth. He didn't say another word. He knew that we had convincingly cut them all down to size – cadets and instructors.

Another humorous incident occurred on a Sunday church parade. We had to fall in on the parade ground and then march 'ashore' to our respective churches. Thus we had Anglicans, Roman Catholics, Presbyterians and Methodists as the main contingents with odds and sods making up the 'other denominations'. Some bright spark had discovered that the Salvation Army Church was about three miles away from HMS *St Vincent* and to get there one had to pass three pubs. The pubs would be open from 11 a.m. until 2 p.m. so about a dozen Kiwis decided that for that Sunday we would pay our respects to the 'Sallies'. We were duly marched off the parade ground under command of our ace practical joker 'Butch' Muir. An hour or so later we presented ourselves at the Salvation Army Church where we were accorded a right royal welcome by sundry SA Officers, men and women. Following certain lessons and hymns the Captain in charge invited anyone in the congregation to come forward and contribute their homily.

Without prior warning 'Butch' stood up and said he would like to say a few words.

To our amazement, 'Butch' launched forth into a very respectful address suitably interspersed with religious references. Our problem was to maintain straight faces and some of our chaps had to hide behind the pews because they were doubled up with mirth. Whatever one's religion may be, one cannot deny that the 'Sallies' are really true practising Christians.

At the end of our course we had to sit practical and written examinations in all subjects. This revealed that the English education system apparently turned a blind eye to cheating or 'cribbing' as the Poms called it. This had been unheard of in New Zealand schools, but it was obviously quite prevalent in the English Grammar and Public School systems. Moreover, the Petty Officer Instructors made subtle suggestions as to what questions would be asked in both the verbal and written tests. So what we saw were Pommie cadets equipped with their 'cribs' which they slid into the sleeve of their jacket or inside their socks. The subjects which they could not cheat on were semaphore – Aldis lamp – morse code – ship and aircraft recognition. Those tests sorted the rats from the mice.

The day of reckoning fell on 29th November. The suspense was overpowering.

Three lists of names were read out:

No 1 list – to travel to the United States of America for flying training at United States Naval Air Station, Pensacola.

No 2 list – Elementary Flying School at Elmdon, near Birmingham.

No 3 list – Elementary Flying School at Luton, Bedfordshire.

Happily we only lost one of our close associates – Arch Foley who went on the Pensacola draft. All other members of our 'gang' were on the Luton draft.

The unlucky chaps who 'dipped' (failed) the course, could apply for a 'rescrub' (second attempt) or elect to continue in the Navy in the seaman branch. Some later achieved commissioned rank by entering HMS *King Alfred* as officer cadets – seaman branch.

The successful cadets were authorised to sew on their new badge of rank as 'acting leading Naval Airmen'. Prior to that we had been the lowest form of humanity in the Navy – 'Naval Airmen 2nd class'. The badge took the form of an anchor referred to as a 'Killick'. This also entitled us to a minute increase to our already meagre pay of 5 shillings and 6 pence per day from which we had to make a weekly allotment of 14/- which was to accumulate in New Zealand until the war was over. A few weeks later when we commenced flying training we were to receive a further small increment.

Just before we left *St Vincent* a new draft of Kiwis arrived. I happened to be walking across the parade ground when one of these new entrants approached me.

'I believe I have met you before. You are Masters, aren't you?'

'Yes that's right, but I'm afraid you have the advantage of me. I can't recall where or when we met.'

'Well I'd better introduce myself. I'm Dick Mackie. We met face to face in the front row of a rugby scrum. I was hooker for Wanganui Collegiate when you defeated us in 1938 by 24 to nil. You New Plymouth chaps gave us a hell of a drubbing that day.'

'Well fancy that, Dick. You have a remarkable memory.'

This was my second meeting with Dick whose friendship I have valued ever since. This was also the second time a rugby opponent had sought me out and confessed to a torrid encounter, the first being Joe Brough. By some strange quirk of fate the paths of the three of us have crossed at many times. Joe and I served together later in 1944, and Joe and Dick served together in the *Indomitable* in 1945.

The Rugby match to which Dick Mackie referred was a fixture between Wanganui Collegiate School and New Plymouth Boys' High School played at New Plymouth on 3rd August 1938. New Plymouth Boys won 24 to nil but the really unique feature of this encounter was that of the 30 players on the field six would be serving in the Fleet Air Arm before the close of 1941. They were Dick Mackie, Matt Farrer and Tony Renshaw from Wanganui, D'Arcy Self, Alister Macleod and the author from NPBHS.

This surely qualifies for the Guinness Book of Records!

After leaving HMS *St Vincent* we were all drafted to HMS *Daedalus* at Lee-on-Solent. Prior to the war this was the main FAA station, but since the heavy bombing raids it was used principally as a base for trainee pilots, observers, air gunners, mechanics etc awaiting posting to other training establishments. The Pensacola and Elmdon drafts proceeded on their way fairly quickly, but our Luton draft was destined to spend about four very long boring weeks here. There were so many matelots in transit that no one knew what to do with us. Periodically we went on route marches around the countryside and at night time we were given armed guard duties at various salient points in the vicinity.

Christmas was a good excuse to get us out of sight for a few days, so most of us headed for London to whoop it up for a few days on what little money we had.

EFTS – Elementary Flying Training School

When we arrived at Luton, we found the whole countryside blanketed under a very heavy cover of snow which in some places was several feet deep. The temperature was below freezing, so we were somewhat relieved to find that our billets were at a large country mansion called Putteridge Bury about seven miles from the city of Luton. Putteridge Bury was the country seat of the Cassells family who had graciously handed it over to the Navy for the duration of the war.

Like most English buildings of the day, it lacked any form of heating, so we found ourselves to be as cold inside the building as outside. To make our existence even more spartan we were called at 5.30 a.m. each morning to catch a bush to our airfield at 6.30 a.m. Anyone who was 'adrift' would be in deep trouble.

Once at the aerodrome we had to wait around in the freezing temperature for the dining hall to open at 7 a.m. The temperature was so low that the huge fire fighting tanks for holding reserves of water for use during air raids were all frozen solid.

Our first breakfast was the most unimaginative and unappetising meal I had ever had. The catering was by private contract. They were obviously determined to make a good profit out of us.

We were given a plate of shredded wheat which was floating in some watery solution which served as milk and decorated with water cress. After that one slice of bread, some lumpy margarine that was so cold you could not spread it and a dubious version of plum jam. This was topped off with a mug of wishy-washy tea. At least the tea was reasonably hot – nothing else was.

Our course was joined by three lieutenants, Royal Marines – Smith, 'Titus' Oakes, and Howes-Dufton. These officers obviously found it somewhat embarrassing to be training with such insignificant forms of humanity as acting leading naval airmen. They lived apart apparently in officers quarters and the only time we saw them was in the crew rooms or classroom. To protect their rank they held themselves aloof from the common herd, but we nevertheless got the impression that even they were somewhat awed at the authority we Kiwis exercised over the Brits.

The course was divided into two watches, port and starboard. The Port watch would have ground school (navigation, signals, aircraft recognition, aerodynamics, engine handling, theory of flight etc) in the morning session, and flying when possible in the afternoon. Starboard would do the opposite.

My first flying instructor was RAF Sergeant Paul who introduced me to the Miles Magister, a monoplane training aircraft. My log book records my first flight on New Year's Day 1942 – Air Experience Cockpit Layout – Effect of Controls – Straight and Level – 40 minutes.

That same day I had a second trip with Sgt Paul – adding to the lesson – taxiing, climbing, gliding and stalling. I flew again for short periods on the 2nd, 5th, 6th, 9th, 10th, 14th, 21st, 22nd and 30th January – by which time I had amassed the total of 8 hours 20 minutes dual instruction.

At that point the CFI (Chief Flying Instructor) came to the conclusion that none of us would ever go solo under these conditions.

I can recall several occasions being up with Sgt Paul who was a very fine and considerate instructor being told by him, 'You have got her – now fly me back to the aerodrome.'

I would look over the side of the cockpit and everywhere I looked the ground was covered with snow. A novice could not possibly identify any landmarks. The fact that there was no horizon because of the 'white out' effect made it difficult to keep the aircraft flying straight and level.

But one had to put on a bold front – one could not say to the instructor through the Gosport tube (means of pilot/pupil communication) that one did not know where the hell the aerodrome was. One simply made a wild stab at it and steered in any direction at all just hoping it might be the right one. Well, eventually Sgt Paul's calm voice would come through the Gosport tube: 'O.K. I have got her, turn in the opposite direction and take us safely back to base.'

This climatic condition known as 'white out' was precisely the same as confronted the pilots of the ill-fated Air New Zealand flight to Antarctica which crashed on Mt Erebus. Pilots who are trained in temperate climates would seldom encounter such difficult weather conditions when the ground, the sky and the horizon seem to merge into one.

I shall never forget the day, 9th January, when Sgt Paul put me into my first spin. He demonstrated that by closing the throttle and pulling the stick back, the aircraft would stall.

The nose would drop – add some left or right rudder – and it would flick over on its back and enter a violent spinning sensation with the ground whizzing round and round, faster and faster. Apply some opposite rudder, push the control column forward and the Magister would gladly resume normal straight and level flight. The most horrifying moment was when one hung in one's straps upside down expecting to fall out and use one's parachute.

Since that day I have done hundreds of spins in all types of fighter aircraft, but none were as spine tingling as that first one.

One of the few highlights of our time at Luton airfield was to witness the test flying of the prototype Typhoon fighter-bomber which was about to be supplied to the RAF squadrons. We watched this enormously powerful fighter take off, climb like a rocket and come in to land at a phenomenal speed. Would we someday be sitting at the controls of such an amazing aircraft?

Fifty years on, my memories of Luton are being perpetually cold and perpetually hungry. The quality and quantity of food was atrocious. The Naafi canteen which came to our crew room when we were on flying detail was a welcome supplement, but alas we had very little money to spend on their unappetising sawdust buns.

The Brits bore their hunger even worse than we Kiwis. The Brits were always first in the food queues. The poor devils were almost obsessed about food.

The decision was announced that our course would be going to Sealand, near Chester to complete our EFTS training on a different aircraft, the better known biplane, the Tiger Moth.

It was about this time that we all became very concerned about the war situation in the Pacific. The Japanese fleet had delivered a devastating blow to the United States navy at Pearl Harbor on 7th December 1941 and since then there had been a succession of defeats: Hong Kong, the Philippines, the sinking of British battleships *Prince of Wales* and *Repulse* on 10th December and the final humiliation, the surrender of Singapore on 15th February 1942. By this time few of us ever expected to see our homeland again.

I continued to write letters to my parents and my friend Joan Rees, but in all honesty I doubted whether I would see them again.

Strangely enough none of our chaps expressed a desire to opt out. I believe we all realised that the greater menace was Hitler and the German nation. The first priority was to defeat them and then we could turn our attention to the Japanese hordes.

While we were at Luton a rather curious incident occurred. A Kiwi Naval Airman who was not a member of our course but had somehow been left behind by the previous course, had got seriously offside with the Naval Commander. Apparently he had taken 'French leave' to go up to London to see some 'popsie'. On his return he was on the mat before the Commander who issued a very severe reprimand. Next weekend, this crazy man did the same thing again. This time it was gross insubordination. The Commander had no option but to sentence him to a period of correction at an Army 'Glasshouse', Chorley Military Prison in Lancashire. The offender who was really a small rather inoffensive chap and was obviously hopelessly besotted by feminine charm. He was sentenced to two months in this ruthless hell hole. He found himself to be the only matelot among hundreds of Army rebels.

Each day they would have to scrub and polish their equipment, webbing gaiters, haversacks, etc. Our man however, only had one piece of equipment a gas mask and container, so he had to scrub that along with all the many physical and mental punishments they were subjected to.

When he joined our course at Sealand, he was just a shadow of his former self. His spirit had been completely broken by the Military Police regime. It was obvious to all that 'Scruffy' would not reoffend.

Surprisingly this offence, while it would have been recorded on his personal record, did not prevent him from finally winning his commission as a sub-lieutenant. Sadly, however, he was later killed after joining a new Corsair squadron which was forming up in the United States of America. The Corsairs had been involved in a series of inexplicable accidents about this time. It was later discovered that the danger had been caused by a seepage of carbon monoxide gas into the totally enclosed pilot's cockpit.

Our new EFTS was a grass aerodrome at Sealand about eight miles west of the historic Roman walled city of Chester. We arrived on 10th February 1942 and found the climate, accommodation and food much more to our liking. New instructors were assigned to us and we were introduced to our new trainer, a Tiger Moth biplane. Several of the instructors had been Battle of Britain fighter pilots who had been seconded to training command after having survived a long period on operations. Our CFI was Squadron Leader W. H. R. Whitty ex 607 Hurricanes, based at Tangmere.

My own instructor was Warrant Officer Young and I could not have wished for a more likeable chap. Before our departure from Luton most of us were very depressed because no one could see any prospect of being allowed to go solo. We needed a little encouragement and W/O Young was the ideal man to restore our confidence. With the instructor in the front seat and the pupil in the rear seat communication between the two was limited to a Gosport tube. The psychological effect of some angry comment over the tube could be quite devastating on the pupil. While the instructors would have been well aware of this problem, some tended to impatience but didn't really mean to upset the pupil. W/O Young was by nature a very calm person – he had a ton of patience. When I look back over my flying career I feel that my later good assessments were due to his competent tuition. The great day for my first solo came on 28th February after having eight hours 20 minutes on Magisters and five hours and five minutes on Tiger Moths.

From then on we flew consistently, nearly every day, alternating dual instruction with solo and periodic check flights with the CFI.

Chester was a really charming city to visit. There was a railway station close to the camp, so we could go into Chester in the evening and be back on board before lights out. Occasionally each watch would be granted a 24 or 48 hour leave pass, whereupon we would either stay overnight in one of Chester's quaint little hotels and then set out on a pub crawl around the 150 odd taverns in the city area. I recall staying one night in the smallest hotel one could ever imagine. It was the London Bridge Hotel on the second level of the main street. The frontage could not have been more than 15 feet wide, yet it had a tap room, dining room, staircase and a few bedrooms.

On the other long leaves we travelled round the coast to Llandudno and Caernarvon Castle.

But it was not all play. The flying programme was quite intense. Night flying was the next experience and one which I will not easily forget. I was rostered to fly the first night with W/O Young at 1 a.m. in the morning. It was my misfortune to be on the last detail – the chaps who had flown at 7 p.m. had been in the dreamland long ago.

The night was pitch black, the clouds black, not a star to be seen, not a light anywhere except about six lights either side of what was to be our take off path. W/O Young took off, did a circuit and landed, telling me quietly over the Gosport tube what the routine was. Then he said, 'It's all yours.' So I lined up carefully to the six lamps either side and pushed the throttle forward. Once airborne I climbed to the regulated 1,000 feet on instruments, turned 90° to the port again to become parallel to the take off path.

There wasn't a light or star anywhere, so we proceeded on instruments. Eventually I looked over to port and at long last I could see the glimmer of lamps indicating the landing path. Another turn to port, throttled back to lose height, then I could see the entrance lights to the glidepath. We were in the yellow sector so we were safe to lose more height – turned to port again and lined up with the six lights either side of the landing strip. Then we descended into green – so a little more throttle to hold the Tiger there. Happily we did not descend into red, which meant the approach was too low and very dangerous. Well, we made two more night take offs and landings when thankfully W/O Young called it a night.

On my return to the barracks block where all my mates were snoring their heads off, I was so hyped up and the adrenalin was still flowing at such a rate that I simply could not sleep a wink all that night.

So much for night flying – I wasn't too sure that it was my forte.

A few nights later, as if to confirm my fears, a Boulton Paul Defiant two-seater night fighter sought refuge on our aerodrome. The pilot may have been in action and unable to make it back to his home base. He apparently spotted our runway lights and decided to land. Coming over the boundary something went wrong and we heard a most horrible crash and explosion. The crew of two, probably very experienced men, was killed.

The first tragedy on our course occurred about this time. There was a Spitfire OTU (Operational Training Unit) at an adjacent aerodrome Hawarden. It was so close that the two landing circuits coincided so it was a real wonder accidents had not happened previously.

One of our young English cadets named Barnby was flying solo over the Dee Estuary when a Spitfire suddenly appeared and collided with him. Neither pilot was able to bale out, both were killed.

This was a deep shock to us because the Brits and the Kiwis were gradually beginning to accept each other more easily and young Barnby (barely 18 years) was one of the more popular chaps. It was all the more distressing to us because it could not possibly have been Barnby's fault. He was flying a much slower aircraft and the Spitfire pilot was obliged to give him a wide berth. Whether the Spitfire pilot decided to do some dummy attacks on Barnby and underestimated his closing speed no one would ever know.

The New Zealand contingent had been together now for about eight months since leaving New Zealand, so certain individuals had distinguished themselves in a variety of ways and nicknames had become common. Some of the better known were:

Cliff (Lefty) Bissett, Alex (Buck) Ryder,
Murray (Halfie) Heath, Bill (Jerk) Ryan,
David (Butch) Muir, Bill (Paddy) Wallace (Southern Ireland),
Bill (Shad) Nankervis, Harry (Skel) MacKay
(on account of his rotund physique).

There had been news following a series of CFI check-up tests. Several pupils, including Bill Ryan, Reg Hoskin, Bill Nankervis were rejected from further pilot training. It was a very sad farewell, particularly in the case of Bill Ryan, a former school friend who I had influenced into volunteering for the Fleet Air Arm.

The three returned to HMS *Daedalus* (Lee-on-Solent) where they elected to commence training as observers. I believe they were sent to a training station in Scotland initially and completed their course in Trinidad.

One of the highlights of our training course at Sealand was a cross country flight to Wolverhampton and return, a distance by air of approximately 60 miles. We were first required to do this exercise with an instructor to ensure we were capable of map reading and changing course en route to allow for wind variation. My instructor was none other than CFI Squadron Leader Whitty. This could have been a rather awesome experience for a novice, but Whitty was a very decent officer who bestowed a few words of praise here and there and inspired me to a good performance. The following day he authorised me to do the same cross country solo.

With no one in the front seat to make any course adjustment should one's map reading or compass steering be at fault, this was a major challenge. Cross country flights in slow aircraft like Tiger Moths were much more difficult in the densely populated areas of England than they were in countries such as New Zealand, Australia and Canada. Between Sealand and Wolverhampton one passed over dozens of towns and small villages, roads, rivers and railway tracks. It was a case of pin pointing and adjusting for wind on the port beam all the way. After 60 minutes flying I spotted an aerodrome on the outskirts of the city, landed and taxied up to report to the Duty Pilot in the control tower. The Duty Pilot was required to sign a certificate verifying that one had completed the trip and added an assessment for the landing – good – medium – or bad. My log book shows the comment good, so that was very satisfying to take back with me. The return trip with the wind behind me took only 45 minutes.

Some more unpleasant news was given out. Of the original draft of 64 who left New Zealand, 21 had gone on to Sealand, three had recently 'dipped' and now we were to be split into two drafts for shipment to Canada for advanced training. Eleven Kiwis were to leave in the first troopship and seven in the second.

To be included in the second draft was initially a disappointment, but because we had the opportunity of adding another 11–12 hours on Tiger Moths, most of which was solo, it turned out to be a blessing.

The instructors gave us more freedom in the air, which some of us took advantage of by staging unauthorised 'dogfights' well out of sight of the aerodrome. Butch Muir, Pete Wilson and I would endeavour to get on the same flying detail, take off and rendezvous over a large country estate known as Eaton Hall. There we would whirl around, like World War I aviators, in tight turns, trying to get on each other's tails. It was great fun – I believe my flying skill improved 100% during those few extra hours at Sealand.

We left Sealand on 14th May bound for an aircrew transit camp on the outskirts of Manchester. Here we joined up with a complete draft of 33 course pilots from Elmdon EFTS which contained a number of Kiwis, only one of whom I knew. He was Graeme King from New Plymouth.

A few days later we moved on to Liverpool for passage by ferry steamer to Belfast from where we were destined to travel to Halifax, Nova Scotia on a United States navy tank transporter which was curiously named *Sea Train Texas*. Before going on board, however, we were obliged to spend our final night ashore in Belfast.

By this time, we had become accustomed to the incredible vagueness about movement arrangements in the Navy, so it came as no great surprise to us to find out that no one in Belfast had been notified of our impending arrival. Nor did anyone seem to care.

Amidst all this incredible bungling the fact emerged that because no one had received a signal about us, no accommodation had been organised. We would have to accept whatever they could find. Well, in close proximity to the docks there was a vacant skin and hides store. That was the best they could do for us.

The prospect of a night in such a place just about sparked off a mutiny among the Kiwis, who, as usual, were much more voluble than the Brits. After a cursory inspection of the building we toyed with the idea of getting in touch, there and then with, our High Commissioner Bill Jordan in London. Better judgement finally prevailed, however, because it was only a one-night stay and to make our complaint official was not going to achieve much. After a short discussion which was strongly influenced by 31 course members we decided to go out on the town and get sufficiently 'tanked up' so that we could come back and endure the stinking hovel and hopefully be sufficiently anaesthetised to go to sleep.

The following morning we went on board our transport and enjoyed our first decent meal since leaving New Zealand. Everything about the *Sea Train Texas* was first class. Our accommodation was in bunks, not hammocks, the messing facilities were provided in cafeteria style and the standard of food little short of excellent. The Brits had to complain, however, because everything was highly spiced and they couldn't get used to it.

We were part of a large, very slow convoy so although we had plenty of corvettes, frigates and destroyers in the escort screen it could have been a very dangerous trip. At that stage of the war the German U Boats were hunting in packs and chalking up some frightening successes.

Luck was with us, however, and after about 12 days we safely entered, once again, the harbour of Halifax. A day or two later we departed by rail to Kingston, 850 miles west on the shore of Lake Ontario. This was where we were to spend the next four months at a Service Flying Training School (SFTS). En route to Kingston the journey took us through the neighbourhood province of New Brunswick, then followed the St Lawrence River to Quebec. Up until then the landscape had been very bleak, the standard of housing and farms rather primitive. Considering that Halifax and the province of Nova Scotia could hardly be described as a tourist attraction, we had by this time acquired a rather scornful view of the Canadian landscape. This was late spring or early summer so it must have been a very dismal place in the middle of winter. However, once past Quebec and Montreal the countryside and the scenery became easier on the eye. In fact the province of Ontario, in which Kingston was located, would rival British Columbia for the title of the premier province of Canada.

SFTS – Service Flying Training School

Our aerodrome was situated on the shore of Lake Ontario about six miles away from the city of Kingston. It comprised three sealed, quite long runways with several hangars and numerous barracks and classrooms. This station had probably been constructed especially for the training of pilots under the Empire Air Training scheme. Everything was first class – the food – the accommodation and most important of all the weather.

We were again formed into two watches, Port and Starboard, and introduced to our new training aircraft which proved to be an American built Harvard radial engined two seater monoplane. When one looked inside the cockpit for the first time one was confronted with an awesome array of dials, gauges, switches etc. Other aeronautical refinements were a variable pitch propellor, landing flaps, brakes, sliding hood, retractable undercarriage, altogether a very modern and very versatile little aircraft which could comfortably cruise at 170–180 m.p.h. This was a vast improvement on our two earlier trainers which had open cockpits, no brakes, no flaps, fixed undercarriage and a maximum speed of little more than 100 m.p.h.

We were allocated instructors, mine being a youthful Sergeant Pilot Rattray with whom I flew for the next 20 hours dual instruction. After seven hours I received the green light for my first solo flight.

The routine was the same as in England with the two watches attending ground school in the morning and flying in the afternoon or vice versa. Being summer time the weather was glorious, so from the commencement of this course on 1st June to the last flight on 7th September I had accumulated a further 120 hours day and night flying with 144 individual sorties. When on afternoon ground school we would often dash away and have a swim in Lake Ontario which was only a few hundred yards from our hut.

Then climb into our No 1 uniform which was then simply a white shirt and trousers and tear off into Kingston for a couple of beers and a great meal in a Chinese restaurant.

Like all human beings we were soon looking for some variety, so the four of us, Buck Ryder, Harry MacKay, Peter Wilson and I, decided to purchase a motor car. We had a look around several car lots and came across a Buick Sedan about 1929 model for which the vendor was asking a fabulous price of $80.00. None of us were skilled mechanics but we looked it over, inside and out, underneath and in the engine and could not find much wrong, so we took it. We drove back to the aerodrome in seventh heaven – no one else had come up with an idea like this. Unfortunately, however, we had given no thought to where we were to store the vehicle, but when we arrived at the guard house the decision was ready made. Pupil pilots were not permitted to have cars on the aerodrome. There was only one sensible answer – leave the damned thing parked quite prominently outside the gates. This we did.

As the weeks passed whenever we were given a 24 or 48 hour leave we four would clamber into our jalopy and drive off far afield. We considered ourselves to be the most adventurous of all the cadets on the course, but we did encounter a never ending sequence of problems. One thing which we had not thoroughly inspected was the quality of the tyres. It turned out that these were most unreliable and we had several punctures, often in inaccessible places up to 100 miles away from Kingston.

Despite this problem, however, we thoroughly enjoyed these expeditions which not only established our *mana* with our fellow course members but established a great camaraderie among the four owners.

The officer commanding the station was Wing Commander Fryer who also served in the capacity of CFI. On his instructional staff he had a number of ex-operational pilots, one of whom Squadron Leader Peter Lamb had served in 610 Spitfire Squadron. The senior naval officer was Commander (A) G. N. P. Stringer DFC, RN who had previously been batsman in the aircraft carrier *Ark Royal* during the destruction of the German battleship *Bismarck* in the Atlantic.

The flying training became progressively more interesting and operationally orientated. We were given plenty of time for developing our skill and confidence in solo aerobatics etc. If so inclined, opportunity could be taken for some form of unauthorised experiments. I, personally, revelled in the fact that the Harvard was a very sturdy aircraft and the radial engine was ideally suited for inverted flying. I knew that long periods of inverted flying could damage the engine but I could not resist the temptation to try it out. We had not had any instruction in this art so it was a matter of trial and error. Other unauthorised manoeuvres were flick rolls. The Harvard was the only aircraft that I was game to try these on because the flick roll was known to put undue pressure strain on the airframe and some aircraft had been known to break up in mid air. And of course there was unauthorised low flying. This was a fabulous experience as long as you were not caught doing it. The thing to do was to get well away from the aerodrome in some sparsely populated area where there would be little chance of some observer taking the number of your plane and reporting the incident to the station commander. The fact that I did quite a lot of low flying stood me in good stead when I had my final flying test for my 'wings'. I was able to put on a pretty impressive performance right down on the deck, flying over fences, between trees etc. I guess Squadron Leader Lamb who checked me out must have known that I had been breaking the rules.

In addition to more concentrated night flying, we did a lot of instrument flying under the hood including two or three cross country instrument flights on a triangular course beginning with an instrument take off. Suffice to say one had to be a very precise compass flyer to be able to arrive over the aerodrome after having passed the intermediate turning points.

Near the end of our course we transferred to a satellite grass airfield at Gannanoque about 20 miles further up the St Lawrence river in the area called 'The Thousand Islands'. Here we spent a week in tents and concentrated mainly in night flying but also refreshing our forgotten *St Vincent* skills on semaphore and Aldis lamp signalling.

This was an exceptionally pleasant part of our course. The weather could not have been better and the night flying, with all the local towns lit up, was just a 'piece of cake' after the intense black out in the United Kingdom. The instructors enjoyed this respite every bit as much as we did and a wonderful camaraderie developed between us. Possibly they felt that we pupils had now reached the stage that they could not teach us much more so they tended to accept us on their level. Whether this applied to all of our course or not I will never know, but certainly the six Kiwis developed an excellent rapport with these instructors who had come with us from Kingston to Gannanoque.

Several of the instructors had cars and quite often they would invite some of us to climb aboard and drive into the township about five miles away where we would have a mild session at the local hostelry. On one such occasion we were returning to the aerodrome in two car loads. The leading car bore Buck Ryder, Harry MacKay and Peter Wilson as passengers, whilst the other car, a two seater with 'dickey seat' driven by Flying Officer Ross, brought up the rear. Ross's passengers were 'Lefty' Bissett in the front seat with Bob Gray and I in the 'dickey seat'. Both cars roared off down the metalled road towards the aerodrome with Ross who was slightly 'under the weather', trying to bump the car in front of us. This caused much amusement until suddenly a 90° corner appeared and the leading car whirled around in a dense cloud of dust and flying pebbles.

Flying Officer Ross had not anticipated this corner but his reflex was immaculate. He wrenched the wheel to port doing about 30 m.p.h., failed to straighten up in time and we went head on with an almighty crash into a telegraph pole. Following the crash there was a momentary dead silence until 'Lefty' emerged from the front seat, saw Bob Gray's much bloodied head poking through the rear glass window, then abruptly turned and unloaded his lollies in the nearby gutter. Luckily, although I was alongside Bob Gray in the back seat, I was unhurt but deeply winded by the 'dickey seat' frame. Flying Officer Ross emerged from the driving seat quite unperturbed – he had probably seen and experienced much worse than this as an operational pilot.

Fortunately for us there were no traffic police around so the incident was hushed up. Bob had several stitches which did nothing to improve his already rugged countenance and I doubt whether Commander (A) Stringer our Senior Naval Officer had heard a word about the escapade.

Shortly after the night flying programme we sat our final ground school examination and our final flying test.

All who had survived the course to this stage were awarded the coveted pilots wings. Several had been rejected during the Kingston training, one of whom was that very popular personality of our original *Dominion Monarch* draft Dave (Butch) Muir.

To this day, the circumstances of Butch's rejection remain rather vague. From all accounts, he had to make a forced landing in a Harvard, and I believe it was on Amherst Island not far from Kingston on the northern side of Lake Ontario. Just why he came down there is a mystery but possibly he had been doing some unauthorised low flying and damaged his aircraft in some trees. Anyway the first we knew about it was when he confronted us and quite blandly told us, 'Well, I've had it, chaps – I am leaving you.' We pleaded with him to appeal against the verdict, we discussed it unofficially with some instructors who were sympathetic and we finally decided to petition Commander Stringer to have Butch reinstated.

To our amazement, Butch completely rejected this approach and reiterated his acceptance of the official verdict. Whether Butch had in some strange way acquired a premonition about his future as a pilot, one will never know. Subsequently, however, I encountered three distinct occasions when active service pilots experienced these premonitions – two were killed and one probably took the correct decision and survived. Butch returned to the United Kingdom entered the seaman branch of the Navy, won his commission as a sub-lieutenant and served on infantry landing craft during the invasion of France.

Coinciding with the conclusion of our Kingston course we received notice of our promotions and our future service employment. Three or four became petty officers, a few under the age of 21, midshipmen, and the remainder sub-lieutenants, all with the seniority dated 11th September 1942.

It came as a very severe shock to us to find that Peter Wilson, another fine member of the *Dominion Monarch* draft, had been made a petty officer. Peter had all the potential qualities for commissioned rank, plus the fact that he was undoubtedly a good pilot. No one could understand why he had been downgraded. Perhaps he had not performed as well as he might in the ground school subjects.

Happily however, Peter did not hold this status very long. He was eventually commissioned and later served with distinction in one of the fleets' Firefly squadrons. Returning to civilian life after the war, Peter eventually became managing director of Hawkins Construction

Co Ltd, one of the largest building companies in New Zealand. In retrospect this was obviously a case of poor judgement on the part of the RAF and Naval instructors.

At this point we also received our final flying assessments and notification of which operational training unit we were to attend once we had returned to the United Kingdom. There were three such units, Torpedo Bomber Reconnaissance, Amphibian (Seaplane) and Fighters. Whilst the seaplane course was optional, the other two vocations were generally decided by the instructional staff, taking into account a variety of factors, airmanship, navigation skill, temperament, leadership and aggressiveness etc. In my case I had received quite an impressive flying assessment comprising a mid-term 'above average' and end of term 'above average' as a pilot and navigator, 'average' at air gunnery and a very rare 'exceptional' at dive-bombing at the end of the course. I was called before the CFI and invited to make a choice. This was something that had troubled me for some time. Had I been in the RAF, I would almost certainly have preferred to be a bomber pilot. The idea of commanding a crew of five or six airmen in a Lancaster bomber had a certain appeal. It was a team commitment. Unfortunately, however, the reality was that the FAA bombers were at that stage of the war very antiquated aircraft, Fairey Swordfish and Albacores capable of only 110–130 knots. Nothing had been heard at that stage of the Grumman Avenger bombers which were to come into squadron service a short time later. On the other hand, we know that the fighter squadrons were already equipped with Hurricanes and Grumman Martlets (Wildcats) and some deck landing trials have been carried out with Spitfires.

I was informed that the choice was only given to those who had high assessments, so this was a privilege not to be taken lightly.

While I still hankered for the moral support of a team which would include a qualified navigator any qualms that I may have had about the desolation of a fighter pilot trying to find his way back to the carrier over miles and miles of stormy seas were overcome by the knowledge that if I chose fighters I would be flying modern aircraft at least comparable with our enemies.

Having made the decision the CFI then pushed my report across the table, I felt quite humble to read the final comment: 'This pupil has the talent and temperament to become a good service pilot.'

With that we sat down and sewed our gold pilots wings on the left sleeve of our No. 1 uniforms and set off on ten days end of course leave.

Six of us travelled to Toronto where we 'held court' at the most expensive hotel in the City, The Royal York. This was a luxury hotel renowned as the largest hotel in the then British Empire. Even today the Royal York would be considered to be very high class accommodation. Two nights was all we could afford so we then passed on to Niagara Falls and Buffalo. At this stage it became obvious to me that a group of six matelots was too unwieldy and a difference of opinion arose as to where we would spend the rest of our leave. I was determined to go to New York, but the other five nominated Detroit which was not nearly so far to travel. Despite my limited funds I was confident that I could secure plenty of free rides, so I bade the others farewell and set off on my lonesome. After trudging along the main outlet for about two miles I became conscious of someone whistling behind me. I turned around and there was Arthur Herbert Percy Archibald trying to catch me up. 'Hey – Cappy – give us a break man – I'm coming with you.' It was good to have company but I was mystified at his sudden change of heart.

'Now Arch before we go any further please tell me how much money you have got.'

'A little over 20 dollars.'

'Well – I have only got 40 dollars – how the hell do you think two of us are going to exist in New York for four nights with just 60 bucks?'

Arch was supremely confident – he would leave the budgeting to me.

Anyway I could not have wished for a better companion.

We stayed one night at Rochester, another at Syracuse, picking up sundry hitchhikes en route. From Syracuse we were fortunate to be picked up by the driver of a large vegetable delivery van who was heading direct to New York City. Leaving Syracuse we travelled via Utica, Schenectady, passing through dozens of impoverished mining towns in the Catskill Mountains. To see the abject poverty and note the illiteracy of these parts was a revelation. It suddenly registered that parts of the United States of America were vastly different from the image that was portrayed in Hollywood movies. We travelled all day and late into the night, stopping occasionally at roadside cafés for coffee and burger which the driver generously paid for. Finally at about 1.30 a.m. in the morning we emerged from the Holland Tunnel on Manhattan Island where our driver had to drop us off.

A few hundred yards down the street we came across a sleazy looking hotel which offered a night's accommodation for $1.50 each.

We were no sooner in our room than the proprietor who looked as if he was related to one of New York's infamous Mafia families, knocked on the door and enquired whether we would like a girl. Arch who was a quick witted little chap responded – 'Well, if she's free, send her in, otherwise you can tell her to buzz off and find some other sucker.'

Next morning we turned out early and made our way to the only focal point that we knew of, Times Square. From there we were able to pin point a club which had been recommended to us. It was the Phi Gamma Beta club – a type of hotel for university or college students. We were in luck – they could give us a room for four nights and I think the charge was only about 75 cents a night, so we were all set to have a whale of a time on the balance of our combined exchequer. The club officials could not do enough for us. They passed us on to a hospitality organisation which gave us free tickets to a variety of entertainment places. At Madison Square Garden we saw Sonja Henie the Swiss ice skater perform in the *Ice Capades of 1941*. There were free passes to the Empire State Building, free passes on underground rail, invitations to a Jewish synagogue which turned on a lavish meal etc.

We found the average New Yorker was very hospitable to us once we had established to their satisfaction that we were not Limeys (English). The origin of the word Limey goes back to the old sailing ship days when English sailors were issued with lime juice to prevent the spread of scurvy.

For some unaccountable reason, perhaps it was the Boston Tea Party, some Yanks just cannot stand the Brits and quite often we would be involved in some tense situations. The lower social orders are very quick on the draw and invited trouble by referring to us as 'Another Limey – son of a bitch.' Now no Kiwi would stand for that nonsense, so we would take pains to correct. New Zealand? 'Where the hell is that? We ain't never 'eard of the goddamn place. It must be Limey country – you look like Limeys – you must be Limeys.' It invariably ended up by being their guests in the nearest bar where ensued some memorable sessions quite often lasting until about 3 a.m. in the morning.

Time seemed to mean nothing in New York because everything – shops, cafés, bars, theatres – seemed to be open 24 hours of the day.

We went to Greenwich Village, the night club area, Coney Island Beach, the Bronx, Central Park and even had a quick look at Skid Row.

One very interesting event was meeting Nola Luxford, a former Auckland lady who was compère for some weekly radio programmes from New York to New Zealand. There was always a number of RNZAF aircrew on final leave from their training schools in Canada and FAA pilots in transit to or from Pensacola.

Arch and I were fortunate to meet Nola on a day when she was scheduled to broadcast and she very graciously allocated time for us to send a message home.

After five really fabulous days we had to wend our way back to the Canadian border. Happily we still had enough money left to buy seats on a Greyhound bus so we made this return journey in real comfort.

Just a day or so remained to pack up our kitbags and attend to various departure routine matters and we were on the train again bound for Moncton, an RAF transit camp about 30 miles inland from Halifax.

We were held here for about a week pending the arrival of our troopship which turned out to be the MV *Awatea*, the Union Steamship Co vessel which in peacetime was employed on the Wellington to Sydney service. Once again the ship was chock full of trained aircrew personnel from stations all over Canada and the United States of America. There were several troopships in our convoy – they would have been prime targets for the German U-boats awaiting us in mid-Atlantic.

This was to be another fast convoy, but as the submarine menace was even greater than before, we had an exceptionally strong escort comprising fast destroyers, and one rather ancient American battleship.

On the first day out from Halifax I met up with Gordon Huston whom I had known at school in Stratford. Gordon and another old school mate Fred Vosseller were engineers in the *Awatea*. They advised that they would both be off duty at 8 p.m. that night, so perhaps I could come to their cabin for a little hospitality.

We saw each other several times during the crossing. The *Awatea* was later engaged in transporting army personnel in the North Africa invasion. Only a few months after we had taken passage in this lovely ship, she was attacked by German bombers and sunk while discharging troops at Bougie Bay about 100 miles east of Algiers. Fortunately both Gordon Huston and Fred Vosseller survived this attack.

Return to UK – Greenwich College and OTU

Our port of discharge this time was Greenock, in the River Clyde, from where we travelled to another RAF transit camp at Bournemouth. From there we were quickly redirected to the FAA station at Lee-on-Solent where we arrived early October.

The balance of this month was devoted to kitting out in officers uniform which involved several days in London visiting one's selected Naval Tailor. Each new officer received a monetary grant sufficient to provide two uniforms (No 2 uniforms) and a doeskin (dress uniform), plus a greatcoat, shirts, caps, etc.

Once equipped we were again an embarrassment to the Admiralty because the next conversion course at Errol, Scotland would not commence until 1st November.

The purpose of this course was to convert pilots who had trained on radial engined Harvard aircraft on to the Miles Master in-line engined aircraft. Opportunity was also given to those designated for fighter pilots OTU (operational training unit) to go solo on the Hurricane fighter.

The instructors on the staff were not instructors in the real sense of the term, they could be better described as check pilots who supervised our conversion from radial to in-line engines.

It was my misfortune to have to fly on five occasions with a crazy irresponsible red haired Scottish Sergeant pilot. Right from the outset I could detect that this chap had a monstrous 'chip on his shoulder' and he was going to show these sprog sub-lieutenants a thing or two. On my first trip with him, he took charge and proceeded to fly very low up the River Dee. Then he turned and charged towards an escarpment at a dangerously low height, pulling up just before we were about to meet it head on.

In these aircraft, the instructor flew from the rear seat so his vision was not nearly as good as the pupil in the front seat. The object of this exercise was obviously to put the wind up the pupil who had no option but to sit still in the front seat. To grab the control column and pull it back could have spelt disaster. Next day he flew low along the River Dee to a spot where he knew some power lines crossed the river. At a guess they would have been not much more than 30 feet above the water in the middle. He flew the Master underneath this wire. By this time I was beginning to get a little bit alarmed but to complain would have only resulted in ridicule.

On the fifth trip with this madman he did a slow roll at 250 ft while passing over the centre of the town of Cupar, about ten miles inland from the famous golf links at St Andrews. Once again it could have been fatal for me to touch the control column because at that height any tendency to 'belly' out of the slow roll would have ended in disaster. That was the last time I flew with him.

That same afternoon, the lunatic was up with an English sub-lieutenant, Hegarty. He did identically the same thing over Cupar, but this time they crashed on the outskirts of the town and both were killed. Whether Hegarty seized the control column out of desperation or not, one will never know. It resulted in the loss of two trained pilots, one who should never have been designated an instructor plus a very valuable training aircraft.

At the time I harboured a deep sense of guilt. Should I have reported my earlier experiences to the officer commanding the station? Had I done so it possibly could have saved Hegarty's life. But on the other hand knowing the prejudices that existed between the Air Force and Fleet Air Arm, I could have been accused of exaggerating the problem and judged to be suffering from LMF 'Lack of moral fibre'. After all several other sub-lieutenants had flown with this idiot and whilst they were undoubtedly worried about his antics they chose to say nothing. This was a very sad episode.

Near the end of November we completed this rather leisurely course and then proceeded to Greenwich Naval College in London for what was popularly termed the 'Knife and Fork' course. As this implies it resembled a sort of finishing school to smooth off any rough edges.

We were under instruction from a very fine old submarine commander who took us through Naval history, naval law and discipline, wardroom etiquette, duties of officer of the day etc.

The college was a collection of imposing buildings dating back to the days of Wren. The most impressive part of the college was the 'painted hall' which served as the officers' mess during the war years. There we were attended by white coated, begloved Wren stewards who deferentially slid plates of rubberised egg, baked beans on toast and watery porridge under our noses as we sat down at the lines of the beautiful oak tables. This was real luxury living, but what part it played in the grand design of a Fleet Air Arm officers training goodness only knows.

There was, however, one very memorable incident which occurred during our stay at Greenwich. One evening Field Marshal Jan Smuts the Prime Minister of South Africa, made an important speech relayed by radio to every corner of the British Empire. At the conclusion he expressed a wish to meet all the officers in the 'gun-room', which was officially the midshipmen's mess. When we assembled Smuts came in followed by an entourage which included General Alan Brooke, Chief of the Imperial General Staff, the Hon. A. V. Alexander First Lord of the Admiralty, sundry admirals, generals and lesser VIPs. There were insufficient seats in the gun-room, so Smuts very modestly suggested that everyone should sit on the floor. With his white goatee beard and his much bemedalled Field Marshal's uniform Smuts was a most impressive figure. He spoke very informally to the assembly and wished us good fortune in our respective duties.

At the conclusion of the 'Knife and Fork' course, our draft split up once again, fighter pilots went to Yeovilton (HMS *Heron*) bomber pilots to Crail (HMS *Jackdaw*) in Scotland and the odd seaplane pilot to Poole near Bournemouth.

Our training at the fighter OTU Yeovilton commenced on 15th December 1942. This was to be our first association with naval flying instructors, all of whom had had operational experience either during the Battle of Britain, the Norwegian Campaign, the Mediterranean or the Western Desert in support of the 8th Army. Our Chief Flying instructor was the well known ace Lieut Commander (A) Dickie Cork who was No. 2 to Wing Commander Douglas Bader and had been awarded the RAF decoration DFC. The story goes that when Cork returned to FAA service following his period in 242 Squadron during the Battle of Britain, an admiral who noticed the ribbon of the DFC told Cork that he was not correctly dressed.

'No one,' said the admiral 'can wear an Air Force decoration while serving in the Royal Navy. Remove it immediately and put up the DSC, the naval equivalent.' Cork did as he was told.

A short time later, however, Cork had occasion to visit Bader at his squadron base Tangmere. Bader noticed the DSC ribbon, asked Cork why he was not wearing the DFC, heard the edict issued by the Admiral and in true Bader fashion, told Cork to restore the DFC. It had been awarded to him by His Majesty the King and no tinpot bloody admiral could take that away from him.

Cork was wearing the DFC ribbon when he welcomed us to Yeovilton. He proceeded to give us a memorable pep talk which went something like this. 'You chaps have been trained up to this stage by the RAF. Well, from now on you have got to forget a lot of what you were taught and learn quite different naval flying routines. Henceforth instead of entering the circuit to land at 1,000 feet as prescribed by the RAF you will enter at no more than 200 feet. This may sound like 'split arse' flying but you will soon come to understand the necessity for getting on to a carrier as quickly as possible, hence the low tight circuit. Furthermore, instead of using the RAF glide type high speed approach, you will be taught how to make a 'tail down' approach, with bags of motor on and your air speed just a few knots above the stall. When you eventually get to a carrier you will have to do deck landings without even looking at the airspeed indicator. You will rely upon signals from the batsman and learn like World War I fighter pilots – to fly by the seat of your pants. That's all for now – enjoy yourselves at Yeovilton but don't play silly buggers. The navy has invested a lot of money in your training. Don't mess things up by doing something foolish.'

Well, that was the gist of Dickie Cork's welcome. To us he was a hero – and although he put things in a brutally simplistic way, I thought: well, if he could do it so could I.

Sad to relate Dickie Cork did not survive the war. On 15th December 1943 he was appointed wing leader of the 15th Naval Fighter Wing comprising 1830, 1831 and 1833 Corsair squadrons, a total wing strength of 60 aircraft operating from HMS *Illustrious*. This carrier sailed to the Indian Ocean early 1944 preparatory to forming up with the British Pacific Fleet. After an exercise in April

1944, Cork was unable to land back on the *Illustrious* and was redirected to the Naval Air Station at Trincomalee, Ceylon. On coming in to land, he failed to see another Corsair doing ADDLS (assisted dummy deck landings) and despite a warning from the control tower, landed on top of the other Corsair. Both pilots were killed.

This was a very sad end to the highest scoring fighter pilot in the FAA – possibly ten confirmed victories, plus several probables and damaged. At the time of his death he had added a DSO to the DFC awarded during the Battle of Britain.

We commenced flying at Yeovilton on 15th December 1942. With the exception of a few instrument flying checks on a Miles Master aircraft all the flying here was solo on Hurricanes. Instructors would fly with us in other Hurricanes for formation flying, sectional attacks, dog fighting etc., but generally we enjoyed the freedom.

On Christmas Day 1942 we were given the whole day off, so six of us took off to visit a delightful little tavern in the leafy village of Yeovilton which boasted a church, a tavern and about a dozen houses.

We had heard that this tavern had a very good line of Somerset cider, better known as 'scrumpy', and that for a nominal charge that turned out to be two shillings and six pence the proprietor would give you the key to the cellar and you could imbibe to your heart's content.

For anyone who had not previously indulged in Somerset 'scrumpy' the effect was catastrophic. Six very inebriated pilots returned to the wardroom after midday for their rather belated dinner.

It is interesting to note that the first vicar at the Yeovilton parish was a young cleric who later became famous as Cardinal Wolsey.

Because most of our training was conducted on a solo basis it was not difficult to 'nip' off on an unauthorised exercise, provided of course that one did not exceed the duration allowed for the flight.

On one such occasion I decided to fly down to Tavistock, the area where I understood my ancestors had lived prior to emigrating to New Zealand in 1876. Forty four years later in 1987 with some assistance from a Plymouth based genealogist I was able to establish that my great grandparents lived in a village called St Cleer which is not more than 20 miles south of Tavistock.

However, on this day I was paying my respects to any members of the Masters family who might still be living in Tavistock. I suppose all fighter pilots pass through a period of over confidence – I guess I was in one on that particular day. As a parting gesture I decided to do a loop followed by a roll off the top. I came down from 3,000 feet pulled back to 1,000 feet, went into a loop and then attempted to roll out at the top. Horror of horrors – the speed had fallen off and the Hurricane stalled upside down. I was suddenly projected into a dangerous situation – it had all the ingredients for an inverted spin which would not be easy to recover from at that height. Well the lesson I had absorbed at ground school re the theory of flight came back loud and clear. Don't touch the control column – to pull it back or push it forward would create just enough pressure on the airfoil to put it into a spin. So I sat hanging in my straps upside down while the carburettor spluttered and nearly gave up the ghost. Slowly the nose dropped and the aircraft gathered momentum, still inverted and finally I rolled out at barely 200 feet above the fields below. My flying suit was wet with cold perspiration. This was surely the biggest fright I had had to date – I was damned lucky to be alive. I flew back to Yeovilton a very chastened sprog pilot.

It was at Yeovilton that I renewed association with a number of old friends who included Neville Turnbull, (from days at Stratford Primary School), Alister MacLeod, Joe Brough, Martin Turner and a short time later Arch Foley. All except Mac had been trained at Pensacola and were doing a conversion on to Wildcats. Mac had preceded me to Canada, so his course at Yeovilton was a few weeks ahead of mine.

Mac had just received news that his brother Ian, who had been at New Plymouth Boys' High School at the same time, had just arrived in the United Kingdom as a seaman in the New Zealand cruiser HMS *Achilles*.

Ian had been given leave, so Mac asked if I could accompany him to London for a get together. We were all due for a 48–hour pass, so it fitted in very conveniently.

We met Ian at the New Zealand Forces Club at Charing Cross Road and then proceeded to 'wine and dine' him. Ian had a friend Bob Stuart who later became very well known as captain of the All Blacks in the early 1950s.

I could sense that Ian was quite impressed by the fact that his older brother was a commissioned officer in the Fleet Air Arm. You could sense the hero worship, so it was not unexpected when he asked whether it would be possible for him to get into the FAA. By this time we had consumed quite a few pints and were in a delightfully happy frame of mind.

'Sure', says Mac – 'just get in touch with Bill Jordan – he'll fix it.' I kept quiet wondering whether the MacLeod family would approve of two sons in the FAA.

Anyway Ian's application was accepted, he completed his training and like Mac and I joined an operational Seafire squadron.

Sadly, he was killed on 13th January 1945 while practising air to ground attacks in Egypt.

As one would imagine, the training at Yeovilton was essentially operationally orientated. Such things as aircraft recognition, air gunnery, dummy deck landings, oxygen climbs became a feature of a day's work.

To become a successful fighter pilot one needs to acquire a highly developed skill at marksmanship. Shooting from an aircraft is vastly different from firing a rifle at a target on the ground. Unless one is firing from dead behind a target aircraft one had to make allowance for deflection both horizontally and vertically. Adjustment is also necessary for the closing speed, and if one is not flying accurately (with the needle and ball in the centre of the Reid and Sigrist dial) the bullet pattern would be thrown to one side or the other. All these factors have to be taken into account for accurate air firing.

The first and possibly most important factor in air fighting is to identify friend from foe. Our training in aircraft recognition commenced at HMS *St Vincent* and continued throughout the various stages of later training. We had to become proficient at identifying the profiles from all angles, head on, from astern and abeam of all military aircraft used in the European theatre of war. That included British, German, French and Italian aircraft.

The method of identification became more sophisticated as training progressed to the point where the back room boys had developed a simulator which would depict a target aircraft flying cross the pilot's windscreen. The pilot was required to identify the target, lay off deflection and if necessary open fire. Quite often the instructor would announce that a friendly aircraft had been shot down. Other marksmanship skills were developing with very popular sessions of skeet shooting. This developed quick reflex action as well as requiring fine judgement of deflection. In the air the pilot's shooting skill was tested on the camera gun. Every fighter had a camera gun installed in the wingroot. It was activated by the gun button on the control column and as the attack took place the sequence was recorded on the film. In actual combat, the essence of air fighting was to get as close in behind your opponent as possible so that there would be no need for deflection shooting. In practice, however, we were told to concentrate on quarter attacks which meant that deflection was always a factor and this would have to be adjusted as the closing range to the target decreased. The Hurricane fighter had four 303 machine guns mounted in the wings. These were synchronised to give a lethal cone of bullets spread at a distance of 200–250 yards from the target. If the pilot was shooting from say 300 yards down to 150 yards he should have been recording a reasonable percentage of strikes providing his deflection and line were accurate.

All this sounds very simple in theory, but when you have to contend with too fast a closing speed and the slipstream effect of the target aircraft, it becomes quite a challenge.

The effect of a high closing speed on a large target like a Lancaster bomber or Sunderland flying boat can be quite hair-raising and cause the pilot to open fire at too great a range. At 400 yards one of these aircraft looks quite enormous through the gunsight and yet to be really effective one should be close in to no more than 200 yards.

The next experience was the use of oxygen which was essential for flights at high altitudes. Yeovilton was supplied with a large decompression chamber which could accommodate about six pilots at a time. When operating the chamber there was a medical officer outside monitoring the effects on those inside. Gradually the air pressure was decreased to simulate higher altitudes. At a pressure equivalent to about 12,000 feet the doctor would tell the trainees to put on their oxygen masks and would then gradually decrease the pressure until it simulated what one would experience at above 30,000 feet. On the day our group was tested the doctor took us up to 34,000 feet before one of the chaps suddenly complained about pains. The pressure was increased and we were held there until our friend recovered. Then the doctor proceeded to demonstrate the practical effect of lack of oxygen.

He told one of our party to remove his mask and start writing a message on paper. This was OK for a few seconds but one could notice that the 'guinea pig' was getting slower and slower and the writing became a scrawl all over the paper until finally he collapsed on the table. Quite calmly the doctor said, 'OK chaps, put his mask back on.'

With that the 'guinea pig' came to life and immediately his brain resumed where it had left off and he was back to writing his message once again. It was quite a hilarious performance – but the first 'guinea pig' couldn't appreciate the humour of the situation. It did serve to impress upon us how dangerous it could be to run out of oxygen at high altitudes.

Following this we did our first practical experience of a high oxygen flight. Three of us, an Englishman, Bob Gray and I, were taken up by an RNR sub-lieutenant (A) Leeming. Instead of doing the climb in the vicinity of Yeovilton, Leeming purposely led us over the south east coast and into the English Channel in the direction of Cherbourg Peninsula. As it was midwinter we were wearing as much clothing as possible, fleece lined boots, woollen, silk and then leather gloves. The Hurricane aircraft was constructed of fabric behind the cockpit, so it became extremely cold, as we climbed higher and higher. Eventually we reached 31,000 feet where the aircraft was so sluggish that it seemed to be just hanging on the propellor.

Below us we could see the coast of France and behind the coast of England.

Because one had a tendency to become rather dopey and slap-happy when on oxygen our formation of four aircraft became so loose that at long last Leeming became alarmed. Just why he took us into this dangerous area goodness only knows – it was a foolhardy thing to do.

Admittedly our guns were loaded but we three pupils had not had any operational experience whatsoever. We would have been easy prey for any experienced German Me 109 pilot who intercepted us. Happily this did not happen.

On returning to a lower altitude Bob Gray complained of pains so we circled at about 24,000 feet while he recovered. I myself experienced some pain in my finger tips. What with the extreme cold and the effect of oxygen it felt as if the blood was bursting out from my fingers. Quite a nasty experience.

When we finally landed at Yeovilton, Leeming was 'on the mat'.

The RAF No 11 group based at Tangmere had scrambled two flights of Spitfires to investigate some aircraft out in the channel that were not displaying IFF (Identification Friend or Foe) on its Fighter Control Radar Screen.

We must have been pretty elusive or they were poorly directed because we did not see them.

No doubt Leeming received a pretty stiff reprimand and an endorsement in his log book.

This was the end of the 'Hurricane' course at Yeovilton. I was gratified to chalk up one more 'above average' assessment.

One would have expected that after having mastered the Hurricane one would have immediately advanced to a more sophisticated fighter, but this was not the case. Our next training programme was to an antiquated Fleet Air Arm fighter two seater Fulmar aircraft. The Fulmar was really a naval adaptation of the RAF 'Battle' aircraft which went out of the first line squadron operation after the collapse in France early 1940. The purpose of using the Fulmar however, was quite justifiable because we would use it:

(a) for deck landing preparation
(b) for night flying
(c) for air to air gunnery.

In all these respects it was an ideal training aircraft.

My first flight in a Fulmar took place on 23rd February 1942.

While on Fulmars I took the risk of another unauthorised flight, this time to visit my relations at Merthyr Vale, South Wales. I had previously written to them and intimated that some day I would fly over and come down fairly low over the village and pump the throttle so they would know who it was. A problem arose, however, because I had no map of the area. The maps with which we were issued were local maps and these did not extend beyond Bristol. However, I did have a very small pocket Atlas (6″ × 4″), on which I outlined a flight track. I was confident that once I got to the south coast of the Bristol Channel I could easily pinpoint Barry on the north coast, then fly about 355° north and I would hit Merthyr Vale.

Everything went according to plan. This time I did not attempt to show off with aerobatics – I had learnt my lesson at Tavistock.

However, on the return journey I was very nearly blasted out of the sky by some anti-aircraft fire from either Flatholm or Steep Holm islands. These guns put about three rounds across my bows. I didn't realise that I had breached a prohibited air traffic area.

On the way back to Yeovilton I wondered whether my aircraft would be tracked on radar – if so, I would be in dire trouble. Fortunately for me no such threat arose.

On 7th March we flew down to the RAF fighter station at Warmwell where we were scheduled to do air to air firing out near Portland Bill. My efforts at firing at the drogue towed by a Martinet aircraft would not have rated a mention in despatches. Our Fulmars carried four Browning machine guns in the wings, each loaded with 100 rounds of 303 ammunition. My first attempt yielded no hits, my second 11 hits (2.75%), followed by 13 (3.25%) and nine (2.25%), not exactly an outstanding performance, given that the Fulmar was a very stable gun platform. The camera gun proved, however, that like most novices I was opening fire at too great a range – it was only when I closed on the drogue that I registered strikes. Had it been the real thing I would at least have damaged the enemy aircraft.

A tragic accident occurred one day while we were at Warmwell. It was a grass aerodrome and was being used by an RAF operational Typhoon squadron. This area of the south coast was subject to hit and run reprisal raids by fast German FW 190 fighter bombers who would streak over the Channel and drop their bombs with very little warning. Their main targets were towns like Weymouth, Dorchester and Bournemouth. On one air 'firing' detail with Peter Wilson in the rear cockpit as a passenger, several FW 190 fighters carried out a raid on Dorchester.

They probably came through very low over the sea while we were firing at a drogue off Portland Bill. Thank goodness they did not see us – we would have been easy meat for them.

We were warned by the RAF command that if a red alert was sounded, the Typhoon pilots, several of whom were at first degree of readiness, strapped into their cockpits, would have priority over all other aircraft and could take off without further warning in any direction so as to enable them to get to grips with the FW 190's. On this particular day one of our naval instructors, Lieutenant Harrington RN, with Peter Wilson as the pupil, had just committed a Master aircraft to its take off. Two Typhoons on the other side of the airfield saw the red very light go off and came charging across in the opposite direction. These were both very experienced pilots. They had their undercarriages up in a flash and were about to change height when suddenly Harrington's much slower Master loomed up in front of them. The leading Typhoon pilot realised that Harrington could not do anything to avoid a collision so he pulled back on the control column hoping that the Master would pass beneath him. Unfortunately the Typhoon did not have sufficient speed to become airborne.

It suddenly stalled, flicked over and crashed with a horrendous explosion just a short distance ahead of the Master. The pilot of the Typhoon was a highly decorated Battle of Britain pilot, so this unfortunate incident cast a pall over the remainder of our stay at Warmwell. There were some who tended to blame the tragedy on to the Fleet Air Arm.

On our return to Yeovilton we were thrown into deck landing training with a vengeance. It was now 15th March and apparently we were scheduled to do our deck landings on a carrier in the Clyde on 31st March. So every opportunity was taken to do ADDLS (assisted dummy deck landings).

An ADDL entailed a take off followed by a circuit around the airfield at about 200 feet, lower undercarriage, lower flaps, keeping turning onto the runway in an exaggerated tail down attitude with plenty of engine power and speed just to a few knots above the stall. The idea was to lower the aircraft down alongside the batsman then open up and go around for another ADDL. This was really precision flying – the end result of our months and months of training.

In the meantime we also had a short spell of night flying on Fulmars. Night flying in the United Kingdom during wartime was a very different thing from our earlier night flying in Canada. Canada was a piece of cake compared to the United Kingdom.

In Canada it was so much easier to navigate by night, because with no black out the towns were shining like beacons and the airfield runway was a continuous strip of lights.

By comparison at Yeovilton the sky was pitch black unless it happened to be a cloudless moonlight night which was not very often. In the towns and countryside there was not a glimmer of light to assist a pilot in navigation and the runway lighting was limited to a glide path indicator plus about six lights either side to indicate the direction and length of the runway. A few dim red lights had been installed on any flying hazard such as hangar buildings etc. that were close to the runway.

Another problem was the occasional presence of German night fighter intruders who came in over the south coast and waited near a known airfield to catch aircraft taking off or landing. And to compound an already difficult situation, the pilot's view ahead was obstructed by six engine exhaust stubs on either side of the engine. These produced massive gouts of flame which made it extremely difficult to pick up the glide path indicator at the entrance to the runway.

By comparison with the experience of night flying in the Harvards this made the exercise extremely hazardous for novice pilots.

My first experience of night flying at Yeovilton was quite unpleasant. The conditions were not bad, a little overcast but every now and then a star would appear. After flying around a while I noticed what seemed to be a yellow light formating with me. It seemed to hold its track and position. It did not look like a star, so I began to wonder whether this could be a JU 88 night intruder. I turned and the object seemed to follow. Finally it penetrated my over cautious brain that it was only a star after all.

Heaving a sigh of relief I came in to land on the aerodrome and picked up what I thought was the glide path indicator. The light I saw was red, so realising I was too low I gave the Fulmar full throttle to climb into the safe green area. Nothing happened the light was still red. Then suddenly a Very light was fired from the ground so I had no option but to raise the undercarriage and flaps and go around again. Believe it or not I made the same mistake again and yet a third time. It was then that I realised that I was not seeing the glide path indicator at all. In fact what I was endeavouring to do was to land on top of the main hangar! I eventually located the glide path indicator and got down safely. What a performance! That would surely be noted on my course report. This incident did not, however, affect my selection to go on to Spitfire training. Only three pilots on our course were selected. All three were Kiwis, Buck Ryder, Harry Mackay and I.

Following a careful briefing which took us through the starting up procedure, the cockpit check for take off, the necessity to taxi out fast to avoid overheating the engine, the lack of vision from the cockpit when taxiing etc we were each given a flight of one hours duration to familiarise ourselves with this really beautiful aeroplane. Beautiful is not the description one would generally associate with inanimate objects, but the Spitfire was truly a joy to behold. It had the sleek gracious profile of a thoroughbred racehorse – it was so neat and compact – its elliptical shaped wings added a dimension that no other aircraft has ever possessed before or since. It was indeed a case of love at first sight.

I put on my parachute and climbed through the little door panel into the cockpit. I immediately felt as if this little fighter had been especially built for me – it fitted like a glove – the pilot instinctively felt that he and the Spitfire were one entity.

The control panel was very neat with artificial horizon in the centre, surrounded by the altimeter, airspeed indicator, oil pressure gauge, engine revolution counter, boost control etc.

I gave the signal to the matelot on the battery starter trolley and the Rolls Royce Merlin engine spluttered into life. The chocks were waved away and I started taxiing out to the end of the runway. The instructors warned about poor vision soon became apparent. One couldn't see to taxi straight ahead so one had to use the brakes to steer it out in a fish tail motion. Only then could the pilot see what was ahead of him. The engine heat slowly crept up, so I opened throttle a little to taxi faster and thereby create a greater airflow for cooling effect.

At the end of the runway I called the control tower and received a Green Aldis lamp for take off. I completed my cockpit check ensuring that the variable pitch propellor was in the 'fine pitch' position for maximum power on take off. Throttle forward a little to get her rolling – no noticeable swing – more power on and we were racing down the runway. The Spitfire was in a neutral trim position, so I hardly noticed that it had flown itself off with the speed building up at an incredible pace. I handled the control column very cautiously because we had been told that the Spitfire was extremely sensitive fore and aft. I moved it ever so slightly and sure enough the plane bucked like a young stallion. Before I knew where I was I was up to 1,000 feet and I hadn't even closed the hood or raised the undercarriage. It just seemed to be going like a bat out of hell with the speed still building up and the altimeter spinning around. I guess I must have been at nearly 1,500 feet by the time I had lowered the seat to allow the hood to slide over my head and then raise the undercarriage. A few weeks later when I had become accustomed to the sensitivity of the Spitfire controls I was able to lower the seat, close the hood and raise the undercarriage at 100 feet and then commence a fairly steep climbing turn. But this aircraft was one of the earliest models a Spitfire Mk I. Later models of Spitfire Mk V were somewhat more positive on the controls.

This was the most exhilarating flying sensation I have ever experienced. Only one other has come close to it. That was when I had the unusual privilege of flying a Gloster Gladiator biplane fighter in Ceylon early 1945.

At the end of my one hour familiarisation flight I returned to the aerodrome and prepared to land. I closed the throttle to slow down the forward speed but it made no appreciable difference. This was a racehorse indeed. I had to take the throttle right back before I could get the speed down to about 120 knots for my approach. Then lower the undercarriage, open the hood, raise the seat, propellor into fine pitch and finally lower the flaps. Only then did it dawn on me that the vision over the long engine cowling was not what I had been used to.

As luck would have it my landing was quite a 'daisy cutter'. Before leaving Yeovilton I had chalked up exactly three hours on Spitfires.

The next challenge was the deck landing course which we were to do on Fulmars and in preparation for which we had spent every available time on practising ADDLS. My pilot's log book records that I had done 44 ADDLS prior to leaving for the RN Air Station at Machrihanish on the Mull of Kintyre, West Scotland. In retrospect when I think of my later responsibilities as a carrier batsman, this was really inadequate preparation for a novice deck-lander.

At Machrihanish two of us were tumbled into the back cockpit of a Swordfish, no parachutes and were flown out to land on HMS *Activity*, the smallest carrier then in service in the Navy.

As we flew overhead, it looked about as big as a matchbox. The thought passed through my mind that perhaps it may not be too late to opt out. I could understand now why a few pilots having achieved their wings, showed no desire to take part in the shooting war.

The Swordfish pilot landed on with an almighty crunch and we two guinea pigs tumbled out.

It then transpired that the *Activity* had not only the narrowest and shortest flight deck, it only had four wires, which were not hydraulically self centreing. Even the American built 'Woolworth' carriers had eight wires all of which were self centreing. Their Lordships at Admiralty had given us sprog pilots the toughest carrier of all to land on. Perhaps we should get in touch with Bill Jordan in London – he might have been able to rustle up the *Ark Royal.* Then came the briefing which was pretty cursory and callous, to say the least. We were warned that if we could not see the batsman not to 'crab' or skid on our approach. To do this would, in all probability mean going over the side into the 'drink'. If that happened provided one went in right side up, one had about ten seconds to get out and clear before the Fulmar headed for the bottom. Then inflate your Mae West while we heave to and lower a boat to pick you up. Great stuff – a real Hollywood movie spectacle!

Our names were announced in alphabetical order. The first to 'dice with death' was an Englishman named Clarke – 'Nobby' Clark, as all his predecessors had been known in Nelson's day.

'Nobby' climbed into the cockpit, started up, revved up to full power on his brakes, then tore down the flight deck. He sank below the bows then miraculously reappeared still in flight to fly a circuit and come in to make his first landing. The batsman was controlling him, but as he came closer to the round down, it was obvious to us that 'Nobby' was finding it difficult to see the batsman, so he did what he was told not to do. He put on some skid and started to crab in. He was given the cut by the batsman, but when the Fulmar caught the wire, it swung violently to the port side and over 'Nobby' went into the drink. 'Man overboard' was sounded – the carrier hove to and a boat was lowered.

Those of us who were watching the proceedings saw the Fulmar sink and then in the distance a very small black dot appeared on the surface. 'Nobby' had survived the crash.

The second chap went off and happily survived four landings. I was next. The first take off was a weird operation because the Fulmar, even with full power on, literally fell over the bows but just cleared the water in time to get airborne. Coming around to land on, I experienced the problem that all new deck landing pilots have, of dragging the aircraft towards the carrier from a long way astern. Consequently, it is difficult to see the batsman. The only solution would be to go around again and try and judge the approach so that you were turning in to the 'round down' until just before touching down. But pilots of our limited deck landing experience could not possibly do it. So there was, in fact, only one other way to keep the batsman in sight and that was to break the rules and 'Crab' in. Anyway, I did my four landings OK, so I must have been able to straighten up just when I hit the arrester wire.

When finished, three of us piled into the back of the Swordfish, no parachutes, not strapped in, and were flown back to Machrihanish.

We learnt the following day that one of our Kiwis who was to follow me, Harry MacKay, had stalled on his approach and the Fulmar had spun into the sea. Happily Harry managed to get out and I saw him in London a few days later where he was enjoying some 'survivors leave'.

Harry described the incident something like this: 'I let the speed fall off too much then she stalled and flicked over on its back to go into the water. The fuselage broke off behind the cockpit and I was borne down to Davy Jones's locker tied to the engine. It got blacker and blacker while I struggled to get out of the parachute and out of the cockpit. I reckon I was down about 40 feet and getting short of air when I finally got clear. Now what will you have to drink?'

Harry had had one helluva fright but he was putting a pretty bold front on it. We had a good session in the *Sussex Hotel* and when it closed at 2 p.m. we took off to a vaudeville show, at one of the theatres in the West End. I believe the comedian at this show was Tommy Handley. Anyway at one stage of the comedy the curtain goes up and there is Handley on the stage, all by himself, dressed in a weird pair of baggy trousers and pensively peeling a banana. 'One skin – two skin – three skin – five skin.' The audience roared with laughter. 'That fooled you, didn't it?'

Well dear old Harry had a very spontaneous sense of humour which, when combined with a few pints of ale, became almost infectious. There was something abut Handley's performance that really tickled Harry's fancy. He laughed and laughed and laughed – he couldn't stop laughing. It became obvious to all that someone in the audience was really enjoying this performance. All eyes were now on Harry MacKay – it was now he who held their attention. Everyone started laughing – the theatre was in an uproar – even Tommy Handley was laughing. It was great stuff. Little did they know that this portly naval officer had just survived a nerve racking experience in the depths of the River Clyde.

This was to be my last meeting with my friend Harry Mackay who, by chance, was my cabin mate in the *Dominion Monarch*. We had stayed together all the way through our training, we had shared the successes and the failures, we shared the Speights beer and the oranges in Halifax, we were co-owners of the car at Kingston, we were both Spitfire pilots. This was quite an unusual sequence of events.

While I was posted to a Seafire Squadron, Harry and Buck Ryder were despatched to Gibraltar as replacement pilots for Seafire Squadrons.

They both later joined a Firefly squadron along with another 31 course member, Peter Wilson.

On 24th June 1944 Harry was killed in a flying accident near Machrihanish. With this I had lost a very good friend.

Our course at the Fighter School had been completed, so when we returned to Yeovilton it was merely to collect our gear and go on indefinite leave pending a posting from Admiralty.

At the conclusion of the second part of the OTU I received an 'average' assessment which was a slight disappointment, but I suppose the night flying incident messed things up a bit.

On this leave I took the opportunity to revisit my relations in Wales with whom I spent three or four days. While there I happened to get into conversation one day with my Aunty about politics and expressed an interest in visiting the House of Commons when I returned to London. In her capacity as Mayor of Merthyr Tydfil she arranged with the local Member of Parliament, a Mr Williams, to provide me with an invitation and a pass.

On returning to London I took advantage of this and it so happened that on the day Mr Williams received me at the House of Commons, the Prime Minister, Winston Churchill, was scheduled to deliver one of his more important speeches. It was a very impressive occasion, every available seat in the Chamber was occupied. I was surprised, however, at how small the chamber was to accommodate the hundreds of representatives from all regions of the United Kingdom and Northern Ireland.

The public gallery likewise was small, so I felt very privileged indeed to be the only naval officer in attendance.

Just before Churchill commenced his address a door opened in the important personages gallery and who should walk in but Mr

Jim Curtin, Prime Minister of Australia, followed by Mr Peter Fraser, Prime Minister of New Zealand. Mr Fraser was accompanied by a secretary, Mr Frank Corner, who was a resident of the Weir House during the time I was there. Frank Corner was apparently in the Diplomatic Corps and he later served as New Zealand's Ambassador to the United States of America.

Churchill's speech on this occasion was devoted to the possibility of inveigling General Franco, the Spanish Generalissimo, to join the Allies in fighting against Germany. Spain was at that time sympathetic to the German cause, possibly under obligation for German assistance during the Spanish Civil War.

This leave which I spent mostly in London extended to a longer period than usual, so I was able to familiarise myself with the various Kiwi watering holes in the West End.

A visit to the Sussex, the Mitre, the Lamb and Flag (Lamb and Green Peas), the Shandos or the Captains Cabin, would invariably result in a reunion with someone from the navy or air force whom I had known back home.

897 Seafire Squadron

My posting eventually came through and I was delighted to learn that I 'was required to report on board HMS *Daedalus* (Lee-on-Solent) to join the 897 Seafire Squadron under the command of Lieutenant Commander (A) W. C. Simpson.'

This was a magnificent appointment – something that I had hoped for. Only a minority of fighter pilots were posted directly to a first line operational squadron. The majority were sent 'stooging' for several months, sometimes as much as a year, in the second line squadrons whose duties were fleet requirements, communications, transport, target towing etc.

I reported to 897 squadron on 26th April 1943. The following day the CO 'Willie' Simpson told me to take Seafire 1B-AB933 and do an hour's total flying to get the feel of things again. After ten days leave, part of which was spent in hectic sessions in London, it was quite a challenge to climb into a Seafire cockpit, especially as I had only recorded three hours on the type at Yeovilton.

897 Squadron was in the process of forming up. The pilots who had so far joined were the CO Lieutenant Commander (A) Willie Simpson, Lieutenant (RNR) Horace Barr (England), Sub-Lieutenants (A) Doc Davies (Canada), Brian Razzall (England), Hammie Neilson (Scotland), Les Baker (Wales), John Rankin (Belfast, Northern Ireland), Arch Foley and Joe Urlich (both Kiwis from the *Dominion Monarch* draft) and myself. It was a rather cosmopolitan collection to which was added shortly after Tony Perry (London) and Stuart Donnelly (another Kiwi also from our *Dominion Monarch* draft). Out of the 12 pilots which was to be our total squadron complement, it was quite unusual to find as many as four from New Zealand.

Other Kiwis from the *Dominion Monarch* draft who appeared at

Lee-on-Solent about that time were Lefty Bissett, Ralph Cocklin and Bob Gray, all of whom had been appointed to a second line communication and fleet requirements squadron. Lefty and Ralph were both bomber pilots and Bob Gray was a former cabin mate of mine at Yeovilton. Lefty and Ralph eventually joined Swordfish first line TBR squadron while Bob was posted to east Africa and later in Ceylon in second line duties.

Only half our aircraft had been delivered to the squadron when the CO received a signal to leave Lee-on-Solent and proceed to RN Air Station at St Merryn known as HMS *Vulture* on the coast of Cornwall. This was to be the working up base for our squadron over the next two and a half months while we prepared to join an aircraft carrier.

As luck would have it Willie Simpson detailed Les Baker and me to fly two of our Seafires from Lee-on-Solent to St Merryn. Those pilots who had not been detailed had to travel with the ground party by train or road transport.

A move from one base to another is a major logistic operation. Apart from aircraft and pilots there are approximately 150 ground crew personnel with their personal possessions, plus all the squadron maintenance equipment, spare parts, safety equipment, confidential books and squadron records. For a smooth operation the CO requires a good backup from his staff officer, master at arms, all his commissioned officers and petty officers.

So Les and I wrapped our toothbrushes in our pyjamas, climbed into our Seafires and took off for St Merryn, a trip of a little over one hour. I had never been to this station before, so when I circled around and had a look at it, I got quite a shock. Not only was it a very short runway even for fighter aircraft, but it appeared to be on the mound of a low hill so that both ends of the runway were lower than the middle. To make it more difficult one approach was from the sea over a very high cliff with the end of the runway very close to the edge of the cliff. On this day the wind sock indicated a breeze from the north, so we had to approach from the sea and endeavour to get down not too far away from the cliff edge. With only six hours experience on Spitfires or Seafires this was a dicey situation.

The ground staff and the remaining pilots arrived next day with the balance of our aircraft being delivered shortly afterwards. We immediately settled down to squadron exercises and were allocated various responsibilities.

Hammy Neilson, an ex 19 course member who had served in second line squadrons for some time was an admirable choice as the aircraft maintenance officer. Stuart Donnelly, who had previously been training as a chemist in New Zealand, got the job as Staff Officer which is virtually the squadron secretary and in charge of all the paperwork. I was rather pleased about this because with my university background and being almost qualified in accountancy, I thought Willie Simpson might have fingered me for this job. Arch Foley became the armaments officer, another excellent choice because of his army experience and his love of playing with weapons. Joe Urlich became the safety equipment officer, in charge of parachutes, life rafts, distress signals etc. Les Baker was in charge of transport and I was delegated to look after the squadron publications and confidential records. Hoards of 'bumpf' were churned out each week from Admiralty and it was my job to incorporate it in existing manuals by way of deletion or amendment.

I cannot recall what particular responsibilities were allocated to Brian Razzall, Horace Barr or Johnny Rankin – possibly they were back up officers for maintenance, armaments etc. The status of senior pilot i.e. second in command, was given to Doc Davies despite the fact that he was junior in rank to Horace Barr, an RNR two ring lieutenant.

Athough Willie acknowledged Doc's ability as a pilot and as an aggressive personality, it was never an easy relationship between the CO and his senior P. In fact Willie never found it easy to relate to any of his colonial pilots, one Canadian and four Kiwis. However from the point of view of performing his duties as CO Willie was extremely dedicated and fully committed to instilling team spirit and efficiency with all ranks.

His first priority was to build 897 squadron into an effective naval fighter unit and to get to know the respective abilities and flying characteristics of his pilots. I was told by him that we would be flying together next day so that I could learn a new type of battle formation flying that would henceforth be used by 897 Squadron.

Willie explained that up until a late stage of the Battle of Britain fighter squadrons had been flying either in formation of three or line astern. It was Douglas Bader who had advocated the type of formation that the Germans had adopted during the Spanish Civil War and continued to use during the Battle of Britain. The basic unit was the 'Rotte', a pair of fighters, a leader and a wingman who as far as possible endeavoured to maintain contact – the wingman's main purpose being to protect his leader's tail. Two pairs of fighters would then become a flight in our squadron and would fly in a 'finger four' abreast formation with the flight leader in front and the other three aircraft slipped back so as to give maximum coverage of the sky and protect each others' tails.

The space between each aircraft would be 150–200 yards, and when the flight changed direction the inside pilot would slip under and the outside two pilots would slide over to resume a line abreast at formation on the different heading.

Verbally this sounded very simple and even when Willie put the formation on paper and showed how the turns took place it seemed a piece of cake.

So we got in our two Seafires and took off to practice this new battle formation. We climbed to 8,000 feet levelled off and 'Willie' told me to adopt formation at 200 yards distance. Before take off he had explained how I would gauge the space distance on the side of my cockpit canopy. Once in position then his command came over the R/T (radio telephone) 'Break port – go!' As he turned I slid across beneath him until I estimated I would resume the spacing 200 yards apart. When straightened up I seemed to be approximately spaced correctly, but somehow in coming out of the turn I was no longer line abreast but about 100–150 yards behind. Quickly as if to disguise my 'finger trouble' I rammed on full throttle to catch up. I could imagine Willie in his cockpit chuckling inside his oxygen mask at the ham fisted effort this damned Kiwi was putting on.

Once back in position I received another command: 'Break starboard – GO!' The same thing again I ended up 100 yards behind. More throttle to catch up and we went through the routine time and time again. I was beginning to catch on when suddenly the bulletproof windscreen on my Seafire seemed to go all misty and cloudy! I had great difficulty in even seeing where Willie was. It was then that I noticed the leading edge of my mainplane had gone white and the windscreen itself was now completely obscured. ICE! We were now at about 12,000 feet and I had never had any previous experience of icing up. I called Willie on the R/T and reported my problem to which he replied: 'Well put the bloody de-icer on – that's what it's for.' The de-icer – I didn't know the Seafire had one – let alone where it was. Like a naughty schoolboy I had to admit my ignorance whereupon Willie reduced height and we returned to the aerodrome and landed.

When I recall that incident I am almost certain that this performance plus a couple of minor indiscretions later on, blotted my copy book in Willie's eyes. Although I maintained an accident-free record and was one of his best landing pilots he never gave me a better assessment that 'average'. After leaving 897 squadron later and joining 809 squadron commanded by Major Al Wright, Royal Marines, I was immediately reinstated as 'above average'.

Our air drills continued in pairs and then into flights of four until we all reached the stage of perfection in battle formation. From flights of four we proceeded to practising it as a complete squadron with the CO's flight in the middle, 'Doc' Davies high cover and Brian Razzall medium cover. During this period I always flew as No. 2 to Willie, so he must have had some confidence in me.

Interspersed with battle formation we had some concentrated air to drogue firing off Tintagel Point which is supposed to have been the seat of King Arthur and the Round Table.

When on air firing details we were using 100 rounds each on four machine guns and 20 rounds each on our 20 millimetre Hispano cannons. Each aircraft had a capacity for 300 rounds per machine gun, so each pilot's result was assessed by dipping the rounds in different coloured paints. Consequently if your colour was red and there were 40 red 303 holes on the drogue – you were assessed as having scored 10%.

During these flying details I discovered two things. Firstly, that the Seafire being a much more sensitive aircraft to fly, was not nearly as stable a gun platform as a Harvard or a Fulmar. Secondly, my marksmanship had improved. I was scoring quite regularly 30 to 35 hits which was a substantial improvement on the Fulmar results. Poor old Arch Foley, by contrast, was having a very miserable time. It hurt him particularly because not only was he the squadron armament officer but he always had the natural instinct to be a winner at whatever contest he was involved in.

And so it came to pass, one evening, when Joe Urlich, Arch and I were having some drinks in the St Merryn pub that Arch presented us with his solution. By using his 'muscle' as armament officer he was going to arrange for his aircraft to have 200 rounds per machine gun all of the same colour.

Great Stuff! So off he went. This time to his eternal embarrassment his deflection was absolutely spot on. He blasted the drogue to ribbons. There were so many holes in it that it fell to pieces when the target towing aircraft dropped it on the airfield. Poor old Arch – the game simply wasn't fair.

Although Willie Simpson conveyed the impression of being a rather fussy little man, there was one thing that came across loud and clear. He was determined that 897 Squadron would be known as a crack fighter unit – it would be nothing but the best. He cultivated that *esprit de corps* to such an extent that every member of the squadron was intensely proud to be in it.

Willie had also had the privilege of attending several advanced courses. What he learned there from former RAF Battle of Britain pilots he passed on to us. He was also well informed about other options which were available to his pilots. One of these was a three day course at the Rolls Royce engine factory at Derby. The purpose of this course was to provide experienced pilots with a more specialised knowledge of the performance and capabilities of the Merlin engine with which the Spitfire and Seafires were equipped. Those who had been sent on this course could then return to their squadron and relay the knowledge to the more junior pilots.

Willie decided to send Arch Foley and Joe Urlich on this course. I was sent the following week alone.

I booked in at a hotel in Derby and went to the Rolls Royce factory the following morning. Most of the day was spent in lectures delivered by experienced fighter pilots and engineers on the methods to achieve most efficient cruising speeds, best fuel consumption, maximum flight endurance etc.

When I entered the lecture room I was confronted by a large assembly of RAF pilots, mostly highly decorated and all nationalities, British, French, Polish, Czechoslovak, Canadian, Australian, USA, New Zealand etc. As the sole Fleet Air Arm pilot, a sprog sub-lieutenant I felt as if I was an intruder. However, at the back of the lecture room I saw two officers dressed in navy blue uniforms. I heaved a sigh of relief thinking that I might have some FAA friends to associate with. When I approached them, however, I discovered they were not naval pilots but British Overseas Airways pilots. We sat together throughout all the sessions because we were the only three pilots who were not from the Royal Air Force.

During our conversation I enquired how they happened to be attending the course when everyone else was a service pilot. They looked at each other rather sheepishly and then explained that because they were on secret operations they were unable to disclose their background. I pondered for a while about this and decided to follow it up. I pointed out that wherever they were flying from someone must surely know what they were doing. So after a conspiratorial exchange they then told me that they were flying in the new twin engined Mosquito fighter bomber on diplomatic service they were operating from an air base in Scotland which I guessed was probably Drem or Turnhouse and flew by night across the North Sea at very high altitudes, through the Skagerrak to land at Stockholm in Sweden. To keep their weight down they were unarmed civilian aircraft carrying diplomatic mail and occasionally a passenger who would have to be flat in the nose of the aircraft. These passengers they said were often mysterious people, possibly spies being infiltrated to Germany through Sweden. This had all the ingredients of a fabulous thriller.

Another interesting person I met there was the former Head Boy while I was at New Plymouth Boys' High School. This was Athol G. McIntyre. He and I had been in the sixth form together in 1937.

Mac came in to the lecture room on the morning of the first day.

He mounted the stage and stood behind the rostrum and commenced his address. I cannot recall what the subject matter related to, but whatever it was Mac was always able to put it over in a humorous and entertaining way. He was by nature an extrovert character who had a tendency to dramatise the circumstances. It was no time before he had the audience in fits of laughter with his description of baling out at night over the Isle of Wight after having been hit by friendly anti-aircraft fire. Then he went on to describe his second parachute jump when his Hurricane was shot down by a Messerschmitt 110 over Portsmouth. When his session concluded I stood up at the back of the room and waved to him. 'Well for God's sake. If it isn't old Cappy Masters, fancy seeing you here.' Then to the audience: 'An old school chum of mine from New Zealand'.

Mac and I met that night and had a very pleasant session in one of the Derby pubs. I told him how I was receiving mail from our old school master Yank Kerr and we reminisced about many incidents at New Plymouth Boy's High School, particularly about the morning when over 300 boys had been whacked in the assembly hall.

At the conclusion of this course I had to make my way back to St Merryn via London. My travelling companion off the same Derby course was one Art Roscoe, an American Eagle Squadron pilot during the Battle of Britain. Art had recently returned from Malta where he had been awarded the DFC for a good score of German aircraft. By some gentle persuasion I agreed to stay overnight in London so we could take in some of his favourite haunts. I knew that this would be inviting trouble from Willie who was expecting me to return direct with no overnight stop in London.

Well, when I reported to him next day there was all hell let loose.

'Where had I bloody well been?'

'Didn't I realize that there was a war on?'

When his initial furore had subsided I explained that the chief flying instructor on the course was an ex head boy of my New Zealand secondary school and I felt duty bound to accept his hospitality. Hence my slight delay.

Knowing Willie's habits fairly well by this time, I guessed he would check with Rolls Royce to confirm that Squadron Leader McIntyre was in fact a Kiwi and the chief flying instructor. I heard no more about it but I could still detect that Willie still harboured some resentment over this incident.

Once again we were back to hard flying. Willie had received some technical information about a new type of flying suit called the Franks 'water suit' the purpose of which was to increase the pilot's threshold for blacking out under high forces of gravity. This blacking out resulted from the blood being forced from one's brain to the lower body level. This caused a grey curtain to come down over one's eyes to obliterate all vision which would gradually be restored as the forces of gravity declined. The circumstances in which black out took place were when the aircraft was put into a high speed dive and the control column moved back quickly to transform the dive into a climb.

The water suit had been made available for trials and like all other developments Willie was interested to give it a trial. The suit itself was made of rubber which fitted over one's flying suit or battledress and was laced up at the front. The pilot then put on his parachute and staggered ungainly to climb into the cockpit. Once there a naval airman would jump on the wing and connect a water hose to an inlet valve on the water suit. The suit filled up with water to just above the heart level, thus establishing a barrier for the force of the gravity to take effect on before it affected the pilot's bloodstream. Although this sounds a rather 'Heath Robinson' idea, it did, in fact work as intended. For various reasons, however, it was absolutely useless from an operational point of view, because the time taken to get into the suit and fill it with water, made fast scrambles impossible. Furthermore, it would have been extremely hazardous on operation because of the difficulty of baling out of a Seafire cockpit and the horrendous situation which would confront a pilot who had to ditch in the sea. The weight of water in the suit would have made survival impossible.

Despite the limiting factors it was at least interesting to conduct an experiment. Brian Razzall and I went to assess the device. Brian was wearing the water suit while I flew in the common battledress. At the given signal Brian went into tight maneouvres and invited me to follow. The dives and turns got tighter and tighter, but I still managed to keep a bead on him through the reflector gunsight. While I did begin to 'grey out' I did not completely 'black out' so I kept on his tail all the time.

When we returned and landed Brian expressed amazement that I had been able to maintain position on his tail. He claimed that he had made his dives and turns so tight that he was on the verge of blacking out despite the water suit. To him it seemed impossible that an unprotected pilot could keep a bead on him.

My thoughts went back to my medical examination in Wellington when the doctor pronounced that I had a higher than normal blood pressure. Could this have been the reason? But because I knew nothing about aero-medicine I did not mention my thoughts to Brian just in case, he might quite accidentally drop it off to Willie Simpson who might have used it as an excuse to fire one of his rebellious Kiwis.

There were several other Kiwis serving on the station at St Merryn. Some where in the second line target towing squadron while one or two were doing a conversion course on Hurricanes preparatory to joining a squadron. One of the latter was Arthur

Street from Marton, a two ring lieutenant who must have been on one of the very early New Zealand courses at *St Vincent*.

Arthur became friendly with Joe Urlich, Arch Foley and myself.

We would often go ashore as a foursome and have a few pints in a local tavern. One such night Arthur became rather sentimental as if to get something that was bothering him off his chest. He told us how he would dearly love to be in a first line squadron, but he had serious reservations about one English pilot with whom he had to do exercises such as formation flying. It did not occur to Joe, Arch or I, that what we were listening to was a premonition.

The following afternoon Arch and I were making our way from our squadron dispersal to the wardroom when we heard a loud explosion which seemed to be on the other side of the airfield. Two towering columns of dense black smoke erupted from about a mile away.

My thoughts were immediately of Arthur Street and I hoped he was not one of these.

Without hesitation Arch and I took off across the middle of the airfield. We were half-way to the site of the crash when the fire truck, the ambulance and several other vehicles passed us.

Two Hurricanes had, in fact, collided just off the aerodrome circuit. Both pilots were killed. One of these was our friend Arthur Street – killed on active service 27th June 1943. Two very chastened sub-lieutenants returned to the wardroom to drown their sorrows.

On 12th July the squadron bade farewell to St Merryn bound for Machrihanish on the Mull of Kintyre to prepare for initial deck landings in Seafires. We took off in formation of threes joined up as a squadron and made a very low level pass over the airfield. Looking across from Willie's aircraft I could see that we had very neat wing tip to wing tip performance.

It seemed that the entire station personnel were out waving farewell, the Captain, the station officers, the ground staff and the Wrens were out in force to wish us all the best. It really made me feel very proud to be a member of such a good squadron.

En route to Machrihanish we had to land at Penros in North Wales to refuel. Coming in to land we adopted the customary low naval circuit, a stream landing with close intervals and the standard Naval tail down approach technique. The entire twelve aircraft were down on the runway and taxiing to the control tower within five minutes.

Once out of our aircraft we were confronted by a fearsome looking moustachioed Royal Air Force Group Captain, the commander of the station. He castigated Willie Simpson.

'What the hell do you chaps think you're doing? If you want to kill yourselves, don't do it on my station. I've never seen such split arse flying in all my days.'

Willie, very diplomatically endeavoured to explain that what he had witnessed was standard naval procedure. We were an operational squadron and whether we landed on airfields or aircraft carriers the same technique applied. The Groupie was obviously unimpressed. With a gruff acknowledgement he jumped into his utility, clashed the gears and screamed off to his office. This clearly demonstrated the difference and occasional animosity between the two flying services.

We arrived at Machrihanish on 13th July. For the next two weeks it was a concentrated period of assisted dummy deck landings (ADDLS) to prepare for our first deck landing experience on Seafires which had by that time earned the reputation of being the most difficult aircraft to land on a carrier.

There were several reasons for this. Firstly, it was the lack of visibility from the pilot's cockpit. It was virtually impossible to land the Seafire with one's head 'in the office' because one could not possibly see the batsman during the approach to the round down. This meant that the pilot simply had to wear his goggles and put his head out the port side into the slipstream and fly the Seafire without watching the airspeed indicator. To complicate matters even further the Seafire was very sensitive on the controls, particularly fore and aft, so if the approach speed was just a few knots too high the Seafire would float over the eight arrester wires and end up with a colossal prang into the barrier. On the other hand, to let the speed fall too low would mean a stall and an inevitable spin into the drink.

Consequently the pilot had to have implicit faith in the skill of the batsman and to sense any change in the flying characteristics by the 'seat of his pants'. Truly no naval aircraft has ever been more difficult to deck land than this otherwise lovely little Seafire. Even the famous Spitfire test pilot Jeffrey Quill had chalked up trouble when he tried to deck land a Seafire.

Over the next two weeks we were practising ADDLS at every opportunity. My log book record shows that during this period I had done 114 ADDLS before being flown out to our carrier HMS *Unicorn* on 4th August. The pilot of the Swordfish who flew Les Baker and me on board was Graham Finlayson of the *Dominion Monarch* draft.

This was to be a day of terrific suspense. Not a word was said, but I am sure that all were wondering whether one or more of us would not be alive at the end of the day.

Happily all four Kiwis completed four deck landings each without any prangs or burst tyres. Some other members were not so happy. Fortunately we had no fatalities, but there were several superb barrier crashes, where the remnants of the aircraft had to be pushed over the side. Hammy Neilson being the shortest pilot in the squadron had the greatest difficulty despite the fact that he had put his seat into the highest notch and put several cushions beneath his parachute. Hammy was a delightful little Scotsman, seemingly quite unperturbed that he had written off a £10,000 Seafire in the most glorious barrier crash one could ever imagine.

During our short stay at Machrihanish I renewed acquaintance with Alister MacLeod, Cliff Bissett and Ralph Cocklin all of whom were members of the *Dominion Monarch* draft.

Mac was in 834 Seafire Squadron whose pilots, like us, were doing their first deck landings in Seafires. Prior to this Mac's squadron had been working up at Turnhouse, Scotland and was to join the escort carrier HMS *Hunter*. Little did we know it, but we were soon both to sail for the Mediterranean and be involved in our first operation.

Cliff Bissett and Ralph Cocklin were on a training course for anti-submarine warfare. The course involved a lot of night flying in pairs of Swordfish aircraft, one of which mounted a very high powered Leigh searchlight beneath its undercarriage while the other carried depth charges. The course was named after its supervisor 'Bibby's flight'. These chaps were required to fly under the most extreme weather conditions, hail, snow, rain and high winds. There was nothing more demanding than this. It called for an exceptional amount of 'guts' to see this course through. Several of the crews were lost crashing into the hills near Machrihanish. Cliff Bisset himself had a very narrow escape when he had to make a night forced landing. We came to the conclusion that, while landing Seafires may have been a hazardous occupation, the risks were nothing in comparison with 'Bibby's flight'.

On 5th August three Seafire fighter squadrons 809, 887 and 897 officially joined HMS *Unicorn* which was to be our home for the next two-three months.

In addition to the 36 fighter aircraft there were about eight Swordfish TBR aircraft on board.

Whereas until now the squadrons had been working up individually, now they had to work up collectively and with the carrier. Exercises such as homing on the ship's beacon, calibrating the ship's guns, and more deck landing drills were the order of the day.

From now on each time one flew off one would go to the ship's bridge and synchronise one's wrist watch with the ship's chronometer. We had all been issued with Swiss Omega watches which were internationally renowned for accuracy.

If lost at sea the only way we could find our way back to the carrier was by listening in to the ship's beacon which operated on a very high frequency sending out sector letters through 360 degrees.

Some bright person had devised a very simple method for fighter pilots to return to their base, if in difficulties due to bad weather conditions. For reasons of security the carrier could not always give a pilot a course to steer to return, so this very simple 'Heath Robinson' method was devised.

The 360° face of one's watch was divided into twelve segments, each of which was allocated a morse code letter.

When switching the beacon on the pilot would hear over the radio, the letter for the sector in which he was presently flying. Possibly after holding his present course for a few minutes the morse code letter would change.

This new letter would indicate that he had flown into the adjacent sector. By holding this heading until the next change of letter he could then determine whether he was flying towards his carrier or away from it. Having resolved this he would then make the required alteration of course to bring him back into the next sector. The process of zig-zagging course would eventually bring him to a point where he was directly over the carrier, at which point he would receive a steady affirmative signal. He would then proceed to circle and lose height until he could see the carrier and land on it.

This sounds very simple in theory, but like most things it was often vastly different in practice.

Factors which tended to create problems were due to altitude. If the pilot was flying say 50 miles away from the carriers he would not pick up the signal unless he was flying at sufficient height. Static on the radio set was another factor which distorted the signals.

The working up routine between the three squadrons and the ship continued at a frenetic pace. Flying details continued from dawn to dusk. Generally we would return each night and anchor off Lamlash on the Isle of Arran.

On 12th August we finally set sail in company with the escort carriers *Hunter*, *Stalker*, *Battler* and *Attacker*, escorted by several cruisers and a large screen of destroyers.

The *Unicorn* being a light fleet carrier was the largest and the fastest of the fleet, but could only proceed at the same speed as the escort carriers whose maximum speed was about 18 knots.

Our course took us across the northern coast of Ireland and well out into the Atlantic before steering a zig-zag course south towards Gibraltar.

We were now passing through a highly dangerous area where German U-boats were in transit to and from their bases at Le Havre and St Nazaire in France.

It was also an area that was constantly patrolled by German Focke Wulf 200 bombers which would shadow any British ships and report the presence to U-boat headquarters in the Lorient.

A high degree of three stage readiness was adopted. The first degree was two Seafires on the *Unicorn* flight deck, with pilots strapped in, engines warmed up, all ready to scramble in at a moment's notice. The two pilots were backed by two more who maintained a second stage of readiness in the crew room with flying gear and Mae Wests, all ready to dash out and jump in two more Seafires which would be brought up on the lift. The third stage of readiness was two to four more pilots who had to be within a short distance of the crew room.

As luck would have it Brian Razzall and I were the two pilots at the first stage of readiness, helmets on, strapped in tight, radio plugs installed, when suddenly the ship's Tannoy system sounded a Red Alert.

The whole fleet swung around into wind and we were both cleared for take off.

The weather that day was ghastly but standard for the Bay of Biscay. The cloud base was about 1,00–1,500 feet and a heavy swell was running. Looking down the flight deck as I opened the throttle on the brokes I could see the bows plunging into the heavy sea. If I waited a second before letting the brakes off I reckoned I could catch the bows on the upswing and get a good clear take off with no risk of sinking after leaving the flight deck. Once airborne we settled down into battle formation and circled the fleet just beneath the cloud base.

At our briefing prior to these patrols we had been told to observe R/T silence. The carrier could not talk to us unless it needed to give us directions for an interception. If we got into difficulties and were forced to bale out or ditch in the ocean the fleet could not stop, but a destroyer would be detailed to deploy and try and find us. What a comforting thought! I don't know about Brian Razzall but I could almost feel the adrenalin flowing.

Down below us we had five aircraft carriers, several cruisers and perhaps 10 or 12 destroyers. There must have been close to 15,000 pairs of eyes watching the patrol line of our two Seafires. It was the sort of feeling that opening batsmen must experience in a test match at Lord's.

Prior to moving to first degree readiness Brian and I had agreed on what tactics we would adopt if we were fortunate enough to make an interception. We knew that the Focke Wolf Condor was heavily defended against attacks from above or astern so we decided we would co-ordinate our attacks from either quarter thus forcing the target to turn in to the first attacker. Then, if we had sufficient height above the water, we would fire from below where the enemy gunners would find it difficult to bring fire to bear.

As we circled the fleet at a few miles radius in and out of the fleeting grey cloud I made up my mind that whenever Brian turned I would make certain that I had him in sight between me and the carrier. Under these weather conditions it could be dangerous to lose sight of the carrier unless we suddenly intercepted the bogey aircraft.

After stooging around for a little over one hour during which time we had not received any instructions from the fighter direction control room, we received a recall signal by Aldis lamp.

Brian indicated that he would land on first. Considering the heavy swell a split arse stream landing was obviously out of the question, so I flew around for a while and had a grandstand view of Brian's approach. The batsman Lieutenant Tony Fradd wasn't happy so he gave Brian a wave off. He made two more approaches but Fradd was still not taking him. On the fourth approach Brian did land and I watched the hydraulic barrier come down and Brian taxied his Seafire into the parking area.

Now it was my turn. There must have been hundreds of pilots in 'goofers gallery' on all five carriers watching this performance and secretly thanking their lucky stars that they were not trying to get back.

As I came in turning on my first approach I could see the end of the flight deck pitching through what seemed like a frightening height. The deck was also rolling from side to side.

Tony Fradd was not happy about my first attempt. He was probably trying to judge my touch down at the moment the pitch was neutral, but to coincide the pitch and the roll was almost impossible.

I took a second wave off and this caused me some concern. The sky was getting darker. If I didn't get on soon they would have to bring out the lighted bats – that wouldn't be very funny at all.

Anyway on my third attempt Tony gave me the cut. I caught the second wire but the fun was not over yet. Just as I touched down the flight deck rolled to starboard and my Seafire headed in the opposite direction. Fortunately the hook held on the landing wire but my port wheel went over the side. That was a very close shave – I very nearly had a swim. Members of the flight deck handling party rushed out from the catwalk alongside the flight deck and grabbed the plane before it could topple over into the sea. Had they not done so, the Seafire would have turned over upside down with me trapped inside. The chances of escaping from the cockpit under those circumstances were very slim indeed.

This was how I did my 13th deck landing!

A few days later we passed through the Straits of Gibraltar and the *Unicorn* berthed at the mole. Just ahead of us was the fleet carrier HMS *Illustrious* which we visited that evening to renew acquaintance with Jack Parli, Winne Churchill, Joe Brough and

Martin Turner. It was a riotous occasion which ended up with a free for all rugby match in the ward room. Churchill was performing as only he could. He had been half back for the Victoria University 1st XV when Mac and I had played in 1940–41.

We stayed about a week at Gibraltar sailing out to work up each day with a larger force of carriers and escort vessels.

Occasionally we would be required to land at the Gibraltar air strip which was not an experience I found to my liking.

Gibraltar had been notorious for a lot of flying accidents which were probably attributed to the turbulent air current which whirled around the rock. I certainly did not relish putting Seafires down there. You seemed to have to fight your way down buffeted side to side by these quite vicious updraughts.

While we were berthed at the mole, each night from dusk to dawn reverberated with explosions of depth charges in Gibraltar harbour.

It transpired that this nightly exercise was carried out to prevent some very brave Italian frogmen from venturing across Algeciras to fix limpet mines on to the hulls of British warships. Spain was supposed to be neutral but in actual fact the towns of La Linea and Algeciras were havens for rather more dangerous activities than German and Italian espionage.

The arrival or departure of every British naval vessel was known in Berlin within minutes.

During our short stay in Gibraltar we managed to obtain a 12–hour visa to visit La Linea which was just over the border from Gibraltar. In fact one side of the airstrip is British territory the other Spanish. The border was manned on one side by immaculately turned out British regular troops while on the other side, one encountered demoralised Spanish soldiery. To see soldiers with toes protruding from their boots and scruffy torn uniforms was quite a revelation. This was the great dictator's Army – General Franco's men.

Once in the town of La Linea we did the place over. We sampled the anisette and the food and generally had a good time.

We sailed from Gibraltar on 28th August, our next port of call being Algiers. The day after our arrival here was a Sunday so there was the customary Sunday divisions on the flight deck. Anyone of the Roman Catholic faith was permitted to go ashore by liberty boat to attend their own religious service. Arch Foley and Joe Urlich were both Catholic by faith, but could hardly be termed ardent adherents. They decided to go ashore and invited me to join them. I imagined that having got ashore they would head for the Catholic Basilica and confess their sins of which they had an impressive portfolio. Well, I could not see where I was as a Protestant, and not a very good one at that, could become a legitimate travelling companion.

In retrospect, I now regret this decision, because Foley and Urlich had absolutely no intention of taking communion. Once ashore they headed for the Kasbah the district with the sleazy restaurants, night clubs, Arab belly dancers etc. They returned to the carrier suitably rejuvenated, but the Pope had nothing whatever to do with the transformation.

From Algiers we then headed for Malta. At dusk that night as we sailed along the North African coast past Cape Bougaroun Arch, Joe and I were sitting on one of the anti-aircraft gun turrets admiring the sunset. Joe suddenly became sentimental and started reminiscing about his earlier days at Kaitaia. He had been born into a part Dalmatian, part Maori family. His great grandfather had probably emigrated to New Zealand in the latter part of the 19th century and like many of his countrymen had worked in the Kauri gum fields. Joe went on to tell us about his school days, his time at Teachers' Training college and many intimate details of his life prior to joining the Fleet Air Arm. As I listened to this I could not help thinking back to our late friend Arthur Street. Could I be listening to another premonition?

Several days later we arrived at Malta and as we entered Valetta harbour we could see at once the enormous devastation caused by the German and Italian Air Forces during the siege period of earlier months. Numerous hulks of tankers, cargo and a few warships were strewn around the inlet.

We had the opportunity for a brief shore leave but what with the appalling amount of bomb damage and the stringent rationing there was little in the way of entertainment or sightseeing.

Operation Avalanche – Salerno

The following day which must have been 8th September was a Sunday, so as usual we adopted the harbour routine of Sunday Church divisions on flight deck. On this occasion, we were joined by all the fighter pilots from the other escort carriers *Battler, Stalker, Hunter* and *Attacker.* With everyone dressed in white tropical rig of the day it was quite an impressive occasion. In all we would have approximately 130 fighter pilots plus a few TBR pilots in the congregation.

The purpose of this gathering became clear when church parade concluded. Rear-Admiral Philip Vian who had been appointed officer commanding our task force took the rostrum to address the assembled pilots. He informed us that the fleet would leave Malta that afternoon in company with a large force of cruisers and destroyers and make a feint, in daylight conditions, through the Gulf of Taranto to create the impression that we were to attack the big Italian naval base at Taranto. When darkness fell, the fleet would then sail on a reciprocal course turning, passing through the Straits of Messina about midnight. In the early hours of 9th September we would meet up with a large invasion force comprising American Army units and the British 5th Army who would land on the beaches near Salerno.

Vian did not pull any punches. He told us that if successful, this operation, the first major sea-borne invasion of Europe, should significantly shorten the war. On the other hand, he told us that, because the nearest Royal Air force and American fighters were based in Sicily, the Fleet Air Arm would have to provide a continuous air cover over the beach head. His intelligence had informed him that the Germans and Italians could mount a very strong fighter defence comprising German ME 109s, FW 190s, plus Italian Macchis, Fiat G50s and Reggianne 2000s. While the total fighter strength of our task force was 132 Seafires assuming 100% serviceably, the enemy strength was three times this.

This news was greeted with dead silence but Vian proceeded to say that it was quality not quantity that would decide the battle.

He was never one to 'gild the lily' which was probably why he had earned the nickname 'Blood and Guts'.

The next announcement was that if any of our pilots were to bale out or ditch in to the sea, a guard destroyer or submarine would be deployed to search. Great stuff!

The carrier HMS *Illustrious* together with an American carrier and supporting escorts were to provide the combat air patrols with Wildcat fighters while our fighters were engaged in patrols over the beach head and beyond.

The task force sailed from Valetta harbour that afternoon led by the cruiser *Euryalus* in which Admiral Vian flew his flag, then the two cruisers *Scylla* and *Charybdis*, following by *Unicorn, Hunter, Stalker, Battler, Attacker* and ten destroyers bringing up the rear. Once at sea, the force adopted battle formation with the cruisers in the van, the five carriers in the centre and the destroyers on the flanks.

We accordingly headed up the Gulf of Taranto, but as soon as darkness fell we turned about and sailed south west to the entrance to the Straits of Messina.

The military campaign in Sicily had concluded about ten days prior to this with the German and Italian armies withdrawing across the Straits to retire up the toe of Italy. As our fleet passed through the Straits late that night we sailed very close to the town of Messina which was all lit up and we could actually see the Italians celebrating in the streets. They obviously did not have their hearts in the war, they were glad to be out of it.

But perhaps it was something more than getting rid of the Germans that they were celebrating. Over the radio that night we had heard that King Victor Emmanuel of Italy had through his Chief of Army staff General Badoglio sued for peace. Mussolini had been rejected and now sought refuge with the Germans.

On the other side of the Messina Straits we could see heavy

artillery fire which was Montgomery's 8th Army giving the Jerries the hurry up.

This was all very exciting news. Perhaps we would not have to go to into action within a few hours of Salerno. It proved to be a futile hope. The Jerries don't give in that easily as we were to find out with a vengeance.

So it was off to bed to get what sleep we could before being called at 4.30 a.m. This was one night I could not sleep. My mind was in a whirl after all the events of the day. I simply could not stop thinking of the prospect of being outnumbered three to one. Would I have to shoot? Would I have to bale out? What would happen if I had to ditch in the sea?

After a quick breakfast those who were not on the dawn patrol were crammed into 'goofers gallery' at the back of the ship's island to watch the take off. The *Unicorn* flew off eight Seafires, four for high cover, four for low to medium cover. The patrols were one and a half to two hours duration, and we maintained this pattern from dawn to dusk. With four Seafires from each of the escort carriers we were able to maintain a presence of 24 aircraft above the army all day long.

Tragedy was not long in coming. The first four Seafires to return were the low cover provided by either 809 or 887 squadrons. The flight leader landed safely but the next aircraft flown by Sub-Lieutenant (A) MacKenzie was too low in approach. Tony Fradd our batsman gave him an urgent signal to climb a bit higher, then suddenly the Seafire flicked onto its back and spun into the sea only a very short distance from the round down. For those who were watching from 'goofers gallery' this was a very sobering experience.

The only conclusion that we could come to is that McKenzie had allowed his approach speed to fall off and when he received the signal to increase his height he must have pulled back on the control column at the same time as he applied the throttle.

There was worse to come. The Seafires from my own 897 squadron streamed for landing but there were only three. Where was the fourth aircraft? The three pilots to land were 'Doc' Davies, flight leader, Arch Foley and John Rankin. Joe Urlich was missing.

On these sorties we were carrying extra fuel in a drop tank so as to extend the duration of our patrols. In using the drop tank, the pilot was supposed to take off on his main tank and having attained a safe height, switch over and consume the contents of the drop tank. When the drop tank had been exhausted the engine would splutter so the pilot then switched back to the main tank. It was not feasible to do this in reverse, but this is apparently what poor old Joe had done. He took off correctly on his main tank, but in the excitement of the occasion he forgot to switch over to the drop tank. Towards the end of the patrol his main tank ran dry, but when he switched over to the drop tank there was no response. The engine stopped dead. Joe then attempted to bale out using the recommended Royal Air Force procedure of ejecting in an inverted position.

Unfortunately, like many other Seafire pilots before and after, Joe got trapped in the cockpit and had difficulty getting out with the increasing forces of gravity. When he did finally get clear he was far too low. His parachute had just opened when he hit the sea at a collosal speed.

Both Arch and I thought back to the evening when we sat with Joe on the gun turret. This intimate episode had quite obviously been a premonition.

It was not until very late in the war at least a year after this incident that the Royal Air Force method of baling out was rejected in favour of diving over the side in level flight. The Seafire it seems had different aerodynamic qualities from the Spitfire. Perhaps the extra weight of the airframe, the landing hook etc. made a difference. In the meantime many Seafire pilots had lost their lives trying to bale out.

My first patrol was the third one of the day. It comprised our CO Willie Simpson, myself as No 2, Les Baker and Tony Perry. After taking off we switched our radio transmission over to HMS *Euryalus* which was Admiral Vian's flagship and the task force fighter direction ship. We received instructions to climb to 26,000 feet and patrol parallel to the coastline which was a straight line extending from the Isle of Capri to Agropoli in the south.

This was an uneventful patrol and we all returned to land on safely.

At this stage it had become apparent that with absolutely no wind speed and the limitation of the task force to 17–18 knots which was the maximum speed of the escort carriers, a high percentage of Seafires were becoming damaged with excessively heavy landings or floating into the barrier.

On *Unicorn*, apart from the sad loss of Joe Urlich, 897 squadron had so far had an accident free record.

Not so, however, with the two other squadrons. They had chalked up some majestic prangs.

The experience on the escort carriers with their shorter flight decks was even worse. On these carriers there was a tendency for the Seafires to lurch tail up and nose down after catching a wire with the result that the propellor hit the deck.

That night there was a conference on board HMS *Hunter* and the Captain Henry McWilliam recommended that eight to nine inches should be cut off the propellor blades. This was a typical naval improvisation – it would not have been done in the Air Force. Remarkably Hunter's Seafires continued to operate, the crash rate subsided and their air performance was not greatly affected.

My next sortie on 9th September was the dusk patrol. As before we reported on HMS *Euryalus* for instructions. We were to patrol at 18,000 feet and be alert for possible bogeys. We were no sooner on our patrol line than we received an urgent call 'Bogey angels 28 vector 030 buster buster!' In layman terms this meant that the fighter direction officers had picked up an aircraft on radar at 28,000 feet which was not displaying IFF (Identification Friend or Foe). 'Buster buster' was the instruction to push the throttle to maximum boost and highest revs to climb to the required height as quickly as possible steering 30° from our present position. The sun was behind us so we were in a good position for surprise. As we closed on the bogey, *Euryalus* gave us slight adjustments in course, until finally we spotted him from behind. At that height, even under maximum power our closing speed was distressingly slow. The target was flying alone, so obviously Willie would have the privilege of attacking first. If he missed I would be next. It was a tense moment until suddenly Willie screamed out: 'It's a bloody Lightning' – an American P38 fighter.

Now what on earth was a solitary American Lightning doing stooging around at 28,000 feet and not showing IFF? There was something rather odd about this. Nor did the pilot give any indication that he had seen us creeping up on him from behind. From our previous knowledge of United States of America fighter pilots one would have expected an instinctive panic reaction with the Lightning diving away from us like the 'clappers out of hell'.

We proceeded to close on him and formatted, Willie and myself on one side, Les and Tony on the other. We were flying wing tip to wing tip – we waved to him, he waved back. He seemed quite unconcerned and kept flying in the same direction which was towards Naples.

One unusual thing I did notice, however – the pilot was not wearing goggles. But I never gave it another thought until we were being debriefed by our intelligence officers. When we withdrew from the Lightning I went to switch my guns to 'SAFE'. I was horrified to find that in my excitement of the chase I had omitted to switch them 'ON'. Needless to say – this was one thing I didn't crow about.

On landing back on board the carrier we were immediately bustled away to debriefing. The intelligence boys acknowledged that there was nothing that we could have done about it, because it was an American Lightning bearing United States of America colours despite the fact that it was not showing IFF.

Then we were told of their suspicions. Apparently there was a small team of German linguists who were constantly listening in to enemy radio transmissions. They had picked up someone who was very accurately reporting the deployment of major naval units and this was quite logically associated with a lone aircraft which was not displaying IFF. 'I believe you chaps have had the unusual experience of formatting alongside a Jerry pilot without realising it.' It was then I recalled that the pilot was not wearing goggles. 'That adds up,' said the IQ, 'Me 109 pilots quite often fly without goggles because they have to have the hood closed for take off and landing. This makes it all the more certain that he is our man.'

There had been so many landing accidents on that first day of the operation that an urgent assessment had to be made of the remaining serviceable fighters. The naval airmen mechanics and airframe fitters worked diligently all through the night, cannibalising some of the damaged planes to restore those less damaged. On the morrow, those that were completely beyond repair we pushed over the side into the Tyrrhenian Sea.

I recall one sortie that I flew on when, quite by chance, noticed that the Seafire had a metal patch rivetted over the main fuselage spar right in front of the tailplane. When I saw it I said to the Petty Officer, Harry Wragg who was in charge of the airframes, 'What the hell is this all about, Wragg?'

He replied, 'Oh I wouldn't worry about that sir. It's just a little wrinkle in the skin. It had a hard landing!'

I thought to myself, it's OK for you to say that – you don't have to fly the damned thing.

I had a reunion with Harry Wragg in the United Kingdom in 1989. We had a good laugh about this incident. Fortunately we didn't get involved in any violent maneouvres that day, otherwise the tail might have fallen off.

In the morning a decision was taken to fly two Swordfish aircraft, each with two Seafire pilots in the rear compartment, down to Castel Vetrano airfield in Sicily where they would collect four replacement Seafire Aircraft. Brian Razzall's flight, Les Baker, Tony Perry and I were chosen for this operation.

Brian and I clambered in with our parachutes into a Swordfish piloted by Sub-Lieutenant (A) Such. We could not wear the parachutes because of the confined space in the rear compartment, so we had absolutely no chance of baling out if things went wrong.

The two Swordfish then headed south to Sicily, making a landfall near Palermo and then landing at Castle Vetrano a distance of over 200 miles. Castel Vetrano, as a matter of interest, was only a stone's throw from Corleone which is reputedly the international headquarters of the Mafia.

Once there we clambered out rather stiffly from our uncomfortable compartment and searched for the air repair yard where we were supposed to find our very valuable replacements.

It was then that I heard a voice: 'Well for God's sake Charlie, there's Cappy Masters.' With that I turned around lugging my parachute and saw two old high school friends, Stewart Fleming, a navigator and Charlie Patrick a TBR pilot. We stopped and had a quick chat. They wanted me to stay and have some fun but I had to remind them that 240 miles away we were fighting a desperate battle. This was no time for frivolity.

We found our aircraft and signed the A25 forms which signified that we accepted that they were fully airworthy i.e. full of fuel, mechanically sound, radios serviceable, guns loaded etc.

Satisfied that all maintenance was OK we took off on our trip back to the *Unicorn*. Passing the volcanic island of Stromboli on the starboard side we saw in the distance four aircraft converging on us. We tried to avoid them, but they kept on intercepting until we identified them as four American Mustang fighters. The way they were behaving suggested that they were looking for trouble, so all four of us rolled over to display our unmistakeable Seafire elliptical wings. No one but a complete idiot would persist in attacking a friendly aircraft, but this meant nothing to these cowboys. Well, thank goodness the Seafires we were flying were LIIc's which were at that time the fastest fighters in the Mediterranean area up to 10,000 feet. We could show a clean pair of heels to Me 109s or FW 190s, so that was something in our favour. We opened the 'taps' and left these impossible twits behind.

The weather by this time had become very hazy, almost foggy, and visibility was very poor. By dead reckoning we should soon be in the area to rendezvous with the fleet.

The following report which I submitted on 15th September records the sequence of events from that point –

897 Squadron
15th September, 1943.

Report of loss of Seafire IIC Aircraft
(Sub-Lieutenant (A) B. Razzall)

At 1100 hours on 10th September 1943, I took off from the Castle Vetrano aerodrome, Sicily, in company with three other aircraft which comprised Dover Flight. The call signs allocated were as follows:

Dover One	–	Sub-Lieutenant (A) B. Razzall
Dover Two	–	Sub-Lieutenant (A) A. O. Masters
Dover Three	–	Sub-Lieutenant (A) L. J. Baker
Dover Four	–	Sub-Lieutenant (A) A. D. Perry

After flying on a course of 040° at economical cruising (i.e. 1300 revs-lbs boost) for approximately 1 hour 30 minutes our position was 240° Agropoli 12 miles or in position EASY 9 on the lettered grid. Dover One thereupon called Wolfson (HMS *Palomaves*) for a course to steer to Dorking (HMS *Unicorn*). We were instructed to orbit this position and await vector. At 1240 hours we received a course to steer of 240° which we flew on for 15 minutes without any sighting of the fleet. Dover One called Wolfson and reported that this course had not brought us over the fleet and said that he intended flying on a reciprocal. This message was acknowledged by Wolfson. At this stage I suggested to Dover One that I endeavoured to make a homing on the beacon, but I was unable to tune in to any signal on the carrier's frequency. When I reported this discovery he requested Dover Four to tune in his beacon, but he too, was unable to get any signal. Wolfson then gave us another course to steer and asked for a report on the state of fuel. Dover One reported less than 30 gallons, but the remainder reported 37 gallons. Shortly after this I noticed that Dover Four had left the formation and disappeared. We flew on this course for about 10 minutes and failed to see anything, so Dover One requested emergency homing as his fuel was apparently very low. Wolfson instructed us to show distress IFF which we immediately did and also requested us to change the channel 'B' on 11 Handstroke (HMS *Euryalus*) but there was no reply to our signals.

On his own initiative Dover One endeavoured to contact Steambrake and Dorking, but neither was successful. The amount of traffic through Wolfson was so great it appeared that our emergency call received no priority.

Obo Leader who was returning from a sortie called up Dover One and endeavoured to give us a homing, but this was also unsuccessful because apparently he had mistaken us for another formation of aircraft.

Wolfson again told us to orbit and then gave us another course to steer 170° and estimated that the fleet was only 8 miles away. Dover One acknowledged this but stated if he did not sight the fleet within 2 minutes he would be obliged to turn towards the coast because he did not have sufficient fuel to land on. After a short time on this course and still having not sighted anything Dover One turned and flew towards the coast at 3,500 feet approximately. We steered a course of 060° which we estimated would bring us to the nearest part of the coast. At 1330 hours Dover One made his final message to Wolfson saying that the situation was desperate and he was preparing to bale out. He then dived to gain speed because at that stage our air speed was in the vicinity of 115 knots. As he lost height he passed through the cloud and was lost to sight. I called him up on the R/T immediately afterwards, but there was no reply and Wolfson reported that he had already baled out.

Dover Three and myself continued on a course of 060° until we reached the coast. Dover Three eventually crash landed on the beach and I managed to land on a clear strip of aerodrome.

The position where Sub-Lieutenant (A) B. Razzall baled out was about 7 miles due west of Castellabate or position EASY 8 on the lettered GRID.

897 SQUADRON
HMS *UNICORN*

28th September, 1943.

Sir,

I have the honour to submit the following report on loss of clock whilst ferrying Seafire II C LR 664 from Fleet Air Arm storage section at Castle Vetrano aerodrome Sicily to the ship.

I was obliged to force land owing to shortage of fuel at Monte Corvino aerodrome, Italy. Owing to the fact that this aerodrome was still under enemy shellfire I was unable to remove the clock (6A-1104) which I had placed loose in the cockpit.

When I returned to inspect the aircraft twenty four hours later the clock was missing. During this period it was not possible to provide an armed guard for the aircraft.

I have the honour to be
Sir
Your obedient Servant,
A. O. Masters
Sub-Lieutenant (A) RNZNVR

The Commanding Officer,
897 Squadron.

'Willie thought I had pinched the clock!'

I shall never forget the simple but poignant message that Brian Razzall relayed to us as he was about to bale out 'I'm getting out now chaps. Best of luck to you.'

Here was a man in really desperate trouble, yet as our flight leader he was still concerned about our survival.

What happened when he disappeared into the hazy fog no one will know. Presumably he would have tried to get out in the recommended Spitfire maneouvre, but if he had a dead engine this would have been impossible. Did he get trapped by the back of the cockpit and get dragged down by the centrifugal force like poor old Joe Urlich? Brian's body was never recovered.

At this point Les Baker and I had no alternative but to turn and fly in the direction of the beachhead. Les was a section leader, so I automatically followed him. However, when the coastline came into view I realised that he was heading too far south. I remembered from our pre-flight briefings that the coast south of Agropoli was unlikely to be cleared of German troops until after D DAY + 2. I urgently indicated to Les that we should be heading more to the north. He said, 'OK, I'll follow you.'

We were still flying at very low power in order to get the most distance out of what fuel we had left. The landing beach came into sight and we could see hundreds of landing craft loaded with troops, tanks and supplies, shuttling to and from their mother ships. We were flying at about 500 feet so that we would be recognised as friendly aircraft with our red and blue roundels and the easily discernible Seafire elliptical wings. Suddenly a balloon barrage reared up in front of us, so we had to increase power to clear it.

As we staggered over the balloons at no more than 130 knots with Les flying slightly behind on my port side we were suddenly confronted with a seemingly impenetrable curtain of fire. Tracer was coming from all directions plus some black AA bursts fortunately a bit above us. It seemed as if we had been bracketed by landing craft behind, troops on the beach beneath us and isolated pockets of Germans behind the sand dunes.

Out of the corner of my eye I saw Les diving down to port where I later learned that he made a successful forced landing among the impedimenta on the beach.

There was no way in which I could follow either to port or starboard, so I flipped the Seafire over and dived down inverted to roll out again a moment later, right down on the deck and travelling inland.

Just by sheer chance I found myself heading directly towards the airfield at Monte Corvino about four miles inland. It was supposed to have been captured by D-Day plus 2. I pulled up for a quick look being cautious about the amount of throttle applied and to my horror I saw that this grass airfield was strewn with bomb craters. It had apparently been targeted by United States Liberator bombs for several days prior to the invasion.

Then as if some superior being was watching over me, I could see what seemed to be a very narrow line extending from one side to the other where no bombs had fallen. This had to be it. There was no time to circle around, I had little more than a thimble of petrol left.

Undercarriage down, flaps down, hood open and I squeezed the

Seafire in. The motor was still going when I came to a stop but it was a very close shave.

What to do now? I got out, divested myself of the parachute and grabbed my naval cap. There wasn't a soul in sight but I could see a number of damaged enemy FW 190s on the perimeter and extensively damaged hangars. It was really eerie. It was obviously a dangerous place, but which way was I to turn?

I turned to run towards the seawards side of the airfield when suddenly there was a dull 'Cruump' behind me. A cloud of dust could mean only one thing. Someone was ranging on my Seafire with artillery shells.

Almost at the same time I heard some shouting from the hangar side of the field and saw two crouched figures running towards me. Holy hell – now I've got a fight on my hands. Anyway one against two was not impossible and I had the Seafire fuselage for cover. I undid the pistol holster, took out the heavy naval issue Webley revolver and quickly loaded six chambers. By this time the figures were half way across and had seen me behind the fuselage. 'Don't shoot! Don't shoot. We're Royal Navy.' Thinking that this could still be a German ruse to get closer to me I kept the revolver steadily aimed at them over the tailplane. I recalled the movie films where the heroes waited till they could see the whites of their eyes before opening fire. In any case a revolver is not very accurate beyond say thirty yards.

The leading man repeated 'don't shoot' and touched his cap and then I recognised the naval badge. His companion wore a petty officer's cap.

'Come on, follow us. Run like hell. There's another shell coming in.'

Sure enough there was another 'CRUMP', this time in front of the Seafire. We got to the damaged hangar for a breather where they introduced themselves. The officer was Lieutenant (A) Gerry Woods, an observer trained on an early pre-war course at *St Vincent* in August 1939 and Petty Officer Smith who was a radio specialist.

They explained the reason for their timely arrival. They had come ashore with a battalion of the Queen's Regiment with a radio set to maintain contact with report development to Admiral Vian's Headquarters in HMS *Euryalus.* Their prime task was to report when the airfield at Monte Corvino had been captured and whether it was serviceable for operational fighter squadrons. We all agreed that it would be some days before all the craters could be filled and a troop of German Tiger Tanks was still holding out on the South east corner of the airfield. It could have been these who were firing at me.

Before we left the airfield I noticed the remains of another Seafire. Apparently another Fleet Air Arm pilot had to make a forced landing about an hour before me. He was not so lucky: a German tank shell hit him in the engine and he was killed.

As we walked off the airfield we passed what seemed to be a brand new FW 190. I said to Jerry Woods that I would love to have a look inside the cockpit, to which he replied: 'I'd go easy if I were you – it may be booby trapped.' Woods and Smith escorted me, not along the road towards the beach as one would have expected, but in the opposite direction to the front line. They had their little unit domiciled with the headquarters of The Queen's Regiment in what remained of a bombed out country tavern. As we passed across the recent battlefields we saw quite a number of destroyed Sherman tanks plus a few German Tigers. The Shermans had obviously taken quite a hammering. Although it was only the second day of the battle, one could not help notice the unusual sweet sickly odour of death which pervaded the atmosphere.

The high temperatures would undoubtedly have contributed to this.

The following extract from Gerry Wood's book, *Wings at Sea*, published 1985, refers to these incidents:-

'Though the airfield never really fell completely into our hands until the fighting had moved northwards, we were able next day to set up on the perimeter, protected by the RAF Regiment. Droves of Italian prisoners moved south to the cages, ragged, dishevelled, without arms, unshaven, and with their baggy breeches hanging around their ankles. Revolting, but at least for them the war was over. The Germans had their mobile 88 guns well hidden in the hills surrounding the airfield, and rained shells on the beach, dropping onto the airfield just to remind us that they had everything ranged and plotted. It would have been stupid to set up in the control tower for this reason, but also we knew that everything inside was booby-trapped. So we simply maintained contact, giving what news we could, including our ability to take emergency landings with certain provisos. The German gunners' fire was accurate, and anything that moved was shelled. So, we advised Ancon that any emergency landing would necessitate the pilot getting out immediately he touched down and running for the dry ditch that surrounded the airfield.

The first to land was Sub-Lieutenant 'Cappy' Masters RNZNVR, who obeyed our instructions and dived for the ditch. I went round to bring him in. (Many years later, when we met again in New Zealand, he told my wife and I that he had me in the sights of his .45 Webley for some seconds, believing me to be a German because of my khaki battledress. When just about to fire, he saw my cap-badge!) He brought us up-to-date with the news and requirements from the carriers, and during that day and ensuing days, we took 30 aircraft in, losing only a few to gunfire and prangs. Among the pilots of the Seafires rescued were Al Wright of the Royal Marines, whom I should have flown with to Malta in 1940, David Ogle and 'Hooky' Walker. Where the aircraft were serviceable, but couldn't land back on board, the best we could do was to advise the ship that the pilots were safe and the state of the aircraft. Later, when the firing had died down, we could refuel the Seafires, so they could return to their ship if weather conditions had improved, or fly south and land at one of the airfields liberated by the 8th Army moving north (and now only70 miles away from us) or to fly slowly to Malta. Most of them seemed to opt for Malta. Meantime the marauding German 88s in the hills had not been winkled out completely, and were playing cat and mouse with the emergency landings, picking them off desultorily so as to keep us in a state of permanent twitch. Eventually the 2/6th Queen's Regiment made a night attack and sorted them out.

On 12th September an Italian general arrived in a motorcycle combination sidecar, the driver being his ADC, a captain. Both were quite beautifully dressed, covered in gold lead, medals, aiguillettes, and looking more like commissionaires from the Odeon than fighting men. They had come to surrender, having apparently first offered to do so to an army patrol just up the road, but had been referred to us, who did not want them either. 'Cappy' took them down the road to the nearest army post, returning later with their .22 calibre Beretta pistols and the motorcycle combination. Since I already had a Webley and a Colt automatic, I didn't really want a Beretta, and shortly afterwards a British Army major arrived, demanding the return of all the prizes, since the Italian officers were in grave danger of being killed by their own troops. 'Cappy' protested loud, long and lewdly, but in the end had to give in, though we kept the combination. It would be ideal for messenger duty once I'd taught the troops to ride it.

That evening Major Randolph Churchill came to us, demanding priority for his newspaper dispatches by air to Malta. Although eminently recognisable, he insisted on telling us several times who he was, just in case the barrage had deafened us. 'Cappy' knew only one Churchill and this wasn't him, so he told our visitor in Maori to go away. We really were too busy talking to ships and answering queries. Our batteries were beginning to fail until we could charge them that night on the Stuart generator. Churchill strode off, intent, he said, on reporting our none-cooperation to our CO, whom he expected to find in the control tower, still booby-trapped with 'red devils', a fiendish Italian hand-grenade which, when detonated, shot out very lethal sharp steel wire. Even though we didn't like our visitor's manner, we didn't want to upset dad, so one of the telegraphists headed him off.

At midnight that same evening, we had just finished listening to the radio to learn that several battalions had been savagely mauled. The one we should have been with – the 5th Battalion – had been practically wiped out to a man by a tank attack. Dick Ward was right, I should have stopped worrying at Bizerta.

A further shudder ran through us just before dark when an Italian Army engineer came to show us where he had mined the airfield on German instructions. With typical Italian thoroughness he had forgotten to prime them, but, we asked, suppose an 88mm shell had hit one of them? A shrug of Latin shoulders – maybe, maybe not. Since the evening seemed so much quieter, and the control tower had been defused, we took our first shower and shave for four days. It had been a damned close-run thing, and certainly at one time evacuation had been seriously discussed by the American Army commanders, but was ruled out somewhat contemptuously by General Alexander.

Our job seemed to be almost over as the 8th Army approached, and shortly it would be possible for the RAF Spitfires from Sicily to land and give fighter cover. I therefore made a signal to AFHQ Algiers, stating that we had completed what we had to do, and indicating that in default of other instructions, we proposed to return after 48 hours to North Africa. Such impertinence usually brings a snappy reply, but not this time. That night Captain 'Scupper' Geyer of 51st Troop Carrier Wing turned up in a jeep, had supper and stayed with us in the candlelit control tower. He had taken a couple of days' leave, and wanted to see something of the Sorrento peninsula before it got too regimental, so would I join him? He had money side-arms, transport and several cases of 'C' rations, rather more tasty than British Army 'Compo'. It seemed a good idea. I left 'Cappy' Masters in charge, with the ratings taking four hours on and eight off until my return. Before leaving, I took 'Scupper' on a tour of the airfield to see the pranged Seafires, and he estimated that his C47s could haul out the engines and other spares worth recovering, sending them on to Malta. His eyes lit up at the heap of Axis aircraft at the mountain end of the field. The swastika tailplanes and panels alone would fetch very high prices from the chairborne troops. Even German steel helmets fetched $5 each, $10 if one were smart enough to put a few bullets through them first. Geyer had a 'good commercial brain'.

In the passage of over 40 years one's memory of events can become somewhat vague. So much happened to Woods, Smith and myself during 10th and 11th September that his version could vary slightly from mine.

For instance where Gerry refers to me accepting the surrender of an Italian general, I tend to recall that he was a very senior officer in the Italian Air Force, more than likely a colonel. It was also I who removed the colonel's Beretta pistol which he considered he was entitled to keep having given his parole. This caused a minor incident when a captain of the Queen's Regiment appeared on the scene and told me to give it back. I told him in no uncertain terms that I had not come 12,000 miles to behave like an idiot. This colonel had surrendered to me personally and his Beretta was my souvenir. This captain then reported me to his colonel who then confronted me and pleaded with me to be a decent chap and restore his weapon. It was then someone in the Queen's Regiment sympathised with me, recommended that I return the weapon and he would replace it with something much more prized, a German Walther pistol. This proposition appealed to me, so I returned the Beretta to its original owner.

I do recall a brief meeting with Winston Churchill's son but I most certainly did not tell him in Maori, as Gerry alleges, to buzz off.

Randolph Churchill as I recall this incident was the member of a war correspondents' party led by the famous American 'Cholly' Knickerbocker. Knickerbocker was intrigued by the presence of two British Naval officers in the front line of an army regiment.

'How come you are here, Bud?' Knickerbocker asked me.

I told him I was a Fleet Air Arm pilot and had made a forced landing on Monte Corvino airfield. Photographs were taken and I had visions of being featured in the United States newspapers. Whether this did in fact happen I never found out.

With the greatest respect I also think that Gerry's memory of commandeering a motorcycle from the Italian Colonel is a little amiss. My own recollection is that we heard there was an Italian Army Hospital on the outskirts of Salerno town which had some motor vehicles. Because there was no fuel for my aircraft it looked as if I might be delayed here for some days, so why not try and acquire some transport? Not only would it improve our life-style but we might be able to promote our own private war against the Jerries.

So we took off to the Italian depot. Some Italian officers complete with side arms emerged to meet us. I asked Jerry if he spoke Italian. No. French? A little but not very well. So I said I would try.

'*Bonjour Messieurs. Parlez vous Français?*'

'*Oui – Un peu.*'

'*Nous sommes officiers de Royal Marine de la Grande Bretagne. Nous désirons prendre votre motor bicyclette.*'

'*Mais non. C'est impossible – Ce motobicyclette reste ici.*'

The spokesman made a motion to indicate that they would not give it to us. With that Gerry Woods withdrew his Webley and threatened them.

Hell's teeth, this was getting a bit rough – these chaps were all armed with pistols – we could have had a shoot-out on our hands.

Mercifully they did nothing, so I said something like this:

'*Si vous ne donnez pas votre motobicyclette les Allemandes prendront par la force.*'

This was enough; they handed it over. Neither of us had ridden a motor bike before, but they showed us how to start it up and off we went down the road back to the Queens Regiment HQ.

That night the Luftwaffe pounded the beachhead and the airfield area with bombs from dusk to dawn. We could not operate night fighters from the carriers so they had the sky to themselves. During daylight hours, however the German fighters were rarely seen.

That night there was so much metal whizzing around that we had to scratch out some foxholes in an orchard for protection. There were no English steel helmets available, so I donned a German one which had to be picked up. I only wanted something over my head and the German helmet gave me better protection than the British version. It was good for one's morale but it would have been chancing fate to have been walking around in it. Night patrols of the Queen's Regiment were passing through this area all through the night to engage the enemy ahead. During the night the Germans had withdrawn towards the hills, so there was more room to move around the airfield area. Sporadic artillery fire was, however, still coming from the 88mm guns which ranged as far as the beach and the landing craft still bringing troops and supplies ashore.

That afternoon another Seafire pilot made a forced landing on the airfield. This was Royal Marine Major Al Wright, commanding officer of 809 squadron and also from the aircraft carrier HMS *Unicorn*.

I met up with Al who had somehow located a stock of aero fuel. We went on to the airfield to inspect our two Seafires and to our amazement they appeared to be undamaged by the intermittent shellfire. American troops helped with the refuelling process and Al took off to return to the *Unicorn* with instructions for me to follow him if he had not returned to the field after two hours.

It was about 5 p.m. when I climbed into mine, started up and took off down the same track between the bomb craters.

Thankfully the sky was now clear so the visibility in the distance was excellent. After about 30 minutes I located the fleet and flew down the side of the *Unicorn* indicating that I wanted to land on.

The whole fleet turned into wind and I went into the landing circuit. On lining up in my approach I was heading directly into the setting sun which was just sinking over the horizon. Even with tinted goggles it was difficult to see Tony Fradd the batsman.

This was another 'By guess and by God landing.' It was becoming a bit too frequent.

I had brought back with me a number of battlefield souvenirs, some of which were pinched as soon as I had left the cockpit. I did manage to retain for myself the German holster and Walther pistol, a Luftwaffe diary and a tropical shirt with Nazi emblem. I gave Arch Foley a Luftwaffe glengarry cap. Al Wright had apparently landed back on board with loot tied to the cannon stubs.

Within minutes the Tannoy sounded 'Sub-Lieutenant Masters is to report to the Captain on the bridge.'

I duly presented myself to Captain W. D. Graham, a big 6 3,, Irishman. He proceeded to quiz me about progress and developments ashore with particular reference to Monte Corvino Airfield. No doubt Al Wright had already informed him that the airfield was littered with many bomb craters and would take many days to restore to operational standard.

During this debriefing I stood with my hands behind my back holding my prized Walther pistol. The 1st Lieutenant and other watch officers must have been intrigued, but I knew if I put it down somewhere it would be gone in a flash.

Unbeknown to us, the Americans had decided to bulldoze a new temporary landing field at Paestum which was about 15 miles south of Monte Corvino. This enabled the several Sicily based Royal Air Force Spitfire squadrons to provide close battlefield patrols. Our five carriers released all our available serviceable Seafires, now reduced to a total of only 26. They were led ashore by Major Al Wright. On landing at the Paestum strip our squadron very nearly suffered a further tragedy. In coming in to land, Arch Foley ran into some rough ground which resulted in the Seafire turning over and pinning him inside the cockpit. Fortunately for Arch, the aircraft did not catch fire.

These pilots did see some action both with the Luftwaffe and the American Air Force. Our Commanding Officer Willie Simpson shot down two Me 109s and Arch Foley damaged another.

There was an unfortunate incident however with the Yanks. Al Wright was leading a patrol when suddenly they were buzzed by a couple of crazy Mustang pilots. In the rear view mirror of the Seafire a Mustang closing from astern can look very much like the head on profile of an Me 109.

The leading Mustang pulled away in time but the wing man kept closing as if to attack. Al Wright spotted him in time, then jumped on his tail and let him have it. Obviously Al thought it was an Me 109. The Mustang exploded but happily the pilot managed to bale out.

Later that day the American flight leader turned up in a jeep at Paestum strip complete with the usual cigar hanging out of his mouth and sporting two pearl handled revolvers.

With hands on hips in true Cowboy fashion he yells, 'Where's that goddamned Limey son of a bitch who shot my crazy wing man down?'

I don't know whether Al confronted him or went into hiding. He may have only wanted to congratulate Al on his quick reaction and spot on marksmanship!

From that day D Day plus Four the Germans began to regain the initiative both on the ground and in the air. A succession of counter-attacks had driven the British and American armies back towards the beaches.

At one stage, I believe, plans were being made for an evacuation which could have been a very difficult operation.

The Luftwaffe had benefited from the intelligence probably gained from the spy aircraft and commenced hit and run raids on the beaches plus the radio controlled bomb attacks on some ships. The first to be hit was the United States cruiser *Savannah* on 11th September. This was followed by the United States battleship *Philadelphia* and the British cruiser HMS *Uganda* which was lying close in to the beaches giving supporting fire. Over the next few days further warships and cargo ships were hit by these radio controlled flying bombs.

On 16th September the Luftwaffe had its greatest success when one of their bombers escorted by FW 190s launched a flying bomb at the battleship HMS *Warspite*. The *Warspite* was hit, very badly damaged in the boilers, and had to be withdrawn from the area. Under extremely difficult conditions she was towed by a variety of tugs and cruisers all the way back to Malta for repairs.

It was not until the 18th September that the 5th Army regained the initiative and began to force the Germans back. In the meantime the 8th Army advancing up from the toe of Italy was only a short distance away.

ABOVE LEFT: The author at his action station.

ABOVE RIGHT: A perfect Seafire deck landing attitude with the batsman about to give the 'cut'. Note the clipped wings to combat the German F W 190 in the rolling plane.

BELOW: A perfect Seafire touch down - right on the centre line.

ABOVE: A group of pilots from the Fighter School Puttalum Ceylon to do initial deck landings on 5 types - HMS 'Atheling' 16th August 1945. The author is on the right of the group. BELOW LEFT: Six "Sad Sacks". Only one with a glimmer of a smile. Trainee Batsmen at RNAS Easthaven, Scotland. Lieut CDR(A) Paul Whitfield *(centre front)*, Bob Joyce *(right back row)*, author *(left back row)*. Note the school's motto *"Nunquam-Dic-Prangem"*. BELOW RIGHT: Chief Petty Officer WILLMOTT MBE, Master at Arms HMS St. Vincent, Portsmouth.

ABOVE LEFT: The heavily cratered runways at HIRARA–SAKASHIMA GUNTO preventing the movement of enemy aircraft from FORMOSA to JAPAN. ABOVE RIGHT: The raid on the oil refinery Sourabaya 17th May 1944. BELOW LEFT: German Tiger Tank destroyed by American Shermans on the boundary of Monte Corvence Airfield 10th Sept 1943. The commander of this tank had been decapitated. BELOW RIGHT: Avengers bombing port installations Sumatra.

ABOVE LEFT: Pilots from 820 squadron discover a prisoner of war camp on the coast of Japan. ABOVE RIGHT: Prisoners of war assembled on the beach where they had marked a message – Yanks 196 - British 25 - Dutch 75. Food supplies were dropped later. BELOW: Briefing for some bomber crews in 'Victorious' prior to the attack on Tirpitz - Commander Morrison briefing with mock up of Kaafiord.

ABOVE: Lieut Commander (A) Ron Richardson with some of his pilots. Richardson was later killed in the attack on the German battleship 'Tirpitz' on 24th August 1944. He was recommended for a posthumous Victoria Cross.
BELOW: Tirpitz at anchor behind torpedo nets, Kaafiord, Norway.

ABOVE: Barracuda bombers heading for the Tirpitz in Kaafiord, 3rd April 1944.

BELOW: NZ airmen serving in 'Victorious' for the Tirpitz attacks.
(Left to right) Rear - Al French, Matt Farrer, Spence Wright. Front - Bill Ryan, George Rawstrom, Bill Direen, Peter Coltman. Three of the above were members of 31 course.

The naval task force of five carriers and supporting ships withdrew from the scene shortly after sending its serviceable fighters ashore to Paestum. It then sailed across the northern coast of Sicily to anchor off Bizerta in Tunisia.

The fighter pilots were allowed shore leave here. It was not a very inviting place, having been reduced to rubble during the battle leading up to the German capitulation. As far as we could see there was only one solitary building left standing.

Although the American Army was miles and miles away to the west when the German general Von Arnim surrendered, the Yanks swept in and took over this sole remaining building and converted it into their officers club.

We were welcomed as honorary members and proceeded to sample the local vintage which consisted exclusively of very rough Algerian red wine served to us by Bedouin Arab waiters. We ordered our drinks which come in minute ceramic crucibles about the size of the average egg cup.

'This is no good. We're not going to get much mileage out of this. Fill the bloody table up.'

So a queue of waiters emerged loaded with crucibles and deposited these on our table which was soon completely covered from corner to corner.

This was more like it, but how the hell were we going to demolish all this gut rot? Someone beckoned some Yanks to join us so we sat around the table, six Fleet Air Arm pilots and three Yanks and proceeded to empty the crucibles. Despite the harsh taste, the wine was pretty potent and a great party was under way.

When we had finally demolished the crucibles we suggested to the Yanks, all of whom were Army pilots that they might like to return to the *Unicorn* with us for a meal. 'Ya goddam right we would.' So off we went.

Fortunately the harbour was only a stone's throw away from the American Officers' Club which we later discovered had, in its hey day, been a high class French brothel.

Our liberty boats were loading and discharging at the end of a long row of caissons, which were linked together by a chain. To get to the end where the liberty boat moored, one had to spring carefully from one caisson to the next one. With the surge of the waves the caissons were quite unstable, one caisson rolling to port while the next rolled to starboard.

Remarkably we all got to the last caisson without anyone falling into the sea, then the boatswain started the motor and we headed back to the *Unicorn*. By this time the wine had taken its effect and the three Yanks were well and truly plastered.

We got them up the gangway and down to the wardroom but from then on they were a complete loss.

Two of them dropped their 'lollies', so we had to escort them back to the gangway and shovel them into the next liberty boat for shore.

We never heard how they negotiated the caissons after getting out of the boat!

Back in the wardroom, we were accosted by the Commander.

'If you chaps bring any more of those insufferable types on this carrier I'll have your knackers for garters!'

The following day the fleet departed for Gibraltar to discharge damaged aircraft. I recall being told that approximately 80 damaged Seafires from the *Unicorn* and four escort carriers were put ashore for repairs. A very small component of about 20 serviceable aircraft were retained for combat air patrols passing through the Bay of Biscay. Our squadron was joined at Gibraltar by two new pilots to replace Brian Razzall and Joe Urlich.

At this point I should mention the remarkable exploits of another New Zealand pilot who was forced to make an urgent landing on the beaches on D-Day. This was Sub-Lieutenant Donald Cameron.

Don was in one of the escort carrier squadrons. He apparently made his forced landing very early in the day when the troops were discharging from their landing craft. Unfortunately, the area where he came down was still strongly held by German troops. He was captured and quickly taken back inland. At one stage when the German unit was under heavy fire from the Allied forces, Don was given an entrenching tool, with his captors making motions to dig a hole. Poor old Cameron really thought his end was nigh. But all the Jerries intended was for him to dig a slit trench for his own protection. Later in the day he was removed to the rear, put in a truck with a lot of other captured American and British soldiers and driven north over Mt. Vesuvius towards Rome. En route he endeavoured to enlist support from an American to jump off the truck and run for it. The American agreed, so Cameron waited his opportunity and when rounding a corner at a relatively slow speed he jumped off and rolled down a ravine. Apparently his escape was unnoticed.

He headed south and eventually crossed through the Allied lines.

Twenty-one months later Don Cameron was to make wartime history when he was captured by the Japanese having made a forced landing in the sea off the island of Miyako Jima in the Sakashima Gunto archipelago in between the northern tip of Taiwan and Okinawa. Don had been flying a Corsair fighter as escort for Avenger bombers and Firefly fighter bombers when his aircraft was hit by anti-aircraft fire. He attempted to return to his carrier but had to ditch in the sea. He clambered into his inflatable raft and settled down to await rescue by submarine. Unfortunately, during the night the wind had blown him westwards and he awoke to find himself in the surf with Japanese soldiers taking pot shots at him from the shore. He surrendered and was later taken to a prison camp in Japan from which he absconded for the second time. His freedom, however, was short lived. When the Japs recaptured him this time he was accorded some very rough treatment. It is probably fortunate that the war was nearly over because by this time he was also suffering from malnutrition and severe dysentery.

While we were operating in Italy all pilots were supplied with a variety of escape equipment. For once in my life I was a millionaire! Each of us were given a supply of counterfeit Italian lire – hundreds and hundreds of thousands of this paper money which the Allied Governments undertook to honour if and when the war ended. In addition we each carried in various parts of our uniform a silk handkerchief which featured a detailed map of Italy, one button which was sewn on the shirt which when detached became a compass, a metal hacksaw blade which was sewn into the shirt collar, a stiletto which could be plunged into the back of some unsuspecting Hun, and last but not least a heavy Webley revolver.

In addition to this, those of us who were members of 897 Squadron had been briefed by a member of Military Intelligence before our departure from the United Kingdom. The theme of this lecture was about evading capture in the event of being shot down or baling out over enemy territory. The intelligence man had probably put his story over many times before so by the time he visited 897 Squadron he had polished his delivery up to a really theatrical performance. His recommendation went like this –

'If you have the misfortune to be shot down or bale out, the first thing to do is to destroy your IFF set (Identification Friend or Foe). This is highly secret and should not fall into enemy hands. Secondly, you should bundle up your parachute and hide it so it will not disclose your point of arrival. Then try and find somewhere to hide until darkness falls. Do not attempt to travel in daylight. Only move along the edge of fields at night time. When you come to a village or small town circle around it in the darkness and see if you can identify the local brothel. In France, particularly, every little town will have its brothel which is generally the focal point of the resistance movement. Once identified knock on the door and tell the Madame who you are. If you happen to see Huns there, don't panic – they won't be very interested in you. Madame should then welcome you and hand you over to the care of one of her gorgeous protégées. Now this brothel would in all probability have a means of communicating with other brothels right up to the Pyrenees, the border of France and Spain. Along this trail you will have a really delightful time just quietly fornicating your way to freedom. And you won't have to pay for it and Madame will not send you an account for it after the war. Now this sorts the men from the boys!'

Fanciful as he made it sound there was apparently some truth in his recommendation. Some lucky escapers must have discovered it!

The fleet sailed from Gibraltar bound for the United Kingdom. On the return passage through the Bay of Biscay I determined to adopt as low a profile as possible. Following my experience at first degree of readiness on the outward journey, I was not exactly enthusiastic about having to do another deck landing in these turbulent seas.

Consequently I spent quite a bit of time in the hangar engineering shop fashioning a pair of Fleet Air Arm wings from the perspex of a damaged Seafire cockpit cover. This was a present for my friend Joan Rees.

A few days later we arrived back in the Clyde. Our serviceable Seafires were ranged on the flight deck for flying off to Machrihanish.

The carrier turned into wind and the first Seafire was flagged off. This was followed by several more, but when about ten had been despatched it became noticeable that every successive take off path was getting closer and closer to the port side. Those who were watching the fly off from 'goofers gallery' became alarmed because the carrier was obviously not correctly into wind and this was causing the pilots to drift across the deck. Most of those who had become airborne were experienced carrier pilots, but the next one to go was Sub-Lieutenant Neice, the replacement pilot who had joined our squadron on our return to Gibraltar.

Neice had neither flown a Seafire off or landed on a carrier. As he opened up for take off he was unable to fight the drift and his Seafire fell over the port side into the sea with full power on.

The reaction of the spectators was really mutinous. This was a case of inexcusable negligence in steering the carrier. Words like 'you murdering bastard.' 'You reckless bloody Irishman' were heard. The captain always gets the blame whether he is on the bridge or not.

Poor old Neice was not picked up. We learnt later that he had married only a week or two before going out to Gibraltar to join us.

Our next base was to be a Naval Air Station HMS *Ringtail* at Burscough a few miles inland from Southport in Lancashire. Here we were joined by 808 and 886 squadrons to form the 3rd Naval Fighter wing under the command of Lieutenant Commander (A) A. C. Wallace RNVR.

All the squadrons were re-equipped with Seafire LIIC aircraft. This model was powered by a Merlin Mark 32 engine, which gave it superior performance in speed and climb up to 10,000 feet. We also had the lovely elliptical wings 'clipped' to make the rolling action more positive as a counter to the German FW 190.

We had no sooner arrived at Burscough than our senior pilot suddenly departed. Whether he was transferred by orders from Admiralty no one seemed to know. I rather suspect that Willie Simpson may have contrived to move him on.

'Doc' Davies was a fairly dominant colonial personality. He did not have an easy relationship with Willie and some of the other English pilots. Willie always gave the impression that he preferred a more compliant group of pilots in his squadron. This would possibly explain his decision a few weeks later to move Hammy Neilson, Arch Foley and myself over to 809 squadron.

'Doc's' place as senior pilot was taken by RNR Lieutenant Horace Barr and we were joined by three novices fresh out of fighter school to replace our sad losses of Joe Urlich, Brian Razzall and Neice.

Two distressing events took place while we were based at Burscough.

The first was a taxiing accident. One day Arch Foley and I were taking up two of the new pilots to teach them battle formation.

It so happened that I was in the leading aircraft. We moved out for take off and as usual with Seafires we taxied fast to prevent the engines overheating. An aircraft was coming in to land so I applied the brakes and stopped. The next thing I knew was an almighty bang behind me and suddenly the rear part of my fuselage dropped so that from the cockpit I was left sitting and looking up to the sky. This was immediately followed by a slower metal to metal mincing noise.

I turned around and to my horror I saw the monstrous propeller of Arch Foley's aircraft still rotating not more than two feet away from my head.

Then I caught sight of Foley's grinning face – I guess that's about all he could do. The thought immediately struck me that he would be grinning on the other side of his face when the Commanding Officer heard about this.

Well my brand new Seafire LIIC was a complete write off. They would have to give it a complete new fuselage.

To this day Arch Foley still maintains his innocence. He contends that I should have waved some sort of flag or my handkerchief to indicate that I was stopping.

The fact is of course, that taxiing an aircraft is quite different from driving a car. It is the responsibility of the pilot in the rear aircraft to keep a reasonable distance so he can see when the front aircraft comes to a stop. Poor old Arch received a pretty harsh reprimand and an endorsement in his flying log book. He has never forgiven me – but he ought to be thankful that he was not court-martialled.

The second incident occurred one day when the wing leader Lieutenant Commander Wallace organised a low-level wing exercise in which 36 aircraft from our three squadrons took part. The role of our wing was henceforth to be army cooperation, so we were practising a lot of low level operations, air to ground gunnery, low level bombing and low navigation.

Wallace took the wing out into the Irish Sea turning near the Isle of Man, then coming back very low over the water beneath the 'enemy' radar screen and then proceeding to attack coastal targets in Lancashire. The three squadrons were flying at slightly different levels, ours being the lowest on the port side, while Wallace was stepped up slightly in the middle.

When I looked across at Les Baker and Tony Perry I was horrified to find that they were so low over the water that their propellers were churning up a track in the sea.

Presumably mine must have been doing the same – this was too low for safety at a speed of about 300 mph.

Then Wallace gave a change of direction, which meant our 12 aircraft squadron had to slide under his while the outside 12 aircraft would turn and move across over the top of Wallace's squadron.

At that low height it was a ridiculous manoeuvre and could never have taken place on operations. Just fancy 36 aircraft approaching an enemy defended coastline in such a clumsy formation. Few of us would have survived the anti-aircraft fire.

It was a recipe for disaster and sure enough it happened. The outside pilot of 808 squadron collided with the outside pilot of 886. Both were killed. One of them was Ralph Colbeck who was a member of our *Dominion Monarch* draft.

Colbeck's funeral which took place two days later was one of the saddest I have ever attended before or since. All pilots in the No 3 Naval Wing attended along with ground crews, firing party and the Last Post bugler. Military funerals can be the saddest of all. It left us, moreover, with a sullen sense of anger. It should never have happened. The entire operation was an exercise in futility.

We left Burscough to return to Machrihanish and prepare once again for rejoining another carrier. This time it was to be the escort carrier *Stalker.* Up till then no one in our squadron had operated from the much shorter flight deck of an escort carrier, so we had to refresh our technique with a concentrated session of ADDLS.

Happily we all landed on board without incident and for the next few weeks we concentrated on army cooperation work covering invasion exercises on beaches along the Clyde. At this stage there were all sorts of rumours flying around from the invasion of France to preparation for landings in the Andaman Islands in the Indian Ocean.

We were returning from the Irish Sea late one afternoon when an amazing event occurred.

A flight of four Seafires returned to our carrier just before dusk. Three landed on without incident but the fourth piloted by an Englishman George Fry lurched towards the port side after having caught a wire. The undercarriage of the Seafire ran off the deck into the catwalk and the aircraft turned upside down on an oerlikon gun platform. George was trapped inside the cockpit.

Members of the flight deck party and onlookers rushed to his assistance to prevent the Seafire overbalancing into the sea. George fortunately was unhurt, so we urged him to sit still till we could get some strops over the aircraft to hold it in position. Unfortunately, the carrier was then hit by a heavy swell, the Seafire tipped further over and fell into the sea, still inverted with George trapped inside. It sank like a stone. No one would have given George Fry one chance in hell. The carrier hove to, but by the time it had lost way the site of the accident was over a mile astern. Then someone with a telescope picked up a little black dot riding up and down the waves. George had made it. That was really a close shave.

We managed to get ashore occasionally when the carrier anchored overnight in the Kyles of Bute. The town nearby was Rothesay, headquarters for a number of submarines. Arch Foley and I missed the last liberty boat back one night so we had to doss down in a hotel. When we returned the following morning Willie was fuming. As punishment we were to take the whole squadron for drill on the flight deck at 4 p.m. Willie thought this would embarrass his two recalcitrant colonials before the ship's company. Little did he know that we had both been sergeant instructors in the Army!

At the appointed time all ranks, petty officers and ratings in 897 squadron mustered on the flight deck. Hundreds of other members of the ship's crew gathered in the catwalks to watch the 'humiliation' of the two sub-lieutenants.

I cannot recall which of us took the first spell, but we each gave them about twenty minutes concentrated drill from one end of the flight deck to the other. We had these matelots doing army-type drill that they had never heard of. We then had them marching in columns of threes towards the stern of the carrier and at the very last second before the front rank would disappear off the end into the sea, they would get the command 'about turn'. We showed them how to manoeuvre line abreast, form platoon, at the halt form squad etc. Our audience was patently enthralled; they had not seen the like of it before. Meanwhile, Arch and I were absolutely revelling in the adulation.

When the whole exercise was over, the ship's Master at Arms, a chief petty officer in charge of the ship's discipline, approached us.

'Excuse me, gentlemen. That really was a good show. Tell me – where did you learn those skills?'

Needless to say Willie Simpson never referred to the incident, but I doubt whether it had done much to modify his acceptance of the colonials.

Shortly after this we received a signal from Admiralty ordering our squadron to move to a Royal Navy Air Station HMS *Goldcrest* at Dale on the south west coast of Wales near Milford Haven. Apparently some dramatic changes were taking place. 897 squadron was split up with half the pilots remaining and going to HMS *Daedulus* at Lee-on-Solent while the remainder would join 809 Squadron commanded by Marine Major Al Wright. It was not surprising that Willie Simpson took this opportunity to 'unload' Foley and Masters onto Al Wright.

809 Squadron

This was to become a larger 20 Seafire squadron with a complement of 24 pilots. It would be part of No 4 Naval Fighter wing comprising 807, 809 and 879 squadrons each consisting of 20 aircraft.

While we were awaiting delivery of more Seafires to complete our complement we were granted seven days leave. Arch and I headed for the 'Big Smoke' (London) where we knew we would almost certainly met up with other Fleet Air Arm or Air Force crew that we had known in New Zealand.

One such chap we ran into was our old *Dominion Monarch* friend Cliff 'Lefty' Bissett. 'Lefty' was in London on survivor's leave.

He and Ralph Cocklin had been in 816 Swordfish squadron aboard the escort carrier HMS *Tracker.* They were carrying out anti-submarine patrols on Atlantic convoys. In returning to the carrier to land on in a very turbulent sea Lefty's aircraft crashed over the side into the sea. His navigator unfortunately was drowned but Lefty was picked up by an escort vessel.

It must have been a frightening experience. He quite unashamedly declared he would never land on a carrier again. Cliff was the oldest member of our *Dominion Monarch* draft. He was probably about 31 years at this time. He realised that there was no future for him in this occupation. He subsequently trained as a fighter direction officer where he was probably better suited to apply his knowledge of flying.

Our usual routine while on leave in London was to have a morning session at the famous New Zealand watering hole, the Sussex Hotel, Leicester Square. The pubs would close about 2 p.m., so we would then adjourn for a meal, usually a steak, which was horse flesh or sometimes a delightful mixed grill which we had by chance discovered in a little restaurant under South Africa House. Then we might mooch along to the *Chez Moi* Club near Piccadilly. This was the haunt for fighter pilots of all nationalities.

On this particular day Arch and I were sauntering along Leicester Square when suddenly a notion entered my head. I told Arch that I wanted to go to the Post Office at St Martin-in-the-Fields which was only a short distance away.

'What the hell do you want to go there for?'

'I want to send a cable to New Zealand.'

'Well you can send it tomorrow morning – come on, we're going to the *Chez Moi* Club.'

'No Arch – I want to send it now.'

'Well – why the great hurry?'

'I want to send a cable to Joan Rees to propose we become engaged.'

With this Foley grabbed me by the arm, turned me around quite ruthlessly and said, 'What the hell's got into you Masters. Have you gone mad? You'll never see this thing through.'

'No, Arch old man, I want to do it and am going to do it now whether you like it or not.'

A rather disgruntled Foley followed me to the Post Office.

The cable read as follows –

> 'Propose we get engaged – Have asked my parents to buy the best ring available – Will not take NO for an answer.'

When I think about it 50 years later it doesn't sound very romantic. To send a cable message of that type was quite expensive and I realise that I was being rather presumptious in expecting a favourable reply.

When the message arrived in New Zealand it was delivered to the Huntly School Dental Clinic where Joan had a young pupil in the chair for treatment.

The postal lady, full of smiles, handed over the cable. She was probably aware of the contents. I believe that when Joan opened the cable she was so flabbergasted, she turned to her dental nurse colleague Barbara Heale and excitedly said, 'What shall I do?' Barbara made up her mind for her. 'Get on your bike now and tear off to the Post Office. Tell him you accept.' So Joan tore off her nurse's white veil and pedalled off flat out to the Huntly Post Office.

I received her reply when I returned to the Naval Air Station at Dale. It must have been intuition which prompted me to send this cable. We had been writing to each other at regular intervals for over 20 months by which time about 50 letters had passed between us. I concluded that no girl would respond to that many letters unless she was just a wee bit interested. So it was worth popping the question. The element of survival was another matter, but if I didn't declare my intentions soon some other chap might beat me to it. Unbeknown to me, at that time, I did have several rivals one of whom was a New Zealand Army captain who had been awarded a Distinguished Conduct Medal for bravery while holding the rank of Sergeant. He was certainly an eligible suitor.

Back at Dale the new 809 squadron of 24 pilots was reorganised into squadron duties, flights etc. The new Senior Pilot was Ron Richardson a New Zealander from one of the early *St Vincent* courses. Ron was a real daredevil. I was flying with him one day in company with an Englishman when Ron suggested doing some tight VIC formation aerobatics. As the leader of the formation it was probably safe enough for him, but recalling the Arthur Street incident at St Merryn and not knowing the flying ability of the third pilot, I respectfully declined the invitation.

Ron was not to stay with us very long. He was promoted to Lieutenant Commander (A) and given command of the 1840 Hellcat Squadron comprising mostly pilots of the Dutch Naval Air Service.

Ron was later recommended for a posthumous Victoria Cross for his leadership and gallantry in attacks on the German battleship *Tirpitz* in Alten Fiord, Norway. Having expended his ammunition in strafing attacks on the *Tirpitz* he saw what appeared to be a radar station on a peak surrounding the Norwegian fiord, so he dropped his landing hook and dived in, to breach the wires between the two masts. Regrettably this very gallant New Zealand pilot was shot down by German anti-aircraft fire.

While at Dale we received a request from a Sunderland flying boat squadron based at Milford Haven for the opportunity to practise evasion tactics against our fighters. We welcomed this opportunity because we had never previously had the chance to do any affiliation with aircraft of this size.

On this occasion my No 2 was a boisterous Scotsman Jock Morris. We arranged a rendezvous with the Sunderland at St Brides Bay. We had previously arranged to commence our attacks from above coming down on either quarter so that when the Sunderland attempted to evade by turning into the first attacker, the second Seafire would then launch its attack. It was all fine in theory, but this Sunderland crew was very well trained. Although we synchronised our attacks quite well neither of us was able to draw a bead on this enormous aircraft. Despite its huge size and its slow speed it was surprisingly manoeuvrable. The pilot would close down the port motors, open up the starboard motors and the big plane seemed to turn on a penny. With a closing speed of perhaps 100 miles an hour our Seafires would flash past the rear turret without having been able to get the Sunderland in our gunsights.

Head on attacks were not any easier because the pilot would commit the Sunderland to very steep diving turns. Nevertheless it was a useful experience both for them and us.

On 16th March 1944 we moved to the Royal Air Force aerodrome at Long Kesh near Lough Neagh in Northern Ireland.

Long Kesh is now internationally famous as a high security prison for terrorists captured during the sectarian disturbances in Northern Ireland.

The purpose of our move to this area was to enter into cooperation with the American Army stationed in that area and awaiting the call for the invasion of France.

A number of our Seafires had been fitted with oblique cameras in the fuselage behind the cockpit. We developed skills at photographic reconnaissance and were about to commence reporting the fall of gunfire from warships when suddenly and unexpectedly I was the recipient of some very bad news.

A party of us was going into Belfast to have a little fling. Our Commanding Office Al Wright was driving the squadron utility. He asked me to sit in the front with him while the other three chaps in the party sat in the back under the canopy.

We had just left the aerodrome when Al said, 'Cappy, old chap. I have some news for you. I received a signal from Admiralty yesterday requesting me to nominate one pilot from the 809 who would be capable of being a carrier batsman! I am afraid you are it!'

This was like being hit over the head with a sledge hammer.

'You're kidding, Al.'

'No I'm sorry, old chap – it just had to be you.'

Well, I was completely lost for words. It seemed as if my naval career was in tatters. I just couldn't understand because in the short time we had been together I had developed a very good rapport with Al Wright. I was on far better terms with him than I was with Willie Simpson.

I felt deflated but I had one more problem, 'couldn't you change it and choose someone else?'

'No – I know you're disappointed. I probably would be too but you may see it differently in 12 months time. Just try and make the best of it.'

He told me one other pilot from 807 squadron Bob Joyce had also been selected – no one apparently from 886 squadron. We were to leave in three days time by ferry steamer from Larne to Stranraer, thence by train to Easthaven north of Dundee. We would be attending a batsman training school run by Commander (A) Bob Everett.

The Wing put on a fabulous farewell party for Bob Joyce and me the following night. I could sense the sympathy in our impending departure, that was quite touching. It so happened that Arch Foley was the squadron duty officer on this day, so he had the squadron motor bike to ride back to our billets. Arch clambered on the bike with Tony Perry as the pillion rider. They roared off down the gravel road from the officers' mess to connect with the main road which ran at right angles. Directly ahead of them was a canal. Arch was travelling too fast to negotiate the bend on to the main road with the result that the motor bike skidded in the loose metal and instead of turning right, it headed directly for the canal.

Tony Perry hurtled from the pillion over Arch's head to land in the middle of the canal. Arch himself was pinioned under the motorcycle in the rushes bordering the canal. When we came on the scene these two bedraggled muddied creatures were struggling up the bank. They were greeted with gales of irreverent besotted laughter.

Now Arch Foley had never been one to take kindly to ridicule. The fact that he had been dragged out of the muddy water of the canal severely dented his pride. But characteristically he bounced back once he was back on terra firma.

'So you think it's funny, do you Masters? Well, I'll tell you what – when we've got the bike out you can have a go. We'll see how bloody good you are.'

Fortunately the motor of the cycle had not gone under water so when we dragged it up the bank, the engine kicked into life straight away.

I took up Foley's challenge and invited No 2 George Morris to ride on the pillion. We revved up and took off down the same loose metalled road, but like our predecessors we had trouble negotiating the turn on to the main road running parallel to the canal. To prevent a violent skid in the loose metal I had to widen the turning circle and as a consequence ran up on to the grass verge which was very slippery. The back wheel slid into the water and we entered the canal. In the bright moonlight, I remembered seeing George Morris projected off the pillion to execute a very neat somersault and enter the middle of the canal. It was a classic performance. Foley's honour had been restored. Fortunately for me, only the bottom right trouser leg got wet but the other three chaps had to arrange for a complete dry cleaning job in the nearby town of Lisburn.

Next day Bob Joyce and I left Long Kesh on our transfer to Easthaven, Scotland. Our escorts in the 809 squadron utility were Arch Foley, Tony Perry and George Morris. It was not altogether difficult to see that we had their sympathy. It was quite a drastic severance to be ordered away from the prestigious fighter squadrons, but we just had to make the best of it.

Batsman's School

When we arrived at Easthaven we were met by Commander (A) Bob Everett who gave us an introduction. It appears that the Admiralty had decided that all future carrier batsmen would be required to take this course at Easthaven. One of the reasons for this decision was the appalling number of Seafire deck landing accidents at Salerno. Someone on the Air Staff at Admiralty had drawn the conclusion that perhaps some carrier batsmen had not had adequate training to handle speed aircraft like the Seafires in very low wind speed conditions.

Hence the new course at Easthaven. When we assembled we found that the course comprised six pilots, Lieutenant Commander (A) Paul Whitfield RN, previously in command of 847 Barracuda Squadron, three lieutenants and two sub-lieutenants, Bob Joyce and myself. It became obvious that Paul Whitfield was being groomed for a higher rank, but even he was required to do the batsman course. He and I later became associated in mid 1945 when I joined the carrier HMS *Indefatigable* where Paul was the deputy Commander Flying. The three lieutenants were also fairly senior types so Bob and I felt really small fry in comparison.

Neither Bob nor I had become reconciled to our fate and we toyed with the idea of failing the course so that we could return to our squadrons.

Bob Everett was well aware, however, of this reaction, and he made it profoundly clear to us, that if he had any suspicion of a trainee purposely attempting to fail the course, he would make certain that that officer was relegated to second line duties for a very long period.

We knew then that it was useless to try, so we determined to make the best of it. To provide training for these rebellious batsmen there was a squadron of 12–15 pilots whose sole occupation was to fly circuits around the airfield in Swordfish aircraft. After having been there a few days we batsmen trainees began to wonder whether we shouldn't be feeling sorry for these pilots rather than ourselves. If there ever was a dead end job in second line flying this was surely it. I am sure these pilots were so bored by their daily routine of ADDLS that they were just about comatose in their cockpits. They were purely going through the motions. It would not be unfair to say that if they had obeyed implicitly the signals of the trainee batsmen the aerodrome might have been strewn with pranged aircraft.

Two of these pilots I recognised. One was Johnny Johnston who had been a year or two ahead of me at New Plymouth Boys' High School. The other was Tim Anderson who I had known from schooldays in Stratford. My depression, however, was so intense that I scarcely bothered to acknowledge their presence – a fact that I have regretted ever since.

In addition to the actual control of aircraft in a landing pattern we also had to learn the technique of ranging aircraft for take-off from a carrier.

One of the major deficiencies of this course was that our training was confined to slow speed Swordfish aircraft whereas when we were posted to a carrier, most of us would have to handle all types of Seafires, Wildcats, Hellcats, Corsairs, Barracudas, Fireflies and Avengers. In this respect a batsman might be passed out by Everett as competent, but he was still to be confronted by a frightening challenge if and when he joined a fleet carrier.

The course at Easthaven lasted about four weeks. Then we were despatched to the River Clyde to join HMS *Argus* where we put into practice the skills we had supposedly acquired from Bob Everett.

The *Argus* was probably the oldest aircraft carrier in the Royal Navy. It was once an Italian liner, the *Conte Rosso*. It was acquired by the Royal Navy and converted to an aircraft carrier shortly after the First World War. *Argus* had performed a wide variety of operational and training duties. Its last operational employment being 'Operation Torch', the Allied landings in North Africa.

It was unsuited, however, for long-term front line duties so it was now used mainly as a deck landing training carrier both for pilots and batsmen. In profile, it was a strange looking contraption because it did not have the customary island from which the more modern carriers were conned.

Once again the aircraft allocated to this second phase of our training were limited to Swordfish and Wildcats. We spent four days in the *Argus* during which time I had batted 53 Swordfish, 48 Wildcats and two Avengers. My most strenuous day was 50 Swordfish plus ten Wildcats. I soon discovered that holding the bats out in a strong wind of up to 25–30 knots can become very tiring indeed. It was like being in a boxing ring trying to hold your guard up for four or five rounds.

Bob Joyce and I returned to Easthaven for our final assessment earnestly hoping that we would not come up to the standard that Bob Everett had set down for his 'new era' batsmen. Without inviting undue suspicion we had both performed in a fairly 'slap happy' disinterested manner.

Everett apparently ignored our hostility and passed us both with an 'average' assessment. As the trainees were nearly all unwilling conscripts I doubt whether many would have been graded 'above average'.

So I bade farewell to Bob Joyce and proceeded on indefinite leave pending an appointment from Admiralty. I never saw Bob again during the war, nor did I learn what ship he was posted to.

On all previous leaves I had the company of one or two squadron friends but as a batsman I was now a loner. I travelled by train to London where I would almost certainly meet up with someone I knew in either the Air Force or the Navy.

I booked into the Garrick Hotel opposite New Zealand Forces Club. This was a modest all male non-licensed hotel which suited my means particularly if my indefinite leave became rather lengthy. As luck would have it, I ran into several old school acquaintances from Stratford and New Plymouth. One was Neville Turnbull, who had just returned from a lengthy exile at Freetown, Sierra Leone. Apparently Neville had incurred some vague displeasure of the Captain of HMS *Heron*, Yeovilton, and for what was to be seen as retribution was posted to an anti-submarine patrol squadron in a remote part of West Africa. Others were Fred Bamford and Gifford Goldsmith, both of whom were on coastal forces.

An interesting character was Sergeant Pilot Eric Meharry with whom I played in the 1st XV at New Plymouth Boys' High School in 1937. I met Eric at a late hour in the Sussex Hotel. He had just arrived in London on leave from his squadron based in the North.

He had no where to put his head down so pleaded with me to let him share my room.

I could hardly say no, but warned him he would have to be out of the place by first light. The next night I had gone to bed and was fast asleep when I was quite violently shaken.

'Come on your silly old coot – move over.' This was Meharry again. As if that weren't enough – he came at it a third night and followed this up by asking for breakfast!

This had gone far enough – I evacuated the Garrick and took up residence at another hotel in Leicester Square.

I've often wondered whether he used the same confidence trick a fourth night and how the new occupant of the room reacted.

It is really little wonder that Londoners and particularly East Enders have an earthy sense of humour. The social morals were much more permissive than what we had known in New Zealand. Soliciting by prostitutes in the streets was supposed to be illegal, but the police seemed to turn a blind eye.

One of the most humorous cases of this immorality was that of a newspaper vendor whose patch in the night black out was outside Lyons Corner House in Leicester Square.

Ostensibly he was selling the Daily Mail and as one approached him in the black out he would be screaming in a raucous voice: '*Daily Mail – Daily Mail – Daily Mail.*'

Then just as one came abreast of him he would whisper 'Rubbers sir – Rubbers sir.'

There's nothing really quite like Cockney humour.

While the prospect of indefinite leave might have sounded like a passport to paradise, in reality it soon becomes quite irksome. After two weeks I had seen all the worthwhile films and one or two stage shows and my bank balance was almost down to zero. I couldn't stand the uncertainty any longer, so one day I took off to Queen Anne's Mansions, the headquarters of the Naval Drafting office to see if I could get back on duty.

I met a Commander RN in charge of appointments and expressed my feelings quite bluntly. I put it to him that if there was no position available as a batsman perhaps I could be restored in 809 squadron. This was what I really wanted.

No, that was completely out of consideration. Too much money and effort had been expended in developing my skill as a batsman. It would be quite irresponsible to consider my reinstatement in a fighter squadron.

He nevertheless appreciated my concern re lack of employment and promised to consider the matter without delay. I should receive a signal at New Zealand House within a few days.

During this period in London I saw several outstanding films and stage shows. Two films that I recall were *Gone with the Wind*, which I had seen previously in New Zealand. This film was being featured in a Leicester Square theatre when we arrived in September 1941. It was still playing at the same theatre in June 1944. Another classic was Noel Coward's film *In which We serve*. This was a wonderful propaganda film based on the destroyer HMS *Kelly* commanded by Lord Louis Mountbatten. John Mills had a leading role in this film. It was a production which made one enormously proud to be in the naval service.

Two days later when I called at New Zealand House for mail, there was a letter from the Drafting Office at Admiralty ordering me to report on 5th June to a mysterious organisation called the Wellcome Bureau of Scientific Research, 183 Euston Road. This sounded like some sort of espionage outfit.

Anyway I duly presented myself to find that it was nothing more than the headquarters for tropical immunisation. I was attended to by a medical officer who informed me that I was to be innoculated against yellow fever and black water fever. My anti-tetanus vaccination would also be given a booster.

All this suggested that I was in line for a tropical appointment, so I quizzed the medico about it.

He suggested it could be the Indian Ocean or East Africa. With these shots it certainly would not be the Atlantic or Russian convoys.

I chose to ignore the doctor's warning about an allergic reaction and elected to take the three shots at the one time which turned out to be a wise decision because when I returned to New Zealand House that afternoon there was another message requiring me to report for passage overseas on the following day 6th June.

In company with three other officers, we were taken by bus to an aerodrome at Lyneham in Wiltshire. It was at this point that I was informed that my appointment was to a Royal Navy Air Station *Bherunda* Colombo, Ceylon.

There we boarded a Royal Air Force Transport Command Douglas DC3 Dakota aircraft and headed for another aerodrome at St Mawgan on the Cornish coast.

While the aircraft was refuelled we adjourned to the officers' mess for a meal and take stock of ourselves.

Our party comprised a brigadier general of Royal Marines who was bound for the Burma front, a commander RN who had been posted as assistant to the British naval attaché in Moscow and an army major who had been seconded to General McArthur's headquarters in Australia. As a very junior naval officer I felt very humble in this illustrious group of VIPs.

Our aircraft took off about midnight bound for Gibraltar where we landed safely exactly seven and a half hours later. From the Gibraltar airport we were whisked in to one of Gibraltar's leading hotels, I believe it was the Bristol where we showered and enjoyed a very good breakfast. The local newspaper had just been delivered. The front page bore sensational headlines 'Second Front Commences'.

While we were flying across the Bay of Biscay a massive invasion fleet was crossing the Channel to land in Normandy.

The war news only served to deepen my depression, because had it not been for this batting appointment I could have been with my friends in 809 Squadron who were then in HMS *Stalker* heading for the south of France invasion which was to follow on 15th August. Willie Simpson and those who remained with him in 897 squadron were then providing fighter cover and army cooperation from Lee on Solent. It was not easy to accept that I was not involved.

Six days later on 13th June the first VI flying bomb was seen by the Royal Observer Corps at Dymchurch near Folkestone.

Hundreds of these infernal weapons were soon hurtling across the Channel to hit targets in and around London during the ensuing weeks.

At midday we took off on our second leg, this time to Tripoli. This was another seven and a half hour flight. By this time everyone was getting sore backsides through sitting in the uncomfortable metal seats. The Dakota was very much a utility cargo carrier, it had no comforts whatever for its passengers. At Tripoli the aircraft was refuelled and we set off on the third stage, flying through the night to land at West Cairo airfield early in the morning.

There was a change of crew at Cairo for the next leg to Habbaniya in Iraq. Half way there we encountered an enormous unforecasted sandstorm which forced the pilot to turn back and seek refuge at Lydda airfield a short distance from Tel Aviv. This allowed us an overnight stay so the army major and I took the opportunity of seeing this very modern city. By this time there were only three passengers, the commander RN having left us at Cairo from where he was to proceed by air to Crimea and then to Moscow.

The aerodrome at Habbaniya is in a desolate valley close to the Euphrates river and about 60 miles west of Baghdad. Habbaniya had been a Royal Air Force outpost since the end of the 1st World War but in April 1941 an Iraqi chieftain named Rashid Ali was encouraged by the Germans to revolt against the British forces holding Habbaniya. The airfield was surrounded by Iraqi forces and for some time a state of siege existed. Eventually British forces gained the upper hand and the revolt was crushed.

The airfield is also renowned for having recorded some of the highest temperatures on the earth's surface. On the day we landed there in mid summer it was certainly hot. When the doors of the Dakota opened it was just like stepping into an oven. The heat was unbelievable.

Surprisingly, however, the officers' mess had air conditioning, so one walked from an oven into a refrigerator. After refuelling we took off, this time for the island of Bahrain four and a half hours flying time away. From Bahrain our next leg was a six and a half hour flight to Karachi where we had an overnight stay in a very luxurious Victorian era hotel staffed by turbaned Sikh servants.

En route from Bahrain to Karachi I was invited by the pilot to join his crew in the cockpit. When I went forward I found all three of them, the captain, co-pilot and wireless operator sitting around a small table playing cards. The aircraft was flying on automatic pilot, but what really disturbed me was that no one was on watch. Well, I guess the chance of meeting another aircraft over that desolate area would have been more than a million to one. I told them I thought they had a pretty cushy job whereupon the captain disengaged the auto pilot and invited me to fly hands on. I very soon discovered what a boring job it was flying in Transport Command compared with the excitement of a fighter squadron.

From Karachi we had two more stops, Bombay and Bangalore, before reaching our final destination at Colombo.

Katukurunda – Ceylon

I reported to the Naval Air Station HMS *Bherunda* but discovered that my actual appointment was to a TBR Training Squadron No 756 based at HMS *Ukussa* Royal Navy Air Station at Katukurunda about 30 miles south of Colombo.

On arrival I reported to Lieutenant Commander (A) T. T. Miller the Commanding Officer of 756 squadron who briefed me on my duties. I was to prepare a number of Barracuda and Avenger pilots for their initial deck landings. While I would be based at Katukurunda I would also have to prepare for fighter pilots at Puttalam Royal Navy Air Station about 120 miles North. The Puttalam pilots would be flying Seafires, Wildcats, Hellcats and Corsairs, of which I had only previously batted Wildcats.

The most distasteful period of my naval career had just begun. I soon discovered that TBR pilots were a different breed from fighter boys. They may have been more reserved, more responsible and possibly even better pilots, but they lacked the *esprit de corps* and *joie de vivre* that existed in fighter squadrons. The fact that the trainee deck landers had probably come to Katukurunda direct from the United Kingdom to convert on to Avengers and Barracudas created a psychological barrier. Perhaps I could also have been at fault in this regard because I was so browned off with the job and my future prospects.

Finally I got around to having a chat with Miller and suggested to him that if I could get some flying in perhaps it would help me to adjust. I pointed out that it was desirable that a batsman should have practical experience on all types of aircraft he was required to control on the flight deck. A batsman should be conversant with the stalling speed, the landing altitude and the vision from the cockpit. Miller agreed and arranged for me to have two flights in his precious aircraft, one in an Avenger, the other in a Barracuda.

One trip in each was enough. Compared with the Seafire the Avenger was like driving an enormous bus, while the Barracuda resembled an aeronautical 'Christmas Tree'. Neither experience did much to lessen my depression.

Off duty Katukurunda was a dismal place – nothing to do – nowhere to go. I got that way that the only day in the week I looked forward to was a Sunday. This was not for religious reasons.

Every Sunday work would cease at midday when we would adjourn to the wardroom for our weekly ration of one only bottle of beer. This was followed by the most marvellous meal that has ever been my privilege to enjoy anywhere in the world before or since. It was a magnificent Ceylon curry containing just about every ingredient you could think of. There was the usual portion of boiled rice, curried fish, prawns, crabs, pineapple, bananas, meat, chicken, beans and assorted vegetables. One intriguing ingredient was described to me as snake's gourd. Now there were snakes galore in Ceylon so I accepted that this bright green substance must be part of a snake. I was wrong of course, it was some kind of vegetable. These curries did not vary in strength. There was only one standard – very hot. After the first Sunday curry I realised that the bottle of beer should be used to extinguish the oral fire that these strong curries created.

It was about this time that an operational Barracuda squadron flew in from a carrier. I got a marvellous surprise to run into the two people that I knew very well. One was Bill Ryan, of the *Dominion Monarch* draft who had been rejected as a pilot at Sealand but who later successfully qualified as a commissioned observer. Bill's squadron had recently been involved in bombing raids on the German battleship *Tirpitz* in Alten Fiord, Norway. For his part in these operations Bill had been awarded a 'Mention in Despatches'. This was a grand reunion.

The other acquaintance was Gerry Woods with whom I had shared some amazing adventures at Salerno in September 1943. Gerry was now a lieutenant commander (A) and in command of a Barracuda squadron. There would not have been many observers in the Fleet Air Arm at that time who would qualify for the command of a squadron from one of the early pre-war observer courses. We reminisced until the late hours supported by copious nips of pink gin.

By this time I had spent over two weeks preparing the TBR pilots for their initial deck landings. Then I received a call to visit Puttalam HMS *Rataliya* where a group was waiting for deck landing preparation. Here I renewed my acquaintance with several chaps that I had previously known or been on a course with. This was also my first introduction to the fearsome Corsair fighter. I had never seen one before, but its vices and reputation were well publicised. At first sight it looked awful. It was easily three times the size of the very neat compact little Seafire. The Americans seemed to build everything bigger than necessary. It had gull wings and from our early days in studying the theory of flight, I guessed that this had been incorporated to counterbalance some aerodynamic deficiency. They were painted a very dark blue, in fact almost black, so in profile and colour they looked horrible and threatening.

I later discovered that the reason for the gull wing was to avoid excessively long undercarriage legs that would otherwise be needed to provide clearance for the exceptionally large diameter propellor.

Well I just had to get used to them, so I approached the Commander Flying at Puttalam Lieutenant Commander (A) Godfrey Parish DSC and pointed out that if he wanted his pilots back in one piece, it would be a good idea if I had some air experience in a Corsair to familiarise myself with its peculiarities. Godfrey didn't hesitate – 'Sure, off you go, Masters.' He was the sort of person I could easily establish a rapport with. He was an old boy of Eton College, but there was nothing 'honky tonk' about him. He was droll, invariably untidily dressed, socks around his ankles, shirt tail hanging out but as courageous as a lion. Over the next nine to ten months, he and I worked very closely together. I came to value Godfrey Parish as one of the finest Englishmen I was to meet in the Fleet Air Arm – we became very good friends.

The Corsair fighters had been developed by the Chance Vought Co. in the United States of America expressly for use in the United States Navy. Following trials, however, the United States Navy rejected it as being too difficult to operate from aircraft carriers. Test pilots for the United States Navy who gave it deck landing trials were disappointed with the forward vision from the cockpit and the excessive bounce when the oleo legs hit the deck. Instead it was offered to the Royal Navy which was urgently seeking a high performance fighter to replace its antiquated Gladiators, Fulmars and Hurricanes. The first Fleet Air Arm squadron to be equipped with the Corsair Mk I was 1830 at Quonset Point, United States of America, in June 1943. This squadron successfully carried out deck landing trials in HMS *Slinger* a few months later.

On my first familiarisation flight in a Corsair Mk II I was immediately impressed by the enormous power released by the 2,000 hp Pratt & Whitney radial engine. It stormed down the runway like a rocket. It was steadier in straight and level flight than a Seafire, therefore it was a more effective gun platform. With its tremendous speed (417 mph at 20,000 ft) and its heavier weight ($1^1/_2$ times that of a Seafire IIc) it could dive and outclimb any other British naval fighter. In fact the only Allied fighter which was slightly faster at 20,000 ft was the North American P51 Mustang which was rated at 437 mph at 25,000 ft. Possibly the only aspect where the Corsair yielded dominance to the Seafire was in its manoeuvrability and turning circle.

Having familiarised myself with the characteristics of the Corsair, I then proceeded to take the first group of Puttalam pilots for ADDLS. Happily a number of these pilots had been posted to Puttalam from Wildcat operational squadrons for conversion on to Corsairs and Hellcats. They were experienced deck landing pilots, so it was no problem for them to adapt to their new aircraft. When I was satisfied that all were ready to go to the carrier I returned to Katukurunda for a final check out with the TBR boys.

We boarded my old carrier HMS *Unicorn* at Colombo and from 26–19th June carried out initial deck landing experience on Swordfish, Barracudas, Avengers, Seafires and Corsairs. For a new batsman this was a daunting task and I knew there would be some dicey moments. I had little trouble with the three TBR aircraft, but I did chalk up some trouble with the Seafires and Corsairs. Over the three days I batted 108 landings 74 of which were Barracudas, 4 Avengers, 4 Hellcats, 12 Corsairs, 4 Seafires and 10 Swordfish. One of the Corsair pilots was a friend, Evan Baxter. Poor old Evan suffered three burst tyres – but it was not his fault. He was not to know that his were my first Corsair landings – it could have been so much worse. Some months later while a member of 1833 squadron Evan was shot down while escorting Avengers on a bombing raid on Palembang, Sumatra.

He managed to bale out some distance from Palembang, but he was captured by the Japanese. This raid took place on January 28th 1945. Along with about seven other Fleet Air Arm airmen one of whom was another Kiwi, John Haberfield, they were all held as prisoners of war, while the Japanese pondered over their fate. In their uncanny Samurai warrior code the Japanese apparently revered these men as heroes. But in the Samurai code heroes should not become prisoners of war. Their fate was finally decided on or about 31st July 1945 when all were ceremonially beheaded. This was one of New Zealand's most tragic wartime episodes. These pilots have no known grave, nor are their names recorded on the large war memorial in Singapore.

After completion of this course in the *Unicorn* I returned to Katukurunda to resume a boring and lonely existence. The brief interlude at Puttalam with the fighter boys had only added to my despondency. It was then that I came to the conclusion that if I were to improve my lot I would have to take some positive action, possibly without the approval of my superiors. I knew that Katukurunda had an air repair yard where they mended 'broken' aircraft, so they must need a pilot for test flying. I approached the Air Engineer Officer and offered my services. 'No problem – I have a Wildcat ready now – have you flown one?'

'No, I haven't, but if you could give me the handling notes I reckon I would be ready to take it up inside half an hour.'

'OK, mate, she's all yours.'

So I went away in a quiet corner and did some very rapid reading. I knew previously that the Wildcat had an antiquated method of raising and lowering the undercarriage. This was done by winding a handle on the starboard side of the cockpit about 30 turns. Quite an exhausting job following take off. Apart from that I had no problem over the Pratt & Whitney radial engine. It was similar, but more highly powered than a Harvard. The only thing I failed to notice in the handling notes was the need to lock the tailwheel before landing. This omission was to have dire consequences.

I reported to the AEO, signed the A25 serviceability sheet and off I went. The Wildcat was a lovely little aircraft, very manoeuvrable and just made for aerobatics. For 30 minutes I really displayed my talents above Katukurunda in full view of everyone below. I rolled, stalled, turned, looped and rolled off the top spun and then, satisfied that the aircraft was in good order, I came in to land. It was a sweet touch down and everything was going well as the landing speed declined, when suddenly and quite unexpectedly it developed a vicious ground loop. I had never previously experienced a ground loop but if anyone had asked me, at that point, I would have thought a wing would lean over towards the ground and the aircraft would develop a wild swing in the same direction that the wing tip was pointing.

In this case the opposite happened. The Wildcat swung wildly to starboard. I couldn't correct it with the brakes. Then the port wing tip hit the runway with sparks flying in all directions. I knew immediately I was in awful trouble. Firstly, it was an unauthorised flight and it was on an aircraft that I had not been checked out in. I was guilty of gross negligence and excessive confidence. Furthermore I had involved the Air Engineer Officer. It was not his fault but he would be on the mat with me. He had no authority to allow me to fly the Wildcat.

Next day I was arraigned before the Captain RN of the Air Station. He was a four ring Captain (A) with observer's wings, quite an exceptional appointment for that day. He must have been a very senior airman to reach that exalted rank particularly as an observer. There is something about pilots, however, that fosters the feeling that they are a superior breed to observers. Consequently, while I respected his rank I felt that I was being judged by someone who had no practical knowledge of actually flying an aircraft.

The enquiry proceeded along these lines –

'Well, Masters, will you kindly explain this incident.'

I proceeded to give him a brief summary of my previous service and of my great disappointment at being conscripted as a batsman. I thought I needed to keep my hand in at flying so that if I remained a batsman at least I was familiar with aircraft characteristics.

The Captain listened patiently then launched into a broadside.

'Now just get this straight, Masters. I am well aware of your rebellious attitude, but I am telling you now – it's got to stop.'

'You may be disappointed in your posting, but has it entered your puny brain that there are others including myself who would prefer a more glamorous job.'

'You have done a very foolish thing – it is out of my hands. You are to report to RANASIO (Rear Admiral Naval Air Stations) Colombo. It is over to him to deal with people like you.'

As an observer, the Captain formally acknowledged that it was technically beyond his competence to personally judge my indiscretion. That was an admirable decision for him to take.

Hell's teeth – that really was a dressing down, but there was worse to come. I was taken to Colombo under guard and when I entered RANASIO headquarters I was taken before Commander (A) Robin Kilroy RN.

Kilroy greeted me rather sternly.

'Masters, I am told that you have put up a colossal black at Katukurunda – what's the problem?'

Kilroy was a pilot, so I decided to play it the pilot's way.

'Sir, when I volunteered for service in the Fleet Air Arm in New Zealand, it was to be a pilot. Now I am a batsman and I don't like it. I want to get back to a first line fighter squadron.'

I couldn't have put it any plainer than that.

Kilroy responded. 'Now look here young man, some of us have to be batsmen – without them the Fleet Air Arm couldn't operate. You should feel honoured that you've been selected for the duty. In 12 months time it should lead to a promotion. At least a senior P's job – may be squadron command. Now just pull your finger out and knuckle down, otherwise you will regret it.'

'What I propose to do now is to transfer you to Puttalam under Lieutenant Commander Godfrey Parish, but if you cause trouble there you will be exiled to Addu Attol – I might add as No 1C (naval officer in charge). Now get back to your duties – let's have no more nonsense.'

I thanked Robin Kilroy for what was a very fair and understanding hearing, but when I withdrew I couldn't help thinking how attractive the job of No 1C at Addu Attol sounded. It sounded like a tropical paradise with dusky maidens and a little empire.

From later enquiries I learnt that there was in fact a place called Addu Attol. It was in the Maldive group of islands in the Indian Ocean and there was in fact a naval officer in charge. His entire command comprised about six seamen and a native bumboat. His duties were to row out from the Attol and meet any Royal Navy warship that called there.

Puttalam

After that disciplinary session I couldn't get back to Katukurunda and pack my gear fast enough. Next morning I flew up to Puttalam and reported for duty to Godfrey Parish.

While Katukurunda represented my most unhappy period in the Fleet Air Arm, my next seven months at Puttalam were to be my most rewarding.

Godfrey Parish was a marvellous character to be associated with. He was enormously popular with all ranks, but he did not suffer fools easily. He also had that droll charm of manner that seemed to make it easy for him to delegate to others. Within a very short time I was not only responsible for the deck landing training but also appointed to be Godfrey's senior instructor in fighter training. This caused some antagonism from a certain two-ringed RN lieutenant who by virtue of his seniority and permanent commission should have been given the job. This same RN Lieutenant succeeded me in this appointment when I left 757 squadron at the end of January 1945.

This appointment put me in a much happier frame of mind. To be the senior pilot of the training squadron was quite an honour. I was allocated an old Indian Scout motor bike which looked like a reject from the North African campaign. Our accommodation quarters and wardroom mess were on the shore of a delightful lagoon which was about five miles away from the Puttalam airfield. We lived in grass or rush covered huts known by the natives as *bandas*. Each officer had a native servant who always answered to the name 'boy'. Mine was an old campaigner who looked at least 60 years of age. Out of respect I could not bring myself to address him as 'boy'. I found his name was Latif.

Latif would supervise my laundry (dhobiing) which would be

washed and thrashed against rocks in the local stream. With this treatment one's shirts and trousers soon became frayed at the edges, but who cared. This was an all male compound – not a single Wren on the establishment.

Each day I would set out for the aerodrome to arrive there not later than 7 a.m. En route I would pass a long column of Italian prisoners of war who were doing some construction work in the jungle. There were many hundreds in the column – they would have covered easily a quarter of a mile. They had no military guards – they just marched to work each day in passive submission. Like most Italians they had no stomach for war and unlike the Germans they lacked the incentive to escape. I rode my motor cycle past this column, day after day, week after week, but no one made the slightest attempt to attack me. It was really quite a strange situation.

Once at the aerodrome I would check with the maintenance crew who would arrive there at the same time. The Aircraft Serviceability board would indicate the number and variety of aircraft available for each day's training. The flying programme I had drawn up the previous afternoon would then be confirmed.

The training squadron contained an interesting variety of aircraft – Seafires, Corsairs, Hellcats, Wildcats, Martinets (for drogue towing), a Walrus Amphibian (for air sea rescue work), a Gloster Gladiator (the Commanding Officer's pride and joy), a Stinson Reliant (for transport and communication) and two Harvards (for marksmanship instruction). Last but not least on the serviceability board was the squadron tractor, something no other squadron had ever possessed.

It was an aged Ceylon elephant complete with its driver – called a mahout.

This truly was a most fascinating job and I quickly shook off my former depression. My attitude had changed almost overnight. I determined from then to put my very best effort into the instruction routine both in the air and with the deck landing programme.

As my confidence as a batsman increased so I developed a personal style which I hoped would project that same measure of confidence to the pilot of the approaching aircraft. I know that it paid off because one or two of the more experienced deck landing pilots had complimented me.

Oddly enough it was the very experienced deck landers who

tended to cause concern. They were so primed up with their own confidence that they would always try to do their ADDLS in a continuous turn just a knot or two above stalling speed and try to touch down precisely opposite and dangerously close to me on the runway. It would have only needed a slight error of judgement for their aircraft to flick and that could have been 'curtains' for them and me. It is a grim prospect when one recalls the numbers of batsmen who were killed on carriers or controlling ADDLS. Decapitation would have been a horrible way to go. Among the next group of Puttalam pilots were some very experienced men who were converting from Wildcats to Corsairs and Hellcats. Many of them I knew very well – Joe Brough, Martin Turner, Jack Parli and Winnie Churchill. There were 11 from Puttalam and three from Katukurunda, so I had to jump in a Seafire early one morning and spend the day there giving these boys ADDLS in Avengers and Barracudas.

These DLTs (Deck Landing Training) were to take place in HMS *Atheling*, an escort carrier. This was going to be quite a challenge to get these Corsair pilots on to the very short deck, but it went off without incident. In three days we achieved 63 landings.

The first night on board *Atheling* I ran into an old school friend from New Plymouth Boys' High School, Don Fitzpatrick who was in *Atheling*'s Avenger squadron. The *Atheling* had just recently been commissioned in the United States of America and still had generous stocks of goodies like fresh lime juice. I introduced Fitz to my friends from Puttalam and we all had a wonderful session on gin and fresh lime juice.

The following morning I paid the penalty with a hangover, but I still had to be on deck at daybreak ranging aircraft for the day's flying programme. That was a hard day's work in the fierce tropical sun and an above average wind speed.

We returned to Puttalam to find 889 Seafire squadron had arrived and were disbanded there. One of the pilots was Alister MacLeod ex-New Plymouth Boys' High School and *Dominion Monarch* draft who I had not seen for about 15 months. That called for another celebration. 889 Squadron was being disbanded because it had just suffered the loss of its Commanding Officer, Lieutenant Commander (A) F. A. J. Pennington RNZNVR in a collision with another squadron pilot.

My next sortie was to the large fleet carrier HMS *Victorious* at

Trincomalee where I had to give DLTs to three experienced pilots, Lieutenant Commander Hall RN, Lieutenant Edmondson RN and Sub-Lieutenant 'Hoagy' Carmichael RNVR. It so happened that members of a Royal Air Force Spitfire squadron were on board *Victorious* for a few days leave from the Burma front. There was not much to do on leave in this theatre of war, so the Navy often offered these pilots some sea experience when it was convenient.

I was standing alongside the Commanding Officer of this squadron (DFC and bar) when the two *Victorious* Corsair squadrons 1834 and 1836 returned to land on after an exercise.

Understandably they would have been briefed to put on a 'good show' for these Royal Air Force types. They came back in battle formation, then streamed at very tight intervals to land on. They did it with spot on precision and at immaculate intervals.

When all 40 aircraft had been recovered the Commanding Officer turned to me and said, 'That's the most amazing piece of flying I have ever seen – it was really tremendous.'

That coming from a highly decorated Royal Air Force Squadron Commander was a great compliment to the Navy.

My next course early in November 1944 was in HMS *Battler*, another escort carrier. This comprised 74 landings for 17 pilots on three different types of aircraft.

Some days we included air to ground flying practice on targets which were sited out on the coastline. On one such occasion Godfrey Parish told me to go out as a marker with an air to ground radio to comment on their tactical approach and relay their score. Two of these pilots were Martin Turner and Joe Brough. They revealed themselves as very determined and aggressive pilots in fact, dangerously so. They both made good tactical approaches, but in their shallow dive to the target to open fire they both 'mushed' at about 280 m.p.h. and actually flew through some undergrowth before pulling up and away. I was absolutely horrified to see this because I knew what was happening. These two chaps were so keen to score well that they had virtually become hypnotised by the target. They were so close to killing themselves something had to be done. I called them on the radio and warned them what was happening, but I suppose they thought I was exaggerating. They both came in and did it a second time. That was enough – I called the whole thing off. Back at the airfield Joe and Martin were quite *blasé* about the whole affair, but I assured them they were both damned lucky to be alive.

A few days later Joe Brough posed a most unusual question, 'How did I become a batsman?'

'Well Joe – I didn't volunteer for this – I was conscripted – I just had to take the course.'

'Can you volunteer for it?'

'Yes, but you'd have to be a bit off your rocker to consider that.'

'Well, I've been watching you. You seem to get a kick out of it so what's the problem?'

I proceeded then to give him a blow by blow description of the training and the intense depression that I had suffered until I had got this appointment at Puttalam.

I did my best to convince him of my intense yearning to be released from batting and instructional work and be restored to a first line fighter squadron. Only then would I be satisfied.

'But why is it necessary for me to train at Easthaven? Why can't I train here in Ceylon?'

'Well, because Bob Everett is like a God – he is the Navy's master batsman – he would never approve that.'

'Oh, what a lot of crap,' said Joe, 'I don't see why you can't train me here at Puttalam. You could do it – couldn't you?'

'Well, I suppose so – but I doubt whether the Admiralty would approve it.'

'We'll see about that, Cappy.'

With that I forgot the conversation, until a few weeks later when Godfrey Parish lined me up and announced that in addition to the DLTs and the fighter instruction I was now to train Sub-Lieutenant Hilary Joseph Brough to be a batsman.

Well, I was speechless. How on earth could this have happened?

I accosted Joe Brough and asked him to confirm. He told me that following our discussion he had gone to RANASIO in Colombo and lodged an application to become a batsman and be trained by me at Puttalam.

To my eternal amazement RANASIO relayed this to Admiralty in London and a few days later a signal came back approving Joe's application. Whether this matter had been referred to Commander Bob Everett at Easthaven I will never know.

Anyway it was to be the beginning of an interesting and rewarding partnership.

I had known Joe Brough since our initial training days at HMS *St Vincent* where we had some memorable tussles on the rugby field. Later we were both to play rugby and cricket for the Navy versus the Rest in Ceylon.

Joe was a fine sportsman with particularly good ball skills – sharp reflexes and good muscular co-ordination. He should become an above average batsman. This was to be proved later when he served with distinction as No 1 batsman in HMS *Indomitable* in the British Pacific Fleet. He was awarded a Distinguished Service Cross (DSC) for his batting service.

Years later I have wondered why Joe Brough suddenly got this notion of becoming a batsman. Could it have been that incident on the air-to-ground target practice when he flew so low that he was within a few feet of killing himself? It could have been the result of a premonition. Although I have met with Joe on two occasions since the war, first in 1976 and again in 1989, he was so introspective, I failed to earn a comment.

The next course to be taken for DLTs comprised 11 Corsair pilots, 6 Seafires and 5 Wildcats. This session was carried out in HMS *Unicorn*. In the first day, 23rd January, I had my first and only fatal deck landing accident which very nearly took me too.

The pilot was Sub-Lieutenant (A) Frank Marks, a Kiwi. He had done two landings, and as was my custom with the trainees I climbed up on the main plane with a little moral encouragement, a word of congratulation and a pat on his shoulder before sending him off for his next landing. On this occasion I noticed that his windscreen had a slight film over it so I cleaned it with a rag which I carried in my flying suit for this purpose.

Over the noise of the Corsair motor I yelled out.

'Looks like a little oil from the prop – is it troubling you?'

Marks replied, 'No – she's OK,' and gave me the thumbs up, whereupon I flagged him off for his next DLT.

On this approach like most novices he dragged it in from a long way astern and far too low. To restore him to an acceptable height I gave him the signal to go higher and apply a little more throttle. There was no response. This time I bounded out towards the middle of the deck and gave him an urgent 'Go up' sign plus more motor.

He still kept coming – very low and very slow. Something was obviously wrong.

So then I gave him a Wave Off (Go around again). Just at the same time Commander Flying came on the ship's Tannoy.

'Masters – give that pilot a wave off.' What a stupid thing to say. Couldn't he see, I was already risking my neck to wave him off?

This was followed by two red rockets from either side of the stern.

This was all taking place in a very short space of time – something was obviously very wrong. Perhaps the pilot could not see me. He still kept coming towards the round down. It was too late now to make him go around again so I stepped a few paces in board and continued to signal 'more motor' and 'go higher'.

Next moment his Corsair hit the round down and broke the port oleo leg off the undercarriage. This caused the plane to collapse to port and charge directly at me.

Foolishly I stood in front of the charging Corsair signalling 'Port wing up.' It was a futile gesture. Then if I didn't move fast my legs would be cut off. At the very last moment I desperately dived under the mainplane of the Corsair into the steel batsman's net and landed face downwards on top of my 'looker'. The Corsair passed over the top of me, clearing my neck by inches and wrenching away part of the angle iron on the frame of the batsman's net.

The Corsair fell over the port side into the sea with the cockpit hood obviously jammed closed. The pilot Marks was collapsed over the control column so he must have been knocked unconscious when his aircraft hit the round down.

My first instinct was to dive over the side and try to open the hood, but the plane was already filling with water so fast that this would have been impossible.

When the incident was over I became aware of a warm clammy feeling at my back. It was black engine oil all over the back of my white batsman's suit. It had come from one or more of the Corsair's cylinders which had broken in the crash.

Needless to say the flying programme was adjourned while we took stock of the situation. People who had been watching the DLTs from 'goofers gallery' were amazed to see me clamber out of the batsman's net. They had seen me dive, but they thought I had been killed. It was a bloody close one – much too close for comfort.

At that point there was a short conference convened by Captain

Merrewether RN attended by Commander Flying, Godfrey Parish and myself. I was asked if I was prepared to carry on, to which I replied in the affirmative but expressed concern for the trainee pilots who had witnessed this incident.

A crazy thought occurred to me. I put it to Captain Merrewether that perhaps it would boost the morale of those pilots who were waiting if I myself, went up and did four landings. Since being at Puttalam I had always felt that it was good for the pupils' confidence if they knew that the batsman was himself a competent deck lander. The Captain enquired had I done my ADDLS. Fortunately I had, because my protègé Joe Brought had been batting me. The Captain, thereupon, gave his approval but Commander Flying then intervened and asked who was going to bat for me.

It so happened that one of the pilots who had just completed his DLTs in the Corsair was Lieutenant (A) Don Cameron who had been trained as a batsman at Everett's school at Easthaven. After his training Don had been posted to HMS *Shah* in the Indian Ocean. One day off Mombasa, East Africa he was controlling the landing of an Avenger bomber when it hit the round down and exploded only a few yards in front of him. Don was another reluctant batsman who hated the job. Following this crash he handed the bats to his Commander Flying and said he would never bat another aircraft on to a carrier. He must have put on a pretty good act of being a nervous wreck because they let him get away with it. Shortly after he appeared at Puttalam to do a conversion course on to Corsairs.

Immediately following the meeting with Captain Merrewether I located Cameron and told him what I was about to do and would he please hold the bats for me. I knew what his reaction would be.

'No, Masters – you can go to hell. I told you that I would never bat again.'

I pleaded with him. I told him all he needed to do was to stand in position with the bats at 'Roger' (the OK position) and I would do the rest. He finally gave in and I did my four landings for which Captain Merrewether certified my log book as 'above the average'.

The remaining details were then flown without further incident. The death of Frank Marks weighed heavily on all of us, so we returned to Colombo harbour that night. On reflection I felt quite satisfied that he was eminently capable of doing the landings. He was not one of those trainees who required more than the usual number of ADDLS to establish confidence in the deck landing technique. Up to that stage I had only down-graded one pilot as being a potential risk on a carrier. My judgement in his case was vindicated because this pilot had a serious crash at Cochin some months later and was paralysed as a result of his injuries. I was prepared to give any trainee as many ADDLS as were required to enable him to reach a satisfactory standard.

When we disembarked at Colombo, Godfrey Parish had learned that five Avenger bombers were at the Air Repair section awaiting delivery to Cochin. His proposal was that Don Cameron, Joe Brough, Martin Turner and I should join him to deliver these aircraft. We could stay overnight in a posh hotel, have a nice little session there and move on to Coimbatoire where there were several aircraft to be flown down to Ceylon.

This appealed to us, so those who had not previously flown an Avenger had to swot up the handling notes very quickly. The flight to Cochin took two hours, but it was dark by the time we got there. To land under those conditions was quite a challenge – none of us knew how to switch on the cockpit or wing tip lights.

Looking back on this little jaunt I feel certain that Godfrey organised it to take our minds off the awful accident that had happened on *Unicorn*.

Another incident, this one rather amusing, took place in the *Unicorn*. I had just completed the prescribed four landings for one pilot when my 'looker' called me over to the phone in the batsmen's net.

'It's the Captain, Sir. He wants to speak to you.'

I answered the call.

'Masters, how do you feel about the wind speed over the deck? Would you like a bit more?'

Actually the local wind at that time was very light, so we were not getting much more than the carrier's forward speed, possibly 20 knots. I still felt it was reasonably safe but suddenly a rather impish thought passed through my mind – I could speed the carrier up.

So I answered the Captain.

'I think it is safe, sir. None of the pilots have complained, but it would make it easier for them if they had a few more knots.'

'OK Masters, you shall have it.'

'Thank you, sir.'

Now there wouldn't be many sub-lieutenants in the Fleet Air Arm who can say that they indirectly opened the throttle of their aircraft carrier.

That was a classic first if ever there was one.

In the several encounters I had with Captain Merrewether RN he impressed me as a very considerate officer. Some captains behaved like gods in their own domain and junior officers seldom saw them. Merrewether played an entirely different role – he may have been an Air Branch man himself.

Back at Puttalam we had by now built up quite a large pool of trained pilots who were awaiting appointments to various squadrons as and when replacements were required.

A few days later another sad fatality occurred, this time while we were practicing ADDLS on the aerodrome. I had several aircraft in the circuit at the same time. The next one in the stream to approach was a Wildcat piloted by a chap who had just completed his DLTs in *Unicorn*. He had just commenced his final turn when Godfrey Parish ranged up alongside me in the runway and made some comment.

Momentarily I looked around to reply to him and, when I glanced back at the Wildcat again, I was horrified to see it had gone into a spin and was diving into the jungle. There was a tremendous explosion followed by the usual column of black oil smoke. I dropped the bats and several of us tore off down the jungle track in the direction of the crash. There was nothing we could do. The heat was so fierce you couldn't get within 20 yards of the fire. The pilot would have been killed instantly but it was horrible to see him trapped inside the cockpit. There was another night when I couldn't sleep a wink.

Further drama took place a few days later. Don Cameron was on a camera gun exercise with Petty Officer Dyer who was flying a Wildcat. Cameron was flying as target for Dyer while the latter carried out quarter attacks. In one of the three attacks Dyer pressed in so close that in breaking away he collided with Don's Corsair and tore out a good third of its port main plane, destroying the landing flaps and leaving only the main spar in one piece. Dyer's Wildcat dived into the sea before he had a chance to bale out. Cameron immediately called up Puttalam control tower on the R/T and reported the incident. Puttalam instructed him to show IFF so they could get a directional bearing on him and then to bale out. This was Don's second situation, the previous one at Salerno, where it called for a parachute jump, but Don was still not that way inclined. He chose to ignore the instructions and proceeded to fly back towards the coast line. Quite unperturbed he checked the stalling speed of his Corsair at about 4,000 ft – it was around 150 knots. With a third of his port mainplane missing this in itself was quite a hazardous test. He maintained his course back to Puttalam and joined the circuit at about 200 knots. To get into this very small airfield with the damage he had sustained would call for some really precise flying. He came around on his approach – no flaps, because if he selected flaps down one wing would obviously stall and the aircraft would spin into the ground. He brought it into low over the boundary of the jungle and made his first touch down at around 160 knots. The aircraft leapt into the air again but he lowered it by more motor, then proceeded to slow it down by braking alternatively port and starboard wheels. Those of us who were watching this amazing piece of flying could see the smoke from the brake drums as he gradually reduced the landing speed. When finally he brought the Corsair to a halt it was only a few yards from the jungle at the other end of the airstrip. This was the most magnificent display of airmanship that it has ever been my privilege to witness. There are those of course who might say that Don should have obeyed instructions and baled out. Who knows whether, had he done so, he would have been located by our Air Sea Rescue Amphibian.

When his aircraft eventually stopped Don had to be assisted from the cockpit – he was drained with exhaustion. This was the most spectacular piece of flying one could ever imagine.

A few days later we received a signal that King George VI had awarded Don Cameron a King's Commendation for flying services.

Following the death of the young Wildcat pilot I expected to have to appear before a Board of Enquiry at Colombo. Apart from the fact that my attention had been momentarily distracted by Godfrey Parish's comment, I failed to see how this could have been the cause of the accident. It later transpired, following an engineer's inspection of the remains of the Wildcat, that one of the landing flaps had failed to operate, thereby causing one wing to stall. At such a low speed and low altitude there was nothing any pilot could have done to correct the resulting spin.

This incident preceded by the death of Frank Marks and then followed by Don Cameron's remarkable close shave created a lot of tension. To relieve the 'twitch' there was a tendency to let off steam through some rather unwise sessions in the wardroom. Godfrey did not discourage this, probably because he was as much 'round the bend' as everyone else. A practice had also developed for some of the more senior pilots to show off over the aerodrome before coming in to land. Both the Corsair and the Hellcat had pressure injection carburettors as opposed to English fighters which had gravity-fed petrol flow. This difference made the Corsair and Hellcat ideal for inverted flying. Several of us would come down along the length of the runway at about 250 knots, roll at 100 to 150 feet, push the stick forward to bring the nose up and then roll out in an upward zoom. It was a fantastic thrill but incredibly stupid. Eventually we took stock of ourselves and concluded that we were all getting a bit slap happy.

It was also about this time that I had heard that many New Zealand pilots had by that time returned to New Zealand for three months foreign service leave. I had been away since July 1941 so I would have easily qualified for a break. I submitted my application, but I did not feel hopeful about my release from the batsman appointment. I would at the very least have to wait until a replacement was available.

Among the many crazy pranks that took place about this time were two worthy of recollection.

Ceylon, or Sri Lanka as it is now known, was home to millions and millions of crows which are sacred to the Singhalese people. We were having a party in the mess one night when one officer returned from the 'heads' clutching a crow in his hand. Apparently it had been roosting in the toilet block, so he made a dive and grabbed it.

Someone said 'The poor little bugger needs some refreshment.'

With that someone went to the bar and ordered a double gin and water.

'Now someone hold Mr Crow on the table. Someone else open his beak. Then I'll give him something to tickle his tonsils. He won't be crowing for a while when he gets this lot.'

So someone held him and someone else opened the poor little devil's beak while the next chap poured half the contents down its throat. It took only a minute or two to take effect. The crow obviously felt groggy, so he was released on the table top whereupon he staggered around, flapped his wings and rolled over. The poor little devil was well and truly pissed. In this day and age the perpetrators of this prank would probably have been arrested and charged with cruelty to animals. At the time, however, it was greeted with gales of drunken laughter. To chaps who were themselves halfway around the bend it was a great way to relieve the tension.

A short while later the crow interlude had been at the forgotten and the party went on, finally winding up about 11 p.m. Everyone had had their ration and retired to their *bandas*.

Don Cameron, however, was still in the mood to play, so he invited a few chaps to his *banda* for a night cap. Apparently he had acquired a bottle from somewhere. When he went to get this bottle, however, it had disappeared. Some other lousy pilot must have swiped it. Cameron was as mad as a meat axe about this, vowing retribution to all and sundry. To have invited his mates for a night cap and then let them down was just the last straw. So he bade them wait awhile and returned to the wardroom and somehow got into the bar to retrieve another bottle to replace the one he had lost. Back he went to his *banda* and the cosy little party continued.

It was about this time that 'Jimmy the One' (the station first lieutenant) was doing his nightly rounds with the petty officer of the day. They discovered that an unauthorised entry had been made into the wardroom bar and hearing the raucous laughter emanating from Cameron's banda they took themselves there to investigate.

The evidence was there for all to see. 'Jimmy the One' accused Cameron of breaking and entering the bar. Cameron denied it but the scene was set for a grand showdown.

Apparently when Cameron returned to the bar he noticed the drunken crow still flapping on the table, so in sympathy he picked it up and took it back to stay the night with him.

'Jimmy' then went to arouse Lieutenant (A) Reg Bryant RN who was the officer of the day. They were probably considering whether Cameron would be placed under arrest. In the meantime Cameron had gone to bed, but he couldn't sleep due to the animated discussion taking place a few doors away in Reg Bryant's cabin.

He got out of bed, grabbed the crow, put it on his shoulder and marched in stark naked to confront the two senior officers who were debating disciplinary action. Cameron still protested his innocence, but 'Jimmy' would not buy it. This ended up with Cameron telling 'Jimmy' he was just a silly old fool whereupon he threw the crow at him, 'And you can take that too!'

Well, the humorous part of this incident was that 'Jimmy' submitted a report to the Captain the following day giving him a blow by blow description of Cameron confronting him in his birthday suit and throwing a crow at him.

No one knows just how the Captain interpreted this. He probably concluded that 'Jimmy the One' was off his 'rocker' and should be posted to a less troublesome station. From all accounts the Captain decided to take no action.

Two nights after this party I was afflicted by a violent fever. It hit me early in the evening, so I retired early. Because of the heat and the high humidity everyone slept in the nude without even a sheet to cover them. For protection against mosquitoes we slept inside nets. Puttalam was in the middle of a swampy area and on the edge of a lagoon. It was a perfect breeding ground for 'mossies'. While I was at Puttalam there had been many cases of malaria and a few cases of fatal cerebral malaria. At night time therefore we always took the precaution of wearing full uniforms – bush jacket style. On the night of the party, however, I recall hearing a 'mossie' inside my net, but I was too far gone to worry about it. This must have been the little blighter that infected me.

Once in bed I was shivering dreadfully cold and aching all over particularly behind my eyes. I managed to stagger around and find a rug and some clothes to put on, but this had no effect whatsoever on the fever. The pain behind my eyes became unbearable. It felt as if my eyeballs were being dragged back into my brain with a pair of pliers. I remember someone coming in to see me, realised I was unwell and called Godfrey Parish. The last thing I remember that night and for the next few days was a vague apparition of Godfrey and Bill Belcher, a Kiwi, leaning over me.

I had succumbed to an attack of dengue fever, sometimes known as breakbone fever. Just how long I was unconscious for I cannot recall – it could have been two days. When I recovered my senses, I was in a bed in the station hospital. The patient in the next bed was a drole Kiwi, Ian MacGregor.

'I wondered when you were going to surface, Cappy. It's been a bit boring talking to myself.'

I don't know how dengue fever compares with malaria except that it is not recurring, but I would never wish this experience on anyone.

Had it not been for the generosity of a very fine captain and the backing up from Godfrey Parish the next rebellious incident could well have ended in a court martial which would have been the end of my naval career.

While the squawking of the sacred crows was the bane of our existence during the daytime, the hours of darkness were rent with the continual 'hee-hawing' of wild donkeys which roamed around the lagoon and the station area. One night after a good mess party a few of us decided to give these donkeys a good fright and hopefully encourage them to pester the inhabitants of the nearby village. It was decided therefore that two chaps would muster and drive these stubborn animals down the road while a third member would fire a pistol to ricochet bullets off the road. Because I had my German Walther pistol, it was decided that I should have the privilege of putting a fright into these animals. I had fired off several shots which could be heard whining off the sealed surface of the road and landing somewhere in the distant jungle. Suddenly there was a compelling roar, 'What the hell's going on there?' It sounded like the voice of authority, the Station Captain. Apparently he had been walking down the road when he became aware of the shooting and bullets ricochetting over his head. No one could ever have reacted faster. The three culprits disappeared in a flash and were soon in their *bandas* feigning sleep.

Once back at camp the Captain called out the guard, members of which then toured the officers' quarters, waking up those who were asleep and ordering a full muster immediately on the parade ground. By this time I had gone to sleep, but it was not for long. Godfrey Parish aroused me and asked whether I was involved. He knew I had the pistol, so I was immediately under suspicion.

When I joined the parade all the officers were present, in all sorts of weird attire, predominantly underpants and blankets. The captain proceeded to describe his experience and proclaimed his suspicion that one or more officers were responsible. He then called on the officer who had fired the shots to step forward. For a moment there was dead silence – only the breeze in the palm trees could be heard.

At that moment a young sub-lieutenant – 'Red' Middleton, who had apparently been imbibing to excess gave forth an involuntary hiccough followed by another and another. This caused a ripple of laughter and eased the tension.

It took only a couple of seconds, however, for me to realise that if I did not own up to the offence I would immediately forfeit any respect that I may have earned from my fellow officers. So I stepped forward. I felt a real criminal – I knew I was in deep trouble – facing a possible court martial. The Captain then announced that I was under close house arrest and had to report to him at 0900 hours the following morning. This meant I could go back to bed but there was a sentry on the door of my *banda*. The Captain then set out to punish the other officers who were involved in this incident by requiring the entire officer complement to do guard duty all through the night. It seemed at the time that the real culprit, in being sent back to bed, was in fact being let off lightly.

The crunch came at 0900 the following morning.

I cannot recall the captain's name – he was actually a commander RN and a thorough gentleman.

He commenced by reminding me that he was dealing with a very serious offence. Firing at the captain in the days of Nelson would have meant a hanging from the yard arm. In 1945 it could mean a court martial and a possible dishonourable discharge.

Then he adopted a more sentimental approach. He had obviously studied my service records. He referred to the 'black' that I had put up at Katukurunda and how generously I had been treated by Commander (A) Robin Kilroy at RANASIO. Then he got on to the subject of my application for foreign service leave and indicated that he might consider stopping it. Worse was to follow. Apparently Godfrey Parish had been really stretched to put in a good word for me and mentioned that I was hoping to get married while on my leave.

'Now what is your fiancée going to think, Masters, if I detain you here for misbehaviour?'

There wasn't much I could do except to weather this reprimand, but at the same time I sensed that he knew that I was near the end of my tether. He terminated the dressing down by inferring that, if it had not been for my record and the good reference of Godfrey Parish, he would send me off once again to RANASIO and possible banishment to Addu Attol. With that I was dismissed.

A few days later a signal was received advising that my long service leave had been approved. So the Captain had not intervened to stop it or postpone it.

It was now mid-January 1945 and we were due to depart at the end of the month. I still had one unfulfilled ambition. That was to be able to fly the Gloster Gladiator aircraft that had somehow arrived at Puttalam as a wreck after service in the Western Desert of North Africa. Godfrey Parish had made it his personal project to restore it to its former glory. Months and months of work had gone on in the air engineering department fashioning replacement parts for the engine and fuselage, and finally about this time it was ready to fly.

It was Godfrey's own very personal possession. I knew that if I was to get a trip in this precious aircraft it would be a little short of diplomatic coup. The ideal time to put the hard word on Godfrey was late in the evening after having shouted him a drink or two or maybe three.

The ploy was successful. He agreed to let me have one trip for half an hour on condition that if broke it I would forfeit my forthcoming leave.

The Gladiator was the last of the British biplane fighters. It came into service in No 72 Squadron Royal Air Force in 1937. At the outbreak of war in September 1939 210 Gladiators Mk I and 243 Gladiators Mk II were in first line squadron service. The Fleet Air Arm had a further 38 Sea Gladiators. They were used on operations in the Norwegian campaign, the Western Desert, Greece and Malta. At one period of the siege of Malta the total fighter defence comprised three Gladiators, 'Faith, Hope and Charity'. The Gladiator had counterparts in both the German Air Force, the Henschel HS123, and in the Italian Air Force, the Fiat CR42. They were all biplanes of similar performance. The power plant of Godfrey's Gladiator was a Bristol Mercury 725 h.p. radial engine.

It was a real joy to fly, even more delightful than the Spitfire. It was perfection for aerobatics. At 180 knots on my first attempt I did a vertical climbing roll and a roll off the top. I couldn't have done this in a Seafire at 300 knots and I wouldn't have even attempted it in a Corsair due to the danger of spinning. Coming in to land height could be lost by side slipping as we used to do in Tiger Moths. I didn't break Godfrey's precious toy, so he let me have a second trip.

We were notified that we would be sailing from Colombo in HMS

Unicorn on 29th January. We were to report on board at 1600 hours that day.

Don Cameron and I had the privilege of flying down to Colombo in the station's Stinson Reliant.

My friends had always been kind to me in this regard because they appreciated that as a batsman I did not get nearly as much flying as they did, so I was the pilot.

At Colombo Don suggested that we should visit a gem stone merchant and purchase a gift to take home to New Zealand. I recall purchasing a moonstone necklace for Joan Rees.

Following that we parted. Don had some other business to attend to, while I took the liberty boat out to HMS *Unicorn* which was lying at anchor in the harbour.

There was a muster of the Puttalam pilots, most of whom were destined to join squadrons in the Pacific Fleet. All were present and correct except the irrepressible Donald Cameron who was apparently adrift.

By this time the carrier had weighed anchor and the quarter deck quivered with the thrust of the propellers. The Commander with telescope under his arm was pacing up and down the quarter deck muttering dire threats to Cameron if he ever had the misfortune to set eyes on him again.

Knowing Cameron fairly well by this stage, I guessed he had gone into some bar and was having a good skinful of booze.

One of our chaps who happened to be looking in the direction of the naval jetty suddenly saw a native bumboat emerge with an officer clad in a full white tropical uniform sitting in the sternsheets. He drew this to the attention of the Commander who levelled his telescope in that direction. Sure enough it was that rapscallion Cameron urging the native boat man to greater efforts. The carrier had by this time just got way on, so the Commander telephoned the bridge to report that we were being pursued by an officer who was absent without leave. As the bumboat drew closer to the quarter deck the gangway was lowered again. Cameron was now recognisable by the naked eye and provoked gales of laughter from the quarter deck group as he railed at his boatman – 'In – out – In out faster, boy – faster, you clot.'

Finally the bumboat caught up and Cameron leapt from the boat and in a grand theatrical performance he strode up the gangway to salute the quarter deck. The Commander was completely taken aback when Cameron in his most charming manner thanked him for slowing down the carrier to enable Cameron's boatman to catch up.

It was then that we became aware of some plaintive calls as the gangway was being raised. The boatman had been holding on to the step waiting for Cameron to pay him for his services. With a characteristic flourish Cameron went over to the rail and deftly tossed a few rupees into the boat and waved his hire goodbye.

While in transit our contingent had no formal ship's duties, but to keep us occupied we were detailed, whilst passing through the Indian Ocean in particular, for watch duties on anti-aircraft guns. Some chaps actually doubled up on some bridge watch keeping.

We stopped for a few hours at Fremantle just long enough to dash ashore and sample the ice cold Australian beverage. Then on to Sydney where we arrived about a week later.

Foreign Service Leave

After disembarking from *Unicorn* we were hustled into Navy trucks and taken miles out of the city to a racecourse called Warwick Farm. This amenity had been temporarily handed over to the British Fleet as a transit camp. The main grandstand completely open to the elements was to be our sleeping quarters. We were issued with a straw palliasse, a pillow and one blanket and then left completely to our own devices.

There was nothing to do so we hi-tailed it off by train to Sydney, a city none of us had visited before. We very soon discovered that Australia was quite the opposite of what we had left in England. Whereas in England food was very basic and austere, in Australia it was plentiful and in great variety. Beer however was the direct opposite. In the United Kingdom pubs opened 11 a.m. to 2 p.m. and 6 p.m. to 10 p.m. There was never any shortage of beer. In Sydney, however, the hotels only opened between 5 p.m. and 6 p.m. If you were not in the queue it was bad luck.

We were at Warwick Farm for only a few days when news came through that several of us would fly back to New Zealand on an RNZAF Sunderland Flying boat leaving from Rose Bay Sydney at 3 a.m. on 17th February.

Since arriving in Australia units of the task force 57 of the British Pacific Fleet comprising four fleet carriers, *Illustrious*, *Victorious*, *Indomitable* and *Indefatigable*, plus two battleships and sundry cruisers and destroyers, had arrived in Sydney harbour. I had heard that my old school friend Alister MacLeod had just returned from three months leave in New Zealand to be posted to 887 Seafire Squadron which was presently in the *Indefatigable*.

As I would have about 15 hours to fill in before the departure time from Rose Bay I decided to visit the *Indefatigable* which was anchored a short distance from Admiralty Steps. I caught a liberty boat returning to *Indefatigable* and went on board about 7 p.m. to find Mac happily reclining against the wardroom bar. The last time we had met was about eight months previously at Puttalam, Ceylon. I caught up on the news from home and was then introduced to one of their pilots who was returning to New Zealand on the same flying boat. This was Jim Sheerin whom I had not previously met, but knew to be somewhat of a character. I soon gathered that the party in progress was to farewell Jimmy who was entering into the spirit and the spirits with great gusto. The booze was flowing freely and everyone was having a whale of a time.

Jimmy didn't appear to be the slightest concerned about getting his gear ready to go ashore. He was still wearing an open white shirt and a cummerbund – he couldn't return to New Zealand like that.

So we managed to get him down to his cabin, only to find that he hadn't even started his packing. Someone grabbed a kitbag and quickly tumbled Jimmy's belongings in to it. Then it was discovered that he was lacking a conventional shirt and tie so someone else had to lend him the gear and we finally trundled him up the quarter deck just in time to catch the last liberty boat of the night for shore.

We boarded the flying boat and departed from Rose Bay precisely on the scheduled time. The flight across the Tasman took slightly over eight hours and was uneventful. My first sight of my homeland after an absence of over three and a half years was memorable. As we flew over the Helensville-Huapai area I marvelled at the greenness of the countryside, the trees and the neatly cultivated farmlands. It was all so different from what I had seen in the last few years – Canada, North Africa, Sicily, Italy, India, Ceylon and even Australia. This was a country that Richard Seddon had so rightly termed 'God's own Country'. There was nothing like it anywhere.

Our Sunderland flew down Auckland harbour making an immaculate touchdown at Mechanic's Bay. From there we were taken by a Naval pinnace to HMS *Philomel*, the Auckland headquarters of the New Zealand Navy. What trains there were had departed for the day, so we had no option but to stay the night at *Philomel*. Here we had our first taste of New Zealand naval pomposity. We trooped in that evening for a meal in the wardroom and, as was our custom in any warship of the Royal Navy in wartime, when we had finished the meal, we stood up to leave the wardroom. At this point, some 'jumped up' little chairborne officer came up and told us that it was disrespectful to leave the wardroom mess until the Commander had risen.

Our chaps were quite ropable about this. Nowhere on any Fleet Air Arm shore station, nor firstline fleet carrier had we ever been subjected to nonsense like this. It didn't exist at Greenwich Royal Naval College which would have been the ultimate in wardroom etiquette. Anyway to hell with the New Zealand Navy if that is the way they behave – so en masse we just stood up and walked out.

Next morning we crossed over to mainland Auckland and made travel arrangements to our various destinations. This was my first opportunity to advise my fiancée Joan Rees that I had arrived back in New Zealand. She was still based in Huntly with her friend Barbara Heale as school dental nurses for the Huntly area.

This was Saturday 18th February. Schools were closed so there was no way of contacting Joan by telephone. My only means of communication was by telegram from the Auckland Post Office. Without a rail timetable I could only say that I would be arriving in Huntly sometime that day.

Apparently this was a great shock to Joan who thought I was still in Ceylon. In a panic she met two trains before finally I steamed in at 5 p.m., and that was a meeting we shall never forget!

There were about six other Fleet Air Arm pilots travelling in the same carriage and when we arrived in Huntly they were literally tumbling over themselves in ushering me off and passing out my bags. I knew, of course, that this was not out of concern for my welfare, it was only because they wanted a ring side seat at our reunion. I descended from the carriage at the Southern end of the station platform so I had some way to walk to the main concourse. Then suddenly I saw her coming towards me. Neither of us would have wanted to attract undue attention and I was conscious of these characters behind me watching my every move. Joan looked lovelier than ever. She was dressed in a striking pale blue linen suit which complimented her wavy brunette hair. After three and a half years absence it is not easy to retain one's composure. I had experienced some exciting times, but this really sent my pulse rate galloping. We finally met, but both were so overcome and shy that words did not come spontaneously. It seemed an unusual situation. Here we were, almost strangers, yet engaged to be married. Eyeing each other, we liked what we saw and nervously embraced, to the accompaniment of cheers, hand claps and wolf whistles. I turned and waved those roguish naval types away.

I picked up my suitcase and kitbag while Joan carried the parachute bag and together we set off for the little flat which she shared with Barbara Heale. By the time we got there our initial nervousness had gone, but years later Joan recalls that she was plucking grasses all the way along the roadside.

Barbara returned some time later after having been at the races. So here I was with the same two girls who had farewelled me on Wellington Station in July 1941.

Joan had arranged for me to stay with some friends who lived nearby and late the following afternoon I departed by train for Stratford. Joan was to follow as soon as she could obtain leave from the School Dental Service.

After a brief stay in Stratford we were both on the train again heading for Napier. This was a two day journey involving a stop over at Palmerston North.

This was my first meeting with Joan's father and her stepmother. Plans were soon under way for our wedding which was to take place on 20th March. Because of the very tight time schedule we were unable to have banns read so that the wedding service could take place in the Anglican church. We settled on the Presbyterian church as an alternative. Although it was going to be only a very small wedding due to the wartime travel restrictions, I could see that there was a considerable amount of organising to be done. There was not much I could contribute to the choice of dresses, the wedding cake and all the many frills of even a modest occasion, so Ted Rees and I mutually decided that while the bridegroom was a Very Important Personage on the actual day, his presence would not be missed in the run up period.

Joan had no objections so I returned to Stratford and came back to Napier with my parents and my sister who was to be Joan's bridesmaid, on 19th March. In the meantime I had heard that Arch Foley was also home on leave in Takapau. I put the proposition to him that as a penance for almost killing me for cutting my tail off at Burscough he might consider being my best man. He accepted unconditionally so we arranged to meet in Napier on the morning of the wedding.

The 20th March was a beautiful late summer's day – it could not have been better. When Joan was escorted down the aisle by her father I simply could not resist the temptation to have a quick look. She looked absolutely gorgeous in a pale blue dress with mauve accessories, a floral arrangement and pale blue hair veil. To complete the ensemble she was also wearing the moonstone necklace which I had purchased in Colombo. We made all the relevant promises until death do us part and the vicar pronounced us man and wife.

As we both walked out of the church I was quite surprised to see how many people were present. Ted Rees being the secretary of the Hospital Board was a well known figure in the community. There were probably a lot of friends of the family present. Unbeknown to us another Fleet Air Arm pilot Jon Fenwick and his wife Daphne, also a school dental nurse, were present. They had been married the previous day and by some strange coincidence were to meet up with us later on our honeymoon at Lake Waikaremoana.

The wedding reception was held in the lounge of the Masonic Hotel at Napier.

Arch had borrowed his father's car and was returning to Takapuna after the reception, so he agreed to take us as far as Hastings. We had gone only a few miles along the promenade road when a tyre was punctured. I wondered at the time whether this misfortune so early in our married life was an augury for further good or bad luck. It did illustrate, however, how capricious motoring was during the war years. Petrol was stringently rationed and replacement tyres very difficult to obtain.

The following afternoon we took the railcar to Wairoa where Joan had spent her first dental nursing appointment. We were met by Jack Heslop, an old friend of Joan's and possibly an erstwhile rival of mine, and were taken to see Hazel and Ed Krogh with whom Joan had boarded for two years.

Next day we were on the bus to Lake Waikaremoana. The hotel at the lake was a very gracious colonial style building, in very serenebush clad surroundings and perched high up on a promontory overlooking this great expanse of water. The accommodation was first class and the 'grub' simply fabulous after service fare. We could not have chosen a nicer place in all the world. It was a perfect refuge from the mad world I had been living in. We could have remained there for months.

But that regrettably was not to be.

John and Daphne Fenwick had joined us and we were just beginning to enjoy their company when early on the Thursday morning I received a devastating toll call from Navy office in Wellington. There was a Wren on the phone telling me that my promised three months long service leave had been curtailed and I was required to report to HMS *Philomel* in Auckland the next day for onward passage to Leyte in the Philippines.

The conversation went like this:

'Good morning, is that Lieutenant Masters?'

'Yes – speaking.'

'This is the Navy Office Wellington. A signal has just been received from Admiralty in London requiring you to report at HMS *Philomel* on Sunday morning for passage to Leyte.'

'There's something wrong here, lady. I am in New Zealand on three months long service leave and I still have over two months to go. You must be referring to someone else.'

'No, I'm sorry sir. It is to you that the signal refers.'

Now by this time I was getting a bit alarmed and becoming rather cross with this Wren telephonist.

'Would you please get this into your little head, lady, I'm here on three months leave and on that commitment I got married a few days ago. How on earth could the Navy countermand that decision? It's just not me you want.'

By that time the poor little Wren realised that the matter was beyond her competence.

'Would you like to speak to the Drafting Commander, Sir?'

'Yes – put him on please.'

'Good morning, Masters. I am Commander — I gather that you are querying the signal which we have received from Admiralty in London.'

'Yes, I am. It's just too stupid for words. I was sent home on three months long service leave. I've been here barely four weeks and now this Wren is telling me that my leave is finished. Also I have just got married, last Saturday. I can't possibly leave my wife under these circumstances.'

'Masters, I can understand your disappointment, but please bear with me while I explain. This is a secret matter. I am not supposed to be discussing it with you. The senior batsman in one of our fleet carriers has been seriously injured or wounded.

The Admiralty drafting office claims that you are the only trained batsman available in the Pacific area. I am sorry, old chap, but you have just got to go.'

'Oh – to hell with the Admiralty. How the hell could they possibly know my circumstances? The whole thing is absurd – it stinks! Anyway, I haven't got my gear here – it's all in Taranaki.'

'We have been in telephone communication with your father and he has already sent your kitbag and other gear on to Auckland by rail.'

I was really nonplussed to hear this. It seemed as if the whole world was conspiring against me. So I launched another attack.

'There's no way I can get from here to Auckland by Sunday morning.'

'Yes, there is, Masters. There's a bus which leaves Wairoa tomorrow morning and reaches Waikaremoana by 9.30 a.m. and travels through to Rotorua. You can catch a train at Rotorua leaving at 3.30 p.m. and you'll be in Auckland that night.'

From this it was obvious that the sods had thought of everything. It sounded like a Secret Service operation and poor Joan was sitting alongside me, holding her head in her hands.

By this time I had had a real gutsful of the Navy. After my experience in the wardroom mess at *Philomel* and the absurd protocol that existed there, I visualised this drafting commander as a jumped up little twirp of a three ringed RNVR paymaster whose sole job was to push human beings around like pieces on a chess board. He had a cushy job – he didn't have to fight – he was just paid to tell others to do the dirty work. I finally let fly with some angry and disrespectful comment and slammed the receiver down hoping it would burst his eardrums.

Then I had to explain it all to Joan. My initial reaction was that we could pack some gear and take to the bush. If we had provisions we could have survived in the Urewera country for weeks, but I would have been a deserter – a wanted man.

Joan was understandably very upset, but there were no tears, just good family discipline. She realised I had to obey, so then we set off to find our friends John and Daphne to give them the sad news.

Next day the bus arrived in time and we set off for Rotorua. We were both a couple of dejected sad sacks. There was little to talk about but I did marvel at the wonderful bush scenery as we wended our way through the Urewera National Park.

We boarded the train at Rotorua for the long night journey via Hamilton to Auckland. I recall that as we travelled along we were both humming the tune of *Lili Marlene*. I had heard this lovely song and music for the first time when I arrived in New Zealand. It was the theme song of the German Afrika Korps. It was so popular that it had been adopted by the Allied Armies who were opposing them in North Africa. But having been in the Navy and having spent most of my service in the United Kingdom and the Indian Ocean this haunting melody had not reached me.

Joan and I were both sad creatures and *Lili Marlene* was just made for us. It has ever since been one of our favourite tunes, especially when sung by the original Lale Anderson. This lyric was written as long ago as 1923 by Hans Leip, a young German. Fifteen years later Norbert Schultz added the music and Lale Andersen, a Danish German cabaret artiste, featured the song in a Berlin night club. It was not a raging success. The story might have ended there had it not been for World War II.

In April 1941 the Germans started broadcasting propaganda from the Belgrade radio station and between bulletins they played old gramophone records, one of which was Lale Andersen's version of *Lili Marlene*. So popular did it become that the German Afrika Corps adopted it as their marching song. Tank crews of the 8th Army heard it on their radios and they too adopted it. And so it spread through the rest of the Allied forces in the Middle East.

We arrived in Auckland late in the evening and went to claim the luggage forwarded from Stratford, but because I could not produce a claim ticket the Railways employee refused to hand it over. A heated confrontation developed and it was only when I became aggressive and started to jump the counter that he let us in to find it.

With no accommodation booked we went across to the Station Hotel. The only person on duty was a rather elderly night porter who told us that what with Easter and Races all hotels in Auckland were full. I told him our tale of woe and that I had to catch the first naval liberty boat for *Philomel* at 5.30 a.m. next morning. He offered us the Commercial Room, made us tea and gave us pillows and a blanket. His kindness had been a great boost to our morale and I managed to slip him a £2 note which was quite a good sum in those days.

The taxi ordered for 5.20 a.m. did not appear, so sharing the luggage we ran 'as the crow flies', half a mile to the naval terminal jumping railway lines as we went. The pinnace was waiting impatiently, so there was time for only a brief farewell before it pulled away from the jetty. The sun was just coming up and I waved to Joan standing alone in the still dawn and was overcome with emotion. Usually in most situations I believe I am a fairly stoical person but not this time, because I wondered if we would ever see each other again!

On arrival at *Philomel* I was hastened away to the depot headquarters, to be greeted by a paymaster lieutenant who claimed that they had had one hell of a job getting me back. I wasn't in the mood to listen to any of that nonsense and as I was now a two ring lieutenant myself, having been notified of six months accelerated promotion dating from 25 October 1944, I really let this chairborne type have it. I was at the stage when I just didn't care whose toes I was treading on. And when he inferred that the Captain of *Philomel* wanted to see me I told him to go to hell. I immediately assumed that this would be a reprimand for the disrespect I had shown to the drafting commander at Navy Headquarters Wellington.

So I quickly got on the bus and set off for Whenuapai Air Base where I was scheduled to take passage on a Liberator aircraft to Sydney.

I was just climbing up the gangway to the Liberator when one of the station ground staff came running from the Control Tower yelling out.

'Lieutenant Masters is wanted on the phone by the Captain of *Philomel*.'

Holy hell – these buggers are persistent! They are determined to give me the works at this late stage.

Well, I had no option but to go back and answer the phone. It was not the Captain on the line but the Captain's secretary. It was the same little man that I had the altercation with an hour earlier. He asked me to wait because the Captain wanted to speak with me.

The Captain came on the line.

'Is that you Masters?'

'Yes sir.'

'I believe you are very upset about your recall and that you have just got married a few days ago.'

'That's correct, sir. I came home on three month's leave and I've only been here a month, married for a little over a week and this has been dropped on me.'

'Well, you know the situation, but apparently there has been a slight change since the Admiralty signal was received. I have been authorised to tell you that your leave can be extended for a very short time provided you give me a reliable address where I can contact you at very short notice.'

I had to think very quickly. I had nowhere to stay in Auckland, so I asked if I could go and await the call in my wife's flat at Huntly.

The Captain intimated that this would be satisfactory, but did not enquire about a telephone connection. I gave him the address and that was that.

In our conversation he seemed to be a very considerate officer and he made a special point of sympathising with my predicament.

About 17 years later I was to become closely associated with him in a long standing business relationship. My wife and I were having dinner with him one evening about 1970 when I was telling him about this episode. He listened very intently and suddenly said, 'You wouldn't believe this, Masters – I was the Captain at *Philomel* who spoke to you that day.' What an amazing coincidence! He was Captain Jack Hilliard DSC RNZNVR one of the very few reserve officers to reach that exalted rank.

I then telephoned the Railway Hotel hoping that Joan would still be there. She was, having just had some breakfast.

'Hello darling, it's Cappy here. Just stay where you are. I'll be back with you in about two hours.'

'Goodness, what on earth has happened?'

'I can't tell you now – it's all so very complicated, but please just stay in the hotel.'

When we eventually met I gave her a blow by blow report on the incredibly bungling sequence of events.

We caught the first available train back to Huntly, hoping against hope that the Navy would now forget all about me.

This, however, was not to be. On the following day, Sunday, Joan and I were out for a walk around the town when suddenly I was accosted by a police constable. I was dressed in civilian clothes, but because he had not seen me around the locality before it was quite logical for him to stop and ask if I was Lieutenant Masters. Apparently the Navy had discovered that the flat had no telephone connection so the man hunt was passed over to the local police. The constable told me to return to the flat and stay there until further notice.

The following evening a Public Service car arrived from Auckland to pick me up. It was futile to argue anymore. The only things missing were the handcuffs. I donned my uniform, bade a tearful farewell to my wife and then set off for Whenuapai Air Base once again.

In May 1946, six months after I had been honourably discharged from the Navy, I received an account from the Internal Affairs Department for the provision of this Public Service Transport!

Like a fool I paid it.

The date of departure by the Liberator was 1st April – April Fool's Day! Five and a half hours later I was at Mascot aerodrome, Sydney.

Here I reported to the Headquarters of the British Fleet where I was informed that I was required to travel to Brisbane the following night and wait at the Naval Barracks for further instructions.

The first part of this trip to Coff 's Harbour was during the hours of darkness, but from there on I was able to study the countryside. What I saw didn't impress me one little bit. The farmland was very poor in comparison with New Zealand.

The farm buildings were derelict, uncared for, with rusty iron roofs. The whole scene was most depressing. Even the towns we passed through in northern New South Wales and lower Queensland seemed to be lacking in civic pride. Brisbane itself was in those days a dusty, unkempt frontier type city.

As I expected, the RAN Barracks in the Brisbane River knew nothing about me, but on being presented with my travel documents they agreed to provide accommodation and victuals.

A few days passed and no further instructions came through, so I began to wonder what all the panic was about in relation to my departure. A week went by and it was well into the second week when I had to appeal to the Paymaster for an advance of money. This presented a problem because here I was a New Zealand Fleet Air Arm officer as a very temporary guest on an Australian Naval

Depot and seconded to the British Pacific Fleet. Slowly the reality of the situation penetrated the Aussie bureaucracy and they finally gave me some spending money.

This was the second boring and lonely period of my naval career, the first being at Katukurunda in Ceylon. I had no duties – nothing whatsoever to do except wander around and fill in time.

It was many years after the war ended before I realised how this frustrating situation had developed. Apparently at the time the Navy Office in Wellington received the signal from the Admiralty, it was a matter of extreme urgency. The fleet was still engaged in bombing and strafing airfields in northern Taiwan and the Sakashima islands. The fighter and bomber squadrons had been operating continuously for several weeks and had sustained some serious losses. The fleet was not equipped to stay in operations indefinitely and was confronted by a formidable logistics problem. Quite possibly the original plan was that I would be flown to Leyte in the Philippines and then take passage by a destroyer to join one of the aircraft carriers. However, on 23rd April, the American Admiral Spruance, Commander of the United States Pacific Fleet released the British Task Force No 57 to withdraw from the battle area and replenish at Leyte.

This change of operational plans was apparently the cause of my rather prolonged spell at Brisbane.

It was near the end of the third week that the movement order was received from Sydney. I was to report at the RAAF aerodrome at Archerfield just outside Brisbane. Here I boarded another DC 3 Dakota transport aircraft and four hours later landed at Townsville where we stayed overnight. Next day it was a four and a half hour flight to Milne Bay in Papua-New Guinea for refuelling and then on to the island of Momote in the Admiralty Islands group. This was another overnight stay.

The following day the flight took us across the northern coastline of Papua-New Guinea to the island of Biak, a Dutch East Indies possession which had just recently been cleared of Japanese troops. Another refuelling and we were away once more on a four hour flight across the sea to Pelilu in the Palau islands where we again stayed overnight.

The Palau Group consisted of a number of small islands, only one of which, Pelilu, had been captured and cleared of Japanese. It was being used as an aircraft staging post for flights from Australia to the Philippines.

Once captured, the Americans had moved in their 'Seabees', United States Navy construction teams, to clear the island and develop a runway. When we arrived there the island was base for two United States Marine Corsair fighter squadrons who had the interesting job of bombing and strafing Jap positions in the surrounding islands, one of which was barely four miles away. We watched the Corsair pilots take off, drop their bombs on the Jap fortifications, strafe any available targets and then return to base to re-arm. It was almost like flying around the local airfield circuit. The Yanks never take long to provide 'mod-cons'. They had their own officers mess established in a Nissen Hut and it was well stocked with a variety of alcoholic beverages. I enjoyed this night swapping experiences with the marine pilots who were more than a little interested to learn that I was a batsman who had deck landed a Corsair.

Next morning we were off at first light for Tacloban strip at Leyte. Coming in to the airfield across San Pedro Bay I could see a massive assortment of naval ships lying at anchor. I recognised the aircraft carriers as British, so the *Indefatigable* which I was to join must be one of these.

Tacloban was all American territory and I knew that the presence of the British Pacific Fleet was resented by many of the admirals in the United States Navy, so the situation called for the utmost respect and diplomacy.

Once off the aircraft I reported to the control tower where I was referred to a United States naval officer.

'And what can we do for you, bud?'

'I am posted to the British aircraft carrier HMS *Indefatigable* – is she in the Bay?'

'She sure is fella – can we give you a ride out?'

'Yes, I would appreciate that.'

'Well, stick around for a while and I'll get a berth for you.'

Later that afternoon I was taken down to the harbour jetty where a United States Navy liberty boat was about to leave.

British Pacific Fleet

As we drew near to the gangway I marvelled at the size of this carrier. It seemed enormous with the *Unicorn* and the escort carriers I had previously served in. As I lumbered my gear up the gangway I heard a voice 'Good day Cap – I believe you only had seven days.'

I looked up and there was my old mate Alister MacLeod standing at the quarter deck end of the gang way. Now how on earth did he know that I was a passenger in a United States Navy liberty boat or for that matter how did he know I was joining the *Indefatigable*. It was all very mysterious. I guessed that the reference to my short honeymoon must have come from his parents who had been informed by my parents and possibly written to him since my departure.

Once on the quarter deck Mac introduced me to Doug Alexander another Kiwi pilot in 887 Squadron. Then I recognised David Bryce-Buchanan who had been on a course with me at Kingston Canada. David was one of the carrier's batsmen. He then introduced me to the other batsman Peter Roome. It was becoming quite a select little welcoming party when I recognised another chap I knew. This was Lieutenant Commander Paul Whitfield who was on the same batsman's course with me at Easthaven. Paul had been posted to *Indefatigable* as the deputy Commander Flying. He did no actual batting but was in command of the flight deck division and would have to be capable of batting if required. I suppose he was relieved to see me arrive because my presence would dispose of any possibility that his services may be required at the 'coal face'. It was at this time that I discovered the name of the batsman who had been injured. It was none other than Lieutenant (A) Charles Patrick who was an old school mate from our days at New Plymouth Boy's High School.

Charles and I had actually been in the same class at school for 3 years.

David and Peter picked up my gear and escorted me down to the three-berth cabin which we would share when the ship's tannoy announced 'Lieutenants Roome, Bryce-Buchanan and Masters muster on the flight deck for ranging aircraft.'

This was ghastly. Hell's bells, I had only been in the ship half an hour. To make matters worse during my time as a deck landing instructor batsman I always had someone else to range the aircraft and even then it was only one at a time. Now, out of the blue, I was suddenly pitched into a situation where I would have to supervise the ranging, positioning and striking down 30 to 40 aircraft at a time. It was an awesome situation. Fortunately, on this occasion Peter and David were present to show me the ropes.

When I reached the flight deck I was also amazed to see that the carrier was actually under way and that all the other ships were heading out of the bay. I guess if I had not made that United States Liberty boat I might have ended my days as a beachcomber at Tacloban.

It was about 1700 hours that aircraft commenced coming up on the lift. It was a lovely late afternoon and hundreds of crew members were on the flight deck playing deck hockey, quoits or just promenading around the deck. We had just ranged one Avenger from the lift when suddenly there was heavy machine gun fire. Everyone dropped instantaneously. The firing continued. I immediately thought we were under constant attack from Japanese aircraft, but surely they could not be in this area. Finally the firing stopped and people stood up to assess the cause. What had happened was that the last Avenger which had been brought up on the lift with its wings folded back, had 'copped' a runaway 0.5 machine gun in its wing. This was apparently caused by a faulty solenoid.

This gun with its barrel pointing down at one distinct spot on the light steel plated section of the flight deck fired round after round until it penetrated the deck, then the wooden quarter deck below to finally penetrate the bulk head of a cabin below the quarter deck. Once there the bullets in a continuous stream whirled around inside this cabin where three aircrew officers were either asleep or resting. All three were killed in this incredible accident.

This had all happened within two hours of my arrival in *Indefati-*

gable. I began to wonder, what with all the scary incidents that I had been involved in during the past two years, whether my number was about to come up.

These three unfortunate officers were buried at sea from the quarter deck next day as we sailed past the coast of Formosa (now Taiwan). Burials at sea are very sad affairs.

Late in the night of the 2nd May our task force 57 comprising two battleships, *King George V* and *Howe*, four fleet carriers, *Indomitable*, *Victorious*, *Illustrious* and *Indefatigable*, plus five cruisers, *Black Prince*, *Swiftsure*, *Euryalus*, *Gambia*, *Uganda* and 15 destroyers, reached its operational area about 100 miles east of the Sakashima Gunto archipelago. At 0300 hours the following morning a Royal Navy Marine came in to our cabin and gave the three of us a good wakey-wakey. He waited a short while to make certain that we turned out.

We three batsmen then went to the wardroom for a quick 'cuppa' and then up to the dark and windy flight deck to range the aircraft for the first strike which would take off at 0545 hours.

The first aircraft to be flown off were eight Seafires which operated as Combat Air Patrol above the whole fleet. They were followed by Strike Able comprising of eight Fireflies, each armed with eight only 60 lb rockets for ground attack. Once airborne the Fireflies would be joined by the Avenger bombers each carrying four only 500 lb General Purpose or armour piercing bombs. The fighter escort to the target was provided by Corsair and Hellcat fighters from the other three carriers. Each strike would comprise approximately 48 Avengers, eight Fireflies and possibly 36 or more escorting fighters.

The prime purpose of our Task Force 57 was to neutralise three airfields, Hirara, Nobara and Sugama, on the island of Miyako Jima which were being used by the Japanese as staging posts to move kamikaze and other aircraft through from Formosa to Okinawa. These airfields were subject to intense bombing raids for two days out of every three. On the night of the second day the force would withdraw and rendezvous with the fleet train comprising a number of oil tankers, supply ships and other warships, including a few escort carriers. Having refuelled and replenished the force would return to strike at these airfields for a further two days.

Unfortunately, these islands were not suitable bombing targets because of the coral structure. The runways would be cratered in the raids, but the wily Japs would work all through the night and restore them for operational use the following day. This routine went on week after week. Our aircraft undoubtedly did a tremendous amount of damage and prevented the passage of Japanese aircraft from attacking the much larger United States Task Force 58 operating further north of Okinawa.

At this point it is perhaps appropriate to refer to the diplomatic negotiations that preceded the involvement of the British Pacific Fleet.

It was at a Big Three (United States, Britain and Free French) meeting in Quebec 1944 that the formation of a British Pacific Fleet was first mooted. With the war in Europe moving towards total victory, the British political and military leaders were anxious to play a major role in the final assault on Japan. Until that time the war in the Pacific had been largely an American effort with strong support from Australia and New Zealand in island hopping operations.

The Chief of Staff United States Navy, Admiral King strongly resisted the proposal for the Royal Navy to participate in the Northern Pacific waters. He considered that it would be more appropriate for British warships to be used in mopping up operations in Japan's fast disintegrating empire in the Southern area. In many quarters King's attitude was construed as antipathy towards the Royal Navy, but in reality he had good grounds for adopting that stance. His objections were based more on a matter of logistics. He reasoned that the British ships were not at that time capable of being refuelled at sea and would therefore have to withdraw from the battle zone from time to time to replenish and effect repairs.

The American Navy on the other hand had perfected an efficient auxiliary fleet, consisting of many hundreds of ships which were capable of providing everything that the main fighting units needed in the way of fuel, spare aircraft, replacement pilots, spares etc.

It was President Roosevelt who finally overruled Admiral King and paved the way for the Royal Navy to play a major supporting role in the Okinawa campaign and in subsequent attacks on the Japanese mainland.

Task Force 57, as the Royal Navy component came to be known, formed up and after several working up operations against Japanese targets at Palembang and Sourabaya in Sumatra, proceeded to Sydney to make the final preparations for the assault against Japan.

The naval command structure was the United States Chief of

Staff, Admiral Ernest King, United States Commander Pacific Fleet, Admiral Chester Nimitz, Commander British Pacific Fleet, Admiral Sir Bruce Fraser, Commander United States 5th Fleet, Admiral Spruance, Commander British Task Force 57, Vice Admiral Henry B. Rawlings, Commander Group Task Force 57, Rear Admiral Sir Philip Vian, United States Task Force 58, Vice Admiral Marc Mitscher, Commander British Fleet Train Task Force 112, Rear Admiral D. B. Fisher.

The combination of the American Task Force 58 with the British Task Force 57 became a mammoth display of sea and air power. Admiral Spruance had at his disposal more than 1,200 ships of war, including the respective fleet trains.

The British force was deployed to cover the left flanks of the Okinawa operation.

The first strikes against the Sakashima Group, operation Iceberg No I, commenced at dawn on 26th March and continued relentlessly for 26 days. The routine being two to three days strikes followed by one to two days withdrawal for refuelling and replenishment.

It was on 1st April (April Fools' Day) that HMS *Indefatigable* was hit by a Japanese suicide bomber, which hit the flight deck near the base of the island causing a number of casualties and putting the flight deck temporarily out of action. It was under attack like this that the heavily armoured decks of the British carriers proved their worth. Had this been an American carrier which had a wooden flight deck, the *Indefatigable* would undoubtedly have caught fire, the hangers exploded and the ship gone down. The shipwright's party was quickly on hand to fill the big dent with quick setting concrete. The remnants of the Jap aircraft were pushed over the side and flying operations resumed within a few hours.

About this time the American task force was under heavy and sustained attacks from kamikaze bombers. In his book *Action This Day* Rear Admiral Vian records that more than 700 aircraft, of which 355 were Kamikaze, left Kyushu and arrived over the United States Fleet at 1500 hours that day. The United States combat air patrols broke up the formations, but some 400 of the attackers broke through. Three picket destroyers which were deployed to give back-up to the normal radar warning system were sunk along with three other destroyers of the inner protective screen. Eighteen other vessels were damaged, nearly all by suicide attacks. The cost to the enemy was at least 300 aircraft in explosions or shot down.

It was at this stage that Admiral Spruance decided to re-deploy the British Task Force to attack the northern airfields in Formosa from where most of the kamikazes were based. It was in the course of these raids on 12th and 13th April that a friend, 'Winnie' Churchill, was shot down by Japanese anti-aircraft fire. Winnie was another daredevil – a potential Victoria Cross winner if there ever was one. Winnie was a senior Flight Leader in 1833 Corsair squadron in HMS *Illustrious.* His Commanding Officer, Norman Hanson knew of Winnie's foolhardy exploits and warned him before take off not to take more than one strafing run over the airfield. Winnie apparently made two and was really enjoying setting Jap aircraft alight and sending Japs scampering all over the field so he came in like a bat out of hell for a third pass. This time the Jap gunners were right on target.

By this time the Japs' kamikaze force once again turned its attention to the BPF. This time the *Indomitable* narrowly escaped being hit. A further three days strike followed against Sakashima Gunto by which time the Force had just about shot its bolt. There were problems with refuelling from the small slow tankers and many of the aircrews were beginning to show signs of strain. The task force withdrew to Leyte and on 23rd April anchored in San Pedro Bay.

It was here I joined the *Indefatigable* on 28th April 1945 and I was to stay on board for just over one month before a replacement batsman was appointed. These four weeks were the toughest constant physical exercise I had ever experienced. Although there were three batsmen to share the deck landing duties, the hours of duty were particularly demanding. On strike days we would be aroused by the Royal Marine servant at 0300 hours. We did not work watches (four hours on, four hours off) like the seaman branch – we were on call from the first range of aircraft at about 0400 hours to 1800 hours in the evening. In my own case I was required to be the standby night batsman in case of any deck landing accidents on HMS *Indomitable* in which case we would have to take one or more of their night fighter Hellcats on to our deck. It is interesting to note that the fleet's main night batsman was none other than my old friend and protégé, Joe Brough.

That routine meant that apart from the odd rest that I could have during the day in the aircrew room on the island, I was on call for 17 hours on each strike day, during which time I would be required to hold the bats in a 30 knot wind to control as many as 48 landings in a day. This was as tough as being a boxer in a 12–15 round contest.

On many occasions I can recall going down to the wardroom for my evening meal at 2000 hours, meeting my old mate Alister MacLeod who would suggest a quiet noggin, but I was so tired I had to say no. After the meal I was into my bunk to get what little sleep Admiral Vian would allocate to me. Peter Roome and David Bryce-Buchanan agreed to apportion the landings so that I controlled most of the Seafires and they looked after the Avengers and Fireflies. Because the Seafire sorties were of shorter duration I tended to be on the job rather more frequently than they were.

During this period the *Indefatigable*'s two Seafire Squadrons 887 and 894 were achieving a very fast deck landing recovery rate. The overall average landing interval was reduced to 51 seconds with the best performance being the landing on of eight Seafires with an average touch down interval of only 34.3 seconds. Considering the poor visibility from the Seafire cockpit and its fragile under-carriage this was a most impressive performance.

A typical days batting would be;

May 8th 30 Seafires – 12 Avengers
12th 24 Seafires – 6 Avengers
16th 28 Seafires – 12 Avengers – 8 Fireflies

On this last day the wardroom had been hit by food poisoning. Many aircrews were unable to fly, so those who were fit had to fly double the number of normal sorties. Both Peter Roome and David Bryce-Buchanan succumbed to the illness, so for that day I was the only batsman on duty. Apart from one other day, this was the only time I batted Fireflies. No 1770 Firefly Squadron was commanded by a Royal Marine Major V. G. B. Cheesman DSO, MBE, DSC a highly decorated officer. Regrettably, however, Cheesman was one of few pilots who apparently considered a batsman as being superfluous to his requirements. On my one and only experience with Mr Cheesman he completely ignored the signals I gave him, so after he had landed I threw the bats down on the deck, declaring the Fireflies in future could land themselves. It was a calculated insult and an act of professional arrogance on Cheesman's part. He was without question a very good pilot, but in a very rough sea he would have been very much more dependent on the assistance of the batsman. I heard nothing more about it from either the Commander Flying or Cheesman himself. Possibly the Commander may have supported my action.

In comparison, because I was concentrating on the Seafire pilots who had the most difficult aircraft of all to deck land, I received the greatest cooperation. In a few cases I could tell who was in the cockpit by the style of their approach to the deck. One of these was Alister MacLeod. His technique was faultless. Like Cheesman, Mac did not really need a batsman in a calm sea, but he did at least comply with signals when a slight change of height speed or direction was necessary. Doug Alexander was another ace decklander who was easily recognisable. On the evening of 8th May I did make a concession to celebrate with Doug his 100th deck landing, nearly all of which were in Seafires. That was some achievement.

Another cause for celebration was a few days earlier on 4th May when Mac leading a flight of four Seafires intercepted some kamikaze intruders and shot down three AGM (Zero) fighters. Mac, sub lieutenant Charlich and Chief Petty Officer Bird were credited with one each. On this same day Dickie Reynolds shot down another Zero while sub-lieutenant Miseldine and CPO Danile shared a D3A (Val). Five victories in one day from the *Indefatigable* squadrons was a respectable performance by any standard. On the same day nine other enemy aircraft were shot down by Corsairs and Hellcats.

Amidst the many exciting moments we had under kamikaze attacks and the sad moments when aircrews were shot down or returned wounded, there were some lighter moments. One that comes to mind occurred when the fleet was at oiling stations.

Indefatigable was 'hooked' up to an oil tanker on the port side and to a destroyer on the starboard side, a formation which calls for skilful helmsmanship. The destroyer had passed over a breeches buoy and commenced transferring mail and replacement aircrews to the flight deck of *Indefatigable*. I was standing directly alongside our executive officer Commander Whitfield who was watching the transfer through his telescope.

Suddenly in his delightful Irish brogue he proclaimed: 'Good heavens. It's that devil Sheerin again.' At that distance it was difficult to recognise faces with the naked eye, but as the buoy drew closer sure enough it was Jimmy Sheerin. Jimmy was greeted by rousing cheers from the assembled aircrews and as he stepped out of his harness, he clapped his hands above his head in a typical theatrical wrestler's gesture. Despite his many misdemeanours Jimmy was a lovable character, but this time his past had caught up with him. I doubt whether he flew at all on this operation.

I recall two incidents with Firefly aircraft. One was with a replacement being flown over from an escort carrier. The *Indefatigable* had just commenced to turn into wind to take the landing when the Firefly developed a monstrous oil leak which could be seen streaming behind it. The pilot must have noticed a sudden drop in oil pressure, so he determined to get down as soon as possible. This was one of the few Fireflies which I batted, so when I saw him drop his undercarriage I waved him off because *Indefatigable* was still in its turn into wind. The pilot, however, was desperate to land or ditch, so he kept following our carrier round to try and straighten up in his final approach. A further emphatic wave off was given but he persisted in coming on. He also ignored the two red warning rockets fired from the bridge, and finally like it or not I just had to take him on. He touched down like a bat out of hell but thankfully caught a wire. Despite his good luck he received a very stern reprimand from 'Wings'.

On another occasion a Firefly returned from a strike with its eight rockets still on the launching rails. With the additional weight it would require a faster approach speed to prevent a stall. The pilot landed safely but as the tail of his aircraft subsided on the deck the eight rockets went off with a magnificent 'whoosh'. Because the fuselage was now in a stationary position the trajectory for the rockets had become relatively safe and disappeared over the bows without hitting anyone.

I always felt that one of the curses of the Navy was the traditional daily tot of rum. I realise that it was one of the few luxuries that the matelots could enjoy, but it could be a problem particularly when served while the ship was at 'action stations'. The flight deck division which provided aircraft handling parties comprised two watches, both of which were predominantly New Foundlanders. Under normal circumstances, these chaps were quite pleasant, good humoured but not overly intelligent characters. But once they had had their tot of rum at action stations they were almost impossible to deal with. Manoeuvring heavy aircraft like Avengers requires quite a physical effort but these New Foundlanders would be half asleep after their tot. They were quite indifferent to the orders, the threats, and cajoling.

At the height of the kamikaze raids there was a popular conjecture that the Japanese suicide 'Divine Wind' pilots were clad in ceremonial white robes. No-one had actually seen any pilots, because after their attacks they either dived into the sea or if they hit a ship they would have been blown into smithereens. One day however, while the fleet was under intense attack from a large number of kamikazes, one was shot down by anti-aircraft fire just ahead of our carrier. The aircraft had gone into the sea but it was still afloat as we went past no more than 50 yards away. From where I was standing on the batsman's position on the flight deck I could clearly see the pilot still strapped in the cockpit either killed or unconscious. He was wearing a dark green flying suit so that laid to rest the theory about ceremonial robes.

The living conditions in our aircraft carriers in tropical climates were absolutely abominable. While at action stations all scuttles (portholes) had to be closed for damage control so there was no free flow of air from the outside. The steel decks and the hull became very hot in the daytime, so the interior of the carrier developed an oven-like temperature. Skin diseases, prickly heat and impetigo which is contagious, were rife. A high percentage of the aircrew and seamen would be seen with faces and other parts of their bodies painted with gentian violet. Fresh water was also at a premium. There was none for personal hygiene – all showers had to be in cold salt water. It was some consolation, however, to know that there was always a little water to put with our gin in the wardroom.

One of the most memorable occasions was the celebration for VE day, the surrender of Germany.

On 8th May after a really hostile day of kamikaze attacks during which both the *Formidable* and *Victorious* were hit, we received a signal from His Majesty King George VI: 'Splice the Mainbrace.' This meant a special issue tot of rum to every man in the fleet.

The fleet withdrew immediately to oiling stations and that night was one of prolonged celebration.

The tot was served immediately after the evening meal, so some of the 'Old Hands' intercepted the young midshipmen and sub-lieutenants as they emerged from the wardroom mess and solicited them for their tot. A sub-lieutenant's wine bill allowance was £1/10/0 per month, a full lieutenant £2/-/- per month. The duty free price for a nip of spirits was threepence, which meant that a full lieutenant was entitled to 160 nips per month. For some of the 'hard shots' this was not enough, so they resorted to 'borrowing' from some of the more abstemious characters. This night some of the 'hard shots' probably garnered four to six tots from the younger airmen. This was the ingredient for a really good party. At a very late hour that night I recall seeing my friend Alister MacLeod, clad in just a pair of shorts slowly swinging around the wardroom fan. Commander Whitfield came over, placed his hand on Mac's shoulder and said in his lilting Irish brogue, 'MacLeod old chap – this is lamentable behaviour. Be so kind as to remove yourself.'

Then turning to Doug Alexander and myself he said, 'Alexander and Masters, kindly disentangle this remarkable gymnast and escort him off to his cabin. He has obviously had a trying day and I think we can dispense with any encores.'

Two days later we were back in action again. There was a very tense situation at dusk that evening when a flight of four Seafires returned from a sortie to investigate some intruders. The flight leader was Sub-Lieutenant (A) Dickie Reynolds who had by that time become the highest scoring Seafire pilot. By the time they returned light was fading and I had lighted bats ready for use. Reynolds and two other pilots landed without incident but the fourth member was obviously pretty 'twitched' up. His first two approaches were dangerous, so I had to give him wave offs. There was another wave off on the third approach. Then I recalled my own experience of trying to land in the Bay of Biscay. I realised that this young pilot was probably scared stiff. If I didn't get him down in one piece this time he might go in the 'drink' and be lost in the darkness. So on this approach I kept taking him. He was far too high coming over the round down but I gave him a high cut over the third wire and because he was right on the stall the Seafire dropped like a stone. As I batted this young pilot I could appreciate his difficulty only too well. With his head outside in the slipstream on the portside of the cockpit his forward vision at night was obscured by gouts of flame from six exhaust stubs. He could hardly see me. For him it must have been a frightening situation.

It was such a heavy landing that the left oleo leg crumpled the Seafire's wing. But the pilot was alive – that was the main thing.

In a similar situation a Corsair or Hellcat could have been cut from that height and would have sustained no damage whatsoever. As a former Seafire pilot I still loved this delightful little aircraft, but as a batsman I soon came to realise that it was not robust enough, nor did it have the endurance range to be a good naval fighter. In the Pacific theatre it could really be employed only in the defensive role.

Apparently Rear Admiral Vian was watching this incident from the bridge of his flagship HMS *Indomitable* in the rapidly fading light. He made this signal by Aldis lamp to our carrier, 'Congratulations to Sub-Lieutenant Reynolds for leading his men back.'

That was typical of Vian's concern for his aircrews.

Our last strikes were carried out on 15th May following which the British Fleet withdrew and returned to Sydney. It had been at sea for 62 days broken only by eight days in San Pedro Bay. During that time there had been 23 'strike' days, 4691 sorties flown, 927 tons of bombs dropped and 950 rocket projectiles discharged. Seventy five enemy aircraft had been destroyed for the loss of 26 of ours. But we had a further 134 through kamikaze attacks or accidents. Deck landing accidents accounted for 61 of these. We had lost 41 pilots or aircrew killed or missing. A further 44 officers and men were killed and 38 wounded as a result of Kamikaze attacks on the ship.

The foregoing statistics were recorded by Admiral Vian in his book *Action This Day.*

During the 22 days I was in *Indefatigable* I battled 361 sorties without any accidents or fatalities. It had been hard physical effort – I wasn't sorry we were on the way back – with a bit of luck I would be able to get out of batting.

Once back in Sydney I called at the headquarters of the BPF and requested an audience with the Drafting Commander. I was received by Lieutenant Commander (A) Miller RN, the same officer with whom I had been briefly associated with at Katukurunda in Ceylon. Instinctively I did not expect a very sympathetic hearing, but my fears were unfounded. First of all, on the question of my unexpired leave, regrettably this could not be reinstated. So what did I want to do? I was being given a preference – that was a change. So I intimated that the least I was hoping for was a Senior Pilot's appointment, preferably in a Corsair Squadron. Unfortunately, there were no immediate vacancies. How about taking over a 12 aircraft Seafire squadron which was scheduled to form up in Queensland in a month's time? This sounded like a CAP outfit probably based in an escort carrier attached to the oiling fleet. No, that did not appeal – Corsairs were what I wanted. Well, there was a Corsair squadron No 1845 just forming up at Maryborough in Queensland. So far only the Commanding Officer and the senior pilot had been appointed. I enquired who they were and discovered that I knew both of them. The Commanding Officer was Lieutenant Commander (A) R. H. (Dickie) Grose whom I had known when he was Commanding Officer of 879 Seafire Squadron in HMS *Attacker* during the Salerno campaign. The Senior Pilot was Lieutenant (A) Spence Wright who had left New Zealand with me in the *Dominion Monarch* draft.

Well, I did suffer a slight disappointment that I would not have a senior pilot's posting, but at least it was a Corsair squadron, so I told Commander Miller that I would take it. On 1st July 1945 I flew by an Expediter to Maryborough and reported to Dickie Grose. At that stage we only had three Corsairs, one each for Dickie, Spence and myself. On 10th July we received a signal to move the whole squadron to Nowra, New South Wales. On 10th July Dickie Grose detailed me to fly one Corsair down to Nowra and arrange for the arrival of the squadron personnel while he and Spence Wright supervised the movement order for the ground staff, spares etc. This was to be a four hour trip and as the weather report was good I decided to follow the coastline most of the way. A member of the RAAF staff at Maryborough suggested that I should take note of a stretch of beach about 50–60 miles south of the entrance to the Brisbane river which would one day become a big city. As I flew past these golden sands all I could see were stray groups of dilapidated batches with rusty iron roofs, which seemed to be typical of Australia at that time. The prediction was to become true, within ten years this area had been developed as Surfers' Paradise.

On approaching Sydney harbour I decided to come in on a low level beat up of Elizabeth Bay where my Uncle and Aunt had a seaside apartment. I had been staying with them only a week or so previously but never guessed that I would be returning so soon.

Nowra turned out to be an RAAF aerodrome, one of several in and around Sydney that had been loaned to the Fleet Air Arm during the development of the British Pacific Fleet. Ours was to be the only operational squadron in residence at that time. All other Corsairs had been delivered here and 18 more pilots had been posted to 1845 squadron. These included two more Kiwis, Graham 'Kanga' Wiley and Charlie French, both of whom had previous operational experience. With the exception of one two-ring lieutenant who must have spent some time in a second line squadron, the remaining pilots were all young lads straight from training school.

Obviously it was going to take at least two months to work this team into shape. So the working up got going at a frenzied pace, air drills, air to ground firing, dive bombing, camera attacks, ADDLS which I had to take, then Dickie Grose came up with a truly alarming requirement. He informed me that a date had been scheduled for this squadron of relatively 'green' pilots to carry out night deck landings on the carrier HMS *Glory* in Jervois Bay. Holy Hell, this was something no one had bargained for – the prospect was really alarming.

Dickie apologised but said I would have to take the lads for night ADDLS. The curse of being a batsman was becoming a bit hard to wear. No mention was made as to who would be giving me my night ADDLS. What a bloody shambles this was!

It was about this time while at Nowra, that I became conscious of an unusual symptom. I had caught a slight cold and whenever I blew my nose into a handkerchief I noticed that air was expelled from both of my ears. Very intriguing, but I thought no more about it until one day I was combing my hair before a mirror. I had been smoking a cigarette and to my amazement I noticed what seemed to be smoke trickling out both ears. Well, this was really weird. So I had another puff, inhaled and held my nose and the smoke literally poured out. I displayed this phenomenon to some squadron mates who thoroughly enjoyed the performance. One suggested that it could become a popular post-war stage performance. Then someone who knew a little more about the human anatomy than I, declared that both my eardrums had been perforated probably as a result of high pressure dives in aircraft. The fact was, however, that my flying hours over the previous 12 months had been minimal, so there must have been some other reason for the perforations.

It was only when my hearing deteriorated years later that the real cause of the problem was identified. It was the concussion from the anti-aircraft gun fire during the kamikaze attack on 8th May 1945.

At the time of writing my loss of hearing measures over 50%.

On 6th August an awesome event which presaged the end of the war occurred in the sky over the Japanese city of Hiroshima.

An American Boeing Superfortress bomber flying at 30,000 feet from a United States base on Saipan had dropped the first atomic bomb. The devastation caused by this single bomb was horrendous. More than four square miles of the city were obliterated. Of an estimated population of 320,000, 78,150 people were killed, 13,983 missing and over 40,000 seriously injured.

That night I had returned to my cabin early to write a letter to my wife. I had just completed it and was about to go to bed when two breathless characters burst in. They were Bill Belcher who had been on the training course while I was at Puttalam, Ceylon, and Lieutenant Commander (A) P. N. Charlton DFC, RN.

'Come on, Cappy – you'd better come back to the wardroom. The Yanks have just dropped a big bomb on Japan.'

'So what? You jokers are both half fonged that's the trouble.'

'No, this is fair dinkum, Cap,' says Bill.

'This was a special super bomb – they called it an atom bomb.'

I quickly dressed and followed them back to the wardroom where a magnificent celebration was getting underway.

Three days later another atom bomb was dropped on the Japanese city of Nagasaki, again with a frightful death toll.

Another week passed with the Japanese government apparently still committed to the war.

Then on 17th August came the stupendous announcement that the Japanese Emperor Hirohito had ordered his forces to lay down their arms.

The sense of relief was unbelievable, but flying practice continued albeit at a much slower tempo.

The proposal for night deck landings was put on hold, but not before one pilot had made a forced landing one night in the aerodrome circuit.

Thankfully he survived the crash. The postponement of the night deck landings came as a great comfort to me because, after my determined effort to land on the hanger at Yeovilton, I did not exactly fancy my talent as a night fighter pilot. I am certain also that it prolonged the lives of the many inexperienced young men in our squadron.

This was an opportune time to submit a request to see the captain of the air station. I received a very sympathetic hearing and was told to pack up and present myself at the Fleet Headquarters in Sydney for passage home to New Zealand.

I was to join an escort carrier HMS *Vindex* which was leaving for Auckland on 26th August.

In company with several other Fleet Air Arm pilots I travelled overnight by train to Brisbane, but when we arrived at the berth in Brisbane river, the *Vindex* was nowhere to be seen. The Australian naval authorities told us she had sailed down the river about 20 minutes previously.

We quickly took action and managed to persuade the Aussies to provide a naval pinnace so we could try to catch her up before she was out in the open sea. We tossed our gear on board and the helmsman set off at full throttle.

About eight miles down the river as we swung round a bend near the Royal Queensland Yacht Club we could see the *Vindex* in the distance. The gap was slowly closing until finally we were within hailing distance just outside the entrance to the river. The *Vindex* hove to, lowered a gangway and we thankfully climbed on board.

This was becoming rather an unusual habit, climbing on board departing ships and aircraft at the very last minute. Anyway our determination and ingenuity paid dividends, we were at long last on the way home. My level of confidence in the navy was such that if we had missed the ship, someone in Admiralty might have 'yanked' me back for some more batting in some remote and God-forsaken naval establishment.

The four day crossing of the Tasman passed without incident and on Friday 31st August we entered Auckland harbour on a crisp sunny spring day. I could see no reason for renewing acquaintance with *Philomel* after my earlier experience. I gave it the widest berth possible.

Once ashore I headed for the Post Office to send a telegram to Joan who would not have known of my impending arrival. Once again without any knowledge of the rail timetables, I merely said I would be arriving by rail. Joan quite naturally assumed that I would be travelling that day but this happened to be a day when the evening train did not stop in Huntly. She assumed therefore that I must be travelling as far as Frankton, so she chartered a taxi from Huntly only to find that I was not on board. Prudently she had instructed the taxi driver to wait, so she was able to return, albeit rather sorrowful and disappointed. Years later, she told me that this fruitless quest had cost her £5, which must have been almost a week's wages. Undaunted, however, she caught the first train from Huntly to Auckland the following morning, so when I arrived at Auckland railway station, Joan was waiting for me. As I entered I saw her at the far end of the concourse. Even at that distance she looked really lovely dressed in a trim form fitting navy blue coat. It was a vision I will never forget – I was overwhelmed by a profound sense of relief. There was no bashfulness this time – caution was cast aside as we ran to each other. I was one of the lucky ones – for me the war was finally over.

Fifty years later as I pen these lines, I have no regrets. To have served in the Royal Navy and in particular the Fleet Air Arm was a unique privilege. It was an elite service. When we volunteered we were young and the motivation was primarily one of adventure – we got that in good measure. Life was never dull. There were times of frivolity, there were times of anxiety, there were times of extreme danger and there were times of sadness at the loss of one's friends. I feel very humble that I was one of those who survived.

The Final Assault On Japan

Following its return to Sydney on 1st June 1945, Task Force 57 was allocated barely three weeks to repair damage, replenish supplies, and undertake routine maintenance before returning to the battle area. The air squadrons from *Indefatigable, Formidable* and *Victorious* were flown to shore bases near Sydney where any necessary modifications were carried out and tasks such as gun alignment, compass swinging etc. attended to. The logistics problem was stupendous.

The responsibilities covered fuel, water, food, bombs, rockets, anti-aircraft shells, aircraft ammunition, spare parts for aircraft radios, fighter direction, replacement aircrews, medical supplies etc., etc. The requisitioning was endless but it is to the credit of the Royal Navy Supply Branch that the fleet complied with the target date despite the fact that it was dependent on a supply line 12,000 miles away in the United Kingdom.

The main force which had now been designated Task Force 37 sailed from Sydney on 23rd June. It comprised the battleships *King George V*, in which Admiral Rawlings flew his flag and *Howe*, the aircraft carriers, *Formidable* and *Victorious*, the cruisers HMS *Newfoundland*, HMS *Euryalus*, NMNZA *Achilles*, HMNZS *Gambia*, HMCS *Uganda* and 22 assorted destroyers, of which six were Australian. The carrier *Indefatigable* followed shortly after and rejoined the main strike force at Manus in the Admiralty Islands. HMS *Indomitable* had to undergo a short refit and was withdrawn from this operation to be replaced by HMS *Implacable* which awaited the fleet at Manus.

While waiting for Task Force 37 to assemble at Manus, the carrier *Implacable* had been deployed to carry out air strikes against the Japanese base in the Truk Islands. This garrison had been bypassed by the American forces in their island hopping advance towards the

Philippines. It was a convenient opportunity to give the *Implacable* air group at taste of hot warfare before proceeding to the forward area.

The force sailed from Manus on 6th July to rendezvous on 16th with the American 3rd Fleet now under the command of Admiral Halsey. HMS *Indefatigable* was unfortunately delayed at Manus due to a fault in her air compressors rejoining the combined fleet on 20th July.

Admiral Halsey now had at his disposal a massive fleet comprising 10 battleships, 16 aircraft carriers, 25 cruisers and approximately 75 destroyers plus an air sea rescue component of more than 20 submarines and over 50 flying boats.

Several 'fleet trains' comprising oil tankers, destroyers and 'Woolworth' escort carriers were additional to this total.

In his book *Action This Day* Admiral Sir Philip Vian relates how he and Admiral Rawlings were summoned on board Halsey's flagship the USS *Missouri*. Vian assessed Halsey as possessing all the 'attributes of mind and body which go to the make up of a great Seaman to which was added a wide humanity,' Halsey was aware of the logistic problem of the British Fleet which would be operating thousands of nautical miles from its nearest base, whereas the American fleet or part of it could withdraw a relatively short distance to refit and replenish at Pearl Harbour in Hawaii. When it came to the subject of tactical command Rawlings was in no doubt that the combined fleet would act as a single unit under the overall command of Admiral Halsey.

This is described by Halsey in the following passage in the book, *Admiral Halsey's Story*.

> 'When I was informed at Pearl Harbour that the British Pacific Fleet would report to me, I naturally assumed that I would have full operational control, but when I re-read the plan at Leyte I discovered that the tactical control had been reserved. This would force me to present Admiral Rawlings with three alternatives.
>
> (1) Task Force 37 would operate close aboard us as another Task Group in Task Force 38; it would receive direct orders from me but it would be privy to the orders I gave Task Force 38. These it would consider as suggestions to be followed to our mutual advantage thereby assuring us a concentrated force with concentrated weapons.

(2) Task Force 37 would operate independently some 60 to 70 miles away thereby preserving its technical identity at the cost of a divided force (I stipulated that I would consent to this choice only if the request was put in writing).

(3) Task Force 37 would operate completely independently against soft spots in Japan which we would recommend if so desired.

Rawlings did not hesitate. He said, 'Of course. I'll accept the No 1 option.'

My admiration for him began at that moment.'

At Pearl Harbour, however, Admiral Chester Nimitz the American Commander in Chief Pacific, countermanded Halsey's intentions. Halsey, however, persisted with his tactical plan and from that moment the American and British fleets operated alongside each other as one grand unit.

Considering the earlier opposition to the British involvement voiced by Admiral King C-in-C of the entire American Navy this was a magnificent achievement. Undoubtedly the British operations against the Japanese bases in Sumatra, Formosa and Sakashima Gunto and the minimal damage to our warships under Kamikaze attacks had finally convinced the American naval command that we were a competent well trained force.

The main problems now confronting the British Force was the speed differential of its battleships and the relatively short radius of action its Seafire CAP fighters. The British battleships had a maximum speed of 26 knots, whereas their American counterparts were all capable of 30 knots. This meant that the British carriers, cruisers and destroyers were obliged to conform to the best speed of our major units.

The endurance of the Seafires was increased by the use of extra large overload petrol tanks which precluded the carriage of bombs and reduced speed and manoeuvrability in the air until the tanks could be discarded, before going into action. At 1600 hours in the afternoon of 16th July 1945 the mighty combined fleet set course for the position from which aircraft would be launched, the following morning for the assault on the Japanese mainland.

Admiral Halsey had at his disposal 1200 aircraft in the American carriers and 255 in the British carriers. Included in the force was the United States carrier *Bonhomme Richard* which was specially equipped for night offensive operations.

To compensate for the variable speeds of the various groups of carriers and the differences in the duration of CAP fighters called for predetermined times for turning in and out of wind. As Admiral Vian relates the BPF was usually ready, but not without very considerable stress and strain.

The first strike against the Japanese mainland took place on 17th July against part of the coast of Honshu and in between Tokyo and Sendai, but bad weather conditions precluded any effective attacks. Elements of 1834 Corsair squadron from HMS *Victorious* did however fly almost across the island of Honshu and attacked Niigarta airfield on the other side. The distance across Japan at this point was approximately 110 miles.

During the next four weeks leading up to the Japanese surrender on 17th August, the Fleet Air Arm attacked the eastern areas of Japan over a wide area from Tokyo Bay, Nagoya and Tokushima in the South. Operations were interrupted by several typhoons during which fleets manoeuvred hundreds of warships without collisions.

Indefatigable's No 24 Seafire Wing and *Implacable*' No 38 Seafire Wing both equipped with long range drop tanks were now being employed in an offensive role against Japanese airfields and shipping.

It was during an attack on shipping in the Nagoya area on 30th July that Doug Alexander was shot down by Japanese anti-aircraft fire while leading a 'ramrod' of eight Seafires. His death must have been a grievous blow to Alister MacLeod. They had been together for a long time and had developed a close friendship. Although my acquaintance with Doug was more recent I recall him as being one of the finest men I had been privileged to meet in the Fleet Air Arm.

In a most unusual gesture, the English Naval Historian David Brown, who was himself a naval aviator 1957–69, dedicated his book *The Seafire* as recently as 1989 to the memory of Doug Alexander, a man whom he had never known.

It was about this time that Alister MacLeod assumed command of *Indefatigable*'s No 887 Squadron for the final few weeks of operations against Japan.

On 9th August, some huge combined strikes were launched at previously untouched airfields where more than 250 enemy aircraft were destroyed on the ground and many more damaged. The British component claimed 50 of these as well as sinking three Japanese destroyers and damaging three more, plus other assorted vessels.

These successes were not achieved without heavy cost. Seven aircraft were shot down and five pilots lost. One of these was Hammy Gray, a lieutenant in the Canadian Navy who had previously been awarded the DSC for exploits against the German Battleship *Tirpitz*. Leading a sortie of Corsairs from HMS *Formidable*, they succeeded in sinking a destroyer, but unluckily Hammy Gray was caught in the defensive crossfire, his aircraft was badly damaged and he was killed in the crash, alongside the destroyer. He was immediately awarded a posthumous Victorious Cross, the second to the Fleet Air Arm, and the last awarded during the war against Germany and Japan. Only eight days later Emperor Hirohito ordered his forces to lay down their arms.

During the period 10th July to 16th August it is interesting to compare the independent contributions of the two allied naval task forces.

United States Task Force No 38

10 Fleet Carriers
6 Light Fleet Carriers
1191 Aircraft
8 Battleships
19 Cruisers
60 Destroyers

On 13 strike days this force destroyed 2408 Japanese aircraft and sank 924,000 tons of enemy shipping.

British Task Force No 37

4 Fleet Carriers
255 Aircraft
2 Battleships
6 Cruisers
15 Destroyers

On eight strike days this force destroyed 347 Japanese aircraft and sank 356,760 tons of enemy shipping.

Yet to many the British task force rather resembles the British army in Burma. It was almost another forgotten force.

It is also of interest to note the origins of the airmen in the British Pacific Fleet. Whilst the majority were English, the New Zealand Navy provided approximately 25% of the fighter pilots, plus a few from the Canadian Navy. In the final Iceberg operations the Australian Air Force which now had a surplus of fighter pilots were invited to contribute 24 volunteers. The minimum qualification was 500 solo flying hours and preferably operational experience on Spitfires. The response was overwhelming. A number of these pilots had previous experience in the Western Desert, Europe, New Guinea and Darwin, but were required to forego one rank to transfer to the navy.

After intensive ADDLS they successfully carried out deck landings, albeit with a few crashes and barrier confrontations.

However, by the time they were posted to the forward areas as replacement pilots the war was over.

The rivalry between the two Seafire wings Nos 24 and 38 became quite intense; so much so that in the final Iceberg operation 38 Wing eclipsed the creditable deck landing recovery rate for Seafires previously established by 24 Wing in *Indefatigable*.

Implacable's 38 Wing recorded an average landing interval of 42.8 seconds – nearly ten seconds better than that achieved by No 24 Wing off Sakashima. The best landing interval was 31.8 seconds in a 19 aircraft stream recovery. This reflected excellent deck landing techniques plus confidence in the carrier's batsman and a well trained flight deck party.

From the Seafire cockpit, each pilot with his head out the port side in a slipstream, would see the machine ahead of him catch one of the arrester wires and would probably see the hook released and the previous pilot open his throttle to clear the landing area. By that time he would be closing on the round down with his attention then rivetted on the batsman. Because his vision from the cockpit was obstructed by the Seafire's long engine cowling he would not have seen the barrier dropped to let his predecessor taxi forward into the parking area, nor would he see the barrier raised again to catch him should he not be successful in catching a wire. For 19 pilots to perform this feat in a little over ten minutes calls for a very high degree of airmanship.

As the final onslaught on Japan reached a crescendo with American and British aircraft ranging far and wide over the Japanese homeland, the Japanese Foreign Ministry issued instructions on 10th August to its ambassadors in the two neutral countries, Switzerland and Sweden. These representatives were ordered to convey to the representatives of the three allied powers the following message:

> The Japanese Government is ready to accept the terms listed in the joint declaration signed at Potsdam, Germany on 26th July 1945 – with the understanding that the said declaration does not include any demand which prejudices the prerogatives of his Majesty Emperor Hirohito as a sovereign ruler.

Following frantic discussions, the Allied representatives comprising President Truman, USA, Mr Churchill, United Kingdom and General Chaing Kai Shek, China authorised a reply as follows;

> From the moment of surrender the authority of the Emperor and the Japanese Government shall be subject to the Allied Supreme Commander who will take such steps as he deems proper to put into effect the surrender terms.

Following this, a Japanese Government conference was convened in an air raid bunker near the Tokyo Royal Palace. Emperor Hirohito was present and, after listening to the arguments for and against acceptance of the surrender terms, he announced he would address his subjects by radio the following morning. Even as some of his militarists endeavoured to mount a coup, Hirohito cut a recording at the palace with the help of obsequious technicians. Japanese protocol ruled out the possibility of the divine ruler making a live broadcast.

At noon on 15th August 1945, his subjects listened to a completely unfamiliar falsetto voice on their radios. The Emperor spoke in an imperial court dialect which was virtually incomprehensible to the Japanese lower orders.

The text of the message was:

> After pondering deeply the general trends of the world and the actual conditions in our Empire today, We have decided to effect a settlement of the present situation by resorting to an extraordinary measure . . .
> We declared war on America and Britain out of Our sincere desire to ensure Japan's self-preservation and the stabilization of East Asia, it being far from Our thoughts either to infringe upon the sovereignty of other nations or to embark upon territorial aggrandisement . . .
> Despite the best that has been done by everyone . . . the war situation has developed not necessarily to Japan's advantage, while the general trends of the world have all turned against her interest. Moreover, the enemy has begun to employ a new and most cruel bomb . . .
> We cannot but express the deepest sense of regret to Our allied nations of the East Asia, who have consistently cooperated with the Empire toward the emancipation of East Asia . . .
> The hardships and suffering to which Our nation is to be subjected hereafter will certainly be great. We are keenly aware of the inmost feelings of all ye, Our subjects. However, it is according to the dictate of time and fate that We have resolved to pave the way for a grand peace for all the generations to come by enduring the unendurable.
> Having been able to safeguard and maintain the structure of the Imperial State, We are always with ye, Our good and loyal subjects, relying upon your sincerity and integrity . . .
> Unite your total strength, to be devoted to construction for the future. Cultivate the ways of rectitude; foster nobility of spirit, and work with resolution so that ye may enhance the innate glory of the Imperial State and keep peace with the world.

The above transcript contains not a single suggestion of apology, regret, shame or even an acknowledgement of defeat.

It is perhaps interesting therefore to reconcile this ambivalance with Japan's post-war recovery to develop four decades later, into one of the three strongest economies in the world.

With the cessation of hostilities it was opportune to compare the operations of the two naval task forces during the final few months of the war.

Any such comparison should be based on four factors: (1) the ships (2) the aircraft (3) the personnel (4) the commanders.

(1) *The ships.* The US Navy had the advantage of larger and somewhat faster fleet carriers, but with their wooden flight decks they were extremely vulnerable to kamikaze attacks. A large number of American fleet and escort carriers were rendered unserviceable

and many sunk under attacks by determined Japanese suicide pilots. The British carriers, most of which were hit, some twice, were relatively unharmed because of their heavily reinforced steel flight decks. The American carriers however, were better designed for lengthy operations at great distances from their home bases. They were replenished by a highly efficient fleet train which had progressively developed from the earlier island hopping campaigns.

Crew comforts, ventilation etc. were better provided for in the US carriers, thus sustaining good morale for long periods at sea.

While the British carriers may have lacked facilities for dispensing ice cream and cold drinks they were 'wet' in other respects. The men on the lower deck could look forward to their daily tot of rum even at action stations while the aircrews could occasionally unwind with a few drinks in the wardroom.

(2) *Aircraft* At the commencement of hostilities the US Navy was equipped with fighters, torpedo bombers and dive bombers, many of which did not match the Japanese aircraft for performance. It was only with the introduction of the Hellcat fighter and the Avenger all purpose bomber that quality was restored. The Corsair fighter, which had initially been rejected by the US Navy due to the deck landing deficiencies, was later modified and in the closing stages of the war became the most effective all-purpose fighter. When comparing the US naval aircraft with those operated by the British Fleet Air Arm it is important to appreciate the US aircraft were all specially designed for aircraft carrier operations, whereas the British aircraft were generally adaptations of aircraft in use by the Royal Air Force for land based operations. In the Pacific theatre the Seafire which was a naval version of the Spitfire, suffered in comparison with the more robust and somewhat faster Corsairs and Hellcats.

Moreover, the Seafire was probably the most difficult naval aircraft of all to deck land. This was due to lack of visibility over the long engine cowling, the very fragile undercarriage, the sensitive fore and after control surfaces and the tendency to 'float' if the approach speed was much more than 5–7 knots above stalling speed.

It was also restricted in endurance and radius of action to patrols of one and a half to two hours whereas Hellcats and Corsairs could remain airborne for four hours.

These two American fighters were much easier to deck land. One could quite safely approach in a Corsair at 100 knots, cut the throttle and it would drop on the deck with its very sturdy undercarriage. Both American fighters were equipped with very steady and heavily armed gun platforms with 6 × 0.5 Browning machine guns, whereas the more sensitive Seafire had 2 × 20mm Hispano cannon and 4 × 0.303 machine guns.

The Seafire, while it was a lovely aircraft in all respects to fly, was obviously not designed for the type of operations called for in the Pacific. Regrettably it was relegated to a fleet defence role CAP (combat air patrol).

The British Firefly 2 seater fighter bomber proved to be a very versatile strike aircraft. It had a good endurance (1070 miles) which compared favourably with a Corsair (1015 miles) and packed a very powerful ground attack armament of 4 / 20 mm Hispano cannot, plus 2 × 500 lb bomb or 8 × 60 lb rocket projectiles. But because of its slower speed it needed Corsair or Hellcat escorts.

(3) *Personnel* When it comes to a comparison of the aircrews of the two task forces, I have a suspicion, and this is purely a personal opinion, that there was a difference in air discipline. If this is true, I feel that it was based on training in enemy aircraft recognition and in the disciplined use of radio telephone communication.

There was no difference in the aggressive qualities of American and British pilots, but where the British pilot would have been trained to identify the target before firing, the American was more inclined to shoot first and ignore the consequences. Reminiscent of cowboy behaviour of the movie films.

And when it came to inter-plane R/T communication there definitely was a difference in discipline. I learned this at first hand one day in HMS *Indefatigable*. During a break in my batsman duty I took the opportunity to visit the ship's fighter direction control room where I listened to the R/T transmission associated with our strike on the airfields at Ishigaki in the Sakashima Gunto archipelago.

The FDO (Fighter Direction Officer) then switched over to a channel being used by the American task force operating off Okinawa about 200 miles north east of our position. I was horrified by what I heard. Obviously a tense air battle was in progress and the kamikaze aircraft which were generally flown by poorly trained pilots had been led into the attack under the cover of more experienced fighter escorts.

It was absolute bedlam. The channel was cluttered with a confusion of reports, instructions, warnings, frantic calls for help and the odd excited cry of victory.

No doubt with dozens of fighter aircraft milling around, the R/T does tend to become pretty chaotic, but one basic principle in the British system was to indicate the origin of the message. 'Dover Red 2 to Dover Leader – bogey 4 o'clock angels 2 crossing left to right.'

'Roger – I see him stand by to break.'

What I was listening to was a garbled mess – not entirely without some humour.

'Watch it Hank – there's a bastard on your tail.'

'For Christ's sake Butch – break and dive.'

Now there must have been dozens of Hanks and Butchs in the US Navy, possibly several in the same aircraft carrier. How they managed to operate in this sort of shemozzle really puzzled me.

We had to laugh, however, when a typical Texan drawl announced 'Hey man – Ah got me a Jap. Ah got the son of a bitch from behind. Boy oh boy – ah sure set his arse on fire.'

Listening in to this mess took me back to the days in 897 Squadron under the command of Willie Simpson. Willie had been on a course at RAF Central Flying School and later a wing leader's course. What he learned there he imparted to the members of his team.

Two of his priorities were perfection in battle formation and strict discipline in the use of R/T. Adopting the theories of Bob Tuck the experienced Battle of Britain fighter pilot, Willie demonstrated that, if necessary, the squadron could manoeuvre and carry out evasive breaks in dead silence, by using wing signals.

The origin of messages was vitally important: 'Dover Red 2 to Dover Leader' and the use of a clock face to report the whereabouts of enemy aircraft.

To further improve reporting procedure he suggested the 897 Squadron substituted the word 'Bograt' for the more common term 'Bogey'. Despite what clamour there may be on the radio channel this would indicate to Willie that the message was from one of his pilots.

These basic differences between American and British pilots were my personal observations, but I do believe that British airmen were better trained in aircraft recognition and R/T discipline.

But when it came to offensive spirit one had to admit that the American pilots were always willing to fight. Maybe they did not always pause to identify, but no one could accuse them of a lack of aggression. The infamy of the Japanese attack on Pearl Harbour ensured that American pilots always fought with a vengeance.

One particular difference that is interesting to compare is in the aircraft recovery technique. Both services employed a deck-landing control officer, more commonly known in the British service as a batsman.

As the name suggests, the DLCO controlled the approach of the aircraft landing on the carrier with a pair of fluorescent discs, not unlike ping pong bats. The signals which the British batsman gave to the pilot were positive and were meant to be obeyed. On the other hand the signals given by his American counterpart were indicative only. The American batsman's signals merely suggested to the approaching pilot what he was doing wrong and it was then over to him to make the appropriate correction.

Although not all British pilots had complete confidence in their batsman, I believed that if they had the choice of the two systems they would have preferred the command method.

As a relatively inexperience pilot, I shudder to think what might have happened to me when attempting to land on the carrier *Unicorn* in the Bay of Biscay. It was comforting to have the batsman Tony Fadd giving me positive signals.

(4) *The Commanders* In the annals of naval warfare none would enjoy a prouder tradition than the British Royal Navy. It reached its apex following the victory of Nelson over the French at Cape Trafalgar in 1815. Many of the present day naval customs and uniforms have their origin in that era. In fact, many of Britain's erstwhile enemies have adopted similar uniforms to the British *matelot*, the three white brads on the jean collar which are presumed to commemorate Nelson's three victories at the Nile, Copenhagan and Trafalgar. With slight variations they have adopted similar uniforms, cap tallies, etc. and more significantly the design and architecture of warships. The fact that the fledgling Royal Navy Air Service actually pioneered the development of naval aviation meant little or nothing to the seamen and gunnery admirals who comprised the hierarchy of the Admiralty at the outbreak of the second world war.

This prejudice manifested itself in the command structure of the navy to the extent that very few senior air branch men were considered competent to assume command of aircraft carriers. Some senior airmen were posted to the command of shore based naval air stations, but only a few were privileged to command even an escort carrier.

Consequently RN carrier captains were heavily dependent on their commanders flying and the air staff for technical and tactical advice on aviation matters.

A few like Admiral Sir Philip Vian had the foresight to realise that the day of the battleship as a capital unit in the Navy was in sharp recession. It was now the aircraft carrier which packed the offensive power of the fleet.

It is perhaps interesting to note that Philip Vian was one of the last admirals to find a last resting place in St Paul's Cathedral, London. Such was his standing in the modern navy.

The US and Japanese navies, however, had the advantage of assessing Fleet Air Arm operations in the North Sea, the Norwegian campaign, and the Mediterranean battles at Taranto and Matopan. They very quickly appreciated that the offensive power of the fleet had passed from the battleship to the aircraft carrier. The naval war in the Pacific was dominated by naval operations and those in command seemed to have a more realistic and practical approach to the use of aircraft. It seemed that a greater proportion of US Naval captains had seen earlier service in their air arm.

Historic Documents – CCCVII-CCCIX
JAPAN SURRENDERS UNCONDITIONALLY TO THE ALLIES

The official text of the instrument of surrender signed by representatives of Japan on board the United States battleship *Missouri* in Tokyo Bay on September 2, 1945, and the terms of the 'Potsdam Declaration' issued on July 26 by Mr. Churchill, President Truman, and President Chiang Kai-shek are given below.

Terms of Japan's Unconditional Surrender to the Allies, September 2, 1945.

1. We, acting by command of and on behalf of the Emperor of Japan, the Japanese Government, the Japanese Imperial General Head-

quarters, hereby accept the provisions in the declaration issued by the heads of the Governments of the United States, China, and Great Britain on July 26, 1945, at Potsdam and subsequently adhered to by the Union of Soviet Socialist Republics.

2. We hereby proclaim the unconditional surrender to the Allied Powers of the Japanese Imperial General Headquarters and of all Japanese armed forces and all armed forces under Japanese control, wherever situated.
3. We hereby command all Japanese forces, wherever situated, and Japanese people to cease hostilities forthwith, to preserve and save from damage all ships, aircraft, and military and civil property, and to comply with all requirements which may be imposed by the Supreme Commander for the Allied Powers or by agencies of the Japanese Government at his direction.
4. We hereby command the Japanese Imperial General Headquarters to issue at once orders to the commanders of all Japanese forces and all forces under Japanese control, wherever situated, to surrender unconditionally themselves and all forces under their control.
5. We hereby command all civil, military, and naval officials to obey and enforce all proclamations, orders, and directives deemed by the Supreme Commander for the Allied Powers to be proper to effectuate this surrender and issued by him or under his authority, and we direct all such officials to remain at their posts and to continue to perform their non-combatant duties unless specifically relieved by him or under his authority.
6. We hereby undertake for the Emperor, the Japanese Government, and their successors to carry out the provisions of the Potsdam declaration in good faith, and to issue whatever orders and take whatever action may be required by the Supreme Commander for the Allied Powers, for the purpose of giving effect to that declaration.
7. We hereby command the Japanese Imperial Government and the Japanese Imperial General Headquarters at once to liberate all Allied prisoners of war and civilian internees now under Japanese control and to provide for their protection, care, maintenance, and immediate transportation to places as directed.
8. The authority of the Emperor and the Japanese Government to rule the State shall be subject to the Supreme Commander for the Allied Powers, who will take such steps as he deems proper to effectuate these terms of surrender.

The 'Potsdam Declaration' of July 26, 1945.

1 We, the President of the United States, the President of the National Government of the Republic of China, and the Prime Minister of Great Britain, representing the hundreds of millions of our countrymen, have conferred, and agree that Japan shall be given an opportunity to end the war.

2 The prodigious land, sea, and air forces of the United States, the British Empire, and China, many times reinforced by their armies and air fleets from the west, are poised to strike the final blows upon Japan. This military power is sustained and inspired by the determination of all the Allied nations to prosecute the war against Japan until she ceases to resist.

3 The result of the futile and senseless German resistance to the might of the aroused free peoples of the world stands forth in awful clarity as an example to the people of Japan. The might that now converges on Japan is immeasurably greater than that which when applied to the resisting Nazis necessarily laid waste to the lands, the industry, and the method of life of the whole German people. The full application of our military power, backed by our resolve, will mean the inevitable and complete destruction and the Japanese armed forces, and just as inevitably the utter devastation of the Japanese homeland.

4 The time has come for Japan to decide whether she will continue to be controlled by those self-willed militaristic advisers whose unintelligent calculations have brought the Empire of Japan to the threshold of annihilation, or whether she will follow the path of reason.

5 The following are our terms. We will not deviate from them. There are no alternatives. We shall brook no delay:-

6 There must be eliminated for all time the authority and influence of those who have deceived and misled the people of Japan into embarking on world conquest, for we insist that a new order of peace, security, and justice will be impossible until irresponsible militarism is driven from the world.

7 Until such a new order is established and until there is convincing proof that Japan's war-making power is destroyed, points in Japanese territory designated by the Allies shall be occupied to secure the achievements of the basic objectives we are here setting forth.

8 The terms of the Cairo declaration shall be carried out and Japanese sovereignty shall be limited to the islands of Hionshiu, Hokkaido, Kiushiuh, Shikoko and such minor islands as we determine.

9 The Japanese military forces after being completely disarmed shall be permitted to return to their homes with the opportunity of leading peaceful and productive lives.

10 We do not intend that the Japanese shall be enslaved as a race nor destroyed as a nation, but stern justice will be meted out to all war criminals, including those who have visited cruelties upon our prisoners. The Japanese Government shall remove all obstacles to the revival and strengthening of democratic tendencies among the Japanese people. Freedom of speech, of religion and of thought, as well as respect for fundamental human rights shall be established.

11 Japan shall be permitted to maintain such industries as will sustain her economy and allow the exaction of just reparations in kind, but not those industries which will enable her to re-arm for war. To this end access to, as distinguished from control of, raw materials shall be permitted. Eventual Japanese participation in world trade relations shall be permitted.

12 The occupying forces of the Allies shall be withdrawn from Japan as soon as these objectives have been accomplished and there has been established, in accordance with the freely expressed will of the Japanese people, a peacefully inclined and responsible government.

13 We call upon the Government of Japan to proclaim now the unconditional surrender of all the Japanese armed forces and to provide proper and adequate assurances of their good faith in such actions. The alternative for Japan is complete and utter destruction.

The Effects of the Atomic Bombs at Hiroshima and Nagasaki

Hiroshima stretches over flat ground in all directions for roughly two miles from the centre. The main commercial and residential area of Nagasaki lies on a small plain near the head of a long bay. From here the valley of the river Urakami runs north for three or four miles, and a smaller valley branches north-east for less than two miles; both valleys are narrow and are separated and flanked by abrupt hills rising in places to 1,000 feet. The smaller valley is crowded with dwellings without plan. The Urakami valley contained large steel, engineering and armament works, together with smaller factories and a host of home workshops with an attendant jostle of workers' dwellings.

Hiroshima had been virtually undamaged by air attack before the atomic bomb fell. The bomb exploded near its centre and thence spread its destruction with great uniformity. Directly or indirectly, it initiated innumerable fires among the wooden houses and workshops, which burned unchecked for days and gutted the Old Town and the industrial zone enclosing it. The more modern industrial buildings on the edge of the town, however, at one and a half miles and more from the centre, escaped with only minor damage.

In Nagasaki the centre of damage was in the industrial area in the Urakami Valley. The harbour and the commercial area, nearly two miles distant, escaped with only minor damage: and so did the housing in the smaller valley, screened by the intervening ridge of hills.

Both in Hiroshima and in Nagasaki, the scale of the disaster brought city life and industry virtually to a standstill. Even the most destructive conventional attacks had no comparable effect in paralysing communal organisation.

In great areas of destruction, rising here and there like islands, reinforced concrete buildings remained showing few signs of external damage. Reinforced concrete buildings of normal construction were usually safe from partial collapse beyond 600 yards from the centre of damage, and from structural damage beyond half a mile. Reinforced concrete buildings of very heavy construction in Hiroshima, within 200 yards of the centre of damage, remained structurally undamaged.

Light single-storey concrete buildings, such as are employed for factories and warehouses, failed at about a mile from the centre of damage in both cities. The most striking feature of damage to steel framed single-storey factory sheds was their mass distortion, in the direction away from the explosion.

Of the machines housed in these sheds, only five per cent had suffered serious damage from the atomic bomb. This low figure is to be ascribed to the absence of fire. Nearly two-thirds of all machines in the Urakami valley had been housed in smaller workshops and sheds of timber. These shops were burnt down almost without exception to a distance in excess of one and a quarter miles from the centre of damage; fifty per cent of the machines in them were destroyed or irreparably damaged.

Japanese houses are constructed on a frame of 4-in, or 6-in. square timbers. The roofs are a source of weakness, their covering of pantiles bedded in mud on $^1/_2$ in. boarding being disproportionately heavy. The walls are of bamboo covered with three inches of mud, which is sometimes protected by $^1/_4$ in. boarding; much of the wall space is occupied by paper-covered screens. Complete collapse of these buildings from blast extended to one and a quarter miles from the centre of the damage in Hiroshima, and to an average of one and a half miles in Nagasaki. Fire completed the destruction almost to the same distance.

People who were directly under the explosion in the open had their exposed skin burnt so severely that it was immediately charred dark brown or black; these people died within minutes or at most hours. Very severe burns were occasionally reported at nearly one and a half miles from the centre of damage; mild burns at a distance of two and a half miles and more.

Fire was not confined to wooden Japanese houses, but raged fiercely in many concrete buildings, in some machine shops, and in other buildings not normally subject to fire. It is certain that fire spread did occur in both cities, but more striking is the vast numbers of separate points of fire.

The most important radio-active action at Hiroshima and Nagasaki appears to have been that from penetrating radiation, for convenience called gamma rays. The gamma rays pass through the skin without affecting it. They do not attack cells in the blood-stream, but the primitive cells in the bone marrow, from which most of the different types of cells in the blood are formed. Therefore, serious effects begin to appear only as the fully-formed cells already in the blood die off gradually and naturally, and are not replaced. Deaths probably began in about a week after the explosion, reached a peak in about three weeks, and had for the most part ceased after six or eight weeks.

It is estimated that people in the open have a fifty per cent chance of surviving the effects of gamma rays at a mile from the centre of damage. The gamma rays are capable of penetrating considerable thickness of building and other materials.

The effects of gamma rays on human reproduction necessarily form a long-term study, but at distances up to one and a quarter miles from the centre of damage, pregnant women who survived had either miscarriages or premature infants who died very soon. Two months after the explosion miscarriages, abortions, and premature births throughout Hiroshima were nearly five times as frequent as in normal times, and formed more than one quarter of all deliveries.

Sperm counts made in Hiroshima show that a high proportion of men exposed to gamma rays, up to perhaps three quarters of a mile from the centre of damage have reduced power of reproduction.

Official casualty figures for Hiroshima are 78,150 dead, as well as 13,083 missing. Those killed by air attack during the whole war throughout Great Britain, including London, numbered 60,000. The standard figure for an atomic bomb in British conditions would be approximately 50,000 dead.

Lieutenant (A) Donald Cameron MID

(mentioned in despatches) RNZNVR, later post-war RN.

No book about New Zealanders in the Fleet Air Arm would be complete without reference to the amazing exploits of Don Cameron. Don was a member of 28 course at *St Vincent*, having commenced his naval career about three months ahead of me.

After completion of his training Don was posted to 880 Seafire Squadron in HMS *Indomitable* but later transferred to HMS *Stalker* for operation 'Avalanche', the seaborne invasion at Salerno, Italy.

I had not made his acquaintance at that stage, but we did have rather similar experiences in Italy. Don was captured by the Germans and escaped, while I was very lucky not to be captured the following day. He made military history when on the 10th May 1945 he was captured by the Japanese following a forced landing in the sea off Sakashima Gunto.

I asked Don if he would contribute something towards this book. He has obliged and, apart from adding the odd comma here and there, the following unabridged text records his personal memory of his time on operations and the unbelievable cruelty he suffered while a prisoner of the Japanese.

Salerno, 9th September 1943

After the invasion of Sicily, during which our carrier HMS *Indomitable* was torpedoed at night by a twin engined Savoia Machetti (the pilot deserved the equivalent of our Victoria Cross), my squadron 880, Seafires, was put ashore at Gibraltar, minus our aircraft.

We were re-equipped with clipped wing Seafires, said to be faster and with a better performance below 12,000 ft.

While working up on these new aircraft, we were billeted in the Loretto Convent about three quarters of the way up the slopes of the Rock.

Early one morning I looked out of the windows of our convent and there below in the harbour were six escort carriers, looking incredibly small compared to the light fleet carrier HMS *Unicorn* also in harbour.

I shouted to the rest of the boys to come and see what I was sure would be one of our new homes. The comments, some not very polite, were amusing to hear, ranging from, 'God I hope we get the big one', 'How do you get down on the bloody minnow?' 'Jesus, how do you get off the bastard?'

Our new Seafires had a slightly higher landing speed, and the next few days were spent mainly in practising dummy deck landings on the end of the Gibraltar runway, appropriately marked out with the positions of the arrester wires.

All too soon it seemed, but one beautiful autumn morning, we flew off from Gibraltar and 12 spanking new Seafires safely landed on our new home HMS *Stalker.*

In company with the other carriers and the battleship *Warspite* we proceeded eastward into the Mediterranean.

The Fleet assembled in Malta, and one morning after weighing anchor, we were addressed by our Captain, Captain H. J. Murray-

Smith, and told that we were to provide close air cover for the British, Canadian and American troops who were about to attempt the first Allied invasion of Europe, the place – Salerno, Italy.

On the evening of September 8th, 1943, the invasion fleet sailed up the Straits of Messina, between Italy and Sicily, Mount Etna in Sicily on our left glowing bright red in the darkness as the fleet sailed on.

It was close to midnight, and most of us were still awake, although resting in our cabins, dressed and prepared for the action to come, when our Captain came over on the ship's broadcasting system to tell us that the Italians had capitulated and Mussolini had been deposed, but we were not, on any account, to think that we would be able to get ashore unopposed as the Germans were, even at this minute, sending troops in to take over.

At last it was nearly dawn and the landing craft were on their way into the beaches of Salerno. My flight, Blue Flight, was to be first off and I was to fly as Blue 2 to my leader, the senior pilot, an Englishman, Jack Smith. Our orders were to patrol at 10,000 ft on a line between Salerno and the island of Capri, to prevent any interference by enemy aircraft attempting to attack the landing force.

There was no wind to speak of, and our carrier was steaming at its maximum speed to give us as much wind over the deck as was possible.

The sea was a flat calm, with what could be described as a long heavy, oily swell, lowering and raising the deck, but at the top of the swell, the after end of the ship was fishtailing from port to starboard.

Jack led us off, he seemed to flop off the end of the deck to appear a little later sluggishly clawing his way upwards.

My turn, stood on the brakes, full boost on the throttle, off brakes, stick forward to get the tail up. Hell, I'd run out of deck already, where was my airspeed? Quick – up undercarriage to reduce drag, nose forward and down, the undercarriage was coming up, but so was the sea. Throttle through the gate eased the stick back. Jesus, that was close but I'd made it, climbing away, easing back on the throttle, take off flap up. Where are you, Jack? Ah, there you are up ahead, swing alongside. Our eyes met across our wing tips. We couldn't break radio silence but we were both saying 'Holy Toledo.'

Blue 3 and 4 joined up on us, and we headed for our patrol line.

Well, where were they? We were nearly at the end of our patrol and apart from a little ack-ack, we'd seen nothing in the air. There was a hell of a commotion going on at the beachhead, wished we could go down and give them a hand.

Ah well, Jack was signalling to turn to port, we were heading back to the ship.

Jack made it onto the deck. My turn. Cockpit hood back and locked, undid parachute harness, tightened seat belt, undid helmet chinstrap, pitch fine, undercarriage down and locked, flaps down, hook down, sliding into my landing turn, nose up, m.p.h. about 5 kts above the stalling speed.

Hell! the deck must be rising and dropping at least 40 feet, but it was that fishtailing that was the worry. Nearly there, but the deck was starting to slide out from under me to starboard. The batsman was correcting me, then he crossed his paddles, cut the throttle, Bang! the tail snapped into the air, I'd caught no 2 wire, I was down.

We had taxied across the barrier and parked our aircraft forward in the bows. Three of us were down and then came Blue 4.

He seemed a little high and the batsman was lowering his bats to bring him a little lower.

Seemed OK then. Yes, the batsman had given him the cut, but the deck was dropping away and starting that terrifying slide out to starboard.

Hell, he was committed now, and the height between aircraft and deck seemed to be increasing.

Crash! he hit the deck, the port undercarraige leg collapsed. The propeller splintered into a thousand pieces. The result of the ship's fishtailing now became apparent, the aircraft was sliding towards the port side of the ship. Had he caught a wire? No, the force of the impact had thrown the hook back up into the locked position.

We watched horrified as Geoff slid over the side, his aircraft flipped onto its back and crashed into the sea.

We rushed down the deck, no sign of the aircraft in the ship's wake. Our escorting destroyer had its boom net out ready to scoop up the pilot if and when he surfaced.

The seconds became minutes, the minutes became eternity. Geoff had gone. The Gulf of Salerno had claimed its first victim.

Blue Flight took off on its second patrol of the day at approximately 10.30 a.m. We were just opposite Capri at 10,000 feet when we encountered light but fairly accurate ack-ack.

My aircraft started to slip back out of formation. My throttle was at the same setting, but my engine revolution had dropped considerably. I opened my throttle to catch up, but the engine revolutions dropped more and more and I now found that I could barely retain my height.

I called up Jack and told him of my predicament. He suggested that I might have stopped a piece of ack-ack in the engine and to make for the beachhead and see if I could effect a landing.

As I approached the beachhead from the sea I became the target for every gun in the area. I was now down to about 4,000 ft. I kept waggling my wings and jinking and bunting to no effect. Suddenly there was a loud bang and my right arm was slammed off the stick and something hit me in the top of my head. The inside of my right arm felt like I had been branded with a red hot iron, while blood from my head was running into my eyes. The top of the hood was shattered and I thought, this is no place for me. I dived for the beach about the middle of the bay which seemed nice and clear and quiet. Locked my hood (or what was left of it) back, lowered my flaps and did a wheels up landing just above the waterline on what I took to be the firmest sand.

I thought I'd pulled it off when the aircraft suddenly stood on its nose and slammed over on its back. I am not sure if I was knocked out, but when I next became aware of things, I was stuck fast in the inverted cockpit with a solid mass of sand around my head and shoulders.

After a short time, I heard German voices and the blade of an axe came through the side of the cockpit, followed by more blows until I was literally hacked out of the aircraft and onto the beach.

I stood up and undid my parachute and was then told to '*raus*', '*raus*!' up the beach to the sandhills prodded along by the German equivalent of a Tommy gun. Once behind the sandhills I was led to a small copse of trees. Under one of the trees was a collapsible green baize topped table, and behind the table sat a German officer. He looked me up and down for some time. Here I should like to add that I was not in the regulation dress for a sub-lieutenant but was wearing navy blue trousers, brown suede shoes, a soft green shirt, navy battle-dress jacket and Mae West. The officer finally said, most sarcastically and looking down his nose, 'Yankee Gangster', and contemptuously waved me out of his presence.

Once more in the sandhills, I was given a shovel and told to dig a trench a Jerry had traced out on the sand. I had some thoughts (not all pleasant) as I dug away. I was then given a blanket, a mug of water, a thick slice of brown, nearly black bread, and told to hop into the trench.

I'm glad I did, not long after I heard the sound not unlike a large projectile reaching the end of its range and toppling end over end, then a God almighty blast. This kept up until dusk when a German appeared with a cup of black coffee and the aforementioned slice of black bread. 'OK, Yankee, you like boom boom.' I was to find out later that it was the *Warspite* shelling the positions of the 15th Panzers.

I should like to say now, that I liked and admired these grenadiers. They treated me fairly and shared what they had with me, and each one I spoke to had the same opinion that Britain and Germany should be fighting Russia as allies.

During the night I was hurriedly put in the bottom of a half track vehicle in the company of about 20 armed Germans. As we set out a terrific battle flared up and we jolted across country, not on roads as I could see, between being trodden on and showered with spent cartridge cases.

The next morning we arrived at Avellino and here I was placed in a makeshift prison camp already occupied by Canadian Fusiliers, the English Hampshire regiment and American Rangers.

I was approached by a middle-aged German doctor who tended to my head wound and was amazed at the wound in my arm.

There was a complete piece of flesh about 2″ square missing from the inside of my right arm and it had been neatly cauterised by the red hot piece of whatever it was that hit me. I can still place my left finger in the cavity left to this day.

The doctor lent me his razor but I was unable to use it as my face was covered with mosquito bites. He asked me my age and when I told him 21, he tutt-tutted, shook his head, then my hand; he was a gentleman.

A German Feldwebel, with an American accent now addressed the POWs and told us that he was short of guards, that we were to walk not run when required to do anything (queuing up for food etc.), and that for every one POW who escaped, he and three others would be shot.

It was here that I first met an Italian/American 1st Lieutenant, for the life of me I cannot remember his name, but he told me that he had represented his country at the Olympics in Foils and Epée, and best of all he spoke fluent Italian.

We were loaded into open lorries, about twenty of them, holding about 60 men standing up.

A German guard sat with the driver, and another guard sat with his back to the cab, armed with a sub machine-gun. I will call my Italian/American friend Tony, he and I were about the middle of the truck.

We proceeded north towards Rome. I noticed that sometimes in the hilly sections of the road, the truck in front of us and the truck following were out of sight of our truck for long enough for someone to drop off the back of our truck and make a break for it.

I explained to Tony that if we quietly made our way to the back of our truck, our guard would not be able to see us for the standing prisoners. But we would have to be quick and drop off each corner of the truck when the following truck was still out of sight.

Our chance came just north of Frosinone. On a hilly section of road we quickly hung off the back and dropped. My next step would have won the long jump award of the world and I rolled to the left (as I went head over heels) into the scrub at the side of the road.

I lay there as truck after truck roared past. Crawling out I was joined by Tony from the other side of the road and we took to our heels south into the thicker scrub.

That evening we came to a farmhouse on the outskirts of Frosinone. We decided to take the risk and Tony spoke to the Italian family. Thankfully they welcomed us, took Tony's uniform and gave him civilian clothes. In my case, I only had to take off my epaulettes to pass for a civilian. We both kept out badges of rank in case we were recaptured. It could be sticky even with them.

The Italian family told Tony that there was as train coming through from the north and stopping at Frosinone in the morning. It was mainly to take Italian servicemen back to their homes; but if there was room, and there should be when it got this far south, then civilians could pay for their trip. God bless them, they gave us 100 lire and told us that the train would only go as far as Cassino.

Tony got the tickets next morning. I was to pretend to be deaf and dumb, Tony would do all the talking. If anyone spoke to me, I was to shrug my shoulders and point to my open mouth. I don't think I fooled anyone on the train. But these chaps were going home, and they were happy. What did we matter to them now?

There was no conductor on the train, but civilians would have to hand their tickets in at the end of the trip.

We arrived at Cassino, and sure enough, to get out of the station, we had to pass through a turnstile. A German soldier stood with two Italian station employees at the turnstile. Tony presented our tickets and we walked through. I don't think the German could have cared less about us.

We were now getting into dangerous country and we avoided the main roads. We were hungry and helped ourselves to the many grapes and tomatoes growing in the fields. We used to joke on who would have to down trousers first. This diet seemed to pass right through you.

The signs of war were all around us now and after passing a German artillery unit we had a narrow escape, and had to take cover, crawling into road culverts, to avoid Liberator bombing attacks. We now saw for the first time some dead Italians, terribly swollen, lying in fields on the side of the road. Were they shot by the Germans or caught in the many air raids we were now experiencing?

We passed through Capua, looking by now more like Italians than the real McCoy.

Hunger was the real problem and we took the risk time and again by asking Italian farming families for something to eat. We reasoned that if the farmers were hostile to us, we had a better show of getting away than in a crowded city or town.

At last we came to Casserta and things were getting decidedly dodgy. We could see Vesuvius smoking away, but between us were the Germans and the front line.

Tony said to me that he thought we should have a better show from now on, if we split up.

We shook hands, wished each other luck and promised to have a reunion if we made it.

I walked to the southern outskirts of the town, only too aware of the curious stares I was attracting, especially it seemed to me, from the women. Should I take the risk and declare myself? No, you have a show in a country farm home, none at all in a town.

I took a bearing on Vesuvius then crept under a hedge to wait for darkness. You really feel up against it on your own.

I set out in the dark, pausing every now and then to listen. I made slow but careful progress and morning found me at about a mile from the slopes of Vesuvius. What next? I could hear the sounds of gunfire, aircraft were active overhead, so I stayed undercover. About an hour after dawn I heard female Italian voices, I walked through the trees and saw three women near a well. Ah well, now or never, I walked up to them, and I think they were more frightened of me than I of them. They positively froze. I pointed to myself and said 'Englisi Tenente'. Silence. They looked at each other then back at me. Then the younger and I thought prettier one came up to me and took my hand. I could not understand what she said, but caught the words Bella Englisi. I allowed her to lead and followed her to a cluster of farm buildings. Many Italians crowded around me and I was made welcome. The old man, the head of the family, took my epaulettes and hid them, then pointing to his mouth, led me into his house. I can still see him at the head of the table, holding a long loaf of corn bread to his shoulder and cutting it into slices, the blade slicing towards his chin and the slices falling off his forearm.

I was to stay with this marvellous kind and happy commune of Italian farmers for all of ten days. I watched them tread their grapes for wine (which they drink with every meal, including breakfast). I helped them harvest their walnuts (how hard it was to remove the stain), and accepted from them a rarity, a whole egg for my breakfast. I shall never forget them, and I hope that my report to the Allied Intelligence officers gained them some reward.

On the tenth night of my stay there arrived at the commune, five young Russians. It appeared that they had been working as labourers for the Germans, three of them had blue marks on their faces, which, as far as I could gather, came from being caught in a blast while they were employed in a coal mine.

My Italian friends now became very agitated and worried at this new influx, so I asked if someone could guide us up Vesuvius where we could hide until it was possible to make a last bid to reach our own lines.

A young Italian youth, I would say not more than 13 or 14 years of age, volunteered to lead us. He said he had been up to the crater many times, and that we could shelter in the cable car terminus.

That night, the 28th of September 1943, we proposed to set out. It was pouring with rain; all the better, I thought. The Italians gave us packets of food and, as a last gesture, the dear old head of the family presented me with my sub-lieutenant's epaulettes. I gave the old fellow a big hug and said he was to keep them, and one day I would come back to retrieve them.

So we set out, immediately behind our young guide and the small ravine we climbed had turned into a small creek.

Higher and higher we went, drenched to the skin, not knowing where we were, except that we were still going up.

I became aware of a strong smell of sulphur, reminiscent of our thermal region of Rotorua back home in New Zealand, and shortly after our guide stopped, gathered us around him, and then proceeded to show us in mime that we must remain silent, watch where we put our feet, be careful not to dislodge any rocks, and do exactly as he did.

We must have crept along in single file for over an hour when our guide stopped again, and this time he pointed down the slope of shale and rock and said something to me in which I caught the word 'terminus'.

He then shook hands all around, waved, said something in Italian again and left us.

It was still pouring, and we couldn't see very far, so by sign language I suggested that we stay where we were, try to get what shelter we could, and wait for daylight.

It *is* possible to sleep in the rain, if you are tired enough. The rain had cleared with the dawn and we ate some of our corn bread, guinea pig and tomatoes washed down with a little rough wine.

The view as terrific; you could see Naples and all the bay, heavily built up with villages all around, to the south a range of hills, and on the other side I knew was Salerno.

But better still, half a mile below us was the cable car terminus, a solid concrete building. We were just preparing to descend the shale and rubble slop when some Germans came out of the building, saw us and immediately opened fire.

We took off, half running, half sliding, around the slope of the mountain, the Russians leaving me way behind in our flight.

I was not to see them again for two days.

Further on, I found shelter in the form of an overhanging rock, not quite a cave, but it gave me a clear view back the way I had come, and a chance, I hoped, for a safe retreat.

Unknown to me at the time, but providentially, the Germans we had seen were in fact leaving their post at the terminus and beginning their retreat to the Volturno River.

I remained in my semi-cave for a further two days, with no sign of the Russians. I was shaking and shivering, sometimes hot, sometimes cold; not hungry, but very, very thirsty.

On the morning of the third day I was surprised to see a young Italian boy climbing the shale towards me.

Calling 'Inglisi, Inglisi, bon giorno', he produced a note and handed it to me.

Here are the exact words:

'Mister, English and Americans stay in Torre-del-Greco. If you want something, come to the country house, together with your friends, where, after having eaten, you can go to meet the troops.

Antonio'

I hugged the little boy, clapped him on the back, and spoke every Italian word I had ever heard. He must have thought me half crazy.

We descended the mountain to his home where surprise, surprise, there were the Russians.

I slaked my thirst, thanked Antonio, refused food, didn't wait to find out how the Russians came to be there, but waved to them to follow me.

This has always puzzled me, the Russians shook their heads, grinned, and indicated that they were staying where they were.

I took off down the hill. It was pandemonium. Unless you've been in a liberated Italian village, you will have no idea. I fought my way through the crowds of excited Italians to the side of an American MP, who was directing trucks filled with our troops.

In one breath I blurted out, 'I'm a Fleet Air Arm pilot, captured by the Germans at Salerno and escaped.'

I can hear him still, 'Yeah buddy, well I'm busy here, stand aside.'

To say I was deflated would be an understatement. Maybe he had taken me for an Italian, or worse? God knows I was dirty, bearded, haggard and ragged to say the least.

Just as I was plucking up courage to have another go, a jeep appeared in the convoy.

Beside the driver sat an RN Commander. I rushed out, arms in the air, and shouted, 'Sub-Lieutenant Cameron, Commander Sir, escaped from the Germans.'

(Oh, the delightful English), 'Great show lad, hop in.'

As we drove along the commander heard my story, and then informed me that we were on our way to Naples where he was to report on the harbour facilities. I told him, 'with all due respect sir, I consider we're going the wrong way.'

However, we found Naples empty of Germans, the port a shambles of sunken ships, and blown up installations.

We returned to Castellamare where I was firstly interrogated, secondly bathed and shaved, thirdly wined and dined, fourthly issued with clean underwear, khaki battledress, shoes and socks, and fifthly bedded down between clean sheets.

I was taken to Algiers from Salerno by LCI 299, from Algiers via Marrakesh, Morocco and then to Gibraltar by an American Liberator.

I was due to fly out from Gibraltar to England on an evening flight, but imbibed too freely in Spain, and the aircraft captain refused to take me. The aircraft was never heard of again.

The RN captain at Gibraltar informed me that this incident would not be reported due to my past experiences. But a convoy of LCIs was leaving in the morning for Milford Haven. They were short of officers and I would have to do eight hours on, eight hours off, all the way. My LCI? You guessed it – LCI 299.

Batsman Indian Ocean

After my Salerno experiences, I rejoined my Squadron (880) at Ballyhalbert, Northern Ireland.

My first evening back I was clapped into sick bay, inoculated, shaved from head to foot, and smothered in blue butter.

The first Sunday in hospital my nurse brought in the Sunday papers, all in a tizzy and making a great fuss of me. I opened the papers and found that overnight I had become a media hero. More was to follow, for after leaving hospital I received an important looking letter in my mail. It was from the Master of the King's Household requesting my presence at an afternoon party at Buckingham Palace.

As the party was the next afternoon, I asked my CO Lt/Commander Martyn if I could have a Seafire to keep this appointment.

His reply, 'As this amounts to an Order from the King, I suppose you'll have to have it.' I should have liked to tell him that it was not my idea, but let it pass.

The next morning, the weather was clamped right down, even the seagulls were walking. Still, an order form the C in C has to be obeyed and off I went in my best doeskin uniform.

After some harrowing incidents at chimney top height, I was forced to land at an RAF aerodrome at Derby. (Well, Bonnie Prince Charlie got this far on his march to London.)

I had no alternative but to ring Buckingham Palace and explain to one of the secretaries what had happened.

The weather was better the next day and I returned to Ballyhalbert. The next morning an article appeared in *The Times* that among the NZ guests at Buckingham Palace was yours truly.

Things just didn't seem the same in the Squadron and when

volunteers were required for service as batsmen in the East Indies Fleet, I volunteered and was accepted.

The training school for Deck Landing Control Officers, to give a batsman his full title, was HMS *Blackcap* at Stretton in Lancashire.

This school was ably and delightfully run by Lt/Commander Bob Everett, an oldtimer who was reputed to have physically attacked his observer when they had been forced to land in the ocean after failure to find the carrier. Bob had also ridden in the Grand National Steeplechase, and when he asked me if I should like to fly his pet, a Gloster Gladiator, he walked on water as far as I was concerned.

Well all our course duly passed out as DLCOs and I was posted to HMS *Shah*, East Indies Fleet, to take passage out in HMS *Ameer*, also joining the fleet.

The journey was uneventful, except for an incident as we passed through the Suez Canal.

The captain and commodore were taking their morning constitutional along the deck when a big black negro appeared on top of the canal bank. Throwing his white gown over his shoulder, he proceeded to masturbate the biggest penis accompanied by the biggest grin I have ever seen. The captain and commodore came to a full stop, and the captain rising up on his toes, shouted 'for two pins I'd like to fire every gun in this ship at that bloody wog.'

We duly arrived in Colombo, headquarters of the East Indies Fleet, only to find that *Shah* was out on anti-sub patrol, and was next expected to berth in Mombasa.

I was given a passage in the frigate *Findhorn*, also joining the *Shah*'s screening force.

The heat was nearly unbearable aboard *Findhorn*, so I slept out on the deck collecting a large haul of flying fish; the Captain (2 1/2 RNR) loved them for his breakfast.

One afternoon action stations was sounded and I reported to the bridge to see if I could be of use. *Findhorn* had a ping on a suspected sub. The Captain turned to me (I was standing at the back of the bridge, well out of the way): 'Here – you are Cameron, you want to be useful. Grab the smoke float, stand on the wing bridge and toss it over the side when I tell you.'

I grabbed the float, positioned myself on the wing bridge, read the instructions on the label (thank God I did, you had to tear the toggle on the top of the float to make it smoke after contact with the water), and waited.

The *Findhorn* started her way in, guided by the pings from the Asdic operator, 'Right Cameron, now!' I tore the toggle off and tossed the float over. It smoked beautifully. The ship turned 180° and headed off on a timed run. Turning 180° again, it bore down on the smoke float '*Fire Hedgehog*'. Concentric circles of bombs arched gracefully into the air and descended to circle and enter the water around the smoke float.

Loud crumps and explosions and the sea around the float foamed.

Cheers now rang out all over the ship 'Stop engines. See what you can find, No 1.'

The ship was manoeuvred over some floating debris, buckets and boathooks were employed to scoop up what they could, and that night in the tiny wardroom, the captain delivered his verdict.

'Well, gentlemen, subs under attack are known to fire gash out of their torpedo tubes. But on the credit side of the ledger, there is no Asdic contact, and Hedgehog bombs only explode on contact. It sure weren't no whale, dressed in overalls, and sucking oranges.' The drawling Canadian accent seemed to confirm a kill as far as we were concerned.

We arrived in Kilindini Harbour, Mombasa, to find the *Shah* undergoing a boiler clean. After making my number to the commander, I was taken to meet Captain Yendell.

A charming gentleman, he greeted me with the words 'Congratulations Cameron, I have received a signal that you have been awarded a Mention in Dispatches for your exploits in Italy. Welcome to our ship and remember my door is always open.' And she was a happy ship, hosting four Avengers and six Wildcat Fighters. During our stay in Mombasa, I went ashore to Port Reitz aerodrome and cadged the loan of a Swordfish from the Naval Squadron based there. That afternoon, I took the Engineer Commander and the Paymaster Commander up for a flight around the harbour.

Pays to keep in with these gentlemen, especially the latter, when one is running short of the necessary, and the former, when one wants a fresh-water shower, as opposed to saltwater, with saltwater soap.

We roamed the Indian Ocean in company with *Ameer*, *Findhorn* and various other escort vessels. It was a matter of pride with our Captain that we always beat *Ameer* at flying off and landing on.

We covered a rough triangle of ocean between Colombo, Mombasa, Aden and sometimes the Seychelles.

One afternoon in Mombasa, I received a phone call to inform me that my presence was required that evening at a posh Mombasa hotel for a celebration party.

Arriving all dressed up in my mess undress, blue trousers, cumberband, and white bum-freezer jacket, with epaulettes and wings, I was confronted by the whole ship's company from *Findhorn* and they were really roaring. The Captain approached me with two pink gins in his hands. As he approached he shouted out, 'My lucky mascot, my lucky mascot, welcome Kiwi.'

It appeared that *Findhorn* had been credited with the sub kill and the skipper had been awarded the DSC.

I came aboard *Shah* the next morning via the freshwater barge, *Shah* had moved out into the harbour, and a distinctly less dapper Lieutenant (A) RNZNVR requested to 'come aboard sir,' to his grinning commander peering down from the flight deck.

During another stay in Mombasa, I flew the paymaster and engineer commanders up to Nairobi, in a borrowed Swordfish, for a week's glorious leave. We had a Ford station wagon made available to us by the Naval Station Commander and stayed at the famous Norfolk Hotel. The guest register read like Peers register of lords and ladies.

Then to end it all, the 'shit hit the fan'.

I was batting in an Avenger one afternoon. He was too high and I lowered my bats to bring him lower. He virtually pulled the throttle back to its stop and I rotated my bats for him to give the engine more power. He must have pushed the throttle open too quickly, for there was a belch of black smoke, and he continued to descend like a lift.

In a last despairing effort I rotated my starboard bat above my head to wave him away for another attempt.

The aircraft stalled onto the quarterdeck, below the round down of the flight deck, wiping out an entire guns crew and exploding.

The death toll was seven, with some of the ship's crew suffering bad burns.

It was deep gloom in the Wardroom that night, with veiled insinuations that I had left my wave off too late and that the landing should have been aborted long before I acted.

The next morning I requested to see the captain. I came straight to the point and said that the general opinion was that the tragedy was my fault. The captain replied that it was up to him whether there would be an enquiry to allot the blame for the accident. I then requested that I be released from my duties as a batsman and be posted back to an operational squadron. The meeting closed with the captain agreeing to see what he could do.

I served in *Shah* from the 1st May 1944 until the 16th of October 1944.

I left the ship in Colombo and was posted to HMS *Rajaliya* at Puttalam in Ceylon for a conversion course onto Corsairs.

When you leave a ship in the RN the captain issues you with what is called a 'flimsy'. It is a report on your conduct during your service under his command.

To end my career as a batsman I produce an exact copy of that 'flimsy' below:

16th October 1944

This is to certify that:-

Ty Lt (A) Donald Cameron RNZNVR has served as a DLCO on board HMS *Shah* under my command from the 1st day of May 1944 to the 16th day of October 1944, during which period he has conducted himself:-

To the best of his ability. It is however recommended that he should not be employed again as a DLCO. In all other respects he has conducted himself to my entire satisfaction. An intelligent and smart officer.

W. J. Yendell
(Acting Captain RN)

Commanding Officer
HMS *Shah*

Mid Air Collision Puttalam 3rd January 1945

Near the end of my conversion course on Corsairs at Puttalam, Ceylon, I was detailed to act as target aircraft for three Corsairs, who were to carry out cine gun camera quarter attacks on me.

I steered a steady course at 8,000 ft out to sea and waited for the attacks to begin.

After a while and with no sign of these attacks, I called up on the R/T and said, 'Shake it up fellows, we're getting well out to sea. I shall have to reverse course soon if you don't get cracking.'

Still nothing happening, and I pulled up in a left hand turn, rolled onto my back to pull back on a reverse course and maintain 8,000 ft.

While still on my back there was a terrific bang and I found myself spiralling down, still inverted, with about half my port wing shaved off from the wing root to the wing tip. I applied full power and held the stick over to starboard as far as it would go. The aircraft came right side up. I slammed the hood back, undid my straps, and disconnected my R/T plug. The left wing was dropping again, and for some reason the sight of the shark-filled sea made me resume my seat. Whilst half way out of the cockpit I had seen another aircraft falling in the manner of a sycamore leaf with only one wing attached to the aircraft.

I wound on full starboard trim and applied full starboard rudder. I increased power again and closed the cowling gills.

I found that at approximately 150 kts and with the stick and rudder hard as it would go to starboard I was flying slightly port wing down.

I was flying at just above 4,000 ft and headed for the shore. While I still had height to bail out, I decided to lower my undercarriage. The port wing started to dip again and I applied full power and locked the throttle locking nut. At 160 kts I found that I could keep the port wing at about 5–10° below straight and level.

The cylinder head temperature was in the red, but I daren't reduce power or open the cowling gills.

With my left hand I plugged the R/T back in and called the Puttalam tower requesting they keep the runway clear.

I was descending slowly and lined up with the runway. The worst part of the approach was to see the palm trees flashing back under the aircraft and the wing threatening to dip beyond recovery.

At last, the end of the runway, I just flew the aircraft onto the end, and as the wheels started to run along the runway, eased back on the throttle and with the tail still in the air, started to see-saw on the rudder, applying alternate brake.

The end of the runway was rushing to meet me and with all power now off, I pulled the stick back, banging the tail onto the runway, applied slight right rudder and as the aircraft started to turn to starboard, applied port brake and the aircraft slid off the end of the runway about 45° off the centre line.

The aircraft kept sliding sideways in clouds of sand and dust but the port undercarriage held up (I thought it would have folded inwards under the terrific strain imposed upon it) and I finally came to rest. All silent except for cracks and splits from the overheated engine. I gazed at the coconut palms at the end of the runway, not more than a few yards from where the aircraft had stopped.

I thought that if I had run off the end of the runway at the speed I was travelling, and with no cockpit straps fastened, I'd have shot out of the cockpit like a rabbit pursued by a weasel and splattered myself against the trunks of the palms.

My thoughts were interrupted by a jeep pulling up beside the aircraft with a screech of brakes. It contained the CO Lt Cdr Godfrey Parish and his second in command, Cappy Masters.

'What the bloody hell do you mean by coming in like a bat out of hell with no flaps?' he demanded.

Ah! to savour the moment.

'Why don't you come around and look at the other side of the aircraft, sir,' I enquired.

I sat back and waited for the reaction. 'Jesus Christ, come and look at this Cappy,' said Godfrey. Then later:

'I always thought you were bloody well mad Cameron, now I'm sure of it.'

'Hop out of the plane, Cameron. Cappy, run him to the sick bay for a check up.'

Cappy and I laughed all the way to the Sick Bay, and after being checked out OK, I said to Cap that I'd like to go up again, just to avoid a sleepless night.

'There's a dive bombing exercise laid on in a few minutes, care to have a go?' Cappy said. 'Sure Cap, it's just what I need,' I replied. And so it was, I landed after the exercise relaxed, a little tired, but sure in myself that the Corsair was a great plane and I could cope, come what may.

Some headquarters bods came up from Colombo and photographed the Corsair and yours truly standing where part of the wing used to be. There was an inquiry, and later there arrived the following:-

Sir Arthur John Power, Knight Commander of the Most Honourable Order of the Bath, Commander of the Royal Victorian Order, Admiral of His Majesty's Fleet, and Commander-in-Chief of His Majesty's ships and vessels employed, and to be employed on the East Indies Station.

9th April 1945

Commendation by the Commander-in-Chief

I have received a report on the 3rd of January 1945 that you displayed great courage and exceptional flying skill in bringing back and safely landing Corsair II JT 265 after this aircraft had been severely damaged during an air combat exercise.

I commend you accordingly.

Arthur J Power
Admiral

Temporary Sub-Lieutenant (A)
D Cameron RNZNVR

But the best of all was a letter from Captain W. J. Yendell of *Shah*.

He congratulated me on 'once more surmounting a temporary setback, and wishing you continued success in your career.'

The parachute packer came to see me shortly afterwards and said,

'Would you come down and see your chute, sir? It's ready for repacking.'

I followed him to the shed and there looking like a pile of confetti was my chute. Then it struck me. About a week before the collision I had been practising inverted flying. One of the ground crew had failed to secure the top of my battery. Luckily I had the hood open and my goggles and oxygen mask on at the time. I remember being badly stung about the exposed portions of my face, and in the morning I looked like a brown and white spotted pony. I reported to sick bay and the doc said that it was just as well that I was perspiring so much in the heat, as the salt had counteracted the acid to some extent. I had forgotten about my chute, but my tropical helmet and Mae West had to be replaced.

Had I bailed out after the collision, I'd have plummeted down like a stone. (Some one up there likes me.)

We did four deck landings each on the *Unicorn* then parked my Corsair for the last time in the Puttalam hangers. Proceeding to Colombo by road, we once again boarded *Unicorn* for the voyage out to Australia to join the British Pacific Fleet.

On arrival in Sydney, I was posted to 1833 Squadron, Corsairs, in *Illustrious.*

I found that the Corsair wing from the ship 1833 and 1830 squadron had flown off before the ship reached Sydney, and was now on an aerodrome at Nowra, Jervis Bay.

Commander Wallis, the Executive Officer of *Illustrious*, suggested I catch a train next morning and join them. I told the commander that I had a brother at Rose Bay, whom I had not seen for 14 years, and would like to spend the evening with him and his family, to which he only too gladly gave permission.

I had a great evening with Bill, Brenda and son Barry, and Bill dropped me at the railway station next morning.

Arriving at Nowra the next day, the only familiar face was that of the batsman, Johnny Hastings, one of our batsmen in *Indomitable* in the Med.

'Hello Cam, what are you doing here?'

'I'm a replacement pilot for 1833.'

'Great! How many deck landings have you now?'

'Sixty eight at the last count, Johnny.'

'Some replacement that's more than anyone in the Squadron,' said Johnny.

'Your CO Lt Commander Hanson's away seeing the sights of Canberra at present, but I'll introduce you to the Wing Leader Mike Tritton.'

Mike was an old Med and Malta land DSO, DSC etc., ex-Etonian, very reserved, but a great pilot.

'Right, we're having a Balbo formation shortly, I'll get you an aircraft and you can fly my No 4, OK'

We left Nowra a few days later and rendezvoused with the *Illustrious* off the coast.

The BPF was really something to see *Illustrious, Victorious*, *Indomitable*, *Indefatigable, Howe*, *King George V*, and cruisers and destroyers galore.

We exercised at sea, once repelling an attack by land-based aircraft of the RAAF.

At our first stop, we anchored in Manus in the Admiralties where all the natives had blonde hair (from the peroxide bottle).

Next step, Ulithi Atoll, and here our C-in-C Admiral Sir Bruce Fraser offered his fleet's services to Admiral Nimitz of the USN, the C-in-C Pacific.

Task Force 57 BPF
Sakashima

26th March – 9th May 1945

The BPF was now to be known as Task Force 57, under the overall command of Nimitz.

Our job was to neutralize the airfields on the islands of the Sakashima Gunto; and thus, stop Jap reinforcements from interfering with the landings at Okinawa.

There were three New Zealanders in 1833, Jack Parli, Winnie Churchill, Ben Heffer, and among the replacements apart from myself, Mat Barbour, Mike Ritchie, Jim Clark and Doug Hartshorn.

As a replacement pilot, I seemed to be in different flights and in various flight positions as the need arose, whereas the regular members of the squadron were settled into permanent flights.

On the 26th March 1945 we took off as dawn was breaking. I was flying at No 3. Our orders were to escort the Avengers and give them cover as they bombed the airfields of Miyako. We were then to strafe any aircraft, gun positions and installations we saw on the airfield. Our whole squadron was airborne, and after the bombers had left, we circled above Miyako, with our own wing 1833 and 1830 there were wings from the other carriers. There must have been at least 60 fighter aircraft orbiting when our wing leader gave the order to attack.

When you see films of the hero diving calmly down from a great height to accomplish his mission, let me stress emphatically: 'It just ain't so.'

With mouths dry as cotton wool, screaming and yelling to release the pressure in your eardrums; the Jap gunners would have only to have seen you, and they would have taken you to their scrapers.

Selecting our targets as they came into range, we fired and kept firing until the moment of pull out.

Then it was a case of bunting and jinking across the airfield, hoping to dodge the flak. Collisions were narrowly avoided and once out of range of the ack-ack we climbed back to 15,000 ft and reformed.

The pattern was repeated until the wing leader decided we must have expended our ammunition, or it was time to leave for home.

This mode of strafing was foreign to everything I had been taught or indeed practised.

Diving at an angle of 45–60° from say 15,000 ft gives the AA gunners all the time in the world to line you up in their sights and as you get lower, the light AA joins in. You have aircraft all around you, so you are forced to fire at what is in front of you when you are in range. You dare not change direction in the dive; you might get away with it, but the risk is too high.

As far back as 1942 in the invasion of North Africa, we were taught, by all means fly in high, identify what you are going to attack on the airfield, then fly away out over the sea or land, whichever was the case. Build up your speed as you dive to sea level (you will vanish off the radar screen) and keep down all the way in. You have the element of surprise, only some guns on your approach side can be brought to bear, and if you're low enough, cannot depress their muzzles enough to get a sight on you. Hit and get, keeping low until out of range.

Ours is not to reason why, but to do and die. And die they did. Nottingham, Millard, Marritt, Garland and Churchill. What of the casualties in the other carriers? The bravery of Alec McCrae, his leg almost severed by a cannon shell, as he flew all the way back to his carrier injecting himself with morphine capsules to deaden the pain. I heard it all on the R/T. He took enough morphine (on advice from the ship's doctor) to kill a horse, but such was the loss of blood that the morphine was going out as fast as it went in. Alec landed, was lifted from his cockpit nearly unconscious, and was awarded an immediate and richly deserved DSO. Where are you now Alec? Alec has never been known to attend an FAA reunion.

On the 6th of April about 3.30 in the afternoon, I was flying a combat air patrol as No 3, with Matt Barbour as 4. The names of my flight leader and his No 2, escape me. Cloud ceiling was about 2,000 ft, dangerous kamikaze weather (they flash out of the cloud and hit you before you know it).

The Fighter Direction Officer gave us a vector to steer and told us to climb to 12,000 ft.

As we climbed in thick cloud our Flight Leader called me and said his artificial horizon was on the blink. I acknowledged and moved forward so that they could formate on me.

A short time later, I was surprised to see that the Flight Leader and his No 2 were no longer formating on me, a glance out on the starboard side confirmed that Matt was still there. At 12,000 ft we were in the clear but with a further layer of 10/10 cloud about 3,000 ft above. I called the the FDO and told him we were at angels 12. 'Right 303, you should see a bogey ahead at your height.'

I peered through a fast de-fogging windscreen and saw something the size of a sandfly ahead. I thought it was something on the windscreen, but as I stared, it seemed to be increasing in size.

It had to be an aircraft. I yelled over the R/T 'Tally ho' and to Matt, 'Buster matt'. With throttles through the gate we took off. It was indeed an aircraft, but it looked a bit like an Avenger from the rear. I eased off throttle and from my position, below and behind applied a little port rudder, as I skidded out, I saw on the fuselage, the Big Red Meatball. Quickly sliding in behind I opened fire at about 200 yards. I could see incendiaries sparkling on his port wing root.

He slammed into a split-arsed turn to starboard and climbed for the cloud. I followed, still firing long bursts and as we both entered the cloud, he blew.

His port wing came off and I followed as he sycamored through the bottom cloud layer. Spiralling down through the cloud I came out below the base just in time to see him hit the sea in a big saucer of foam.

I yelled to Matt to confirm it. I shall never forget his reply. 'Confirm it? The bastard nearly fell on top of me!'

I called the FDO and said, 'Splash one bogey. Have you any more for me?'

'Negative 303. The screen seems clear,' and vectored us back to the ship.

We landed back on to find the ship had suffered a kamikaze hit on the front of the bridge and there was debris all over the deck.

As I walked to the island entrance, I saw what I took to be a small Jap flag near the scuppers. Bending to pick it up, I was surprised to find that it was a linen flying helmet, with the Rising Sun painted on the top.

I was even more surprised on looking in the helmet to see the top of a skull about the size of an ashtray with little red veins forming a mosaic in the bone.

I stuffed my find into my Mae West, reported for debriefing to discover that I had shot down a Judy, the first to be credited to 1833, and as the ship was released by *Formidable* on April 13th, the only one to 1833's credit.

We left the area to rendezvous with the fleet train to replenish aircraft and pilots.

That night some of us managed to lay our hands on some bottles of gin, vodka and whiskey, and it was decided to hold a party in one of our cabins.

This was strictly forbidden, but as we were out of the operational area for a time, we bent the rules a bit.

I am not exactly proud of what follows, but it is necessary to remember that we were all very young, we hated the enemy, it was kill or be killed, and I have promised to write it as it was.

I am not too sure who was present at the party. We were six decks down, one very gloomy light, condensation continually dripped from the pipes that came through the ceiling.

As the party got to a stage where we were all great fellows, we could beat any Jap etc. someone produced a brown eye, looking for all the world like a tadpole, it was floating around in a bottle of gin or vodka. The motion of the ship induced the eye to circle endlessly around the bottle as it stared out at us.

Not to be outdone, I staggered off to my cabin and came back with my piece of skull in which we took great delight in stubbing our cigarettes out.

As previously mentioned, the *Formidable* arrived to release the *Illustrious.*

I was surprised one evening when Jack Parli said to me, 'Whacko Cam, we're going home on leave.' 'Not me Jack, I'm on the list to be transferred to *Victorious*', I replied. 'Hell, you've been on ops longer than any of us, I know', he said.

'Well that's the way it is. Jack you'll have to keep one or two on ice for me,' I said.

As the evening wore on, and those going home were regaling us as to what they were going to do when they got home, I started to feel a bit 'hard done by'. The bar closed, and by now nicely primed I decided to call on Lt./Commander Hanson, my CO, on my way to my cabin.

I knocked and was told to enter. Hans was lying on top of his bunk with a towel across his loins, a book in his hands and one leg sticking out to one side of the bunk.

'Before you say anything, Cameron, I know what you're going to say,' he said. 'At any rate, it's out of my hands and there's nothing I can do.'

I hadn't said a word, but drawing myself up to what I thought was a dignified attitude, I said, 'Well, I wish you goodbye, Sir', and reaching out I bypassed his hand, grabbed hold of his foot and yanked him out of the bunk.

It is amazing how a couple of quarts of tuppenny Pink Gins can deaden the senses to all abuse and threats of retribution.

After breakfast we outcasts paraded on the quarter deck, our captain, Captain Lambe, shook each of us by the hand and wished us luck.

On arrival at *Victorious* the Wing Leader sought me out in the Wardroom and said, 'I have been asked by the powers that be in *Illustrious* that you are to be a flight leader in 1836 Squadron and that you be allowed to pick the members of your own flight. Let me know their names by this evening.'

And so, we went back to Sakashima. My first flight with my new squadron was uneventful. Combat air patrol over the battleships as they bombarded Formosa.

On the afternoon of the 9th of May, I was briefed to take my flight to Miyako as escort to a squadron of Avenger bombers. After they had bombed and departed, I was to carry out a patrol over Ishigaki. If I saw anything on the airfield, I could attack at my own discretion and set course no later than 1720 hours from a certain cape (the name escapes me now) to find the fleet.

We took off about 1530, at least three of us did, my No 2 never left the deck due to engine trouble. We were escorting the Avengers to the target when my No 3 said he was returning to the ship with low oil pressure.

That left No 4 and myself. After the Avengers had finished their bombing runs, the two of us carried on to Ishigaki. There seemed to be quite a lot of activity on the airfield below and I had the impression that I had seen an aircraft land on the runway.

Calling to my No 4 (who was carrying two 500 lb bombs – one under each wing) I told him to pick his target, tell me when he was going in, and I would come down with him, to split the return fire.

'Going in now, 501,' my No 4 called, and we both winged over together. At about 2,000 ft I pulled up to port in a skidding climbing turn and see-sawed my way back to 15,000 ft. No sign of No 4. I called repeatedly but no reply. Slowly circling I saw a large fire burning amongst the hangars of the airfield.

That had to be No 4 I thought. I looked at my watch and it was just after 1700. I thought, God what a balls up, one didn't get off, one turned back and now No 4 gone. Noting what looked like a large aircraft at the corner of two hangars below, I headed out to sea and when about ten miles out, I winged over and dived to sea level on a reciprocal course. Belting along as fast as I could go, and right on the deck, I hit the airfield at about 45°a to the main east/ west runway. I headed across the field firing continuously towards the hangars which were rushing to meet me. I had a fleeting vision of men running and jumping down from an aircraft outside a hangar, then I was flashing over open country and out to sea in a matter of seconds.

I kept down on the sea for about another ten miles and then climbed up to 15,000 ft again, all the time keeping a good lookout.

Time for one more run, I headed east to come in on the east/ west runway this time and hit the buildings at the eastern end. Same drill, wing over, full throttle, keep low coast rushing up, I'm a bit right this time, correcting onto the buildings, open fire.

I streaked up the runway at nought feet and as I passed the hangars at the far end, there was a terrible bang and the aircraft seemed to jump sideways. Bits of cowling shot over the hood and the cockpit filled with smoke.

Keeping low I shot the hood back with my left hand and the airflow enabled me to see ahead. I was by this time out to sea, and I kept going, the aircraft still handled normally apart from the burning smell, and the smoke had practically ceased, but a glance at the instrument panel brought me up with a jolt.

There was no oil pressure at all, the cylinder head temperature was off the clock, and as I looked the engine started to sound like my mother's old Whiteway washing machine. I eased the throttle back, eased the nose up a little and tried to get what height I could. At about 2500 ft I called, 'Mayday, Mayday 501 ditching 20 miles west of Ishigaki.' I repeated the call again, locked the hood back, undid my parachute, tightened my harness and pulled out the R/T plug. I wasn't very high above the sea now and I decided to ditch along the swell, in the last seconds I dropped full flap, wound the trim back, closed the throttle and eased the stick back. As I hit along the swell I threw my left arm across my face.

The aircraft hit the sea, shot into the air again, hit again in a slightly nose down attitude and the deceleration practically shot me into the instrument panel.

Off harness, out on wing, reach in and tear dinghy off bottom of parachute, turn on small CO_2 bottle, the dinghy inflates, and I jump into the sea with it.

Now came the hard part, trying to get into the small dinghy. I had to let the air out of my Mae West and after repeatedly tipping the dinghy over onto myself managed to hold one end under the water while I got the top of my body on top by kicking my legs, raising my behind, and pulling towards my knees with both hands, I finally flopped into the bottom of the dinghy with the bottom half of my legs still over the end.

As I lay there practically exhausted, I felt the sides of the dinghy starting to close in over me. I turned over slowly, sat up and after searching awhile for holes, saw air bubbles coming up the side of the dinghy. Sliding my hand down the track of the bubbles, I felt the CO_2 bottle and found that the nut holding the bottle to the dinghy was loose. I tightened it with my fingers as hard as I could, and glory be, the bubbles stopped. A further miracle, strapped to the side of the dingy was a small rubber bellows. Undoing the CO_2 bottle, I screwed on the nozzle at the end of the bellows, and after pumping for a while, I had a nice steady little ship.

I took off my shoes and used them to bail out the water in the bottom. There were two paddles and a large yellow rubber cape with a hole in the middle. By attaching the edges of the cape to buttons around the edge of the dinghy and putting your head through the hole, one could stop the dingy filling with water from the chop of the waves.

The aircraft had, of course, long since vanished, and I could see the smudgey outline of Ishigaki on the horizon.

Now to sit back and wait to be rescued. As it happened I had to wait three months and three weeks.

Luckily the sea was calm, but during the long night I felt several bumps on my behind. 'Sharks', I thought. I carefully lowered a paddle over the side and, much to my amazement, felt what seemed to be a sandy bottom. Further prodding confirmed that the sea bottom was about 2 ft from my behind.

I got out of the dinghy, held onto one end, and proceeded to walk very carefully. After a good 50 yards, the sea started to come up to my waist, so I retraced my steps and the sea duly dropped to my knees again.

So there I was in the middle of a strange ocean, in the middle of the night, walking up and down for a couple of hours.

The sea started to rise and I got back into the dinghy; how simple an operation this time.

In the faint light that precedes the dawn, I thought I could make out a large darker piece of sky to my left, and as it got lighter I saw it was land and a large long beach stretched as far as I could see. It was deserted, but after about half an hour, a lone figure appeared, looked out to where I was vainly endeavouring to paddle away, turned, and vanished back into the sand hills.

In no time at all about a dozen figures appeared on the beach and proceeded to fire at me with rifles. Little spouts of water appeared around the dinghy, so I raised my hands above my head, and the firing ceased.

Some more figures appeared, carrying between them two canoe-like boats, and proceeded to paddle out towards me. I tied my maps and beacon chart to my revolver and dropped them over the side.

Japanese POW

10th May – 27th August 1945

The first boat arrived and pulled my dinghy to its side, and to the accompaniment of shouts and blows to the face and head, I was towed to the shore.

I was pulled from my dinghy, and promptly fell over in the shallows. I didn't seem to have any feeling in my legs.

After falling a second time I was pulled to my feet by my hair and ears and what I took to be the man in charge, waded into the water, took off one of his wooden sandals (similar to our present day sandals) and gave me a gawd almighty bash above the left eye. I went out like a light.

I came to on the floor of a bare wooden hut, at the door stood a Japanese guard complete with rifle and fixed bayonet. He amused himself at odd intervals by grunting something and lunging at me with his weapon, which fortunately stopped inches from my face each time.

Later some more Japs arrived in a truck, my hands were handcuffed behind me and I was blindfolded. I thought, well this is it, but instead I was thrown onto the back of the truck and accompanied by some Japs, we drove off. I was later to experience a worse ride but not much. At every bump and jolt I was thrown into the air only to crash back on to the unyielding tray of the truck. The guards thought it was great fun.

Finally we stopped, and I was shoved into another room and my blindfold and handcuffs were removed. A guard came into the room with a bowl of rice and what looked like slices of parsnip but tasted like radish. I was also given a small bowl of very hot water to drink.

I never tasted cold water, except rain, during my time as a POW.

Later in the evening some guards arrived, and handcuffed, I was taken to what I presumed was an officers' mess.

I was pushed down onto a long bench already occupied by other Japs. A long table was in front of me and on the bench at the other side of the table sat another row of Japs. They seemed better dressed than the others I had already seen, and all wore half Wellington boots.

A Jap facing me got to his feet, came around the table and swinging a pair of handcuffs in his hands proceeded to march up and down behind me, all the time, ranting and raving.

Suddenly he lashed out with the handcuffs, this time, striking me above the right eye. I was knocked clean off the bench, and finished up in the corner of the hut. I was not unconscious but very groggy and had a vague impression of some Japs picking me up while some others were restraining my attacker.

I was led back to my hut and a Japanese lit a cigarette, placed it in my mouth, gave me what I took to be a friendly squeeze on the arm and left me.

I was given the same meal again in the morning, and later some guards came, took off my handcuffs, gave me a cigarette and took me up a hill, (painfully I might add, in bare feet) to what I took to be a sick bay. I was sat in a chair and a Jap in a white coat with the help of a female Japanese cleaned and examined my head. 'I will break scab over left eye and stitch so it will heal,' he said. 'The bone over your right eye is broken, but I will also stitch it and it will mend,' he said.

The nurse stood behind me, hands on my shoulders, and when the doctor had finished, I swear she gave me a friendly squeeze with her hands.

Days passed and I sometimes found that my old mates were only a few thousand feet above me at times, as they went about their business of bombing and strafing.

One afternoon an American was pushed into the hut with me. It appears he had been picked up by the Japs in his dingy, after being shot down, and floated all the way from Okinawa. His name (if my memory serves me) was Abe Ginsberg, a Southerner.

One night we could hear the Japs having a party in the next hut, and we decided to have a go at getting away, and try to get back out to sea in any boat or canoe we could find.

Abe said he would ask to go to the toilet and while he was outside, he would try to get hold of a rock as a weapon. When he returned, and the guard opened the door I was to grab him while Abe bashed him (the guard) on the head.

Hopefully the other guards wouldn't hear and we could make a break for the coast in the dark.

Everything went as planned, except that Abe didn't hit hard enough or the rock was too small, because the guard kicked up merry hell, shouting and screaming as I held him and tried to stop him. I let the guard go, and Abe and I dived into our accustomed places against the wall of the hut.

Some more guards arrived, listened to the assaulted guard's highly pitched and rapid explanation of what had happened. A guard came into the hut, shone his lantern on what he saw were two sleeping prisoners on the floor, grunted something and then proceeded (as we drowsily pretended to wake up) to slap our guard repeatedly across the face all the time shouting something to him.

The door was locked, and the guards went back and resumed their party. The only change we noticed was that our guard, when he was on duty, would never let us go to the toilet.

One evening we were handcuffed behind our backs and taken to a small harbour and put aboard what seemed to be a motorized 50 ft open barge. A ceremony was performed by what seemed to be a priest, and we put to sea.

At dawn we put into another island and spent the day, trussed up, and the object of curiosity from young kamikaze pilots.

From our miming actions, they were so interested in us that they took off our handcuffs so that we could show with our hands what we were trying to explain. They didn't seem to have much flying time and I made the mistake of showing with my hands an attacking manoeuvre, accompanied by a rat-a-tat-tat and was promptly punched in the face and re-handcuffed. Abe was more diplomatic.

We island hopped at night, and rested during the day, except for one night as we neared our destination. A night I shall never forget. A drunken guard – they seemed to have access to plenty of saki – explained with a little English, that the island was infested with snakes. One small variety, 'the sting of fire', was instant death. So he was being kind to us by tying our feet as well as the usual handcuffs.

We were literally eaten alive by sandflies and mosquitoes. We rolled in the sand, buried our faces for as long as we could hold our breath and cursed our guard that long night away.

The reason for the night stop was explained the next day, because about midday, we sailed alongside the wharf of a fairly large village and our guard proudly announced: Taiwan, Taipei.

Still handcuffed, we were taken ashore and into the village. An air raid siren sounded and we were taken into what I took to be the post office. We where placed in a hole in the floor and left to ourselves. If you have ever been on the receiving end of a bombing attack, let me assure you, that it is only the bombs that don't hit you, that whistle.

During the bombing, Abe and I heard a sound like a train approaching through a tunnel and then with a sound like a giant piece of calico or canvass being ripped apart, the building collapsed upon us. We could hardly breathe for dust, we were certainly deaf, and I became aware of an old fashioned wall telephone I had seen in the room, it was only inches in front of my nose.

We lay there, it was deathly quiet, but I don't think we could hear anything anyhow.

Timber and wreckage was pulled away from the top of us, and we were dragged out into the light and blessed fresh air.

We were aware of people running in all directions and a young female was carried past us by the hands and feet, the middle of her body covered in blood.

Although I for one couldn't hear anything, the crowd had formed around us and were waving arms in the air and behaving in a threatening manner. Our guard had drawn his revolver and was waving it at them.

We were joined by other soldiers with rifles and bayonets and a path was cleared through the crowd, but still not wide enough for us to escape numerous blows to the head and back.

We proceeded up the road and after about an hour, the soldiers left us and we carried on with one lone guard.

I was now to experience what I still consider one of the most soul destroying and despairing incidents of my life.

We stopped half way through the afternoon at a small village and the guard took Abe behind a house and returned alone. He then led me to, what I thought was a bamboo crayfish cage. Blindfolding me, he pushed me into it.

He closed the front of the cage, and I lay there with my knees drawn up to my stomach, there wasn't any more room to stretch out. It started to rain quite heavily and I had a good drink as it ran into my mouth. Suddenly I was jabbed in the face and body by something, by tilting my head back I could see a little down the sides of my nose. I could make out that I was being poked with sticks by a group of giggling school children.

Fearful that a stick would pierce an eye, I turned onto my knees and buried my head between the bamboo rods and into the mud of the cage floor. This seemed to increase the poking and my head and rectum became the chief target for the little monsters.

I had just about given up all hope that I would live through this, when the guard, whom I presume had heard the commotion, shooed the devils away. I rolled over on my side, aching all over, and for the first but not the last time, blubbered like a big kid.

That evening we arrived at our destination. It was a large concrete four-storey prison in Taipei. I was put in a cell complete with the first wooden bed, wooden toilet, tub and a blanket that I had seen since becoming a prisoner. I was in a single storey wing running beside a road which I was to be thankful for later, as it turned out.

One afternoon, the air raid siren sounded and we were handcuffed in the front, blindfolded, and led outside, each prisoner holding the trouser top of the man in front. We stood outside during the raid which seemed to go on and on. I was frequently jolted by blast and occasionally pieces of rubble and God knows what else fell on and around me. But I don't think any of us were seriously injured.

There was in this wing of the prison an American prisoner, who I named 'More Rice Murphy'. We had for our three meals a day a bowl of rough rice and a small bowl of hot water. After every meal, without fail, this prisoner would bellow out, 'More rice, you bastards, more rice, you yellow shits.' And every time without fail you would hear the patter of running guards' feet, and the sounds of a beating being administered by the guards. And by the sound of it, not all one-sided. He was a very brave man, or as I half suspected, his mind might have gone.

Late one afternoon, we experienced a heavy air raid and we were left in our cells. The prison was hit several times and I remember curling up in the corner of my cell, hoping to make myself as small as possible. The insides of my feet became sore with the continual rubbing by the shaking of my legs. The ceiling of one cell had a hole punched in it, and a prisoner gave us a running commentary as the Liberators came over.

I had a feeling that this could be the end of the road for most of us, and that night I hung from the bars of my cell window by one hand and slammed my toilet tub into the light well of my cell. No guards came running, so after a while I stood on the tub and pushed the timber of the well upwards. It gave easily, leaving a hole about a foot square. I quickly placed my tub at the head of the bed, draped my blanket over it to give the impression that I was curled up asleep. Not very good, I'm afraid, but I had no time to lose.

Holding the bars of the window again, I swung out and grasped the edge of the light well. Letting go of the bars I swung across and with both hands pulled myself through, one shoulder at a time, into the ceiling. I replaced the light well, waited a little to become more accustomed to the dark and trod very carefully, making my way to the hole in the roof. There was a hole in the ceiling below the hole in the roof, but the cell of our commentator of the afternoon was empty. Carefully I removed the loose tiles from the edge of the hole, tested it to see if it would take my weight and, with some difficulty, pulled myself up and onto the roof. I quietly stole along the top of the roof and at one stage I paused and heard guards' voices below me. I came to a wall of the prison proper, and on my behind edged myself down to the guttering.

It seemed a hell of a height above the road, dim below me in the dark. Well if I sat here I'd certainly be shot off in the morning, so I removed my battledress jacket and wrapped it around one bare foot, my white polo-necked sweater around the other, hung from the guttering and dropped.

It seemed a long way down, but I hit, knees folded, and rolled to one side.

A parachute instructor would have been proud of me. Bruised but nothing broken, I dressed, rolled my trousers up in the approved fashion I had seen to just below the knee, and set off walking but dying to run.

I walked through deserted streets, there must have been a curfew, but now and again I heard the notes of a flute. I was to find out later that the local policemen in Formosa advertise their presence in this way.

I tried to keep going in the one direction, sure that, if I did so, I would eventually come to the outskirts.

A little before dawn, I came to a river with a single railway line across it. Waiting a while to see it was not guarded, I hopped across sleeper by sleeper.

I noted the direction of the river flow as it gurgled against the piles. It was still dark, but I could make out the build-up against the piles on one side as opposed to none on the other. I crossed some paddy fields, was scared witless by a dog barking.

Pulled a cabbage-like vegetable from a field and ate it as I walked. It was starting to get light as I veered off to a bushy covered hill and made my way up it, and finally curled up in the bushes to wait for the dawn.

My life seems to run in cycles of good and bad luck, and it was the time for more bad luck to arrive.

About an hour after dawn, I was congratulating myself on having made it and with a good chance of making the coast. After all I knew that the river must run to the sea, and from the distance we had marched to the prison when we arrived, it could not be far.

Down the hill and across the road from me appeared to be a large block of military looking buildings. There was a parade ground and a flagstaff.

A bugle call sounded and I cringed in my shelter as about 100 armed Japs appeared and fell in. They went through the raising of their flag ceremony, much like ours, and then dismissed.

I sat there, knees up under my chin, and gazing ahead when I heard voices above me. The next minute warm water started to fall on my head and shoulders. I daren't move, but I knew I was actually being urinated on. I stayed motionless, then after about five minutes someone jumped on me from above, and in a few seconds I was once again a prisoner. I had been hiding in the front garden of a house.

The usual bashings as I was pulled stumbling down the hill and across the road to the parade ground.

A small fat middle-aged officer came down the steps of the buildings and seemed to look at me for a long time.

I experienced that bamboo cage feeling again and averted my head, as silent tears ran down my cheeks. I thought, well this really is the end now. They won't forgive me my escaping, yes, old son, it's really the end of the road for you.

The officer said something and I was dragged up the steps into a room and sat in an upright chair in front of a desk like table.

The guards stood at the back of the room and were joined by another younger officer and then in came the middle-aged one and sat down facing me.

In pretty good English, he said, 'You are now the prisoner of the Imperial Japanese Navy, state your rank and number.'

I said, 'Lt Donald Cameron, Pilot, HMS *Victorious*, British Naval officers don't have numbers.'

He replied, 'Ah Soka, the army wants you back (I could guess why). Depending how you answer my questions, then I will decide,' he said.

I would like to say here that we had been briefed to say all we knew if captured, because all we knew would be harmless. We never knew what we would be doing the next day, where the Fleet would be, and any information on ships and aircraft we possessed was already well known to the enemy.

Opening a cupboard at the side of the desk, the officer produced a cloth bag of biscuits. They looked for all the world like the biscuits we had as children covered in pink and white icing, but smaller. I think we called them animal biscuits.

'Let us begin,' the officer said. And then I faced the strangest interrogation I have ever experienced.

'How many aircraft in your ship?'

'What is the top speed of your ship?'

'What is the tonnage?'

'Where were you operating when you were shot down?'

It went on and on and after each question that seemed to please him, he would slide a tiny biscuit across the table to me. I couldn't get enough of them.

Finally he rose to his feet, came around the desk where I was sitting cross legged, gave me a hard slap across the face with his open hand, and departed.

The younger officer led me to a room, closed the door and left me. A while later he returned and said, 'You very lucky man. The

ABOVE: HMS Formidable.
BELOW: The shambles on the flight deck of 'Formidable' following the Kamikaze attack, 8th May 1945.

ABOVE: HMS Indomitable.

BELOW: A Hellcat runs amok in 'Indomitable'. The pilot got out with a slight headache!

ABOVE: HMS Starling, command ship of Captain FJ Walker RN CB DSO and three bars, going to investigate an asdic bearing on a German U Boat.

BELOW: The pilot's view coming in to land on the MAC SHIP 'ADULA'. Note the Swordfish parked forward to indicate the very narrow width of the flight deck.

ABOVE: A typical flight deck scene when ranging aircraft preparatory to a sortie. With dozens of propellors whirling around, one needed to be a ballet dancer.
BELOW: Stormy weather atlantic - Hellcats ready to scramble - pilots hope not.

ABOVE LEFT: To survive a batsman must be a good judge of speed and possess fast reflexes. This batsman ducking under the wing narrowly escaped decapitation. The pilot, unfortunately went over the side and was drowned.
ABOVE RIGHT: One way to arrive but at least the pilot is not in the 'drink'.
BELOW LEFT: Seafire 'decapitated' on the barrier, but the pilot walked away.
BELOW RIGHT: Lieut Cliff Bissett seen clambering out of his Swordfish which went over the side during a rough weather sortee mid Atlantic. Bissett and his air gunner were rescued but the navigator was not recovered.

ABOVE: Members of the highly successful night fighter flight of No.1839 Hellcat Squadron in 'Formidable' *(Left to right)* S/Lieut (A) Harry Taylor (English), Lieut (A) WHI Atkinson DSC (Canadian), Lieut (A) Dick Mackie DSC (Flight Leader) NZ, S/Lieut (A) WMC Foster (English). *(Their achievement)* 10 enemy aircraft destroyed, 28 night deck landings, No prangs – 1 only burst tyre, *some credit must go to the batsman.*

BELOW: No.19 Torpedo Bomber course at Crail, Scotland. *(Back row - in middle)* Ron Spackman, Jack Cramp. *(Middle row - 4th from left)* Peter Holthouse. *(Front row - 2nd & 3rd from left)* Alan Lawrence, Harold Hawken.

ABOVE: Peter Jacobsen, Jack Cramp and Harold Hawken, March 1942. On leave in London - strolling down Fleet Street heading no doubt for the Sussex Hotel - the famous Kiwi watering place. BELOW: A Russian supply ship comes alongside HMS Chaser at KOLA INLET North Russia, March 1944.

ABOVE: The invasion of North Africa - November 1942.

BELOW LEFT: Escort carrier torpedoed North Sea.
BELOW RIGHT: Malta convoy under attack.

ABOVE: HMS Duke of York, Nelson, Renown and the carrier Formidable in the distance as seen from the carrier Victorious. BELOW: The German Focke Wulfe 190 fighter which the author wanted to souvenir at Montecorvino airfield, Salerno 9/09/1943.

ABOVE: Joan and Cappy on their wedding day, 20th March 1945.

captain is flying you to Nippon to the Imperial Japanese Navy's interrogation camp Ofuna. You will leave tonight.'

'Excuse me,' I said. 'Why did the captain slap my face?'

'You very bad mannered, sit in front of captain and cross your legs.'

The usual manner, handcuffed behind and blindfolded, I was put aboard an aircraft, twin engined, and in company of at least two other prisoners. By the old trick of tilting my head back, I could see a little down each side of my nose.

Luckily we did not take the direct route to Japan, we would never have made it. Instead we flew up the Chinese coast stopping in many places on the way.

I still remember sitting blindfolded as usual and handcuffed behind my back in an airfield waiting room. It must have been a civil aerodrome as well, because I was approached by an old Japanese civilian and heard the question, 'Why are you here?' The only answer that came into my head at the time couldn't have been the right one. 'I'm fighting for my country,' I said. Bang in the face, and arse over kite again.

We landed, I found out later, in Yokosuka, at the Naval Air Station.

And the trip lying on the tray of this truck was definitely the worst I have ever experienced.

The driver seemed to find every pot hole and rock on the road, and after one jolt into the air, I thought he must have hit the concrete curb and I would miss the truck completely when I came down.

The Jap guards were laughing their heads off and for all I knew were laying bets as to who would go the highest the 'Ocoocoo' or the 'Rocoocoo', Japanese for Englishmen who have been well baked in the oven as opposed to the Americans, who are not quite English and so have only been half baked.

We arrived at Ofuna eventually and were put in solitary confinement for a week.

You were fed three times a day with a bowl of rice and a bowl of boiling hot water.

You were fed through a trap door in the bottom of the door and as you held your small bowl out for boiling water, the guard instead of pouring it into the bowl, would pour it on your hand and wrist so that you dropped the bowl and gave him an excuse to come in and beat you up.

It didn't really matter because each guard when he came on duty would introduce himself by coming into the cell, made you stand on your bed, (so that he had room for a good swing) and bash you on behind (if you were lucky) or the base of the spine if his aim was out.

I should like to write the following in the form of memories:-

The memory of – The interrogating officer, a civilian Oxford or Cambridge graduate, he never exactly said. Flawless English, hated his landlady's rice pudding in England and despised us. Did they catch you, Handsome Harry?

The memory of – The end of solitary confinement and being led into the prison compound for the first time. The feeling of horror as I looked at these skeletons staring ahead, no-one was talking. I was reminded of a lunatic asylum. As I took my place on a bench I said to the poor devil beside me, 'Where are you from?' I was bashed across the face by a guard who screamed, 'No speako, Bimbo presento.' So that was it, you were not allowed to speak.

The memory of – My friend in camp, Captain Arthur and regular academy man. Shot down in a P38. His chute opened too late, he broke a leg; his medical treatment, a pair of bamboo crutches. He received the same treatment as the rest of us but in 'Art's' case it took longer. As they bashed him off his crutches with their 'Bimbos' they had to prop him up properly for the next blow.

The memory of – Bath night, fortunately few and far between. Rushing to get Art, 'Leave the crutches, we haven't got time.' Helping Art to get near the front of the queue. 'What's the hurry, you weren't going anywhere, I hear you say.' The bath was a large concrete vat; it held at least 20 prisoners. There was a wood fire burning underneath. The guard felt the temperature of the water, and the first batch climbed or were thrown in. No soap. But after a while the top of the water became thick with pus and scabs and the temperature was increasing until the last batches of unfortunates, and usually the sickest and slowest, were literally clubbed into the water. Have you ever heard a dog run over?

The memory of – An American Lt Col, old to most of us (what was he doing flying?). He was being punished with what we called the Ofuna crouch. You stood on your toes, bent your knees, raised your arms to shoulder height, then bent them so you were balancing on your toes in the hands-up position. As soon as your heels touched the ground you were knocked onto your face by the Bimbo. As long as you got to your feet again quickly, for further punishment, a few more bashes seemed to satisfy the guards.

In this case, after the first blow the Col stayed on his face. The enraged guards pulled him to his feet again and again.

I saw a film once of baboons attacking a sick or wounded leopard. There was no difference. The guards, thoroughly berserk by now, jumped on and bashed the heap of clothing into the ground. I whispered to those near me, 'Never forget this. If we ever get out of here, never forget this.' Some hope. We had already been told that if Japan was invaded, every man, woman and child would be needed to fight the invaders. We would in their own words 'get the chop'.

The memory of – The brute, a sergeant, and I think a Korean. I was standing by the wire fence one day when he approached me and said, 'Oh Cameron san. You escape from the Germans (how he knew I'll never know), you escape from the Imperial Japanese Army, let me see you escape from the Imperial Japanese Navy.' He took out his revolver (funny how mere sergeants in the Jap service carried revolvers) from his holster and waved up the wire. I looked at him and thought, he's going to shoot me anyhow, when a voice behind him said, 'Don't do it, Cam.' The enraged bull of a man turned and beat Lt Max Parnell of Marrietta, Georgia repeatedly across the head and face, forcing him across the parade ground until he finally collapsed. The brute stalked off to wherever brutes stalk. We picked Max up and took him back to his cell. There was nothing we could do for him except bathe his face with water.

Max recovered and made it home to his beloved South knowing he had risked his life for me and that I was eternally grateful.

I have his letter in front of me now. Sent at the first Christmas after the War.

The memory of – The beri-beri victims lying on their backs trying to breathe, their bowels uncontrollable and then their Shinto or Buddhist (I never found out which) burial.

The memory of - Finding I had beri-beri (but trust me, it started in the head) and I couldn't see out of my eyes until close to midday.

The memory of – Another Southerner. Saying when out of

earshot of the guards. 'Cam, I don't think I'll last the winter, would you come over the wire with me. We could kill a Jap and eat him.'

The memory of – A guard throwing a slobbery covered cigarette butt onto the ground and the glee as he watched us scramble for it.

The memory of – The last time I cried as a prisoner. They brought in a young American airman. He had a horse bit in his mouth, his head strapped back, and the corners of his mouth split open. But worst of all, the whole front of his body was badly burnt. He was carried into one of the solitary cells. After a couple of days I asked if I could see him, and received the usual punch in the face.

Then after his solitary time was over (must stick to the rules) some of us were allowed into the cell. This is the most enduring memory of all. As we entered the cell, I thought the body on the bed was moving. It was, it was a mass of writhing, feeding maggots.

I don't go to RSA, KEV or ex-POW functions, except bowling tournaments.

I learned long ago that when discussions arose: 'What unit were you with?'

'Oh, you were a Jap POW, must have been tough?' That when you did attempt to explain a few of the more believable incidents, you saw the looks of disbelief in the eyes, and I stay away now, to avoid the embarrassment of it all.

I received a letter from Art after the War and I quote:

> Like you say, it's all behind us now, and there just isn't any use in trying to explain about it. However, I assure you, I haven't forgotten about it, and don't think I ever will.
>
> I have been in hospital for two months now and they tell me I have six more to go. I definitely have a stiff left ankle so I don't know about the Army career. I'm fully expecting a retirement. However, I guess about all I can do is wait and see.
>
> Take care of yourself, Don. The best of luck to you and write me again at your convenience.
>
> Art
>
> PS: Keller stopped in to see me last week and he sends his regards.

The commander of the camp congratulated us on winning the war. All the guards had changed places with guards from other camps during the night. Aircraft dropped food and clothing to us. We were told to stay put as the population might not know the war was over and we could be attacked. Men gorged on canned chicken, vomited and gorged again. I, with a Chief Petty Officer from submarines, were taken out one evening in a jeep by the RAN. The first out, we were taken to Yokosuka and the next morning out to a hospital ship. A young two ring doctor examined me and said, 'What was your weight when you were shot down?'

'12st 3lbs,' I replied (I was 7st 12lbs at the time.) 'You were never 12st 3lbs,' he said. 'I tell you, I was 12st 3lbs,' I said. 'Never,' he said, 'Look, you jumped up little bastard, I haven't been through hell to have you call me a liar,' I said. He replied, 'You're alright Lieutenant, go through the door on the right.'

It wasn't long after, that I found he was testing me. A lot of the POWs were broken in spirit and went through the left door for further treatment.

I finally got to Sydney aboard *Indefatigable*. Was invited to lunch by Rear Admiral Sir Philip Vian. Got drunk with my brother and forgot about the appointment.

Had to report to him the next afternoon, stayed sober and kept it.

'Vian of the Cossack,' was a great man. After a short chat he said 'What were you doing before you joined the Navy, Cameron?' 'I was a gunner in the Coast Artillery at Fort Dorset in Wellington,' I replied.

'No career to go back to then?' 'No, sir.' 'Would you like to stay on in the FAA?' 'Yes please, sir.' 'Good, I'll see what I can do,' said the great man.

I flew back to Wellington, I don't know what aircraft but we sat along the aircraft on a bench, each side, with a packet of greaseproof wrapped sandwiches for our lunches. Wellington, especially the Hutt, had grown. I was taken for a medical at Shelley Bay across the harbour. Given a generous amount of pay until they could sort out what was owing to me. I hired a taxi, stopped at a florist to get a bunch of flowers, knocked on the front door, and there was Mum. I took her in my arms crushing the flowers between us and said, 'I told you I'd be back, Mum.'

The Wreck of the Georgetown Victory

In December 1945, I received a cable from the Admiralty stating that subject to my passing a medical examination I was to be commissioned for a four year short service commission to commence on the 9th November 1945.

I had been in the Royal Navy, and on pay, for over a month it seemed, so I immediately made arrangements to have my medical.

My weight had shot up to 14 stone, and, apart from the fact that I could not bear to have anything even moderately tight around my waist as it caused a rash to appear, I felt pretty fit.

I secured passage in the *Wanganella* to Sydney, where I fitted myself out with new uniforms and was billeted in Pettys Hotel.

Pettys was a lovely little Victorian hotel on the direct route to the Harbour Bridge, the entrance to the bridge only about half a mile up the road. Pettys was run as an RN ship with RN cooks and stewards, wardroom with RN bar opening hours; very handy as Sydney's hotels still remained open all day, closing at 6 p.m. just when we opened, to close at 11 p.m.

As I entered the foyer of Pettys I ran into Commander Sarel who had been our commander flying in *Illustrious*. 'Cameron, just the man I want, stay put here until you hear from me, I'll square it with RN headquarters,' he said. Then he was out the door and off. I had a glorious two weeks in Sydney reporting every day to headquarters to enquire if there were any orders for me, and in the evenings enjoying the nightspots, occasionally with my brother, but most often with a young lady I had met.

Finally one morning, I reported to HQ and was told that I was to take passage in the *Georgetown Victory* for England.

The ship was full of RN ratings going home to be demobilised, and we had a real peacetime send off, paper streamers, bands, the lot.

Our ship was one of the many hastily built during the war and manned with officers and men who were rather rudely called pressure cooker sailors, having only had about six weeks instruction, such was the demand for ships and crews to sail in them.

We put into Fremantle, and at about 4.30 p.m., the Senior Naval Officer aboard sent for me and explained that the ship was due to sail at 6.00 p.m. and that nine ratings were adrift. I was to take a three ton covered truck on the wharf and, with six marines, attempt to bring them back to the ship before we sailed.

We drove down the main streets of Fremantle, stopping at every hotel and grabbing any sailor we found with an HMS hatband. One sailor, out of the dress of the day, no collar, no cap, was standing on a corner, his arm around the waist of a local lass. The marines grabbed him, and he fought like a tiger, but eventually overpowered, he was tossed onto the back of the truck, and held down by the 'Jollies'.

I reported back with my 'catch' and feeling pretty bucked with my success, and the ship duly sailed. The sailor who had caused all the trouble was in the brig, under guard.

About two hours after we had sailed, the SNO sent for me. 'Well done, Cameron,' he said. 'But it seems we have a problem, we were nine men short, and you brought back ten. The odd one is a member of the RAN who was on leave in his home town. Our next stop is Colombo, so I advise that you avoid lone walks on the upper deck until we leave that port. Dismissed.' I spent the voyage to Colombo forever peering back over my shoulders, in fact I nearly developed a permanent 'twitch'.

We sailed through the Suez Canal and out into the Med. The captain of the ship used to put on quite an act, and always attracted a large crowd of spectators.

He would play chess against his opponent with his back to the chessboard. He had of course to remember his opponent's moves as well as his own, and many was the time that I saw him end the game, 'Now my knight to square nine, checkmate,' or whatever was appropriate. He was never known to lose.

I remarked on this method of playing chess to an RNR Lieutenant who shared my cabin. His prophetic reply, 'I hope he doesn't navigate that way.'

One afternoon, the same lieutenant said to me, 'Pop up on deck Kiwi, there's a glorious view of the coast.' I went to the port side of the ship and could see nothing but ocean, turning around, I took a jump backwards. We were so close to what could only be the coast of Spain that I thought we were in danger of running aground.

A strange way indeed I thought, to find Gibraltar. In carriers we had only seen the coast of North Africa until we sighted Gibraltar.

One night we were sailing up the Irish Sea hoping to berth in the Clyde at Greenock or Gouroch the next morning.

We were steaming, at what I estimate at about 14 kts, when I went down to the cabin and turned in. I was asleep when there was a terrific 'crash' and the ship's bow seemed to be climbing and juddering upwards.

We in the cabin grabbed our greatcoats, caps and lifejackets and hurried up to the deck.

The forward end of the ship seemed too high and dry and above the hubbub and general din all around us, we could hear faint voices calling out from ahead of the ship, 'Christ, we've hit the Isle of Man,' I said to the RNR Lieutenant. 'No way, Kiwi,' he said. 'Those voices we can hear out there are Irish.'

And so it proved to be. Our ship had charged up onto the coast at Killard, Northern Ireland.

The tide went out and the dawn came up and the ship stretched over the rocks, and with a hell of a bang, broke its back.

One of the American seamen collapsed on the deck, frothing at the mouth, obviously in the throes of a fit. I said to the bosun as he hurried past, 'There'll be hell to pay over this.' His reply I have never forgotten, 'You kidding? We've got plenty more back in the States.'

As no-one seemed to be in charge, as far as we could see, we brought all our cabin luggage up on deck, cut a large Carley float free, and about a dozen of us climbed down a rope mesh that had been dropped over the side, and paddled through some channels between the rocks to the shore. I still have a newspaper photograph of us coming in.

The Irish women plied us with cups of tea and sandwiches, and the Irish men with questions on what we were carrying in the holds.

Finally all the RN personnel were assembled on the foreshore, and no-one was found to be missing. A column of army trucks appeared and the SNO detailed me to take charge of about 120 naval ratings and take them to the Larne Ferry for passage to Stranraer in Scotland. I hopped into the cab of the leading truck and the army driver said, 'Cutting it a bit fine weren't you, sir. You only scraped into Northern Ireland by about 100 yards. Could have been interned.'

I had finally checked my charges aboard the ferry and was about to ascend the gangway when an RN engineer commander hailed me. As he strode towards me, he said, 'Bit of a dicey do, Lieut, come and have a drink.'

I protested that I was in charge of the troops in the ferry, but he said, 'Tons of time Lieut, we'll hear their blasts before they sail.'

So we repaired to a small hotel just off the wharf and during drinks I found that the commander had been Vian's engineer in the *Cossack*. Common ground for lots of reminiscing and the time flew. Sure enough, later in the evening I heard the hoots from the ferry, and suggested we take our leave. 'No hurry, Lieut, that's not our ship, I know her blast,' he said.

About closing time we finally left the hotel and made our way to our ship. I shall never forget it, no sign of the ferry, and as I remonstrated with the, by this time, slightly tipsy commander he said, 'But I thought you were in my ship', and pointed further up the wharf. God almighty, what to do?

I reported to the Naval Transport Officer on the wharf, and after a very heated exchange with accusations flying back and forth, I booked into a hotel in Belfast. Caught a private plane to Prestwick Aerodrome, Scotland, missed my charges by a matter of about an hour, and reported to Admiralty in London. I explained that I was from the ill fated *Georgetown Victory*, received a uniform allowance, and was posted to Lee-on-Solent for a flight check. It's funny, but I quite forgot to mention that I had lost my draft of fellow survivors. I spent six months instructing at Eglinton near Londonderry, Northern Ireland with 51 Training Air Group and on many occasions looked down from above with my flight of Seafires, and told my pupils that the wreck below was the ship that brought me to Northern Ireland. I was delighted one day to hear a pupil say, 'Cutting it a bit fine weren't you, Sir?'

I was invalided out of the RN in February 1949 with the very exotic sounding complaint of 'Post Concussional Depression', another way of saying 'Fed up with it all'.

I served four years, as an Air Traffic Controller Officer at Nadi, Fiji, with Civil Aviation.

Another 14 years of leasing hotels in many parts of the North Island. And five hotels later I retired, in July 1981, aged 59 years.

My wife (we were married in Lee-on-Solent after the war, and were blessed with two boys and a girl) and I are now grandparents, and live in a lovely mid-North Island town which reminds us of England, and quite often during a drive in the countryside around us stop the car and say, one or the other, 'Doesn't that remind you of such and such?'

My greatest thrill now is to remove the opponent's shot bowl from the jack, during a game of bowls.

And as they say in the old country, 'I wouldn't call the King my cousin.'

Author's Note When Don Cameron recorded these events he did so in longhand. Don's handwriting is not something he is particularly proud of – it is not exactly what one would describe as copy plate. He decided, therefore, to obtain the services of a typist and was recommended to a lady in a firm of chartered accountants in Cambridge. Don explained his requirements and cautiously asked for an approximate quotation. The figure of $145.00 plus GST was given.

Then followed several weeks of close liaison, with the lady telephoning several times daily, seeking interpretations and spelling of technical terms etc.

The day finally arrived when his manuscript had been completed.

Don duly called to collect it, took out his cheque book and enquired how much.

Imagine how emotional it must have been to learn that this firm of chartered accountants had decided to waive the charge: 'Mr Cameron, we feel that you have suffered enough.'

There could be no more magnificent a gesture than this – 47 years after the event. 'If ever a naval airman was deserving of a "gong" it surely must have been Don Cameron, at the very least an MBE. Sadly his sensational exploits went unrecognised except by Vice Admiral Sir Philip Vian.'

Lieutenant (A) Ralph E Cocklin, RNZNVR

Ralph Cocklin sailed from New Zealand with the author in MV *Dominion Monarch*, July 1941. They entered HMS *St Vincent* as members of 31 Pilots Course and were closely associated during all stages of training up until Operational Training Unit when Ralph elected to serve as a bomber pilot. He subsequently flew Swordfish aircraft from the smallest carriers in the most hazardous and inhospitable seas of the world.

Stringbag the Sailor

Any pilot who flew Swordfish aircraft on operations during WW II would want to start his account of service with an appreciation of one of the most remarkable aircraft of all time, the aircraft that gave the Fleet Air Arm its reputation and is the symbol of British naval aviation.

The original order for the Fairy Swordfish to be built was given in early 1935 and eventually 2391 were constructed, the last one coming off the production line in December 1944. At the start of the war thirteen Fleet Air Arm squadrons were flying Swordfish and at the end of the war nine squadrons, including No 119 of the RAF operating from airfields in Belgium, were still flying the aircraft on operations.

Originally three operational roles were required of the Swordfish:

(a) Reconnaissance for the fleet.
(b) Torpedo or bomb attacks with a load of 1500lbs.
(c) Spotting for the guns of the fleet.

These roles exemplified the motto of the Fleet Air Arm, 'Find, Fix and Strike.'

As well there were two machine guns, one which fired through the propeller operated by the pilot and one on a swivel fired by the telegraphist air gunner.

The basic Swordfish I became the Mark II which was the first Allied aircraft to carry rocket projectiles as the main armament. Later a large radome was fitted under the nose of the aircraft giving it the appearance of advanced pregnancy. This housed the PPI or 10 cm radar set which was a very accurate type. This Swordfish became the Mark III which was used later in the war on the Arctic route to Russia. The crew normally consisted of three, a pilot, an observer and a telegraphist air gunner.

The Swordfish operated in all theatres of war from the tropics of the Indian Ocean, and Africa, the Mediterranean, including Malta and the Western Desert, the North and South Atlantic and the Arctic route to Russia.

Among the outstanding efforts of the Swordfish and its crews was the crippling of the Italian Fleet at Taranto by only twenty aircraft, two of which just were lost. Only the successful attacks by Swordfish from HMS *Ark Royal* made the sinking of the *Bismarck* possible, and despite the relatively small numbers of the aircraft produced, FAA Swordfish sank more enemy ships than any other aircraft.

Although a somewhat slow and simple looking aircraft the Swordfish had a wingspan of 46 feet reducing to 18 feet when folded for storage on an aircraft carrier. It was 37 feet long and stood nearly 15 feet high. The top speed was 154 m.p.h. and its range 750 miles. With an overload tank and crew of two the endurance was almost ten hours. Despite its appearance to the contrary the Swordfish was an intricate but incredibly reliable aircraft with cockpit instrumentation as complex as any of its single engined contemporaries.

After the disastrous Channel Dash in which six unescorted Swordfish led by Lieutenant-Commander Eugene Esmonde were shot down, the torpedo role of the Swordfish was no longer used in daylight attacks.

In this attack the German battle-cruisers *Scharnhorst* and *Gneisenau* left Brest to go through the English Channel to a German port. Although the RAF were keeping a constant watch on Brest, the German fleet escaped unobserved and were only spotted accidentally by two Spitfires chasing a Messerschmitt when the battle-cruisers with an escort of a cruiser, six destroyers, 34 E-boats and several flak ships were already 300 miles on their way. Esmonde's 825 Squadron took off from RAF Manston expecting to be escorted by five squadrons of Spitfires and Hurricanes of Fighter Command. Of these only ten aircraft of No 72 Squadron arrived and in the poor conditions these soon lost contact. Esmonde's squadron carried on and with great gallantry attacked the German Fleet now escorted by over 200 fighter aircraft. All of the Swordfish were shot down and only five of the eighteen aircrew survived. Later in the day 242 RAF bombers escorted by over 500 fighters were sent to continue the attacks. Most of these failed to locate the German ships and those that did could not attack because of low cloud. Twenty-eight Beaufort torpedo bombers also heavily escorted failed to hit any of the enemy ships. Fortunately, Coastal Command aircraft had laid mines ahead of the Germans and both battle-cruisers were quite badly damaged by them.

As W. A. Harrison states in his book *Swordfish Special*, 'The Swordfish was, of course, just an aeroplane; its legends, its achievements, were only as good as the skilled and gallant crews could make them.'

After finishing our flying training in Canada we returned to UK, did a commissioning 'knife, fork and spoon' course at RM College at Greenwich and were then sent on for advanced flying training at RAF Errol near Dundee. After some routine flying on Master I and II aircraft we were asked to make the choice between torpedo bomber and fighter schools for operational training. I was offered the further choice of special training as a flying instructor. For me the choice was simple, the glamour aircraft was the famous Swordfish and it offered the possibility of much more flying than in fighters. In addition the type of flying involved a degree of steadiness and accuracy that appealed to me. From Errol would-be bomber pilots were sent to RNAS Crail for training in torpedo work. After some local flying we were sent out to do low flying practice. Until this stage, theoretically, our low flying exercises had not been below 200 feet. We were somewhat surprised when told to go and practice rate four turns (maximum) at 50 feet. As this meant the wing tip was about 25 feet from the water we made sure of perfect turns every time! Most of the two months of training at Crail was devoted to the classic method of torpedo attack. This consisted of flying at about 10,000 feet in sub-flights of three aircraft and approaching the target ship from ahead. Going into line astern the three aircraft would dive vertically while watching for the kick in the ship's wake which would indicate the direction of its evasive turn. The pilots would then turn in their dive to be on the outer bow quarter and aim to reach a point about 1000 yards away from the target and 50 feet above the sea. For a successful drop the aircraft nose had to be up or down within one degree and the wings within two degrees of level. Needless to say, this required a high standard of flying and judgement.

The routine of training was enlivened by a couple of incidents. In one a pilot was somewhat embarrassed when, after a practice attack, his propeller fell off as he headed for home. Luckily he had sufficient height to glide to shore but his embarrassment continued when he found he was committed to doing his forced landing in a field studded with anti-invasion posts. Quite remarkably he landed with only minimum damage. The second event involved the captain of the station. There was a shortage of senior officers with flying experience, and so when a non-flying officer was appointed to command an air station, he was given a course in Tiger Moths and if this was completed successfully he was given a Gloster Gladiator to play with. The Gladiator was the last of the biplane fighters famous for its part in the defence of Malta and an aircraft most pilots would have loved to fly. On this particular day there was a low mist over the aerodrome and with the sun shining along the runway our skipper made two or three tentative attempts to land. Finally he came in on a rather erratic approach accompanied by the sepulchral intoning by one of the watching instructors of 'Over to you God, over' in the traditional manner of handing control of an aircraft from one pilot to another. However, the skipper did make it.

After the torpedo training was finished we transferred to RNAS Arbroath to learn the difficult art of deck landing an aircraft on a carrier by day or by night. At Arbroath part of the runway was marked out to represent the deck of a carrier. The deck landing technique consisted of completing a turn close to the end of the dummy deck and approaching with nose high and the aircraft in the attitude for a three-point landing. Speed in the approach was controlled by the joystick and height by the throttle, the reverse of normal landing procedure. On the approach the DLCO or batsman used his bats, shaped like table tennis bats, to signal information about speed and altitude and, if the approach was satisfactory, to give the command to cut the throttle and land. A good batsman was invaluable in carrier flying. As well as landing training we were introduced to the arts of dive bombing and dropping depth charges. In a final flight from Arbroath Cliff Bisset and I were sent up in a dual Swordfish to do instrument flying practice, which soon became some unauthorised low flying. We duly landed to be met by a mechanic demanding our names. Naturally we assumed that we had been reported for our activities. It was with a mixture of relief and dismay that we received the news that another aircraft had dived into the ground from a thousand feet killing two of our course mates.

After a month at Arbroath doing ADDLES or Aerodrome Dummy Deck Landing Exercises we passed out as trained FAA pilots by doing four or five satisfactory landings on the training carrier HMS *Argus*. First impressions of this tallied with the wit who described it as 'trying to land on a matchbox running away from you at high speed.'

After this Cliff and I were sent to HMS *Daedalus*, the headquarters of the FAA at Lee-on-Solent and for about two months flew aircraft on communication and delivery duties all around the UK.

At the end of this pleasant and relaxing period we were posted to 816 Squadron which was to operate from RAF Exeter hunting E-boats in the Channel at night.

The squadron was reforming after being on HMS *Dasher* when she blew up in the Clyde, due to petrol fumes igniting, with a considerable loss of life. At this stage 816 was a six-aircraft squadron with an acting CO, Peter Pryor, who, with his observer, was about to leave to fly night fighters with the RAF. The new CO turned out to be a RN Lieutenant-Commander whose main ambition in life seemed to be to spend most of his time in the bar, the older hands taking it in relays to keep up with him. It was here in a little local pub that Cliff and I were introduced to the delights of the varied ciders available with the natural accompaniment of real Cornish pasties. There was always one officer on duty, though his most important job seemed to be the collection of those who were not flying from the pubs of Exeter at closing time. In the morning the Duty Officer also had to collect bods from the rented house where the married officers had installed their wives. For obvious reasons this house went into 816 lore as 'Letch Cottage' and the single men were not allowed within a mile of the place. 'Ropey' Horsfield, who was in charge of our transport, had the task of explaining away a four page deficiency list when we left Exeter, Transport consisted of a one two-ton truck, a petrol bowser and a station wagon which, with considerable discomfort, could hold fifteen officers and one huge and incredibly stupid bull mastiff bitch. Amazingly his claim that the faults were all due to operational demands was accepted even if it was not believed. All pilots and observers had administrative jobs as well as flying duties, which meant that FAA squadrons were self contained units with no non-flying bureaucracy. The naval system of regarding flying personnel primarily as officers meant that there was no equivalent of the unfortunate term LMF used in the RAF when an airman's nerve gave way. If an airman developed 'twitch', a quiet word or two with the doctor saw the flier being assigned to another type of duty away from the squadron where he could still perform a useful service to the navy. These two factors were undoubtedly important contributions to the high morale.

After Exeter the squadron was sent to RAF Fearn in Scotland to practice ADDLES prior to embarking on a carrier. ADDLES usually involved a sweepstake competition for the entire squadron and I was flattered to find the ratings had established my crew as the favourite 'horse'. Prior to going out for the competition one of the stewards came to me at breakfast to say that he could not wake the CO and that his cabin was in a mess. I told him to try again in half an hour. After the competition had gone on for some time, a bleary eyed CO appeared, took a look at the proceedings and decided to show how deck landings should be done. He demanded a helmet, goggles and an aircraft, climbed in and took off. On his first attempt he nearly collected the fence at the near end of the runway and on the second he repeated the process at the far end. A rather shaken pilot climbed out of the plane and stalked off without a word to anyone. By the time we returned to the mess he was gone, another victim of twitch, incurred in his case at Malta. A few days later a new CO arrived, Lieutenant Commander Freddy Nottingham DSC RNVR, a very experienced pilot, quiet mannered and efficient. He became extremely popular with the entire squadron which by now had been built up to a full sized one of 12 aircraft. From Fearn the squadron flew low along Loch Ness to HMS *Landrail* at Maclihanish which was far from being the most popular station in the FAA. Here we said goodbye to our black Stringbags and received the new aircraft. We were the second squadron to receive the new rocket projectiles as main armament. These gave the Swordfish a firepower equivalent to a broadside from a light cruiser. As the aircraft were painted white, Jack soon had the squadron artist painting a crest on one of the engine panels. This was the usual semi-clad female figure and was named Shemol, a combination of the names of our respective wives, Sheila and Mollie, the latter far away in NZ. As aircraft succeeded aircraft that engine panel was transferred to each new one. As well as getting acquainted with the new rockets we carried out some experiments in methods to locate U-boats at night. One such was rather hair-raising with aircraft working in pairs, one to fly low over the submarine and fire a special Very cartridge as an illuminating flare for the other aircraft to attack with depth charges. Another was to use a version of the Leigh Light used by Coastal Command. The searchlight was mounted under the port wing of the Swordfish. When my turn came the conditions were atrocious with very heavy rain and as we approached the target and the light was switched on a dazzling reflection from the propellor made flying hazardous. On return to base we found one of the other crews had crashed. All told we lost three aircraft during this period but luckily no aircrew were injured.

Soon we flew out to embark on HMS *Tracker*, an American built escort carrier. At this stage we were joined by a fighter component of Six Seafires, two of their pilots being fellow N. Zers – Gerry Hooper and Bruce Taylor. On joining a new carrier a squadron spent about a fortnight training or 'working up' to develop the team work necessary for efficient operation by day and night, so that continuous flying was the order of the day. It was during this that I discovered a serious defect in the Stringbag, it lacked a very essential component – a pee tube. I was going into the heads one day just prior to take off when a Mayday signal was received from one of our aircraft. Ignoring my bodily requirements I rushed to take off to search for the aircraft in trouble. After half an hour I had reached bursting point so called Jack Durban and Jock Liddell who by now were my permanent crew to pass through a suitable container to me. Unfortunately, the aircraft was a new one and there was not even a Very cartridge in the cockpit let alone anything else. After further urgent pleading Jack passed through the only thing he could find – a condom. He being a happily married man and just back from leave had not emptied his pockets. One fill of the condom and instead of emptying it and refilling it I, like a fool tossed it over the side to the distress of Jock who received the spray. In 15 minutes I was desperate again so we gave up the search and returned to the carrier to find that the missing crew had managed to land at RAF Ayr and were happily supping gin in the Mess. As I was squadron armaments officer one of the armourers was briefed from then on to hand me a protective cannister from a rocket motor immediately before take off. It was not long before most of the other Stringbag pilots followed this ritual.

During the working up period we lost an observer and TAG in an accident. The observer was one of the ones who had recently joined the squadron and while we were waiting one afternoon for night flying exercises he, with others, had headed ashore for some recreation. Being a particularly smooth operator he soon found a like minded lass and rowed with the girl back to the carrier which was anchored just off shore. A visit to his cabin and then a row back ashore made for an energetic afternoon. Obviously all these activities were too much for him as he drowned when the aircraft crashed into the sea that night.

Tracker had as captain one 'Dangerous' Dan McGrath, an ex-destroyer man who, the squadron claimed, would, if we ran into an enemy warship, steam full astern and use the four-inch guns on the quarterdeck instead of using the aircraft with torpedoes. Like most escort carriers *Tracker* had been built in the USA on a merchant ship hull. It had a displacement of 14,200 tons when deep loaded. The flight deck was 440 feet by 82 feet with eight arrester wires to catch the arrester hook hanging down, when released by the pilot, from the tail of the aircraft. If an aircraft missed all the wires it would hit the barrier which was like a badminton net but was made of steel cable. With typical irreverence the last wire was known as the 'For Christ's Sake' wire and the barrier as 'Amen'. Both barrier and wires were lowered flush with the deck when landings were not taking place. There were two lifts to transfer aircraft to and from the commodious hangar, but unlike the fleet carriers there was no armour plating. The top speed of 18 knots made flying operations in low wind conditions rather tricky, especially as the Americans with considerable ingenuity had managed to build into the ship an ability to pitch and roll that was unequalled by any other carrier. This, combined with the efforts of a somewhat less than able batsman nicknamed 'Loopy', made deck landings on *Tracker* even more hazardous than normal. One day during working up the aircrews were piped to go on deck to watch Lt Cmdr Bill Bailey, the CO of the deck landing squadron at Machrihanish, do his 500th landing bringing on board an American journalist who was to spend a few days aboard.

Although conditions were remarkably calm and the ship for once steady in the water, he belted up the deck missing the wires and crashed! A shaken journalist clambered from the wreck. It took several gins to steady his nerves – not helped at all by some aircrew who assured him that it was the normal method of landing in the RN. Several days of flying however convinced him otherwise.

Soon we sailed on operations with the 4th Escort Group to take part in the longest battle of all – the Battle of the Atlantic in which 2353 ships out of a total of 2717 sank during WWII incurring enormous casualties. Of the 782 U-boats sunk 585 of them were sunk in the Atlantic by warships and aircraft. At the time we sailed the most dangerous area was The Gap, an area about 500 miles across, which could not be patrolled effectively by shore based aircraft. It was to help plug this gap that escort carriers and macship carriers were provided. After a short time we were detached to function with the 2nd Escort Group as an Air Support Group with the redoubtable Captain 'Johnny' Walker CB DSO with three bars in overall command in HMS *Wren*. Captain Walker with his group of Bird Class sloops sank over 20 U-boats. His ability to operate his group in hunting U-boats was uncanny and most successful. The function of an Air Support Group was to operate as a hunting group as an independent unit, but also to provide additional support to any convoy threatened. The aircraft patrolled constantly especially at dawn and dusk, the times when U-boats were most likely to be on the surface. If the U-boat remained on the surface it would be attacked, but if it submerged the sloops could be homed to the area and an Asdic search carried out. Forcing the submarines to submerge helped to keep them away from the convoys, because of their slow speed when under water, and this was a major aim in anti-submarine warfare. Whilst on patrol off the tip of Greenland 'Lefty' Bisset, my cabin mate and friend of long standing, crashed while landing during a gale. Bats had brought him too high and with the ship rolling and pitching badly, as usual, the aircraft bounced high, the ship rolled from under and the plane caught the bridge a glancing blow and flopped into the sea. Captain Walker in *Wren* displayed superb seamanship by closing to *Tracker*'s side to pick up the aircrew. The two ships were so close that *Wren*'s mast was swinging over the carrier's flight deck in the heavy seas. Both Lefty and his TAG were rescued, but John Stretton, the observer went right under *Wren*. Two sailors dived into the icy seas to help John, but he was too far gone and they could not support him. Lefty, after survivor's leave, gave up flying and became an aircraft controller. As both of us had lost our cabin mates I moved in with Jack Durban. I missed Cliff for we had been students together, had worn the blue of Otago in the same rep. team, done all our training together and joined 816 at the same time.

Our next trip was also with the 2nd Escort Group and on board was a War Correspondent, A. Devine from the *Daily Sketch*, who eventually wrote a series of articles about our work. *Tracker* seemed to attract writers, because we had the author John Moore on our previous trip from which he produced a small book *Escort Carrier.* Well out to sea we ran into a series of gales in one of which, described as the worst in living memory, we rolled a record official 52 degrees and slowly straightened up – a most unnerving experience! At one stage the steel lashings on some of the aircraft snapped and they started charging around the hangar. Eventually all was brought under control but some of the squadron and ship's crew had taken appalling risks to get the aircraft tied down. A few days after this when the weather had moderated a little we were sent on patrol well away from the group. As it was November 5th Jack made the suggestion that we pop off a Very cartridge to celebrate Guy Fawkes, but while the idea was being debated there was a loud noise from the engine and with a loss in power we started going down. Everything possible was thrown overboard and I fired off the rockets which I suppose could be regarded as a celebration. With some difficulty I managed to get the aircraft up to 300 feet, a Mayday was sent and we headed for home. The carrier was already into the wind and prepared for an emergency landing, so we went straight in. Later I found that broken rods had cut out power from two of the nine cylinders, but the good old Peggy engine had still got us home. That night the escorts obtained an Asdic contact and Walker signalled the group that he had a firm contact and would sink the U-boat at 0700 hrs, which meant that he had to maintain contact for the remainder of the night – not an easy task! Promptly at the designated time the first depth charges exploded and in half an hour came a typical Walker signal: 'Have picked up human remains and other trophies.'

Overnight Shemol's engine had been repaired though the special tensioning spanner for tightening the cylinder heads was not available on board, so I was not surprised when we returned to the carrier after our next patrol and once again the engine gave a mighty bang. The group was well down towards the Azores at the time and was hunting a U-boat which had been forced down by one of the aircraft. It was a beautiful day, so I decided to ditch as the Peggy was having a bad dose of hiccups and with each we sank a little further. Jock was looking for a spot on his tunic where he was going to sew the Goldfish badge for having used his Mae West life jacket and we were already below masthead height when Jack called over the intercom to say that the carrier was preparing to land on. I came in from well astern with plenty of height to spare because of the hiccups. We had two on the way in so that by the time we crossed over the rounddown we were at the ideal height for landing and plonked onto the deck. I opened the throttle to taxi forward and there was a deathly silence. Having got safely down the Peggy had finally expired. Apparently coming in we had made an impressive sight with oil and flames spewing forth. Later the escorts fired their depth charges and we soon had a signal that the second U-boat was confirmed sunk. During all this the maintenance crews had been working day and night, as after the gales only three of our twelve aircraft were in flying condition.

The gales soon returned and one night a mechanic testing a Very pistol pulled the trigger without checking to see if it was loaded. In a moment the aircraft was on fire and the dreaded call 'Fire in the hangar' came over the tannoy. Leading the rush to the hangar were the aircrew who had survived the disaster on *Dasher*. Carriers had enough fuel on board to keep the aircraft going for three months and also enough diesel to refuel the escorts. The fire was extinguished in record time, but at the height of the excitement there was an explosion, a U-boat had fired two torpedoes at us, but fortunately these had exploded a short distance away.

By now the fuel supplies were getting low and the weather conditions were not conducive to refueling at sea, so the group headed for Newfoundland and the American Lend Lease base there. After a month at sea the group docked at the Argentine naval base to the music of the group's signature tune 'A-Hunting We Will Go' played by a US Navy band. It was a tribute to the fame of Captain Walker who unfortunately died a short time later as a direct result of the stress and strain he had subjected himself to in the war against the U-boat menace. As a result of tremendous efforts by the maintenance crews six Swordfish and the Seafires were flown ashore and rather shocked the Americans by the carrier type of landings done putting the aircraft down in the minimum time. The stay at Argentina was a revelation, transport readily available, no shortages of anything and fantastic recreational facilities, though the formality of their Wardroom and club surprised us. We were also astounded that all this luxury counted as overseas service for the Americans and that they received a medal for being there. Among the lighter events of our stay ashore was the reaction to the Seafires, the astonishment caused by one Swordfish winning a bet by taking off across the runway instead of along it and also the interest shown by many of the sloop's officers who came with us on joyrides. Two of our Scottish engineers persuaded fellow Scotsman Bobby Creighton to take them night flying after a good session in the wardroom. When one of them saw that the altimeter read the equivalent of ten minutes before closing time at a pub he tried to climb out for a final drink. Fortunately, his friend was just sober enough to haul him back into the cockpit.

As *Tracker* needed repairs at a proper dockyard we left the escorts and headed for Norfolk in Virginia and parked near the *Indomitable* which was also being repaired. Norfolk provided plenty of relaxation while the dockyard experts did the repairs and repainted everything in sight which did not move. Two members of the squadron spent this break buying up the city's supply of white millet to the complete mystification of the rest of us. When we reached the Clyde these two displayed a quite unusual interest in the squadron stores, including, of course, the cartons of millet as they were sent ashore. At the railway station the millet cartons were carried to one side and relabelled. When we returned from leave we found that white millet, which is the essential ingredient in bird seed, was a banned import and our two smugglers had made an enormous profit on their effort.

Other chaps headed for the lingerie shops to obtain goodies to impress wives and girlfriends back in UK. Ivor, a Welsh fighter pilot, was overheard in the following exchange with a nice young assistant, 'What size panties would a girl of my height and rather slim take?' 'About 32', came the reply. Quoth Ivor, 'Better make them 36 then, and allow room for play.' Jack also distinguished himself by purchasing a nightdress for Sheila and rather horrified the assistant by some of his requirements. The nightie had to be black and by inspection he had to be able to see his hand quite clearly. All the way back the nightly routine was for Jack to unpack his purchase and hold it up with his imagination running riot along obvious lines. The sight of Jack at these times provided a cause for much ribaldry. He had grown a rather wispy beard during the long trip and apparently when he met Sheila was told the beard had to come off before he entered the marital bed. I believe it was just about the fastest shave in history.

After a work-up in Chesapeake Bay we headed north for Argentina escorted initially by a blimp of the US Navy. A short stay this time and in a blizzard we left to join a homeward bound convoy. The old routine of flying patrols in less than satisfactory conditions was enlivened by one of the Seafires being sent off to intercept an unidentified aircraft – it was a Liberator. This was the only operational flight by the Seafires in the entire time we were on *Tracker* and the Swordfish pilots felt really sorry for the fighter boys in their frustration. We arrived back in the Clyde for Christmas and as the squadron was leaving *Tracker* a wardroom party was soon underway. The aircrew were soon well away celebrating the end of the drought, but the highlight of the evening was the commander, a popular figure with the squadron, debagged and standing on one of the tables giving a well sung version of the old classic 'Cats on the rooftops etc.' So, after a great party we said farewell to *Tracker*, had some leave and joined a sister ship HMS *Chaser*.

Chaser, under Captain H. McLintock RN, proved to be a very happy ship and luckily in view of what was to come, it had a first class batsman. Rapidly ship and squadron settled into the routine of working-up exercises though I was somewhat embarrassed on my first night flight from this ship. As I took off the ASI needle dropped off depriving me of any speed indication so I had to settle down and fly 'by the seat of my pants', which was not the ideal situation at night. Jack Durban called the carrier for permission to land ashore, but unfortunately the signal was misunderstood and we were told to land on. A night landing is always a little more tricky than one at day and with no accurate speed indication the three of us were particularly pleased to touch down safely. When Jack and I reported to the skipper the latter was all set to give us a good bollocking because the signal from Jack had been misinterpreted as ASV (Radar) u/s instead of ASI (speed indicator) u/s. When this was sorted out it was compliments all round. On the completion of the trials we were duly inspected by FOCT (Flag Officer Carrier Training) and off to join the 2nd Battle Squadron of the Home Fleet at Scapa Flow. After a few days flying from the shorebase at Hatson we rejoined *Chaser* and set sail with the anti-aircraft cruiser HMS *Black Prince* and a very strong escort to form the escort for convoy JW 57 bound for Russia. Convoys to Russia provided a stern test for both the Royal Navy and the Merchant Navy for the weather was as bad an opponent as the enemy U-boats and aircraft and usually there were plenty of these. Our convoy was made up of 43 merchant ships, mainly American, and, including a covering force of heavy cruisers, an escort of about 30 warships. For comparison an Atlantic convoy was pleased if it had more than half a dozen escorts. For this trip we had a fighter component of six Wildcat fighters from 878 Squadron. They had arrived in style with landings which would have wrecked any Stringbag and were, like most American aircraft designed for naval flying, marvellous for deck landings. Among the pilots was Peter Bethell, another Kiwi and John Nicholls who had recently joined 816. There were now three of us on *Chaser*.

When we picked up the convoy a Swordfish and a Wildcat were sent off to fly around the convoy for a couple of hours to make sure that the rather trigger-happy American gunners could identify the protecting aircraft. As the skipper put it, 'McLintock wants his angels back.'

For a few days all was well and the patrolling aircraft kept strict radio silence, but after five days had elapsed we knew that we had been spotted by the German reconnaissance aircraft. Unused to Arctic conditions we were unprepared for the effect of the cold on crews and aircraft. The Admiralty, in its wisdom, had issued the Swordfish crews with its idea of protection against the cold in aircraft with open cockpits – woolly longjohns.

These irritated the skin so much that most of us preferred the cold and just used our normal flying kit. The Wildcat pilots had the benefit of closed-in cockpits and a heater and so were not so badly affected. On the first patrol when severe icing conditions were met three of us had the same experience. Soon after take off all the pilots noticed that the oil temperature was off the clock which only read to 80 degrees. It had climbed to an estimated 143 degrees, and the oil pressure which had a lower operating limit of 55 pounds per square inch for five minutes was down to 30 pounds. If flying over land a forced landing would have been the correct thing to do as an engine failure was very likely. With the Arctic sea below there was no option but to keep flying. However the reliable Pegasus kept rumbling on. Three subs were sighted ahead of the convoy. I was patrolling astern to force any U-boat on the surface to submerge and by so doing make it impossible for it to catch the convoy which was rated as a fast one in comparison with the Atlantic ones. This was a role of anti-submarine aircraft. We had the pleasure of the company of the German shadowing aircraft, a Blohm and Voss 138n flying boat on a parallel course to ours but five miles away. On landing we found that the oil problem was due to the oil in the external air coolers freezing while the planes were waiting for take-off. The mechanics went to work on the problem and soon had it solved (the petty officer in charge of engine maintenance got a well deserved MBE for his work on this operation). Huge tent-like hoods were placed over the engines with hot air piped into them and immersion heaters were put in the oil tanks. The aircrew problems could not be solved and thawing out after flying became part of the routine. As we approached the Arctic circle it became part of the daily duty for the deck handling crew to chip and sweep the ice and snow off the flight deck to make take-offs less hazardous. Snowstorms and visibility could not be controlled and Frank Borlace landing on in a blizzard hit the round-down and sheered off the undercarriage. The lower wing buckled and he missed all the arrester wires and hit the barrier. This effort became known in the squadron as the 'Borlace Leap'. The aircraft was a complete wreck, so it was pushed along the deck while mechanics worked frantically to remove equipment before the wreck was jettisoned over the stern, the last mechanic being dragged out of the cockpit as the wreck slid overboard. On my second patrol we sighted a U-boat on the surface, but there was no suitable cloud cover and it dived before we could attack. By now Admiralty estimated that there were 32 U-boats in operation against the convoy. On our fifth night out from Scapa the destroyers sank U713. Later there was a large explosion as the Tribal Class destroyer, *Mahratta*, was hit by a torpedo. Only seventeen of the crew of 250 were saved despite determined and highly risky attempts by other escorts.

Many German aircraft were patrolling at a distance around the convoy including FW 200s, BV 138s and an occasional JU88. The fighter boys made many attacks but without much luck. Their Wildcats were equipped with 0.5 in. machine guns and against the heavy armour of the German patrol aircraft the bullets simply bounced off. The convoy sailed north until we were only 900 miles from the North Pole and then turned South to head for Kola Inlet which was our destination. About 100 miles from Russia we saw our first Russian fighter and from here on we had an escort of Russian fighters until we anchored in Kola Inlet. The merchant ships continued on to Murmansk but the warships stayed in Kola. While anchored offshore the carrier kept up a full head of steam and a continuous anchor watch was ready to slip the anchor so that the ship could head out to sea if German aircraft appeared – there was a German airbase only 70 miles away, but fortunately they left us in peace for some reason.

Only a token group was allowed to accept an invitation to lunch at the Red Air Force base and so go ashore. All apparently went off very well indeed, but the vodka in large quantities proved too much for most of our representatives. Our junior doctor arrived back with a beatific look on his face laden with loot as well as vodka. He had found that condoms were a high value trading commodity and had exchanged most of *Chaser*'s supply for desirable souvenirs. That night we had the choir of the Russian Northern Fleet on board to entertain us in the hangar on an improvised stage. The choir put on a magnificent show of singing and Cossack dancing which was much appreciated by us all. In the wardroom afterwards we entertained the Russian officers who proved surprisingly susceptible to whisky and rum, so we managed to even the exchange up somewhat. At dinner they amazed us by their capacity for white bread, pickles and sauces the group of three that I entertained consuming four jars of mustard pickles at the meal. In harbour the squadron officers shared duties with the ship's officers, and so Bob LePage as Officer of the Watch had to get all the Russians collected up to go ashore. As they went onto their picket boat each of the 100 or so members of the choir insisted on kissing Bob heartily on each cheek, an embarrassing experience for a phlegmatic Englishman. I was next on duty and all went quietly until my relief was due. When he did not arrive I sent one of the ratings to give him a shake-up, but when that proved unsuccessful I went down and found him still flaked out. A towel soaked in icy seawater applied to his midriff had excellent restorative properties so I headed off to my bunk. Before I could get to sleep a messenger arrived to say that Ropey had not turned up. We found him in the back cockpit of a Swordfish trying to navigate the plane somewhere – I gave up and stood his watch for him.

The following day the carrier moved out as part of the escort for the homeward bound convoy RA 57 containing 32 merchant ships. On the first day a strong gust of wind lifted one of the Wildcats right off the deck and it plunged down the open lift well without injuring anyone. Off Bear Island we lost our only merchantman to a torpedo but the entire crew was rescued. By now the U-boats were concentrating for an onslaught on the convoy, which gave the squadron their opportunity and most crews made at least one attack. Three U-boats were sunk and five damaged with a few survivors being picked from two of them, but some of these died from the effects of the cold after being taken on board the escort. All the submarines attacked were very heavily armed and put up a thick curtain of flak. Their gunners, however, seemed incapable of allowing for the slow speed of the Swordfish none of which sustained any damage. This was in spite of the fact that the attacks were carried out in a shallow dive starting from about 2000 yards from the target and firing the rockets from a range of 600 yards or less. Wind conditions were so light that one day my rocket load was reduced to six projectiles, a fact of which I was unaware and in an attack flew very close trying to get rid of two rockets which were not in place. In the evasive turn away at sea level Jock eagerly seized his opportunity and let fly with his machine gun, but the sound of his gun popping away made me think the flak was getting more accurate and so the evasive action became more violent. The next day the wind over the flight deck dropped right away and when signals were picked up from a U-boat two of us were sent to find and attack it. Each aircraft was armed with only one depth charge – Swordfish could carry six as a normal load – and the air gunners were left behind. Luckily the submarine had dived by the time we got to its position.

All this time the Wildcats had been chasing away the shadowing German aircraft. The Luftwaffe made no concerted attacks on the convoy, probably because of our fighters. This was contrary to the usual practice of continued attacks by both torpedo and bomb carrying aircraft. A few days after the height of the battle we sailed into Scapa Flow.

As the squadron readied for take-off there was a call from the tannoy 'Range Sub-Lt. Mason.' This was the command given to get aircraft on deck and Jim who was one of the pilots with a sub to his credit was operated on for the removal of his appendix a day later. The other pilots with confirmed kills were Pete Beresford and Ben Bennett.

Before we left *Chaser* there was a flurry of congratulatory signals and a report on *Chaser*'s part in the battle.

From the official report:

> 'The battle was over and due to the determination and courage of the flying crews the old Swordfish had completely defeated a large U-boat pack (estimated at 32 submarines). . . . . Credit is due to all officers and men for successful and cheerful teamwork but the honour of *Chaser*'s part in the battle goes without any shadow of doubt to the aircrews of 816 Squadron whose courageous flying in appalling Arctic conditions in snow blizzards and fair weather alike was to the highest merit.'

The squadron flew down to the Donibristle to check out the damage done to the engines by the extreme cold and were delighted to find the Peggies had withstood the conditions unharmed. We were not so delighted that *Chaser* had dragged her anchor in a gale and had been damaged. *Chaser* had been due to take the squadron to lay mines on the first of the attacks on the *Tirpitz*. Freddy Nottingham was then given the choice for the squadron of either transferring on to Avengers and going straight out to the Pacific or to stay with our beloved Stringbags and go down to Cornwall in support of the invasion. So off we went to Perranporth.

Reports had been received from intelligence sources that the Germans were developing some new types of U-boats, and it was thought that one of these, the W-boat, could be operational at the time of the invasion of Europe. These subs were equipped with a special type of engine which could run submerged off high test peroxide fuel at a speed of up to 25 knots and this would have made many of the escorts useless against them. Several of the more experienced FAA squadrons were hurriedly sent to cover the convoy routes from Lundy Island around the Scilly Isles to Kent. Avenger squadrons were to cover the day patrols and Swordfish did the night flying. It was a good posting for us as there was a good beach for relaxation, the village was a pleasant place and the billets for 816 aircrew were in Droskyn castle, a peacetime hotel, were excellent. Regular patrols gave us plenty of flying, but our stay was marred by an unfortunate accident. One of the newer crews with no experience in dropping bombs was sent up to drop a live 500 lb bomb. The plane was seen going well below the minimum safety height for release and it was blown to pieces with the loss of the crew.

From a personal viewpoint my observer Jack Durban became ill and had to give up flying duties, and as we had been together for some time I certainly missed him. My new navigator was Dick Mably and he soon proved to be as competent as Jack. The latter went as director officer on a carrier in the Pacific.

After three and a half months at Perranporth in which the threatened menace of the W-boat did not materialize we were told to dispose of all flares which gave a good pyrotechnic for the locals. The accumulated mess funds went on a great party to which many of the locals who had offered us hospitality were invited. Jumbo Kay who had drawn the short straw for the first patrol of the night was so frustrated that he carried out a first class 'beat up' of Droskyn Castle watched with considerable interest by the RAF Station Commander who must have appreciated the performance since he made no official comment. Earlier in our stay we had lost Freddy who had been sent to take over an Avenger squadron in the Pacific. He was replaced by an RN officer with no operational experience which was not a satisfactory situation. Soon, however, we were on the way to RNAS Maydown near Londonderry. Here 816 was disbanded with some crews going for a break from operational flying and others joining 836 Squadron which was the Navy's largest squadron with about 90 aircraft. This squadron operated in flights of three or four aircraft on MAC ships or merchant aircraft carriers. These were a British concept designed to give close support to the convoy they were in. A grain ship or a tanker had its upper works removed and a small flight deck about 450 ft by 60 ft was installed. The grain MAC's had a small hangar below the flight deck, but the tanker ones did not have this luxury and all maintenance was carried out on deck. There was a small island or bridge on the starboard side for control of the ship and aircraft. On each MAC there was a resident RN group of Doctors, signalmen and gunners under the control of the Air Staff Officer who also controlled flying operations. Each flight consisted of a flight commander and two or three pilots with their crews and also a batsman. The flight also had twenty to thirty ratings who did all the aircraft handling and maintenance. The accommodation for the flying crews was quite good and general living conditions excellent. The ship's master and all the crew were Merchant Navy and each ship carried about 90% of its normal cargo of either grain or oil products as usual. Only Swordfish could operate from such small flight decks, especially as the top speed of such ships was only about 12 knots. To P Flight were allocated John Godley as flight commander, Jim Mason and myself as pilots with our usual crews and Pete Beresford another ex-816 pilot as batsman.

The 19 MAC ships started coming into operations in 1943 and continued until VE Day after which most were returned to their normal MN function. Usually patrols were flown around the convoy or ahead and astern to provide an immediate protection to it. However, if signals were picked up by HF/DF detection crews might be sent a considerable distance away looking for the U-boat. The Germans never realised that each time a sub surfaced and signalled bearings were taken by the High Frequency Direction Finding gear from both warships and shore stations. This meant their positions could be plotted and convoys re-routed or escorts and or aircraft sent to locate and attack.

P Flight was allocated to *Adula*, a tanker MAC and one on which John had served before joining 816, so we melded in quickly with the ship's personnel, especially with the Chief Officer Bob Allen, who took an almost fatherly interest in the aircrews and entertained us with his stories about life on passenger liners which he had left, we were lead to believe, because of exhaustion not due to his professional duties. His friendship did much to make *Adula* a particularly happy ship. As all the aircrew and ratings were experienced at carrier operations no work-up was necessary and we sailed to join a Halifax bound convoy almost immediately.

The U-boats by this time were equipped with the schnorkel device. This was a hinged tube which could be erected and used as an air intake by a submerged U-boat so enabling it to run underwater on its diesel engines at a higher speed and also to charge its batteries without coming to the surface. These abilities gave a new lease of life to the U-boats. To try to locate the schnorkels we carried out patrols at 50 to 100 feet but it was like searching for the proverbial needle in a haystack. The antisubmarine war was, in fact, shifted to the waters around the UK. Twice I saw burning tankers just a few miles off the shore of Northern Ireland torpedoed in sight of land. Some convoys were routed through the Irish Sea, but the U-boats lay in wait very close to or even inside Irish territorial waters. The escorts kept up an almost constant barrage of depth charges making sleep impossible and, instead of relaxing so close to home, patrols were still necessary. Schnorkels and the new faster types of submarines being developed could have had a considerable influence if the war had continued much longer.

Sometimes the stops at Halifax were not without event. The usual routine was to fly the aircraft off RCAF Dartmouth which was only a ferry ride across the harbour from Halifax and this allowed maintenance to be done under comparatively luxurious conditions. Because of the licensing laws in Nova Scotia we made sure of stocking up for the usual parties which were usually held at the Lord Nelson Hotel. The waiters there would solemnly bring us whatever additives were required and just as solemnly the bottles would come out from under the table so that the additives could be suitably diluted with the chosen essential. As a full bottle of Scotch, for example, cost us only five shillings at duty free prices we were understandably popular with the Canadians. On the way to Halifax our mess bills tended to be rather high, but on the way back our purchases were much more restrained as Canadian Rye replaced the Scotch and we had to pay six shillings for only a half bottle. Most aircrew would drink very little at sea as we had to be prepared to fly at any time of the day or night, but the parties in harbour more than made up for the drought and fortified us for the next time at sea.

On one occasion while in Halifax John Godley and his observer Jake Bennet were duty crew aboard the ship while the rest of the flights had adjourned to the Lord Nelson. Just after our arrival there John breezed to tell us that we had to fly patrols as soon as he got back. Apparently there was a report of a U-boat a few miles off shore and despite the large number of RCAF aircraft including

Liberators and Hudsons we were nominated to carry out the search. John and Jake duly went into the ops room for briefing by a rather earnest RCAF officer and Jake was loaded down with maps seemingly of the whole Atlantic, signal codes for all theatres of war, flares and emergency rations etc. They also had to surrender the contents of their pockets. The climax was reached when Jake was handed a large covered box and the question and answer session followed.

'What is in that?' asked a horrified Jake.

'A pigeon,' came the reply.

'What on earth is it for?' said Jake.

'In case you are forced down at sea and it can carry a message to base,' was the answer.

'Give me back my cigarette lighter,' demanded Jake. 'If we are forced down I will cook the bloody bird.'

On one crossing the SOE was picking up signals from U-boats with the HF/DF and so we were flying constant patrols. Although our aircraft were equipped with an improved radar, so were the Germans and they could pick us up before we had a contact. The threat posed by the presence of an aircraft caused them to submerge immediately. John Godley was doing a dusk patrol several miles ahead of the convoy one stormy evening when the ASO signalled him that SOE had picked up a signal from a probable U-boat a short distance from the aircraft. Jim and I were scrambled and then flew out to rendezvous with John so that a concerted attack could be carried out. The three aircraft searched the area thoroughly, but could find nothing although the SOE was still reporting radar contact. By this time it was completely dark so we formed up and flew back to the carrier in formation. Despite the weather conditions and a forty knot wind along the deck all three aircraft had landed safely in ninety seconds. The probable explanation was that the U-boat had dived and the radar operators on the escorts had mistaken John's aircraft for the sub and so we were flying around looking for one of our own.

After three months on *Adula* John Godley was promoted to Lieutenant-Commander and sent to 835 Squadron as CO and I replaced him as Flight Commander. A new crew joined us and it turned out that the pilot had been on a shore station for some time before being quietly ushered off on 'ops'. He had been discovered in a compromising position with the Mess Secretary's Wren on the wardroom billiard table. We never learned whether it was because she was the Secretary's Wren or because it was the sacrosanct billiard table that the pilot was so rapidly transferred.

Not long after John's departure Jim and I with our crews were summoned to the Squadron Commander's office. We duly reported worrying as to which series of 'blacks' had been discovered, but on arrival found that a rather restrained officer had been directed to read us some letters of commendation from C-in-C Western Approaches and also FOCT. We were being commended for:

(a) Completing over 100 landings on a MAC ship without accident.
(b) Our night operational flights under severe conditions.
(c) Landing on *Adula* while she was refuelling escorts at sea.

Apparently these incidents were novel as far as MAC ships were concerned although all were regarded as routine events on escort carriers.

Although we did not know it at the time we had severed our connection with *Adula*, which was much to our sorrow for she was a very happy ship and the relationships with the MN excellent. Our next MAC ship was *Miralda*, also an Anglo-Saxon tanker MAC, and the same old routine of patrols day after day continued except when the weather was completely hopeless for ordinary patrols. We did, however, learn a further use for condoms. One of the problems of the aircraft on deck all the time was that the electric terminals needed to fire the rocket projectiles became badly corroded by the sea air. Various methods were tried to cure the problem but with limited success until the Doc came up with the perfect solution and so the three Stringbags proudly wore a total of 24 condoms. On reaching port however we received a message:

'It is appreciated that protection is necessary but need you make it so obvious.'

On *Miralda* we tended to be a much more self-contained unit and a feature of life on board became the flight party held the night we entered harbour. We found that all interested ratings and officers, could crowd into one of the two-berth cabins. Our killick in charge of engines, and one of the pilots proved to be skilled tellers of tales and singers of suitable songs and the rest of us provided the choruses. Unfortunately tape recorders were not available as we could have done with one. Pete Beresford tried valiantly on most occasions to keep up with proceedings until, inevitably, his writing became completely illegible. After one such party two of us had to carry the killick down to his quarters and toss him on his bunk. The following morning we had to fly off to our base at Maydown and I was warming up the engine of the Swordfish when a very hung-over face appeared on the wrong or starboard side of the cockpit and shakily said:

'Gee Sir, I want to say thanks for last night, it's the first time I've been put to bed by my CO.'

I was feeling rather seedy myself and did not appreciate the humour of the situation until later.

When we landed at Maydown I was met by the news that I was being given three months leave in New Zealand and so, after farewells and a fortnight before VE day, I sailed for home and Mollie whom I had not seen for over four long years.

Ode to the 'Stringbag'

Between a cloud and a cloud
I saw you glide
in the last light, lees of the cup of day.
your good old 'Peggy' bumbling away:
the sky, and the night, and the sea beneath you, wide
and lonely, three infinites of grey.

But you had purpose, Swordfish. You were going
about your business at that steady amble
which seems so comic to those who have not seen
your shaking, snaking path when you are throwing
yourself about the sky, shell-bursts between
each bank.
or out turning a fighter in the gamble
for hitting-space.
You fraud of a Stringbag, you.

What can you do with a Stringbag?
What *can't* you do?
You can aerobat; you can stand her on her tail;
go into a vertical dive – and pull out sweetly
(you won't find the Stringbag doing a high-speed stall!).
You can take her up in any weather at all
that can be flown in.
You can trust her completely
even if visibility's next to nil,
or you have to land in a mid-Atlantic gale.
Whatever the job you give her, she will not fail—
if there are kills to be made she'll be in at the kill.
Bombing? She carries more than a Blenheim does—
and watch her spot for the guns of the Battle Fleet!

She'll torpedo a cruiser as soon as she gets the buzz,
and (you ask Doenitz!) the U-boats are her meat.

Oh, they spoil you for other aircraft for good, do Swordfishes—
they've always looked obsolescent: they've never been obsolete:
they give a fellow the feeling of confidence and ease
like a seasoned pipe, or dog you've trained, or old shoes kind to the feet.
For crews have learned to trust them who have had time to learn:
in long lone hours of night flight when the sky is a dry point plate
as in the infinite instant of the first evasive turn
after the fish strikes water, and they open up on the crate.

Well. They've stopped producing Stringbags. And doubtless They know best.
I'll fly the kites they give me – and think of my earliest love.
They're grand are the Barracudas, and the Seafires, and the rest.
but – I know what the Psalmist meant, now, when he sighed for the wings of a dove.
And after the war is over, when the Brave New World appears
with planes to suit all pockets, and a seat in a sky-train's cheap,
if I cannot purchase a Stringbag to solace my latter years—
as, once, men took to a bathchair, perhaps I'll take to a jeep.

R. C. S.

Lieut (A) A. B. Foley RNZNVR

Arch Foley was one of the characters of the *Dominion Monarch* Draft. He served in 897 and 809 Squadrons with the author. He flew Seafires in the Fleet Air Arm as he played all sports – rugby, later golf and more recently lawn bowls – with a judicious mix of aggression and at times provocation. Arch had an interesting and decidedly adventurous career, particularly after the author was 'shipped' out of the 809 Squadron on 17th April 1944 to be trained as one of Bob Everett's 'new era' batsmen. It is also interesting to note that on 20th April, only three days later, Royal Marine Major Al Wright transferred command of 809 Squadron to Lieut Commander (A) H. D. B. Eaton RNVR, so he obviously knew he was due for a move when the author received the 'push'.

On 2nd May 1944, 809 Squadron rejoined HMS *Stalker* in the Irish Sea and set sail for Gibraltar where the aircraft were flown off to North Front Airfield on 24th May. The squadron remained there until 5th June when it flew out to Blida about 30 miles south west of Algiers.

From this point various pilots were temporarily seconded to RAF fighter squadrons in the Desert Air Force based at Orvieto, Fabrica and Perugia in Italy.

Arch takes up the narrative from his arrival in Perugia where he was seconded to RAF 145 squadron (spitfire Mk VIII) commanded by the famous test pilot Squadron Leader Neville Duke and part of the fighter wing commanded by the Battle of Britain ace Group Captain 'Cocky' Dundas.

RAF 145 SQUADRON
Perugia, Italy
Spitfire VIII, CO Squadron Leader, Neville Duke.

July 5, 1944
I flew from Algiers to Rome by Dakota
Rome to Viterbo by Anson
Orvieto to Perugia by Fairchild.

I was the only FAA guy at that time. We flew mostly dive bombing trips on roads and bridges, all defended targets. There was plenty of flak about. I did three bombing trips on July 10th. I had told the CO I wanted experience, I sure got it. The guys in the BPF would have pooped themselves. I think now, anyone would have to be silly to fly low level, but you never heard anyone saying they were scared. I suppose we were apprehensive but were concentrating so much on what we were doing, we never had time to be scared. I was a stooge, a No 2 in Italy and had volunteered for some of the trips to get the experience. I suppose we were just doing what we were trained for, mostly it was marvellous, quite exciting really. It was all good fun – until I got shot down.

My number came up on 15th July, 1944; dive-bombing transport. There was plenty of 80 mil and 40 mil about. I had just dropped my 500–pounder – fortunately – when I got swiped by a 40 mil. Talk about Elvis 'shaking all about'. Sparks out of exhaust ports, oil temperature off the clock. Turned the key off, with just enough speed to get up to 10,000 ft, heading south. Picked out a good field, but it was occupied by Germans, bent on my demise! I stretched my glide but hit an embankment, my plane exploded and burnt out.

I was picked up by Italians and my carcase taken over by Pom patrol to 19 Casualty Clearing Station, Orvieto, their General Hospital in Naples. I had a collapsed lung, and abrasions.

The Germans had been waiting for us that day. Our flight had been led by an RAF Flight Lieutenant, a Scotsman and better than most. I just happened to be the unlucky one that day – there was always someone unlucky. The rest, like me, had just dropped their bombs and were heading home, but not me, I was making a forced landing. The Flight Leader had kept an eye on me though and was able to report what had happened.

The Italian peasants had looked after me and summoned the Pom patrol. I felt quite buggered when I came to with an Italian priest leaning over me pronouncing the last rites. I summoned up sufficient energy to rise up and tell him to Taiho! On discharge from hospital I was given a slip, stating I was not fit to fly for the next three months. I hid the chit.

I rejoined *Stalker* by getting a ride in a corvette to Corsica from Naples. 809 were in ground attack role in the South of France. We were supporting the invasion with ground attacks on designated targets, mostly strafing transport. We didn't do much, except lose Jeff Jefferson. George Morris landed in the sea and got picked up by a MTB. He said he was several fathoms down before he got out. Good guy – George. Eventually he died of overdoses of whiskey in Glasgow.

Tyson Davidson was with us in the Med. We were involved in a working up exercise off Gibraltar, before we headed to Blida.

Tyson came in on a dead stall landing approach – his usual which Tony Fradd allowed. He tried to fly straight into the hangar deck but hit the round down and plastered himself on the after gun platform. I was a pallbearer at the only naval funeral at sea which I have ever seen. We put his carcass over the side, sewn up in canvas.

Just before Perugia, I led a flight from Gibraltar to Blida, refuelling at Oran. It was one of the longest flights, certainly the longest for me. I led the flight over the sea, moving with the carrier which was getting ready for the south of France.

In Blida, we'd be on standby at the airfield, four aircraft on standby at a time. It was ludicrous really. We were on constant readiness for JU88s which were doing hit and run jobs. They'd be flying past at 300 knots! We never took off!

I did have the pleasure of a flight from Blida to Reghaia, to take a Seafire L2C to a group captain who wanted to fly the aircraft. In exchange he let me fly a Spitfire 9, a high-level Spit, a two-speed, two-stage super-charger!

Aegean Sea

Stalker's base was Alexandria. As was the case in Algiers, the Squadron was sent ashore to Dekheila for safety's sake because there were still frogmen with limpet mines about. I didn't mind sleeping in a tent, as in Blida. We had transport. Grog up by day on *Stalker*, sleep at Dekheila by night. Plus hard lying money, 6/- a day, I think.

Tough War!

The objective of the Aegean Sea operation on the first trip was to harass the German garrisons on Kos, Leros and Rhodes, and to provide minesweeper cover. A minefree route had to be cleared for the next phase. Tony Perry hit a church steeple on Rhodes after a low level attack, and died later of his injuries, according to a signal.

The second phase was to dive bomb and strafe the retreating Germans from Valos Harbour to Larissa and beyond on the inland road north. The fleet took care of the coastal road and railway. Graham Moore and Les Baker bailed out on mainland Greece. They rejoined *Stalker* fairly quickly. 809 did quite well in the Aegean but some pilots would exaggerate the numbers of transport destroyed. An interesting thing about the Aegean, we had to find our own targets. We did this by armed reconnaisance – 500lb bombs, etc., at first light. I was the flight leader, so I would go to the main road between Valos and Larissa, and north. We would take about eight aircraft, and if there was a lot of transport about we would dive bomb the bridges or transport to slow them down.

My assessment from Al Wright, Above the Average: My assessment (final) from Eadon, Above the Average as a fighter and ground attack pilot.

A few pertinent remarks about the ground attack. It requires first of all a good CO and Senior Pilot. 809 had neither in my time. A leader must be able to fly Above the Average at low level, be a good shot and dive bomber and be able to plan a good tactical approach. He must brief himself and his flight on where and how he will do the job and the likely flak positions. He must be silly enough to fly Seafires and Spits, on low level operations, which they were not designed for. Neville Duke was a top fighter pilot, but he could not map read or navigate, just like Al Wright couldn't.

Debits!

(1) My record shows that I wrecked two Seafires at RNAS Burscough. NOT MY FAULT – Masters failed to fire off a Very light to indicate he was stopping in front of me.

(2) Landed a Seafire upside down at Paestum strip Salerno NOT MY FAULT
(3) Exploded in a Spitfire VIII at Perugia. NOT MY FAULT. *In other words a blameless record.*

Credits!

(1) Damaged Me 109 at Salerno.
(2) $^{1}/_{4}$ share destroyed Dornier flying boat at Volos, Greece.
(3) Scared the living daylights out of Huns, Italians and Greeks.
(4) Beaucoup de la sortie à maison de passe espagnol (très bon Monsieur – Pour les Jeune Chasseur pilotes c'est le repose et la récréation)!

Frights!

A South African pilot landed at Perugia after a dive bombing sortie with a 500lb bomb hung up. He failed to defuse it by the cockpit switch. It dislodged on landing and blew him to smithereens with me just ahead of him – no good for the nerves!

Author's Note

It is sad to report that my great friend Arch Foley answered the call to Valhalla on 14th May 1995.

The following epitaph composed by his four daughters aptly epitomises his unquenchable desire to prevail. Despite Arch's penchant for candidness he was farewelled by a very large number of friends and naval airmen.

FOLEY, Archibald Bernard (Arch), Regt No 2831, Lieutenant A. Fleet Air Arm RNZVR, WW2. – At his home in Napier, Sunday, May 14. Beloved husband of the late Mollie, *incorrigible* and much loved dad of Sandra, Wendy, Val, Kay, and father-in-law of Neil Edmundson, and loved grandfather of his 8 grandchildren, and 4 great-grandchildren.

Lieut(A) Jack A Cramp DSC RNZNVR

When war was declared in September 1939 I had just recently left Hamilton Boys' High School to take a position with Wright Stephenson & Co Ltd, the stock and station merchants. I was under age to join the Army, but the prospect of an adventurous life in the Air Force seemed rather attractive. With my parents' approval I applied. For some time there was no response and I began to wonder whether I had been rejected. Then out of the blue came an invitation from the Navy Office asking whether I would consider taking a medical examination preparatory to joining the Fleet Air Arm. I knew nothing whatsoever about this service so I had to do some quick research. What I discovered sounded very exciting, so I duly mustered for the medical check at HMS *Philomel*. My very first acquaintance in the FAA was a burly bloke by the name of Peter Bethell – we've been great mates ever since. We attended the same medical exam and he subsequently joined me in a draft of FAA recruits who sailed from Lyttleton in MV *Akaroa* in August 1940. There were 38 of us in the draft. My cabin mate was Tom Bassett. I was one of the youngest members, having celebrated my 19th birthday on 31st May.

We disembarked at Liverpool whence we were despatched by rail to Portsmouth. Here we were indoctrinated into the Navy at HMS *St Vincent*. These large barracks were originally the training establishment for seamen boy entrants, but on the outbreak of war a large area was allocated to FAA recruits.

We spent about two and a half months here being taught the rudiments of life in the Navy.

Those who survived this course, then proceeded to EFTS (Elementary Flying Training School). We, aspirants for torpedo bombers, went to Luton, north of London while the fighter boys went to Elmdon near Birmingham.

This was now mid-winter and the weather was atrocious. At Luton we were virtually snow-bound for the next three months. There was no consistent daily flying and some of our course were in despair because they had not gone solo by 15 hours which in good weather conditions should have been 8–12 hours.

From Luton we proceeded to SFTS (Service Flying Training School) at Netheravon near Salisbury where we flew Hawker Harts and Hinds, two delightful training planes.

The TBR boys, who had by this time won their 'wings' proceeded to Crail for a torpedo dropping course and later to Arbroath, both near Dundee, for a deck landing course.

At Crail and Arbroath we came under Royal Naval flying instructors. These were mainly permanent service chaps who were veterans of earlier war service in the aircraft carriers *Ark Royal, Eagle, Courageous* and *Glorious.* They generally tended to be more aloof than the RAF instructors who had taught us the rudiments of flying at Luton and Netheravon. Some in fact couldn't hide their resentment at having to deal with naval reserve officers and in particular colonials who had joined the service for hostilities only.

This unfortunate attitude manifested itself one day at Arbroath when the chief instructor Lieut Commander Bob Everett RN declared his feelings during the course of a lecture. He inferred if he had his way there would be no colonials in the service. This prompted one of our members Harold Hawken to stand up and challenge Everett to repeat his statement. Everett complied whereupon Harold said, 'Now excuse me, sir, we chaps came 12,000 miles to help you people, not to listen to nonsense like that. If we hear any more if it – you will be reported.' Now Everett was well known in the service for his arrogance, chimed back, 'and who do you propose to report me to, Hawken.'

There was dead silence – you could have heard a pin drop.

Harold stood up again: 'With respect, sir, if this occurs again we shall immediately report it to our New Zealand High Commissioner, Mr Bill Jordan.'

Everett was flattened – he had got the message in no uncertain manner. Everyone in the Royal Navy had a profound respect for Bill Jordan. Even officers of flag rank had been known to tremor at the very mention of his name. They were dead scared of provoking a political incident which could have destroyed their professional careers. On reflection, I have no doubt that the stand taken that day by Harold Hawken would have handed out a very sober message to other naval instructors and would have been beneficial to future New Zealand recruits.

To be fair, however, not all instructors were like this, but they never seemed to socialise with us as freely as the RAF men, many of whom were like ourselves, volunteers and had fought during the Battle of Britain.

Following the deck landing course I received my first posting along with Harold Hawken to 830 TBR squadron which was then based at Malta. This was an elite squadron and had been in the thick of things during the siege period.

Harold and I took passage from Milford Haven in one of the latest fast cruisers HMS *Dido.* She was crammed to the gunwales with essential supplies and personnel. She had the speed to run the blockade.

Harold and I didn't exactly have a comfortable trip, we slept on the floor in the wardroom all the way to Malta. She was travelling so fast that the bulkheads were shuddering and it was not easy to relax. By the time we disembarked at Valetta, had we been merchant seamen we would have qualified for hard lying money!

Peter Jacobsen also from our course joined our squadron shortly afterwards.

Our base was at an aerodrome called Hal Far on the south east corner of the main island. Bombing raids by German and Italian aircraft were a daily occurrence. Most of our own operations were at night, minelaying, bombing and torpedo attacks against enemy shipping passing either way between Sicily and North Africa past the island of Pantellaria. Some of the convoys leaving to return to Italian ports were reported by intelligence sources to be carrying prisoners of war. Consequently, some of our sorties had to be aborted.

Life at Hal Far during the daylight hours was pretty hectic and not without incident. When the air raid alerts were sounded the Maltese workers would immediately disappear. I can't say that I blamed them, but try as one might one couldn't get any work out of them until the all clear sounded.

Occasionally enemy aircraft were in the vicinity before the alert had been sounded. I recall one day while at Hal Far when I had some duty to attend to at the opposite side of the airfield. I chose to make a short cut across the field when suddenly there was a hell of a clamour screaming down behind me. Metal was flying all around me. It was an Me 109 strafing the field. His 7.9mm bullets were ricochetting in all directions. I just about had kittens – by dint of some inelegant ballet steps they missed me – Thank God. That was too bloody close for comfort.

When I joined 830 Squadron the commanding officer was an RN observer, Lieut Cdr (A) Frank Hopkins. Frank was a very fine officer – no nonsense about him whatsoever. He was there to do a job and did it well. He mucked in with the lads and created a good team spirit. When his six months tour elapsed he was replaced by another RN observer Lieut CDR (A) John Roe – another good type.

Obviously the Admiralty was pretty discriminating in their choice of commanders for this squadron.

The night sorties were pretty demanding, often calling for sorties of four and a half to five hours. That's a long time to be strapped in to a Swordfish cockpit.

However, my most frightening experience occurred in the daytime. On most night operations, we dispensed with the third crew member, our telegraphist air gunner.

His compartment was converted to take a 50 gallon saddle tank to give us extra endurance.

On one such operation my observer and I took off in a Swordfish armed with a 2000 lb torpedo plus the extra fuel tank. This was a very heavy load, especially as we had very little wind to climb into. I had a hell of a job getting it airborne and barely cleared the roof of a large hangar at the other end of the field. I actually had visions of flying through the hangar, but I gave one almighty yank on the control column and we cleared the roof with a few inches to spare. Whether it was the sudden change of altitude or not, I don't know but the generally reliable Pegasus engine spluttered and went silent.

Stick forward quickly and in front of us I could see a series of small vegetable plots each surrounded by a stone wall. I had to act fast, so I decided to 'mush' it into what looked like a quarter acre onion plot. This wiped off the undercarriage and we came to a stop amid a tangle of broken bits and pieces. The torpedo – Christ – I screamed to my observer who fortunately was unhurt 'Get out and run like hell – the torpedo will heat up.'

We scrambled over one wall then broke the world's record sprint time to dive over another where we thought we were at a reasonably safe distance. I had guessed that the air bottle would have fractured in the crash and the torpedo would heat up and soon explode. Sure enough there was an earth shattering bang and our lovely old Stringbag disintegrated – debris flying to all points of the compass. Another close one!

Some days later our CO summoned us to the crew room where he announced that we had to carry out a daylight torpedo attack against an Italian cruiser force which was near the island of Pantellaria. A day sortie like this would be nothing less than a suicide mission. He said he would prefer to have volunteers rather than issue orders. New Zealand had to be in it, so I stuck my hand up and was selected to pilot one of the four aircraft which was all we had serviceable. John Roe our CO was to be my observer.

We took off on a glorious sunny morning – not a cloud in the sky. There would be no way that we could shadow the enemy force – it was a real suicide job if ever there was one.

After flying for a little over one and a half hours we spotted the ships down sun – two cruisers and three destroyers. John said he would leave the tactical approach to me – we were then at about 6000 feet and the targets would have been about ten miles away. To attack out of the sun was our best option, so the four Swordfish commenced a long controlled dive to bring us about 50 feet above the water at a distance where we could drop the 'fish'. I selected one of the cruisers and had approached to a little over 1000 yards before they spotted us. I let go at about 900 yards by which time all hell had broken loose. The air was full of metal, black puffs, tracer and we were hit several times, but luckily nothing serious. Having dropped our fish I immediately took evasive action, but I happened to see two other Swordfish launch their torpedoes. One skipped on the surface and went under while the other one was a good drop and was heading for a destroyer. Because I was weaving I couldn't see what had happened to mine, but John reported that it was tracking well. A few moments later there was a big flash 'You hit her, Jack – jolly good show, old man.'

The other Swordfish had hit the destroyer near the stern, so two ships had been put out of action.

With that we got to hell out of it as fast as our lumbering Stringbags could go. Down on the deck – full throttle – Malta here we come!

There was no sign of enemy fighters. Perhaps we had attacked after they had left to refuel and their next patrol had not arrived on the scene.

An aerial reconnaissance later that morning confirmed that two ships had been badly damaged and our submarines were called up to supply the *coup de grace*.

That same afternoon our squadron received a further order to repeat the attack, this time with the remaining three Swordfish, mine being unserviceable. This was really inviting trouble; there was no need for it. It was really a suicide mission even if they had fighter cover, which regrettably they didn't. The submarines were already converging on the crippled ships, so why put lives of fine young men at unnecessary risk? As another naval airman has said, 'Their's is to do and die. And die they did.'

When the three Swordfish came within torpedo launching distance they were pounced on by an assortment of Maachi Reggiane and Me 109 fighters. They didn't have a hope. All were shot down. Six precious lives lost to the whim of someone in authority.

Because all 830 squadron had now been destroyed we were obliged to amalgamate with 828 squadron. By this time we had started to get replacement aircraft some flown in at night from Egypt and Spitfires flown off the US carrier *Wasp.*

Elements of the US Navy had become operational in the Mediterranean following the declaration of war in December 1941.

The *Wasp* was later torpedoed and sunk by Japanese aircraft off Guadalcanal in the Solomons 15th September 1942.

When the excitement had subsided John Roe approached me a few days later to tell me that Harold Hawken, Peter Jacobsen and I were now time expired men and would be flown back to UK as soon as an aircraft became available. Several nights later we left Malta on a Wellington bomber to land at Gibraltar early the following morning. From Gibraltar we took passage on a very fast liner in convoy with several others for the UK.

After a brief leave I received a posting to 766 Squadron at Machrihanish. This was under the command of Lieut Cdr (A) R. E. Bibby DSO and specialised in the night attack light torpedo course. I hadn't been there long when I was posted to 835 Squadron, a relatively new outfit that was forming up. This was to be the most unhappy period of my time in the Navy. The CO was an impossible little twirp. An RN Observer, ex *Ark Royal* Lieut Cdr (A) J. R. Lang. Like many RN types he couldn't stand reservists and because I was a Kiwi he just hated my guts. In my book he was nothing more than a spoilt little brat and there were times when I let him know it. He also had a 'twitch' which manifested itself in a constant blinking of his eyes. When we had a few drinks together I would refer to him as 'Blinkey'. God, did he hate me. Anyway it was one way of getting out of it. It was a hopeless squadron. The only pilots with operational experience were the senior pilot and myself.

Of all places to send us for working up, it had to be Hatston near Scapa Flow in the Orkney Islands. A more desolate place you couldn't imagine. The weather was abominable – it rained, it snowed, it hailed, it sleeted with howling gales for days on end.

Finally we left there to spend a short time at Stretton near Liverpool and later to join HMS *Activity*, a new small aircraft carrier.

It was at Stretton that I saw a notice calling for volunteers to train on multi-engined aircraft with a view to progressing to the new Mosquito fighter bomber. This was one way to get out, so I applied and *mirabile dictu*, I was accepted.

After a short course on Ansons and Oxfords I was posted to No 151 RAF Squadron then based at Colerne a few miles north of Bath. Here I had my introduction to this beautiful stream lined aircraft the Mosquito. After the lumbering old Swordfish this was pure magic. It developed nearly 3000 h.p. from two Rolls Royce Merlin engines giving it a capability of over 360 m.p.h. at about 14000 feet. Over three times the speed of my adorable old Swordfish. It had a service ceiling of 35,000 and an assortment of armament of four 20mm Hispano cannons and 303 machine guns, all mounted in the front of a fuselage. On the radar night fighters the machine guns were dispensed with, to allow for the night fighting detection equipment. Much of the fuselage and wings were made of plywood, so it was a very light aircraft with tremendous lifting capacity and dragged around by two monstrous engines. It was a delight to fly – I fell in love with it at first sight.

Following my familiarisation I took part in a variety of operations and served with 151 squadron continuously for the next two years. From Colerne we moved at intervals to other bases.

16/08/43 Middle Wallop – near Andover
24/03/44 Predannack – Cornwall
07/10/44 Castle Coombe – near Bath
19/11/44 Hunsdon – north of London
01/03/45 Bradwell Bay – Essex
17/05/45 Predannack – Cornwall

The operations were mostly at night – defence of London – night intruder flights over France and in support of the D-Day landings in France. This was a very interesting and satisfying period of my service in the Fleet Air Arm. My observer and I were the only two naval officers in 151 Squadron.

I was finally released for long service leave and arrived back in New Zealand in May 1945 just before VE day. I had been away for nearly five years.

Author's Note: Jack Cramp's remarkable feat in launching an aerial torpedo and sinking a fast moving Italian cruiser is unique in the annals of naval aviation.

There are few recorded incidents of warships being sunk by aerial torpedoes and in most cases the targets have been lying at anchor in harbour. The infamous Japanese attack at Pearl Harbour and the Fleet Air Arm victory at Taranto harbour, Italy are two such cases.

But to hit and sink a warship travelling at high speed requires a very high degree of skill and precision flying. Apart from courage in the face of intense anti-aircraft fire from the target, the pilot must select the ideal position and height from which to commence his dive. The speed must be controlled and the height of pull out over the water must be within certain prescribed limits. Having committed his aircraft to the attack, the pilot must maintain a precise height and speed above water and make an even more delicate allowance for deflection so the torpedo will hit the target at the selected point of travel. In the meantime the target could be changing direction.

On 25th May the German Battleship *Bismarck* was intercepted by a strong British naval force in Denmark Strait near Greenland. Swordfish torpedo bombers were flown off from the aircraft carrier HMS *Victorious* and one of these recorded a hit on the hull of the *Bismarck*. The damage, however, was minimal and it failed to slow down the enemy vessel.

The following day, further sorties were flown off the carrier HMS *Ark Royal* by Swordfish aircraft from 818 and 820 Squadrons. These attacks resulted in two hits, neither of which penetrated the heavily armoured hull, but one hit the stern and severely damaged the rudder of the *Bismarck*. This caused the enemy vessel to go into an uncontrollable turn to reduce speed.

This allowed the somewhat slower British battleships, *King George V* and *Rodney* to close on the *Bismarck* and pound it into submission with heavy calibre shells. Ablaze from bow to stern the *Bismarck* was delivered the *coup de grace* by the cruiser HMS *Dorsetshire* which sank it with torpedoes.

Another naval action during which Fleet Air Arm aircraft launched aerial torpedoes was at Cape Matapan off the south coast of Greece. On the 28th March 1941, the Mediterranean Fleet under the command of Admiral Cunningham, intercepted an Italian naval squadron which comprised the battleship *Vittorio Veneto* in company with several cruisers and a number of destroyers. Albacore torpedo bombers were flown off the carrier HMS *Formidable* and were successful in registering two hits on the mid section. While these did not penetrate the armoured hull, they caused the *Vittorio Veneto* to reduce speed from 30 to about 15 knots.

Unfortunately, the British force was unable to catch up, so the enemy ship was able to withdraw towards Italy under the cover of darkness.

In the course of searching for the *Vittorio Veneto* in the fading light, one Albacore pilot sighted the three cruisers. He attacked and hit the heavy cruiser *Pola* which lost all engine and electrical power. It was later sunk by gunfire during the night action that followed.

In each of the foregoing incidents enemy warships had been bit by aerial torpedoes but none had actually been sunk as a result of the damage inflicted.

One naval action in which the use of aerial torpedoes was completely and decisively vindicated was the sinking of the battleship

Prince of Wales and the battle cruiser *Repulse* by Japanese aircraft on 10th December 1941 off the coast of Malaya.

As a junior officer Jack Cramp's exploit earned him an immediate Distinguished Service Cross, but had he been of slightly higher rank, he would undoubtedly have been awarded the more prestigious Distinguished Service Order.

Lieut (A) Richard F Mackie DSC MID RNZNVR

When war was declared against Germany in September 1939 I was a first-year student in the Law Faculty at Canterbury University. Like many other young chaps of my age I found it hard to resist the call to arms. I was under age for the Army Service overseas, so I applied for the Fleet Air Arm and was accepted.

Our draft left New Zealand in November 1941. We entered the RN Barracks at HMS *St Vincent*, Portsmouth early in December of that year, but unfortunately for us, there had been a prolonged hold up on earlier courses due, no doubt, to the very severe winter which affected flying training, particularly at Luton.

Consequently, our draft was consigned to a 'pool' of recruits for 2–3 months until such time as we finished our naval indoctrination at HMS *St Vincent* and could then proceed to elementary flying school.

Following courses at Elmdon, Kingston (Canada) and Yeovilton I was eventually posted, in July/August 1943, to 1839 Squadron which was formed and working up at Eglinton, Northern Ireland. This was the first squadron to be equipped with the new Grumman Hellcat fighters. Our commanding officer was Lieut Commander (A) D. W. Jeran RN who was later succeeded by Lieut Commander S F. F. Shotton DSC RNR.

On 26th February 1944, following the shore based working-up period we joined the aircraft carrier HMS *Begum* and sailed via the Mediterranean for Indian and Ceylon to join the Eastern Fleet. Our squadron became one of two which were later to become No 5 Naval Fighter wing under the command of Lieut Commander T. W. Harrington RN and based in HMS *Indomitable*, which we joined on 25th July.

It was about this time that some very high level negotiations were being pursued between the British and US Naval Commands re the establishment of a British pacific Fleet. Winston Churchill was particularly keen to see the Royal Navy operating in close partnership with the US Navy in the final stages of the Pacific War.

The US Naval command, however, was far from enthusiastic about this proposition, despite the official blessing given by the US President, F. D. Roosevelt.

Admiral King, the commander in chief of the US Navy, had suffered from anglo phobia dating back to the First World War. He was adamantly opposed to the proposal, but not without some good reasons. He reasoned that the British Fleet which was unaccustomed to operating at long distances from bases, would never be able to provide the logistical support for the type of naval operations which would be required in the Pacific theatre.

Churchill, on the other hand, was equally adamant that the Royal Navy could, and would, play its part.

Thus a very complex logistical plan was born. Hundreds of ships, naval and mercantile, had to be assembled initially for the Eastern Fleet to attack territories taken by the Japs in the Indian Ocean, and later in Australia, to provide the necessary supply line for a fleet which would be required to operate several thousand miles north of the Japanese home territories.

At one stage, the British Commander in Chief, Admiral Sir Bruce Fraser, set out in the battleship HMS *Howe* for discussions with the American Admirals King and Nimitz. His Scottish persistence won the day and the Americans agreed to co-operate with the Royal Navy provided it could guarantee to be completely self sufficient, apart from the supply of bulk fuel at forward bases such as the Admiralty Islands and Leyte in the Philippines.

Pending the build up of this logistical support, the RN Fleet carriers, battleships and cruisers which had by this time assembled at Trincomalee, Ceylon, would carry out a series of operations in the Indian Ocean against Japanese bases at Sabang, Padang (ships and airfields), Indaroeng (cement works) – one Corsair lost, the Nicobar and Andaman islands, Sumatra, Sigli – one Barracuda lost. Some Hellcats carried out photo-recce during these and all later raids.

The first of these raids took place on the 24th August 1944 in the Medan area – seven aircraft were shot down, we lost one Avenger, but crew recovered – to be followed later by concentrated attacks on the ports and at Nancowry (Hellcats shot down three – lost one) and oil refineries at Belawan Deli, Pangkalan Branda, Pladjoe and Songei Cerong, Palembang in Sumatra.

The carriers *Indomitable, Victorious* and *Illustrious* (now under the command of Rear Admiral Sir Philip Vian) supported by three cruisers and five destroyers headed for the Malacca Straits where 27 Avengers each armed with 4× 500lb bombs and supported by escorting Corsair and Hellcat fighters, were launched to attack targets at the oiling port Belawan Deli. Bad weather unfortunately obscured the primary oil refineries but considerable damage was done to harbour installations. Later that day Corsairs and Hellcats returned to attack airfields on the island of Sabang.

A third and final operation, coinciding with the departure of the Fleet for Sydney was carried out on the 9th January 1945. At 0615 hours a force of 43 bomb-carrying Avengers were flown off from a position 35 miles off the coast. The oil refinery at Pladjoe was successfully bombed despite the presence of a protective balloon barrage. Escorting Corsairs and Hellcats intercepted Japanese fighters, many of which were destroyed. Following this attack the Avenger bombers headed for their rendezvous 15 miles to the west of Palembang. Unfortunately, they encountered a heavy concentration of anti-aircraft fire and found a number of enemy fighters lying in wait for them.

These operations, while they reduced the productive capacity of the oil refineries by half, were not without cost. We lost a number of good aircrews, some of whom were captured and later executed by the Japanese. Many Japanese aircraft (99 in fact and ten probables – 40 damaged) were destroyed in the air and on the ground. These figures cover strikes on January 4th, 24th and 29th.

On the 26th and 27th the fleet refuelled at sea and set course for Sydney, arriving there on 10th February.

Here, Vice Admiral Rawlings with his flag in the battleship *King George V* assumed seagoing command of the entire fleet.

Rear Admiral Vian had joined the Eastern Fleet on 2nd December 1944 to take command of the carrier force and flew his flag in HMS *Indomitable.* Admiral Rawlings, Commander-in-Chief, in his battle wagon, was too slow. He slowed the fleet down, so Vian asked him to stay at home with his battleship.

The next few weeks was a period of intensive activity in preparation for the move north into the battle area. While the air group continued working up at shore bases tons and tons of equipment from victuals to armaments, aircraft spares, etc. were hurriedly loaded aboard. One of the major tasks, however, was the need to convert from the RN signals procedure to the American system. This entailed a tremendous amount of work. Signal flags, Aldis lamp flashings, radio procedures, signal books, manoeuvring signals, all had to be changed to comply with the US Naval methods.

Before the fleet went north, five of the New Zealand fighter pilots were suddenly advised that they would return to New Zealand on three months leave. (Mackie was one). But after only a short time they were recalled to report back to base in Sydney within 48 hours. Three of them, Maclennan, Ruffin and Mackie, returned on the Sunderland flying boat from Auckland to Rose Bay, and reported to Schofield, a naval fighter aircraft based in western Sydney. The expected recall to the ship did not come, despite heavy losses being sustained. We awaited the fleet's return.

On 25th February the main fleet had left Sydney and headed for Manus Island in the Admiralty Group, where it refuelled prior to joining up with the American Navy. But even at this late stage Admiral King was to reveal the depth of his antipathy to the Royal Navy.

The final plot was to try and get the BPF assigned to Admiral Kincaid's 7th Fleet, which came under the jurisdiction of General MacArthur. This would have meant that the BPF would have been relegated to a relatively minor role from a naval point of view in mopping up operations around Borneo. However, Sir Bruce Fraser's rather more dogged diplomacy finally prevailed and on 18th March the BPF sailed from Manus to the 5th Fleet under Admiral Spruance, which was presently engaged in operations off Okinawa.

At Ulithi in the Caroline Islands the ships refuelled once again, and at dawn on 26th March commenced their first strikes at airfields on the islands of Ishigakishima and Miyakoshima to prevent the passage of Japanese aircraft from Formosa to the Okinawa theatre of operations.

During this period the fleet came under determined attacks by kamikaze pilots, all our carriers being hit, some twice. The damage was generally quickly repaired and they were operational again within a short time.

These operations against Formosa and the Sakashima archipelago continued, except for a brief interval spent at San Pedro roads, Leyte, until 25th May when the entire fleet withdrew to Sydney for repairs to battle damage, refits, etc. The squadrons on *Indomitable* flew off to Nowra – a Naval air station south of Sydney. The *Indomitable* had sustained bomb damage which necessitated a longer than usual stay in the dockyard. This was exacerbated by the decision of Australian watersiders and harbour employees to go on strike. English shipwrights and engineers had to be flown out from the UK to repair the damage.

Admiral Vian had no option but to transfer his flag to the carrier HMS *Formidable* which was commanded by Captain Ruck-Keene RN. It was at this time that, as a very junior officer, I became involved in some very sensitive decision making re naval strategy. At the time I was still flying at the RN Air Station at Schofields. It was here that I received a signal from HMS *Formidable* requiring me to report to Admiral Vian's Cabin.

My immediate reaction was one of surprise. It is most unusual for a mere sub-lieutenant to be called before an admiral. I tried to think of any indiscretion I might have committed but nothing came to mind. In any case, had I been guilty of some misdemeanour, it would have been the executive commander or, at the worst, the ship's captain who would deal with it.

I duly presented myself, knocked somewhat timorously and was commanded to enter.

'Good morning, Mackie. Please be seated – I have a problem I wish to discuss with you.'

That the admiral wished to discuss a problem with a sub-lieutenant struck me as a most unusual, so I was more or less stumped for a comment.

'Well Mackie – we have a spot of bother on our hands. Our American friends have imposed certain conditions which we must comply with before they will allow us to rejoin them in the final stages of the war against Japan.'

'With respect, sir – I can't quite see where or how I can be of assistance.'

'Well, if you will kindly bear with me – I will explain the situation.

As you are no doubt aware the Americans were most reluctant to allow us to be here in the first place, but so far we have been able to overcome all the obstacles and prove to them that the BPF has the capacity to wage an effective war in the Pacific. But now that we are about to return and launch attacks at the Japanese mainland itself the Americans have pinpointed one rather serious deficiency in our arsenal.'

Still puzzled, I had to ask the question: 'What is that?'

'Well, quite simply Mackie, it is the lack of night fighter capability particularly and a "photo recce" team – and something very urgent must be done about it, otherwise they will simply relegate us to secondary targets where there would be minimal prospect of enemy night attacks. They have, in fact, said that they will not provide any night defence for our ships. It's as simple as that.'

'Well, sir – I still can't quite see how I as a junior officer can resolve the issue.'

'The fact is, Mackie – you are just the man who can provide the answer. Now, what I want you to do before we leave Sydney is to take some of your chaps down to Nowra and do some intensive night ADDLS.'

'Well sir, again, with every respect, I am only too willing to do what I can but I must point out that I have had very little night flying experience, in fact, none for over two years and none whatsoever in a Hellcat. Furthermore, sir, I have never yet made a night deck landing on a carrier.'

'Mackie, I have studied your record – I am confident that you can do it. Now, off you go – brief your men and get down to Nowra as soon as you can. And, by the way, you will be transferring to *Formidable* when you return because *Indomitable* will be staying on in Sydney for repairs.'

'One final question, sir – How long will we be able to have at Nowra for ADDLS?'

'Just one night, I'm afraid Mackie.'

With that I was dismissed. Holy Hell – my mind was in a whirl.

All I could think about was that part of a famous old Fleet Air Arm song: 'A25 to the air of "Charlotte the Harlot".'

The words were:-

'I'll fly for a living and not just for fun,
I'm frightfully anxious to shoot down a Hun,
But as for deck landings at night in the dark,
As I told "Wings" this morning –
F— that for a lark!'

Night flying off carriers in single seater fighters with no navigator or sophisticated navigational aids (not even a radio altimeter) would be enough to give anyone the 'twitch'.

However, an order is an order – it had to be obeyed, so off we went.

When we arrived at Nowra the weather conditions, high winds and clouds, were most unfavourable to night ADDLS. That night we got a few circuits in before it was cancelled due to the conditions. Then we received a signal ordering us to leave for Sydney Heads.

When we rendezvoused with the carrier, we found it steaming very slowly into a 40 knot gale. A tremendous sea was raging, the worst I have ever seen. The carrier's bows were dipping under swell. It was pitching to an alarming degree.

We received the OK to land on, so I tackled it first. I aborted on my first two attempts but got down safely on the third. Happily all six of us made the grade without mishap. That should have convinced anyone in the flying game that we were competent deck landers.

But one very important person was unimpressed. No sooner had we clambered out of our cockpits than the leader of the Hellcat fighters was summoned to report to Captain Ruck-Keene. I duly presented myself whereupon he said: 'So you are in charge of the Hellcats. You're only a sub-lieutenant – I expected a Lieutenant Commander, or at least a full Lieutenant.'

To which I replied: 'I am due for promotion, sir, but it hasn't come through yet.'

'Well, be that as it may, Mackie, while you are in my ship you are a sub-lieutenant until I am notified otherwise.'

'Yes, sir.'

'Now, how much deck landing experience have you chaps had?'

I proceeded to ensure him that we were all thoroughly competent, but he was visibly unimpressed.

'Well, Mackie – you will all have to get into the air again, now and prove to me that you are as good as you claim to be.'

Now this really had me worried. Nobody in their right senses would attempt to do familiarisation deck landings in weather like this.

I diplomatically stressed the danger of loss of lives and valuable aircraft, but Captain Ruck-Keene was unperturbed.

What I did not realise then was that he was deeply resentful of having to accommodate Admiral Vian and his staff in his ship and consequently anyone remotely associated with the admiral was an anathema to him.

However, I had no option but to go, but I qualified this by informing him that I would take off first and would report on conditions before the other pilots took their chance. To compound our problems we heard that the ship's batsman had not had any previous experience in controlling deck landings of Hellcats. Consequently, he would not be familiar with the approach speed and the landing attitude of our aircraft.

Only three of us eventually flew and successfully completed two or three landings each, but it would have been foolhardy for the exercise to continue. Whether Commander Flying intervened or not I will never know, but the rest of the programme was cancelled.

We had left Sydney in company with *Victorious* and headed once again for Manus where we were later joined by *Implacable* and *Indefatigable*. Task Force 37 then comprised the four carriers, the battleships *King George V* and *Howe*, cruisers *Newfoundland, Euryalus, Achilles, Gambia, Uganda* and 22 destroyers.

On 16th July, rendezvous was made with Admiral Halsey's 3rd US Fleet, a massive assembly of naval power, stretching across the ocean as far as the eye could see.

My Hellcat team, ten in all, one of whom was Lt (A) J. C. Ruffin RNZNVR, (one of the two PRU pilots who flew at dawn and dusk over the Japanese mainland every day during the operation there), who were Vian's pets, did not have a comfortable time in *Formidable*. The accommodation was under such pressure that initially we had no cabins, so we had to sleep in passage ways.

The most exciting time we had was on the night of 25th July, 1945. At about 2200 hours Harry Taylor, Bill Foster (both English), Bill Atkinson (Canadian) and I were brought to immediate readiness because the ship's radar had detected a formation of unidentified aircraft approaching the Fleet. Harry had trouble starting up, so he had to be left behind and once airborne Bill Foster discovered that his radio was unserviceable, so he reluctantly had to return and land on. Atkinson and I followed the vector given to us by Lieut-Commander Colin Keay, our Fleet's very competent Fighter Direction Officer (also ex-*Indomitable*).

Moments later we received an urgent call from Colin 'Bogeys are just above you and slightly ahead. Buster – Buster (meaning full throttle).'

We peered into the murk and, sure enough, we picked up the exhaust flashes of four aircraft with others further away.

For a moment I hesitated because they appeared to have gull wings – could they be US Naval Corsairs? I warned Bill to hold fire while I edged in closer to positively identify them. No – they were Japs alright – probably Grace torpedo bombers. I confirmed this with Bill and we both attacked. My first target blew up in front of me and I crossed over quickly to get my sights on a second one. Bill in the meantime had shot down the other two. He went after another, guns ablaze and I had lost him. He called to say he was out of ammunition and was returning to the ship. I remained in the area for a while until I was intercepted by some US night fighters, from their specialist night fighter carrier to the *Bonhomme Richard*. By this time I had been airborne for about 40 minutes and was probably about 80–100 miles from our carrier.

Colin Keay recalled me giving me a course to steer for 'home'.

When we returned it was to a joyous welcome. The FAA night fighter component, small though it may have been, had proved itself in no uncertain manner. When the Yanks heard our claims they were inclined to disbelieve us until early the following morning one of their destroyers picked up some bodies of Japanese airmen who had apparently been shot down in the area of our interception.

They then generously acknowledged our success and invited Bill Atkinson and me to fly over to their command carrier for official recognition. This was indeed a great honour – the Americans can be very generous when the occasion demands.

This made up for the antipathy that had previously been demonstrated by several admirals of the US Navy and in particular their Commander-in-Chief, Admiral King.

It was not long after that event that Japan surrendered and I returned to New Zealand.

About the time I was discharged from naval service, I was, I recall, made aware, with some pleasure, that a goodwill visit to New Zealand by Admiral Vian in the aircraft carrier *Indefatigable* was being made.

Before leaving Sydney for Wellington, he sent me a cable asking me to report, in uniform, at the gangway at 1030 hours on the 1st December. When I arrived there I found that Keith MacLennan had also received a similar invitation. The officer of the watch escorted us to Vian's cabin. We received a very warm welcome and partook of morning tea. He amused us with his impressions of local politicians who had just recently been his guests. Little would he have known that one or more of them could have been conscientious objectors in the First World War and some had preferred to spend time in prison for their seditious actions.

When told that my parents had come to Wellington with me, he promptly ordered one of his staff to telephone the hotel and invite them aboard. I was proud and privileged to have served under such a fine gentleman and leader of men.

On Sunday 2nd December, Vice Admiral Sir Philip Vian KCB KBE DSO and 3 bars, was invited by the New Zealand Government to address the nation over the main national and commercial radio stations.

The following is an extract of his address:

'Nearly ten per cent of the pilots who fought through this war in the Air Arm of the Royal Navy came from this country, and they were in it at the beginning as at the end, for there were New Zealand airmen in the successful dive bomber attack on the German Cruiser *Koenigsberg* in early 1940 – the very first warship to have been sunk by dive bombing – as there were, also, your naval airmen in the last bombings of Japan.

I should say here that it has been my experience in command of the British carrier force that New Zealanders are naturally possessed of the qualities which made for eminence in air combat; and I expressed as much in a signal sent in September last to the New Zealand naval Board, which read:

'As I understand it is likely that the majority of the RNZNVR pilots who left us in August for leave will not now return to this command,

> I wish to assure you how great has been their part in the British Carrier operations against Japan.
>
> I consider the pilots from New Zealand to have been second to none, and to have excelled in the offensive spirit. I hope the close and happy association of our naval airmen, welded in the war, may be continued in peace.'

Here are three examples, typical of the fighting spirit of New Zealand pilots.

When operating off Sumatra last, year, the fleet was attacked by Japanese aircraft of the suicide type, all save one of which were shot down in time by our guns or fighters.

One penetrated the screen into the main body of the fleet, where it was a menace and difficult to hit by gunfire through fear of hitting other ships; and it was hard to attack by our fighters on account of the fire of our guns.

A Hellcat piloted by Sub-Lieutenant Keith Alexander McLennan RNZNVR of HMS *Indomitable*, my flagship, was flown off at this time. He had to take off while his own ship's guns were firing at the enemy. Without hesitation he flew through the gunfire of the fleet and shot down two of the attacking aircraft.

A second example was provided by Lieutenant Alexander Macrae, DSO RNZVR of HMS *Indomitable*, who was severely wounded in the thigh when carrying out a low strafing attack during the first fighter sweep our aircraft made on the Sakishima Gunto airfields. Although in great pain, he carried out two more attacks. It was not until he ran out of ammunition that he told his leader that he was wounded and was returning to his ship. Encouraged by messages from the ship, he flew back 100 miles alone, injecting morphine on the way to ease the pain. On arrival he found he could not lower the wheels. His right leg was now useless and he was weak from loss of blood, but he made a perfect crash landing on the deck. He was lifted unconscious from the cockpit.

On a further occasion, more recently, the British Pacific Fleet was operating alongside three American carrier task groups off Japan. During the day, Japanese shadowing aircraft had sighted the combined fleets; at dusk, a concentration of hostile aircraft was detected by our radar. For some reason this detection was not accepted by the US Fleet, who, therefore, did not send out their specialised night fighters, with which they were equipped, to intercept the enemy. *Formidable* carried the six Hellcats, and ten pilots, which were not equipped for night fighting and whose pilots were inexperienced in night flying. Two of them were flown off, led by a New Zealand pilot, Lieutenant Richard Mackie, DSC, RNZNVR of Hawke's Bay.

It was now dark and the position critical, because heavy ships in mass at night are particularly vulnerable to attack by torpedo bombers, which these aircraft were adjudged to be. The radar showed us that the Hellcats were close to one group of the enemy. Suddenly there was a ball of fire falling in the sky – some plane had been hit. A fighter pilot's voice – Mackie's – announced over the radio the destruction of a torpedo bomber, then another, and another, and a fourth hit.

US fighters now arrived to drive off the remaining enemy group and an ugly situation was saved. Admiral Spruance signalled, 'Well done your radar team and pilots.'

But while these are the men – the pilots and the aircrews – who did most of the actual fighting, never forget that in naval flying these men would be ineffectual without the help of the thousands of others who man the aircraft carrier . . . the gun crews, the signalmen, the first aid parties, and all the countless others who have to perform vital duties to keep the ship in action. But from amongst those may I say a special word for the men below in the magazines, the boiler and the engine rooms, who, should the ship be torpedoed or bombed, are usually in the greatest danger of all.

It is these men – the pilots and aircrews and ships' companies of *Indefatigable, Urchin* and *Wizard* – who are visiting your shores today.

They have all longed to come to New Zealand – it is a great wish of any sailor.

May I thank you so much for all the hospitality and kindness you are showing them.'

Broadcast Sunday 2nd December. Main national and commercial Stations.

Author's Note My association with Dick Mackie dates back to 11th August 1937 when he and I confronted each other across the front row of a rugby scrum. New Plymouth Boys' High School was playing its annual fixture against Wanganui Collegiate on their college ground. NPBHS was defeated by 11 to 8 but as it was in a building up cycle, the result was reversed in 1938 when Collegiate was defeated by 24 to nil. Dick still recalls this as one of the sternest games of rugby he had played in.

He excelled at all ball games – rugby, cricket, tennis and later golf. In fact his enthusiasm for golf was also developed at Wanganui Collegiate where they had established a nine hole course.

Shortly after leaving school he had the misfortune to suffer some serious burn injuries to one foot and on the advice of doctors he relinquished his love for both rugby and cricket.

Such was his competitive spirit, however, that he chose to ignore this and did actually play some rugby and cricket while in the navy.

In the early post war years he continued his interest in cricket by representing Southern Hawkes Bay in cricket at the Hawke Cup level.

But golf was his real forte, which he perfected to the point that he was for some time playing off a scratch handicap.

Probably Dick's most memorable golf performance was the day when he broke the Hutt amateur record with a slashing round of six under par!

For many years Dick continued his association with golf as club secretary, president of the Hawkes Bay Association, and representative of the New Zealand Golf Council where his legal knowledge was put to much advantage on the Rules Committee. Other offices were non-playing captain of the New Zealand team to the Commonwealth golf tournament at Sydney, in 1963 and later to the Eisenhower Cup in Mexico 1966.

Then in December 1971, Dick suffered an incurable injury in a motor cycle accident which left him a quadriplegic and confined to a life thereafter in a wheel chair.

Dick, however, had the spirit and determination to excel despite his disability.

In the golf world he became President of the New Zealand Association, was accorded a life membership and became New Zealand Delegate to the World Golf Conference at St Andrews, Scotland in 1980. He also served on the World Administrative Golf Committee.

In his innate modesty Dick dismisses this with a simple statement 'All I can say is – they were rather brave people to appoint me.'

Despite his disability and at the age when most people have long since retired Dick can still drive a car and conducts his own legal practice in Waipukurau.

No words are adequate to acknowledge the attention and encouragement he has received from his devoted wife Mitty.

Lieut Commander (A) A. S. Macleod DSC RNZNVR

Alister MacLeod recalls that when the British Pacific Fleet Task Force 37 met up with the United States Fleet Task Force 38 for the final assault on the Japanese mainland, his Seafire Squadron No 887 aboard HMS *Indefatigable* was employed primarily in a defensive role carrying out combat air patrols (CAP) over the whole fleet.

The Seafires were soon to be equipped with 90 gallon long range drop tanks which effectively extended their radius of operations and allowed them to carry our fighter escort duties for the Avenger Bombers and Firefly rocket aircraft.

Mac's logbook about this time records the following sorties:

July 22 Fleet CAP duration 1 hr 30 mins.
July 24 Fleet CAP duration 3 hrs 30 mins. (his aircraft had obviously been fitted with a long range tank)
July 25 Escort for Bomber Strike 3 hrs.
Sub-Lieut (A) Ken Gall crashed into the barrier on landing and was killed.
July 28 1st Fleet CAP – 2 hrs 15 mins.
July 28 2nd Fleet CAP – 3 hrs 15 mins.
(By this time Mac and his fellow pilots must have been suffering from sore bottoms!)
July 30 Ramrod (an offensive sweep over enemy territory) 3 hrs. 30 mins.
(Doug Alexander hit by flak and is missing)

Mac describes this last patrol as follows:

'Doug was the leader of the eight Seafires briefed to attack shipping in the Inland Sea. I was leader of one flight of four aircraft. We patrolled for some time but failed to find anything worth attacking.

Doug then led us along the coastal inlets searching for alternative targets. The visibility was poor and although there was only a comparatively thin layer of cloud it was down to about 500 feet. Eventually, we came across a large factory of some sort and with Doug leading we went down to strafe it with cannon and machine guns. I don't know whether Doug had actually opened fire but he suddenly pulled up with Glycol (engine coolant) streaming from his aircraft. He had obviously been hit by anti-aircraft fire. We all followed and I tried to contact him over the radio but there was no response.

I then switched to the emergency channel to contact the American rescue submarine, but again there was no response.

During this time, Doug had entered the cloud layer, but by the time the rest of us had got through he was nowhere to be seen. I took the remaining seven Seafires down through the cloud and searched up and down the coast and out to sea, but there was no sign of the aircraft having crashed either on land or in the sea.

I think that we can take it that his aircraft had been hit by anti-aircraft fire and he was probably badly wounded, because he did not answer my calls.

My big regret, even after all these years, is that I don't know what happened.'

Doug and Mac had served together in four different squadrons over a period of more than two years. I can well imagine how distraught Mac must have been as he led his six young men back to land on the *Indefatigable*.

I was likewise very distressed when I learnt of Doug's death, only 15 days before the war ended. He was one of the best. He had a wonderful spontaneous personality and an impish grin that would captivate anyone, male or female.

It was about this time that Lieut Commander (A) J. Crossman DSO of 894 Squadron was shot down and captured by the Japanese. Mac was then promoted to the command of 894 with the rank of Lieut Commander. This must have been quite a challenge for him, as in the space of a few weeks, he had been promoted from Sub-Lieut to Lieut Commander and had lost a very close friend in Doug Alexander.

He then recalls that from 1st August up to the date of surrender by Emperor Hirohito and for some time after, the Seafire squadrons maintained a constant CAP above the fleet to ward off any further kamikaze attacks.

Admiral Vian in his book *Action This Day* recalls that air battles were still taking place following a dawn bombing raid on August 15th the day of the surrender.

Indefatigable's strike aircraft were intercepted by twelve Zero fighters, following which a brief engagement took place. Eight Zeros were shot down by Seafires and others damaged for the loss of only one Seafire.

In this dogfight, which terminated only a few minutes before the surrender was announced, the United States Navy and the Fleet Air Arm fighters which included Corsairs and Hellcats from other British carriers, jointly destroyed 35 Japanese aircraft during the first hour after dawn.

In view of the intensity of this resistance, Admiral Halsey ordered that normal fighter CAPs would be maintained until further notice.

Mac had the rather unique record of serving in five operational squadrons, Nos. 884, 834, 889, 887, and finally in command of 894.

Early in December 1945 Admiral Vian despatched the carrier *Indefatigable* on a goodwill tour to New Zealand. This was no doubt to acknowledge the quite significant part that New Zealand pilots had played in the British Pacific Fleet.

The ship's squadrons proceeded to 'show the flag' in various parts of the country, December 4th Wigram and Woodburne, December 6th Ohakea, December 7th New Plymouth and Ardmore, December 9th Whenuapai returning to land on HMS *Indefatigable* in the Hauraki Gulf on 11th December.

Regrettably one Seafire crashed on landing in the Marlborough Sounds and carried over the side.

Lieutenant Commander (A) L. Gordon C. Reece DSC RNZNVR

Gordon Reece arrived in England in November 1940. He was a member of a draft which was absorbed into No 22 Pilots Course at HMS *St Vincent*.

These are his recollections of service in the Royal Navy.

In the Fleet Air Arm: One Man's Memories 1939–45

Britain and France declared war on Germany on September 1st 1939 when the Germans invaded Poland. The British Dominions quickly followed.

I had lived in Wellington for four years and had turned twenty-one just three weeks earlier. Like many others angered by the Nazis and their fatuous ranting leader, but also tempted by the prospect of war adventures I joined the air force immediately the war began and so did large numbers of others of similar inclination. By early 1940 the number of aspiring fliers was 4,300, a figure far and away beyond the capacity of the then New Zealand air training facilities.

After some prodding by Acting Prime Minister Peter Fraser (his Prime Minister Michael Joseph Savage was mortally ill), the British Government indicated a number of specific and vital requirements for the expansion of their armed forces. Among these was New Zealand providing suitably educated men for training as pilots and air observer/navigators in the Fleet Air Arm of the Royal Navy.

By April of 1940, three men had been sent for Fleet Air Arm flying training, and these and two observers were to be the total allocation for the whole of 1940. The New Zealand Navy Office asked the British Admiralty if more were needed. In May the Admiralty asked what numbers could be sent and the Navy in consultation with the Chief of Air Staff advised twenty men a month would be available from the approved candidates waiting to be called up by the Air Force. The number was modified upwards by the Air Force a few days later to 250 in one or more drafts if and when required. The Admiralty accepted the twenty a month as a basic figure and the first group of twenty left in July, 1940. Admiralty asked that the second and third groups be forty men. In fact the second in August was thirty eight and the third in September thirty seven men.

There was a fourth in October of twenty two. I was in the third group which arrived at Liverpool in early November, 1940 and went at once via London to Portsmouth where at *St Vincent*, a first school in naval training, two months would be spent as naval airmen (2nd class) – what the first class ones were I never knew – before pilot or observer training began.

That pattern of so many a month leaving New Zealand for the Fleet Air Arm would continue throughout the war. Later entry would be direct through naval recruitment and not through the Air Force, and there were a number of other modifications to the arrangement as circumstances changed.

The late Moss Holden was one of the first three New Zealanders to travel to England to join the Fleet Air Arm in the first few months of the war. By December 1941 he was flying a Walrus amphibian from the battle-cruiser HMS *Repulse* which in company with the battleship HMS *Prince of Wales* was off the coast of Malaya north of Singapore seeking to counter the Japanese invasion that had begun in the north of Malaya two days earlier on December 8th, just about simultaneously with the attack on Pearl Harbor in Hawaii on the 7th. Moss was on patrol when he and his crew spotted large numbers of aircraft approaching. They were Japanese torpedo and dive bombers and they flew right past the Walrus with no attempt it seemed to shoot it down. It was noon and both the *Prince of Wales* and the *Repulse* were quickly sunk by the torrent of bombs and the succession of torpedos unleashed against them. There was much loss of life including the Admiral in charge and the Captain of the *Prince of Wales*. Moss Holden landed near the survivors after the sinkings and with men on and clinging to the hull of the Walrus taxied in to the Malayan coast a short distance away. In all 840 officers and men died when the two ships were sunk, 513 from the *Repulse*. But many survived, the complement of the two ships exceeding 2,500.

There is another story concerning Moss Holden that I heard of only after his death. Determined to transfer from amphibian flying to fighters, he conceived the plan of a 'beat-up' of the naval air station at Donibristle just north of Edinburgh on the Firth of Forth. He reasoned that a demonstration of his flying skill in carrying out difficult manoeuvres and aerobatics in a Walrus would so impress the authorities that a transfer to fighters would be assured. And it was. He ended the war in a Grumman Hellcat naval fighter squadron. Obviously I could not authenticate this account with Moss himself but an authority that would be regarded by many as even better than Moss himself told it to me. He was the passenger in the Walrus during the crucial demonstration.

December 1941 was also the time at which the first group of twenty who left New Zealand in July 1940 had completed training and were being posted to operational fighter, torpedo-bomber-reconnaissance squadrons or to flying duties on the larger warships carrying a single aircraft, usually the Walrus amphibian with its pusher airscrew. The outlook for the British forces and their allies at this time was if not forlorn hardly hopeful, for the Japanese were quickly overcoming the British in Malaya and the Americans in the Philippines. They had destroyed many warships in the Pearl Harbor raids. The other Axis powers as they were called, Germany and Italy, were in a dominating position in the Middle East, the Mediterranean, Europe and with submarines, but not surface vessels, in the Atlantic. But there were two major consequences of Japan's undeclared war moves: the United States with its vast resources was now directly involved and the American aircraft carriers of their Pacific Fleet had been at sea when the Pearl Harbor attack took place and thus were able to launch the crucial fightbacks that began not too many months later in the Battles of the Coral Sea and Midway.

The Fleet Air Arm by December, 1941, also had difficulties. Three fleet carriers had been sunk, *Glorious, Courageous*, and *Ark Royal* and its aircraft, the Swordfish, Skua, Roc, Gladiator and Fulmar had shortcomings as warplanes that pilot and aircrew skill could surmount only in the case of the Swordfish and Fulmar. However, there were good signs: the large fleet carrier *Indomitable* had been commissioned a few months earlier to join the *Victorious* and her sister ships, the *Illustrious* and *Formidable* as 30,000 ton[1] weapons in the Royal Navy arsenal; other large carriers had been laid down and light fleet carriers also started; the United States would soon begin converting merchant ships to escort carriers and also building them to basic merchant ship design but with hangars

[1] Displacement 23,207 tons; fully loaded 28,619 tons; speed 30.5 knots maximum.

and flight decks; Hurricanes and Spitfires were being tried in modified forms as Fleet Air Arm fighters and new American aircraft like the Grumman Martlet or Wildcat would soon be made available; and the training of air crew was proceeding very successfully with facilities in Britain and Canada and in Detroit and Pensacola, Florida, in the United States. The Americans had contributed this assistance from well before they entered the war as combatants.

The training groups each consisted at the start of some 100 or more, mainly British, but with the 19th course as they were called, New Zealanders became a noticeable proportion of each course and there were quite a few Canadians and a sprinkling of South Africans and Australians. I count 114 in my course 22 photograph, the course also being called Collingwood, I notice. Another course named Rodney, I believe, was also at the initial training establishment, *St Vincent* in Gosport, Portsmouth, but a month before or later, I think. After that first couple of months the course would split never to come together again. Initial flying training at first would be either at Luton, just north of London, and Elmdon, near Birmingham, depending on whether a fighter or torpedo-bomber-reconnaissance course was to be undertaken. I do not recall whether this was a voluntary matter or if it was decided through the observations and possibly recommendations of the *St Vincent* staff. Later, much initial flying training took place in the United States.

I went to Luton. We slept in a stately English mansion called Luton Hoo for some reason. It was on a large estate some way from the aerodrome to which we travelled by bus in the early morning and at dusk returned to the exclusive house for the night. It was now February, 1941. It was also very cold and we New Zealanders were feeling it. Peter Picot of 20 course got meningitis, I had a disabling ear infection that put me in hospital at nearby St Albans for a month, and Bob Gyllies got the tuberculosis that led to his being sent home a couple of months later. Bob died in the mid-fifties, an unexpectedly brief life for a man who had been a New Zealand University rugby blue at centre three-quarter and a fine golfer. Peter Picot died in November, 1991. I feel quite pleased to see from my log-book that I became ill after 5 hours 25 minutes of dual instruction on March 4th 1941, returned on April 4th and achieved my first solo at 9 hours 30 minutes of dual. But I am crestfallen to find that after all these years there are no means I have of knowing how vain I should be about that feat. I suspect it is about average with the month's absence giving some grounds for a little conceit.

After Luton and the monoplane trainer, Miles Magister, we went to Netheravon and on to Miles Master IIIs and their radial engines. We still wore the sailor uniform and had the white cap band to show our officer training status but we had skipped a rank from NA2s to ALAs or Acting Leading Airman. I roomed there in a good two-man unit with Gisborne man Ron Richardson, and we were pupils of the same instructor and flew a lot together in formation flying. Ron later commanded a squadron partly of Dutch pilots flying American Hellcat fighters. He was one of the dozen or so New Zealand lieutenant-commanders in the Fleet Air Arm in the last years of the war. Ron led a number of fighter escorts to the Barracuda bombing attacks on the German battleship *Tirpitz* in the Norwegian fiord where it was berthed with heavy anti-aircraft defences on the nearby land and barriers in the sea to impede torpedos. Ron was killed diving in attacks on the *Tirpitz* after earlier daringly using his aircraft's arrester hook to damage radio wires near the *Tirpitz*. He was recommended for the Victoria Cross, but the final judgement of those having the power to make recommendations was that the supporting evidence was not convincing enough for a Victoria Cross to be awarded Ron. He was given a posthumous Mention in Dispatches, it being established that no awards between that and a Victoria Cross can be awarded posthumously. However, after the war it is said the captain of the *Tirpitz* at the time of Ron's exploits commented on his bravery in most admiring terms. The VC was awarded to two Fleet Air Arm pilots during World War II: in February 1942 to Lieutenant-Commander E. Esmonde RN, an Englishman, and on August 9th, 1945, the day the second atom bomb was dropped on Nagasaki, Lieutenant (A) R. H. Gray RCNVR won the decoration. Both awards were posthumous. Esmonde flying a Swordfish and Gray a Corsair were killed during the attacks they were making on enemy forces. Japan surrendered only six days after Gray's brave exploit.

Netheravon was on Salisbury Plain and after four months there and satisfactory passes in flying and ground examinations we were awarded our wings and commissioned as officers, Midshipman or sub-lieutenant according to age. Then it was on to Yeovilton in

Somerset and conversion – as learning to fly a strange aircraft was called – to Fleet Air Arm fighters, the Hurricane and the Fulmar and for deck landings on 'dummy decks' i.e. marked runways with a batsman controlling the approach. The TBR pilots would do their conversion in Scotland at Crail and Arbroath.

The first postings of New Zealanders to operational squadrons were to a variety of squadrons and bases. Some went to the Middle East and were involved with the 8th Army in the desert war, some to fleet carriers: *Victorious* at Scapa Flow, Orkney Islands, or to *Illustrious* and *Formidable* in Ceylon, some to Malta, desperately besieged at that time and well on in 1942, some to land-based units in England. I was posted to 885 squadron flying Hurricanes. It was 20th April, 1942 and the squadron was attached to the Royal Air Force at an airfield called Hutton Cranswick which is not far inland near Kingston in Yorkshire. Its duties were fighter defence of Yorkshire, day and night, and convoy patrols in the North Sea. By that time, having been mauled in the Battle of Britain in July to September of 1940, switched to night bombing after that, and invaded Russia on 22 June, 1941, Germany had become stretched to maintain effective land and air operations, though still and increasingly a deadly menace to Atlantic shipping. Thus in the two months 885 were at Hutton Cranswick my log book records only four 'scrambles' i.e. quick take-off to intercept enemy aircraft. None led to contact. I had my first of two very close escapes from catastrophe and certain mortality at Hutton Cranswick. I had been doing a night exercise with searchlight batteries above clouds and had descended through the clouds and identified the very dim runway lights of the aerodrome below. I began to turn a line up the runway peering sideways to my left for the runway lights to reappear. They didn't. A few seconds passed and there were still no lights. The control column went sloppy. I quickly glanced at the instruments. I was either in a spin or very close to it. Stick right forward, hard right rudder took the Hurricane into a steep dive. The faintly lit runway lights were seen again. Stick back and then to mid-position and I was quickly lined up for landing. I climbed from the cockpit thankfully and my trembling knees determined a less than steady gait to the squadron hut. The runway lights, barely visible anyway, had been obliterated not by power failure or some human error but by my turning into a cloud as I circled to line up the runway for landing and as I turned and strained to bring the lights into view again pulling the control column back. Speed reduced anyway, a stall soon followed this unnoticed flying error. I escaped reprimand for this carelessness because there was no damage done to either aircraft or me and no official written report was required. A rare thing to happen perhaps, but lessons were learned.

Not only was I reprimanded for my second near-fatal escape but by no less an authority than their Lords of the Admiralty, or so the letter of rebuke explicitly claimed. It was probably drafted by a minor writer (naval term for clerk) and signed by rubber stamp. I lost it somewhere, so no validation is possible. But others will have to be the judges of whether or not I should have incurred any wrath at all. 885 6 aircraft 7 or 8 pilot squadron of Hurricanes was the first of that famous fighter to be based on an aircraft carrier. We had moved from Hutton Cranswick in late June 1942 to Hatston Naval Air Station near Scapa Flow in the Orkney Islands. I had landed on a carrier only once previously on the *Argus*, a training carrier, in the Firth of Clyde near Greenock in the East of Scotland. That had certainly not been in one of Britain's top fighters, so there was a certain trepidation to this, our first landings on the 30,000 ton fleet carrier HMS *Victorious*. We flew out to the *Victorious* just North West of the Orkneys and there my logbook shows I completed six landings one after the other during the same flight. It was probably as much to give the carrier batsman experience with a strange aircraft as to give us confidence in landing on. Together with battleships (two probably), cruisers and a destroyer screen (thank heavens) enclosing the larger ships, the strong naval force gave cover to a convoy of merchant ships whose destination was Murmansk in the north of Russia. These warships proceeded at some distance west of the convoy but within quick range of assistance if attack on it by sea or air forces was threatened. Well within the Arctic circle and south east of Spitzbergen Commanding Officer of 885 Lieutenant Rodney Carver RN and I were flown off at 3 a.m. to try to intercept a Focke Wulf Condor, a four-engined German reconnaissance aircraft which had been sighted shadowing the fleet. To avoid being detected visually by fighters on days when there was reasonable cloud cover, the Condors would fly into the cloud, and this was such a day. Not that that was of much interest to me for a few minutes after take-off my Hurricane started spluttering and streaming white smoke indicating a coolant leak into the cylinders of the engine had developed and a brief time was left for the aeroplane to remain airborne. We were flying at no more than 100 feet so my choices were limited. Parachuting was impossible. All I could do was land as gently as possible in the sea, which fortunately was calm on the surface but with a big swell. My difficulty was that at that time of a day, though it was still broad daylight in the six month Arctic summer of all day and no night, I was, if not in a torpor, certainly as hardly as alert as I might have been at 12 noon. Moreover, I had just a few seconds to prepare to land in the sea. I released the parachute but had no time to ensure that the dinghy (inflatable) attached to it was recoverable by me, and in my haste and very early morning daze I released the restraining safety straps that reduce the force of forward impact *before* I hit the water instead of after. I had no time left to open the hood and lock it back so that it wouldn't be thrown shut as the Hurricane came to a dead stop on hitting the sea at 80 to a 100 miles an hour. Bracing myself with legs stiff and hard against the rudder bars and one arm forward rigidly grasping the rim of the cockpit, I used my free arm to steady the control column as the last few feet between air and sea quickly closed. The collision threw me forward, but the blow on the head from the gunsight stunned me only for a few seconds and I was able to start wrestling to force the hood open almost immediately. The Hurricane filled with water and started to sink at once, and it was imperative I could get out before the pressure of water on the hood became too great for me to hurl it backwards along its tracks. Fortunately, neither the catch keeping the hood closed, nor its alignment with the fuselage and its tracks had been so badly affected by the abrupt stop that my task of a successful exit from the cockpit was thwarted. Thus after a tussle it opened and I could get out. I was carried down from 10 to 15 feet by the sinking Hurricane and as a result when I reached the surface, that combined with the exertions of getting out and the earlier blow on the head sapped my physical strength. I was so weakened by then that I could not activate the lever that caused the gas in a carbon dioxide bottle to inflate the life jacket I wore to its maximum buoyancy. Nor could I blow up the life jacket (Mae West) with the tube provided. The sea was very cold, but I had been warmly dressed and this at first must have given some protection against that, but as it became waterlogged it would obviously be an impediment. Partly supported by my ineptly prepared life jacket I trod water and waited as a seabird, possibly a fulmar petrel, circled me. Because of the swell I could not see further than about 50 feet and activity of any kind beyond that I was quite unaware of.

I could not see the fleet and had only a vague idea how far we had flown before my engine failed. But if our speed was between 200 and 30 miles per hour and I had been in the air for three to five minutes I would have been a maximum of 25 miles from the ships. To reach me at that distance, a ship travelling at 30 knots would have taken over 40 minutes at least. Hypothermia and exhaustion would have dispatched me long before that much time had elapsed. Yet even one minute in the air at 200 miles per hour would have taken me over three miles from the ships and a fast ship five to six minutes to reach me. At three to four miles distant I would have been expected to see the taller warships as the swell of the ocean raised me up to its highest point, but I saw nothing of them.

Suddenly, incredibly only a few hundred feet away, a destroyer's bow and bridge magically materialised and turned broadside on to me about 50 yards from me. For a time then nothing seemed to happen and I anxiously called for them to hurry, doubtful if I could keep afloat seconds let alone minutes longer. Then a boat manned by sailors came into view round the stern of the ship and after what seemed an interminable time to me but must have been only two or three minutes, reached me and dragged me aboard. I lay in the boat, grateful and marvelling at my luck that the sea was quiet and sharp eyes had spied my head in that grey-green expanse. Lifted aboard the destroyer, I was quickly enveloped in several thick blankets, given copious brandy, fed and bedded. Ultimately, my shaking and shivering stopped and I was back to robust health within hours. The destroyer captain signalled the fleet that I had been picked up, very cold and a bit silly in the head, but not otherwise in too bad a state.

The destroyer lookouts had seen me crash in the sea, the officer of the watch had taken a compass bearing of the splash and quickly approval was given to proceed at full speed to try to find me, by then a mere dot in the ocean. I don't think that the red or orange coloured dye that immersion in the ocean released from life jackets had yet been introduced as part of the survival gear. I remained on that destroyer for the rest of the operation, calling at Iceland and exchanging hospitality with a couple of American destroyers before returning to the Firth of Forth near Edinburgh. One of the American junior officers was Franklin D. Roosevelt Jnr., a reminder, as were the United States destroyers, of his father's strong support for the British and Allied cause before December 7th, 1941 and the Japanese infamy, as the President called it.

I wrote a very detailed report of that experience because pure and repeated luck and the quick skill and efficiency of officers and crew of the destroyer were the major elements in my rescue from a ditching of maladroit preparation and aftermath. My 23 years old body and my will to live must have been in my favour too. My aim in this comprehensive A 25, as naval aircraft accident reports are called, was to alert others to what to do and what not to do in similar situations. I never have found out if Admiralty Fleet Orders, the regular and imperative publication of instructions sent to ships and shore establishments all over the world, contained any reference, direct or indirect, to my experience. But I certainly learnt from it. There is, for example, no absolute truth in the assertion and – I would say – myth that one can survive for only a minute or two in the Arctic ocean; but perhaps I was the exception that proves the rule. I am not prepared to repeat the experiment.

In other squadrons on the *Victorious* at this time, July, 1942, were pilots from the first two New Zealand groups to be trained for the Fleet Air Arm. Doug Hill (Doug S. Hill from Auckland, not Doug C. Hill from Wellington), Hugh Morrison and 'FAJ' Pennington, all flying the Fulmar two-man naval fighter, and Alan Lawrence, flying Albacores, the TBR[2] aircraft that had been introduced to replace the Swordfish but in fact never did, had been posted for their first operational duties on the *Victorious* a short time before 885 squadron joined it. FAJ Pennington ultimately became the first New Zealander to command a squadron, the first to be promoted to the rank of lieutenant-commander and the first to win both a Distinguished Service Cross and a bar to it. Writing his rank, full name – Frank, Athol, Joseph – decorations and unit designation, Royal New Zealand Naval Volunteer Reserve, required 120 letters or two lines of a normal sheet of paper. Ranks included the words Acting Temporary for us war volunteers. FAJ was killed in a collision between his Seafire

[2] Torpedo Bomber Reconnaissance.

and another in June, 1944, in Colombo, Ceylon. Hugh Morrison also lost his life during the war being shot down in a Norwegian fjord while attacking the U-boat base at Kilbotn, near Narvik. This raid should never have taken place. It happened on 5th May, 1945 and Germany surrendered three days later with Goebbels and his family and Hitler and his Eva Braun poisoned in the Berlin bunker they had retreated to with their staff. This example of fatuity leading to quite unnecessary loss of lives will never be excused by me. British intelligence knew Germany was about to surrender and that this kind of raid could have no influence at all on the war at that stage and orders should have been given by the military commanders in London not to engage in pointless operations. Hugh was buried in Narvik, where a simple headstone carries his name and date of death.

Also on the *Victorious* as an observer in Fulmars was New Zealand man R. M. Richardson. Air engineer officer of the carrier was Bevan Napper and A. S. (Shorty) Long joined 885 squadron of Hurricanes before the carrier left to escort a convoy to beseiged and stricken Malta in early August, 1942. Both were New Zealanders.

In that Malta convoy, FAJ Pennington won his first DSC, one was also awarded to Bevan Napper and to R. M. Richardson and Shorty Long was awarded a Mention in Dispatches.

The Fleet Air Arm were very prominent in both the defence of Malta and in attacks on Italian and German shipping by torpedo-carrying Swordfish. Many New Zealanders served with the greatest distinction in Malta beginning in early 1942, and several of them not only flew the Swordfish and dropped torpedoes as they had been specially and intensively trained to do in day and night operations in the west of Scotland but also persuaded the Commander-in-Chief, Malta, fellow New Zealander Air Chief Marshal Sir Keith Park, to let them fly Hurricanes in fighter missions. Jack Cramp, John Morrison, Colin White and Ernie Pratt all won DSCs in Malta operations. The hazards for those who served there were vast, for Malta was under attack day and night, and the stress was such that air crews were relieved after six months service there. Ernie Pratt was killed there in January, 1943 in a Hurricane almost at the point of his being relieved and so was Owen Richards in a Swordfish during an attack on shipping in March, 1943.

After that Malta convoy in August, 1942, the *Victorious* returned to Scapa Flow, 885 having disembarked to Hatston Naval Air Station there. We flew our Hurricanes, via Arbroath and Hutton Cranswick, to Lee-on-Solent, near Portsmouth where we traded them in for first, Spitfires and then the naval version, Seafires, specially modified in both fuselage and engine for carrier operations. The lifts on the fleet carriers like *Victorious* could not accommodate the width of the Hurricane and Seafire wings, and the aircraft could not be lowered to the hangar deck for stowing and maintenance. They were pushed out on U-shaped outriggers in which their tail-wheels fitted quite snugly so that a good portion of their length was over the sea and the deck of the ship was not encumbered by them and other aircraft could be operated freely. After working up, 885 Seafire squadron joined the *Formidable*, pretty well identical with *Victorious*, in late October, 1942.

On November 8th, 1942, Allied forces invaded North Africa at Algiers and Oran in Algeria and Casablanca in Morocco, and 885 squadron with several others covered the landings at Algiers. We stayed in the Mediterranean for almost a year, having moved at first between Oran and Gibraltar and being based on airfields too from time to time at Gibraltar, and Le Senia and Tafaroui in Algeria. During this year, the Germans and Italians had been gradually forced out of North Africa by British and American armies advancing through Algeria and Tunisia and meeting up with the 8th Army coming from Egypt and Libya. They were forced out of Sicily quite soon into Italy, Malta was totally relieved and the *Formidable* visited it in August and later in the month went on to Alexandria, passage through the Mediterranean being possible again for the larger ships after over three years. In September 1943 landings at Salerno were covered by aircraft from the light fleet carrier *Unicorn* and the now increasingly numerous escort carriers *Hunter, Attacker, Stalker* and *Battler.* Salerno was not far south of Naples and there were 60 New Zealanders among the pilots who flew in this operation, some being in the fleet carriers *Formidable* and *Illustrious*, which were covering the smaller carriers close in near the landings from a less vulnerable position further out. My participation in the Salerno operation was restricted to two flights I refer to as 'Umbrella Force H' (the larger carriers and escorts) and 'Umbrella Force V' (*Unicorn* and the smaller carriers and their screening ships) on the 11th September, 1943, and then on the same day transferring to the *Unicorn*, from which on the following day I flew one patrol over the beach at Salerno and nearby. I recall winds were poor and this resulted in damage to the Seafires through heavy landings. Aircraft from the larger fleet carriers, *Formidable* and *Illustrious*, which had come from England for the operation, were called upon to make up for some of the losses.

My comparative inaction was not shared by many of the other pilots. F A J Pennington now commanded 834 squadron in the *Hunter* and he won a bar to the DSC, the Official History reporting that: 'The six pilots of his squadron completed fifty-one sorties without damage to their aircraft.' There were ten air combats and two German planes were destroyed. Don Cameron had to make a forced landing and was captured but escaped within a few days. He was awarded a Mention In Dispatches. Don's later unique experience of being captured by the Japanese in the Sakishima Gunto operations and being imprisoned in Japan is to be admired but not envied, for he and those prisoners with him were both poorly treated and starved.

I was appointed senior pilot of 879 Seafire squadron in November of 1943. 879 squadron was to be the squadron on escort carrier *Attacker.* I joined it at Andover, about 50 miles west of London on the eastern edge of Salisbury Plain. At first, 879 had only a dozen or so pilots, but during 1944 it increased in size to some 30 aircraft and pilots, formed a fighter wing with 807 squadron of escort carrier *Hunter* and 809 squadron of *Stalker* and worked up as a squadron and wing at Burscough in Lancashire, Long Kesh in Northern Island (now a prison of some notoriety) and in June, 1944 in the Mediterranean, Gibraltar and North Africa with the ultimate purpose of providing fighter cover and reconnaissance for the landings in the south of France. Part of the preparation for that was a week operating with the Desert Air Force in Italy. Dive-bombing and strafing attacks on the retreating German forces – at that time in July 1944 not far south of Florence – were very valuable experiences for the forthcoming south of France invasion.

In June 1944 I had been appointed to command 807 squadron on *Hunter* with the rank of lieutenant-commander. There were many New Zealanders in the wing. My close friends in 879 squadron Gerry Gown (DSC in the south of France), Bruce Taylor, Jim Howden (m.i.d. in the south of France) and Mac Ganley, in 807 squadron just one other than me, Des Graham (m.i.d. from the

South of France) and Doug C. Hill (one of three MBEs awarded to New Zealanders in the Fleet Air Arm), John Jellie (DSC from the South of France and m.i.d. from later operations in the Aegean and Greece) and Arch Foley were some of the 50 or so New Zealanders involved in Fleet Air Arm operations in the south of France invasion and then in October, 1944 in the Aegean Sea and Greece, continually harassing the German retreat from that area. The DSC was also awarded me after the south of France invasion.

The *Hunter* returned to Portsmouth, England after the operations in the Aegean and in November, almost exactly four years after arriving in Portsmouth to begin training for the Fleet Air Arm, I left that old naval port to return to New Zealand on leave. It was a good long leave and during it on May 8th, 1945 the Germans were totally and deservedly crushed and 'surrendered unconditionally' as the Allies demanded. With John Jellie and Eric Benge and a Canadian crew, I flew back to England in a Liberator bomber in July 1945, was appointed to command a training squadron in naval air war tactics and was on a course at St Merryn naval air station in Cornwall when the two atom bombs were dropped, on Hiroshima on the 6th August and Nagasaki on the 9th (my 27th birthday), and the Japanese finally and completely capitulated on 15th August.

The war for me was in Britain and to a limited extent northward from Britain and more dominantly southward in the Mediterranean and the lands bordering it. Others had vastly different experiences, and I have the greatest admiration for those who like my friends Digger Robertson and Jack McAleese served on MAC ships escorting the Atlantic convoys, minelaying along the French coast – as Digger did – attacked the *Tirpitz* and other targets in the Norwegian fiords, shot down V1 flying bombs as Selwyn Hamblett did, flew in operations from the numerous carriers in the East against the Japanese in Burma, Malaya and Indonesia, Palembang oil refinery being the biggest of these, and in the months just before the Japanese surrender flew with the British Pacific Fleet and the United States task forces and repeatedly attacked Japan's military and naval forces in the Sakashima Gunto and in Japan itself near Tokyo and the Inland Sea.

Bibliography: THE ROYAL NEW ZEALAND NAVY, by S. D. Waters (part of Official History of New Zealand in the Second World

War 1939–45) War History Branch, Department of Internal Affairs, Wellington, New Zealand 1956

Sub Lieutenant (A) L. J. (Bill) Ryan MID RNZNVR

I left New Zealand on the 21st July 1941 as a member of a draft of 65 recruits in the MV *Dominion Monarch*.

Following my naval indoctrination at HMS *St Vincent* I trained with several other members of our course as an observer in Trinidad and later in Scotland.

I was appointed to No 829 Torpedo Bomber Reconnaissance squadron then based at Machrahanish, Scotland. The squadron of 12 aircraft was under the command of Lieutenant Cdr (A) D. W. Phillips RN and had recently re-equipped with the new Barracuda II bomber.

We spent several weeks at Machrahanish working up around the Clyde, initial deck landings in the new aircraft etc., and on 8th March we finally joined our carrier HMS *Victorious* to sail to Scapa Flow in the Orkney Islands. Here we became part of Force 1, which comprised the battleships *Duke of York* and *Anson*, the cruiser *Belfast* and six destroyers. This group was later to operate with Force 2, which consisted of the light fleet carrier *Furious* and escort carriers *Emperor, Searcher, Pursuer* and *Fencer* plus three more cruisers, two oilers and ten destroyers.

While continuing our working up period at Scapa Flow a dummy bombing range had been installed at Lock Eriboll about 20 miles west of Cape Wrath, one of the most desolate areas of north Scotland.

Unbeknown to us at the time, Loch Eriboll had been selected because it bore a remarkable similarity to Alten Fiord in Norway where our eventual target, the German battleship *Tirpitz* lay at anchor, waiting to emerge and attack any convoys bound for Russia. The following two weeks were spent in rehearsals for the attack, forming up the bombers and escort fighters, tactical approach to the end of Loch Eriboll and wave after wave of divebombing and strafing attacks on the practice target. The final practice took place on the 28th March.

In the meantime a convoy of 49 merchant ships had assembled in Loch Ewe which was about 70 miles south west of Cape Wrath. This convoy was presumably set up as a bait to draw the *Tirpitz* from its lair in Alten Fiord and entice it towards the heavy battleships and carriers in the combined forces. This, however, was not to be, so the convoy and the covering forces continued across the Norwegian Sea to rendezvous about 250 miles north west of the target area.

The briefing of the *Victorious* aircrews was convened for 0130 hours in the morning of the 3rd April. All intelligence data was presented – the precise position of *Tirpitz* at the end of Kaa Fiord, an offshoot of the larger Alten Fiord – the anti-aircraft defences – the tactical approach to evade radar detection etc.

The attack would consist of two strikes, the first comprising 21 Barracudas from *Victorious* and *Furious*, escorted by 45 Corsair Hellcats and Wildcat fighters. Following this, a similar sized strike would be launched from the carriers before the first sorties returned to land on. The fleet fighter defence would be provided by some of the escort carriers. The Barracuda aircraft would carry either 1600 lb armour piercing bombs, two types of 500 lb bombs or a new 600 lb bomb.

Meantime, air engineers and squadron personnel were working all through the previous day and night, ensuring the serviceability of the aircraft and fitting the necessary weapons.

At 0345 'Action Stations' was sounded in *Victorious* and aircrews emerged on the flight deck to man their aircraft. Weather conditions were perfect, the sea was relatively calm with a wind of 12–14 knots which would assist the launching of the heavily laden Barracudas. At 0415 our Corsair fighters which were in the front of the deck park were launched. The carrier had by this time built up a good speed into the 14 knot wind to minimise the problem of getting the heavy bombers airborne.

The first strike was led by Lieut Commander (A) R. S. Baker-Faulkner DSC of the *Furious* TBR Wing.

My pilot Ben Pawson, an Englishman, and I were rostered to take part in the second strike. We watched the aircraft in the first flight take off. The Corsairs were airborne before reaching the bow, but one or two of the heavily laden Barracudas barely had flying speed off the flight deck. As so often happens in naval aviation it seemed to fall over the bows but miraculously gained sufficient speed to avoid crashing into the sea.

The first strike proceeded at sea level towards the Norwegian coast then at some 25 miles began to climb to the bombing height of about 10 to 11000 feet. About 45 minutes later they crossed the coastline. The fighters dropped their long-range fuel tanks and deployed in several directions to intercept any threats from enemy fighters which were known to be deployed in strength at Bardufoss, about 200 miles south west of Alten Fiord.

The Barracudas were so heavily laden it took ages for them to reach their preferred bombing height. Although it had only recently come into squadron service the Barracuda would never have won a prize for aeronautical design. It was not a pretty streamlined aircraft like a Hurricane or a Seafire or for that matter the American Grumman Avenger. It was designed for a crew of three, pilot, observer and radio airgunner and some would add for the 'ghost of Lord Nelson'. The fighter boys rather disparagingly referred to it as the Admiralty's 'Flying Christmas Tree'.

Despite its ungainliness and its lack of engine power and speed, it had a job to do and this was to be its baptism under fire.

The first strike crossed the coast at just after 0500 hours and about ten minutes later they saw *Tirpitz* nestled in behind her torpedo nets right at the end of Kaa Fiord. Obviously the German crew had gone to action stations because smoke generators had been activated and a dense cloud was passing across the fiord to gradually obliterate the hull of the enemy warship. Soon the hull of the *Tirpitz* became shrouded in smoke but the masts and control positions were still visible above the smoke screen. Many violent flashes of explosions were observed by the escorting fighter pilots as the bombers released their loads on the target.

At 0525 while the first strike was attacking our second strike was flown off. Unfortunately, one of our Barracudas failed to start up. As it could not be relocated in the range of aircraft waiting to fly off a quick decision was made to push it over the side – bombs and all. The remaining aircraft took off, but unfortunately one Barracuda failed to gain height after leaving the bows and crashed into the sea with the loss of its crew of three. This strike was commanded by Lieut Commander (A). V. Rance RN.

We crossed the coast at 10,000 feet and then reduced height to 7000 – 7500 feet. From 35–40 miles away we could see the pall of smoke at the end of the Kaa fiord. Some of our escorting fighters dived down ahead of us to strafe the ship's AA gun positions and keep the 'enemy heads down'. Our aircraft was the second to last to join the attack. We dived down through a heavy box barrage and then lighter anti-aircraft fire. Just before we released our bomb I saw one Barracuda from our squadron get hit by close range flak. The pilot had released his bomb and was pulling out of the dive when the aircraft burst into flames and crashed into the cliffs of the fiord. That wasn't very nice to watch – not something I think about.

Needless to say after that, and having dropped our bomb, we took evasive action and got the hell out of the inferno as fast as our Barracuda could go. As we withdrew I recall watching dozens of Corsairs and Hellcats whirling around in the treacherous confines of the fiord with cliffs rising sheer from the water to 3000 feet or more. They were still strafing the *Tirpitz* and any land based gun emplacement they could find, at speeds of up to 300 m.p.h. How they avoided mid-air collisions one will never know. There was a number of New Zealanders among the fighter escorts. From our carrier alone Spence Wright, Bill Direen (both 31 Course with me), George Rawstron, Al French, Peter Coltman, with Matt Farrer and Murray Rivett piloting Barracuda bombers.

One impression I have retained of this operation is rather odd. It was my admiration of the courage of the German sailors who manned their ship's anti-aircraft guns in the face of withering fire from the Corsairs and Hellcats as well as the holocaust of bombs which hit the upper deck all within the space of a few minutes.

It must have been very frightening to have been trapped on this ship. It wasn't exactly very pleasant having to dive down through the defensive AA fire, but at least we were not stationary like these poor chaps were.

Later when statistics of the raid were released, it mentioned that *Tirpitz* had suffered a deluge of approximately 40 tons of bombs of which 24 direct hits had been verified. In these two attacks which together lasted only a few minutes the German casualties totalled 220 killed and 564 wounded, many very seriously.

The *Tirpitz* had been put out of action, but despite the heavy pounding including many hits by our 1600 lb armour piercing bombs we had still been unable to penetrate the 5 to 10 inch armour plating which protected its vital compartments, engine spaces and magazines.

Because of the lack of damage to the hull and the possibility of repairing the damage to the gun turrets, bridge and control systems further Fleet Air Arm attacks were planned for later in the month of April and early May.

Unfortunately, weather conditions deteriorated and these operations had to be cancelled. Consequently this 56,000 ton monster remained a threat to the allied convoy route to North Russia. As long as *Tirpitz* remained seaworthy, even if not battle worthy, the Royal Navy would still be required to maintain capital ships, cruisers and carriers based at Scapa Flow to prevent any possible sally into the North Atlantic.

Because the Barracuda borne bombs had failed to inflict any damage to the hull of the *Tirpitz* it was surreptitiously moved from its lair in Kaa Fiord to another anchorage in Tromsö Fiord about 120 miles south west.

It was here, on the 12th November 1944 the Royal Air Force mounted an attack on 29 Lancaster bombers each carrying one 12,000 lb – 22 feet long 'Tall Boy' Blockbuster bomb.

This was the *coup de grace* for the *Tirpitz*. Pounded within a few minutes by 155 tons of heavy explosives she finally rolled over and sank. Following the postponement of further attacks on the *Tirpitz*, the fleet put to sea on 26th April to carry out a series of strikes against enemy shipping in and around Bodo and Narvik. On one such incursion a convoy of five German ships plus escorts were sighted off Bodo, and although the weather conditions were very poor, low cloud base, and frequent snow storms three of these ships totalling 15,000 tons were sunk and another 800 tons plus a German destroyer were severely damaged. Our losses on this operation were one Hellcat, two Corsairs and one Barracuda.

On the last anti-shipping strike on 1st June aircraft from the carriers *Victorious* and *Furious* attacked another coastal convoy sinking two vessels and damaging two others, one of which had to be beached.

So ended our exploits in the Norwegian sphere of operations.

On 12th June 1944 HMS *Victorious* sailed from the Firth of Clyde to join the Eastern Fleet and later the British Pacific Fleet.

Sub Lieutenant (A) Ian Stirling DSC RNZNVR

1842 Corsair Squadron

On 4th May 1945, our flight escorted Avengers to Ishigaki in Sakashima Gunto where we bombed the town and jetties. Following that we acted as target CAP for the Avengers. However, in the meantime HMS *Formidable* had been hit by a kamikaze, so on our return we had to land on *Victorious*. I recall, on landing, that I had been airborne for 4 hours 5 minutes, so we were very relieved to learn that *Victorious* could take us on.

Being sort of homeless, we expected to have an easy time in *Vic* until we could return to our own carrier. This was not to be.

With the flight deck occupied mostly by *Formidable* aircraft we were obliged to do a lot of Stage II readiness – strapped in the cockpit, motors warmed up and aircraft ranged for take off at a moment's notice.

Next morning on 5th May, four *Formidable* aircraft on Stage II were sent off to intercept an enemy aircraft that had appeared on the ship's radar. This flight was led by Lieutenant Phil Clarke RNVR along with Alan Ewing and a subsection of myself and Geoff Hartshorn RNZNVR. The fighter direction officer in *Vic* directed us to climb to 30,000 ft. and vectored us on to the bogey which was then about 70 miles from the fleet.

The objective was to prevent it from coming any closer and reporting the position of our carriers.

Because of the extreme difficulty of rearranging aircraft on *Victorious*'s crowded flight deck, I was flying a Corsair which had just been landed by Lieutenant Hammy Gray RCNVR (who was later to win a posthumous Victoria Cross). Gray's aircraft had just returned from CAP, so it was not equipped with bomb racks as were the other three aircraft in our flight. Consequently, my aircraft was somewhat faster than the others and was able to forge ahead. Following a short burst of fire the Jap aircraft exploded and I pulled through a huge sheet of flame.

I got the impression that the bogey was a 'Judy', a two seater with a rear gun. There were several bullet holes in Geoff 's Corsair, so the near gunner must have put up a fight which I didn't notice.

On return to the fleet we were ordered to land back on board our own carrier the *Formidable*.

On 28th July I took off an a 'ramrod' over Japan with Keith Quilter as flight leader, Alan Ewings and 'Smithy' (I think it was Gordon Smith). We crossed the coast near Daio Saki light at very low level and attacked shipping in the harbour.

I am certain that the 500 lb bomb which I dropped hit my selected target, a coastal cargo vessel but the bomb may have gone right through it into an empty hold. We continued up the harbour strafing other vessels, some of which exploded.

Following this we patrolled south east along the coast and encountered more ships about 50 kilometres south. We came in at low level over the town to strafe wharf buildings and then attacked the bridge of a ship which I took to be a destroyer. I released my second bomb and just cleared the target at mast head height when suddenly my Corsair lost power.

I had not felt any significant hit, but I had been subjected to some intense anti aircraft fire. I checked my instruments: the engine was dead, so I opened the hood and lashed down my safety harness and as I was too low to bale out, I had no option but to put it in the sea.

I came to, still strapped in the cockpit with water circling my waist, the Corsair engine under water and heading for Davy Jones's locker.

I released the harness but could not release the radio telephone connection to my helmet. This started to pull me down with the aircraft. One mighty wrench, however, and I was free and floating on the surface.

I found that I had come down only 30 yards from a small rocky island in the harbour, from which I could see some Japs pulling a dory out of the water. They were moving around excitedly on the rocks and I could hear the jabber of their voices.

By this time I became aware that the tide was ebbing strongly so I ditched my shoes and started to swim with the current, with my Mae West giving me bouyancy. I noticed that my watch had stopped at 0630 hours.

After I had been swimming and floating for some time a large fish ranged up alongside me. I suddenly felt very vulnerable so I inflated my dinghy, climbed in and commenced paddling. The dinghy pack had been my cushion seat in the cockpit and was attached to my Mae West.

By this time, I had drifted quite a distance from the island and the harbour had become much wider. On looking skywards, I noticed that the warfare was still in progress, but thankfully not in my vicinity.

I continued to paddle and then managed to erect the little sail so as to take advantage of the offshore wind. This was soon seen by the Japs and I became the target for rifle fire from the shore. This forced me to lower the sail.

At that point two Corsairs from my flight circled overhead presumably reporting my position. I reckoned that I could get clear of the harbour, but again things became unhealthy. The Jap anti-aircraft fire was directed at these Corsairs and I started to collect the flak beneath them so I gave them the wave off.

I continued to paddle and progressed further out into the large bay when suddenly I heard an engine, and in the distance I could see a motor boat heading in my direction.

With excellent timing, two United States Navy Hellcats arrived on the scene and gave the Jap motor boat the full treatment. They stayed and circled for some time but then left and once again I felt very lonely.

Then a most remarkable thing happened. I was still edging out towards sea when suddenly a large black shape loomed up alongside me. I just about had kittens but all was well. It was an American submarine apparently on station for air-sea rescue purpose.

I paddled towards it, but it continued to turn in a wide circle so I had to reverse and finally came alongside. Finally, a bearded sailor threw me a lifebuoy and I was pulled on board. Rather sadly, he punctured my dinghy with a knife and threw it back into the sea. It would have been a marvellous war memento.

Thereupon I climbed up the rungs to the bridge where the captain Commander Gunn welcomed me: 'Pleased to have you aboard Mister.' Whereupon I replied, 'And I am bloody pleased to be here, sir.'

Both were massive understatements.

Imagine my surprise, however, when I descended the conning tower to the control room to be welcomed by my own flight leader Keith Quilter!

He and the others had started to look for me when he was suddenly hit by what he described as a 'nasty little trawler'.

I have visited Keith in the United Kingdom several times since the war and we still marvel at the happenings of that day. During our last meeting in 1990 Keith decided that we should telephone 'Pop' Gunn who had by then retired as an admiral and lived in San Diego. We both talked to him, just over 45 years since he took the tremendous risk of bringing his boat and crew in such dangerous conditions to pick us up.

We spent nearly three weeks on board USS *Scabbardfish* and were finally put ashore at Saipan on VJ Day. The tally of survivors was 14, one of whom had broken a leg in baling out of a Mustang. We all stayed overnight on Saipan and having qualified as submariners we joined the VJ Day celebrations in the Submariners Club.

The following day we were flown to Guam where we spent a week in the very comfortable Flight Officers Rehabilitation Centre. Our only problem in life was the lack of money.

By chance the personal aircraft of Admiral Sir Bruce Fraser landed at Guam on route from Tokyo to Manus in the Admiralty Group. About six Fleet Air Arm survivors travelled in this VIP aircraft to Manus where we rejoined our squadron HMS *Formidable*.

We had been absent for nearly a month and the Commander (EXEC) who happened to be at the gangway when we arrived, wanted to know where the hell we had been!

In October 1973 I was privileged to represent New Zealand at a United Nations Cartographic Conference in Tokyo. At the conclusion of the meeting my wife and I travelled by train to Owase where we stayed for two nights in a Ryokan. We walked along the main street down which I had flown and wandered around the wharf area which we had strafed. There were no other Europeans in the town and the only person who understood English was the Ryokan proprietor.

When told the reason for our visit he gave us every assistance, taking us to vantage points in his car. At one place we could look down the harbour and saw the small rocky island that had been my very close visit to Japan nearly 30 years before.

Author's Note Ian Stirling was a member of 52 pilots course at HMS *St Vincent*. Our naval association dated from about October 1944 when Ian was a member of a Corsair conversion course at the Naval Fighter OTU at Puttalam, Ceylon.

In civilian life Ian was a surveyor in the Government Lands and Survey Department.

He retired as Surveyor General for New Zealand.

This summarises a 'Sterling' career by a 'Stirling' pilot.

Fleet Air Arm Carrier Strength 1939–45 War

Fleet Carriers (14) *Argus* (later as a training Carrier) *Ark Royal* (sunk 13/11/41), *Courageous* (sunk 17/09/39), *Eagle* (sunk 11/08/42), *Formidable, Furious, Glorious* (sunk 08/06/40), *Glory, Hermes* (sunk 09/04/42), *Illustrious, Implacable, Indefatigable, Indomitable, Victorious*

Light Fleet Carriers (5) *Colossus, Ocean, Unicorn* (also used for maintenance and training), *Venerable, Vengeance*

Escort Carriers (44) *Activity, Ameer, Arbiter, Archer, Atheling, Attacker, Audacity, Avenger* (sunk 15/11/42), *Battler, Begum, Biter, Campania, Charger, Chaser, Dasher* (blew up and sunk 27/03/43), *Emperor, Empress, Fencer, Hunter, Khedive, Nabob* (torpedoed 22/08/44 but survived), *Nairana, Patroller, Premier, Puncher, Pursuer, Queen, Rajah, Ranee, Ravager, Reaper, Ruler, Searcher, Shah, Slinger, Smiter, Speaker, Stalker, Striker, Thane* (torpedoed by U 482 off Clyde but towed to Greenock), *Tracker, Trouncer, Trumpeter, Vindex*

Seaplane Carriers (3) *Albatross, Pegasus, Vindictive*

Aircraft Transporters (2) *Athene, Engadine*

Maintenance Carriers (2) *Perseus, Pioneer*

Trials Carrier (1) *Pretoria Castle*

Mac Ships (Merchant Aircraft Carriers), (19)
Tankers: *Acavus, Adula, Alexia, Amastra, Ancylus, Empire MacCabe,*

Empire MacColl, Empire MacKay, Empire MacMahon, Gadila, Macoma, Miralda, Rapana

Grain Ships: *Empire MacAlpine, Empire MacAndrew, Empire MacCallum, Empire MacDermott, Empire MacKendrick, Empire McCrae*

It is very interesting to note that the Admiralty had plans in 1945 to launch a new fleet carrier, HMS *New Zealand*. These plans were, however, cancelled when Japan surrendered.

The naming of this carrier was undoubtedly an acknowledgement of the conspicuous presence of New Zealand airmen in the Fleet Air Arm.

At the end of the war in the Pacific 25% of the fighter pilots were New Zealanders!

HMS Indefatigable

Flying Programme No 128 for Friday 4th May 1945

Operation 'Iceberg Seven'		
Duty Pilot	To be detailed by No 24 Wing	
Parking Officers	S/Lts. Drummond and Fountain	
H–2.0	Both watches of AHP to Flying Stations	
	Range 8 Seafire FIII	
	Range 8 Firefly	
	Spot Avenger Deck Park aft	
H Hour (3)	OFF 8 Seafire CAP	(A)
	Taxi 7 Avenger to BOOSTER	
H + 0.30 (4)	BOOST 7 Avenger)	
	OFF 8 Firefly R/P) Strike 'Able'	(B)
	OFF 5 Avenger)	(C)
	Range 9 Seafire LIII	(D)
H + 2.00 (5)	OFF 8 Seafire CAP	(D)
	ON 8 Seafire	(A)
H + 2.45 (6)	ON 8 Firefly	(B)
H + 3.15 (7)	ON 12 Avenger	(C)
	Spot Deck Part aft	
	Range 8 Seafire F III	(E)
H + 4.00 (8)	OFF 8 Seafire CAP	(E)
	Taxi Deck Park Forward	
	ON 8 Seafire	(D)
	Spot Deck Park aft	
THEN PLAN 'EASY' OR PLAN 'FOX' AS ORDERED		
	PLAN 'EASY'	
	Range 8 Seafire L III	(G)

H + 6.00 (11)	OFF 8 Seafire CAP	(G)
	Taxi Deck Park forward	
H + 6.30 (12)	ON 8 Seafire	(E)
	Spot Deck Park aft	
	Range 8 Seafire F III	(H)
	PLAN 'FOX'	
H + 5.15 (10)	OFF 12 Avenger Strike 'Charlie'	(F)
	Range 8 Seafire L III	(G)
H + 6.00 (11)	OFF 8 Seafire CAP	(G)
	ON 8 Seafire	(E)
H + 7.15	ON 12 Avenger	(F)
	Spot Deck aft	
	Range 8 Seafire F III	(H)
	THEN FOR PLAN 'EASY' OR PLAN 'FOX'	
H + 8.00 (13)	OFF 8 Seafire CAP	(H)
	Taxi Deck Park Forward	
H + 8.30 (14)	ON 8 Seafire	(G)
	Spot Deck Park aft	
	Range 8 Seafire L III	(J)
H + 10.00 (15)	OFF 8 Seafire CAP	(J)
	Taxi Deck Park forward	
	ON 8 Seafire	(H)
	Spot Deck Park aft	
	Range 8 Seafire F III	(K)
H + 12.00 (18)	OFF 8 Seafire CAP	(K)
	Taxi Deck Park forward	
	OFF 8 Seafire	(J)
H + 14.00 (20)	ON 8 Seafire	(K)

Notes 1. Seafires are to carry 45 gallon LR Tanks.

2. 8 Fireflies for R/P strike to carry 8 × 60 R/P.3 Fireflies are to be fitted with LR Tanks.1 Firefly is to have R/P rails fitted and is to be at immediate notice to range in case an aircraft goes U/S.

3. Avengers are to carry 8 × 500 lbs. MC Bombs.

4. Both watches of E.A.H.P. and both hangar Ranging Teams will be required throughout the day at short notice.

5. X H Hour and Flying Plan will be broadcast as soon as they are known.
6. KEEP YOUR COPY OF THIS PROGRAMME.

P. W. HUMPHREYS
COMMANDER (FLYING)

Distribution.

LIEUT CDR P. WHITFIELD
SQUADRON COs
LIEUT MASTERS
SUB-LIEUT ROOME
SUB-LIEUT BRYCE – BUCHANAN

LEGEND H HOUR – 0530 hours (H + 1400–1930 hours)AHP – Aircraft handling party)
CAP – Combat air patrol
LR – Long range (drop tanks)
RP – Rocket projectile
Blackburn Skua
Blackburn Roc
Gloster Sea Gladiator
Supermarine Walrus 1
Fairey Fulmar NF.II
Fairey Swordfish II
Fairey Albacore
Grumman Martlet III
Grumman Avenger II
Curtiss Helldiver I
Supermarine Seafire L.III
Grumman Hellcat II
Corsair IV
Fairey Barracuda II
Seafire L. Mk IIC

Appendix I

Technical Data

The Merlin Seafires

Common Data

WINGSPAN: 36ft 10ins (clipped: 32ft 7ins)
LENGTH: 30ft $2\frac{1}{2}$ins
HEIGHT: 8ft (over cowling) 13ft (over airscrew)
WING AREA: 242sq ft (clipped: 234sq ft)
POWERPLANT: Rolls-Royce Merlin 45 (IB and IIC)
46 (IIC)
50A (IIC)
32 (LIIC and LRIIC)
55 (FIII)
55M (LIII and FRIII)
ARMAMENT: 2 × 20mm Hispano cannon
4 × 0.303in Browning machine-guns
FUEL: Internal – top tank 40 imperial gallons
lower tank 37 imperial gallons
total 85 imperial gallons
jettisonable 30 or 45 imperial gallons
90 imperial gallons (FIII/LIII)
OIL: 5.8 imperial gallons or
8.5 imperial gallons (late production LIII and FRIII)

Weights (lbs)

	empty*	LOADED	45–GALL	90–GALL	500LB BOMB
IB	5,910	6,718	7,122	n.a.	n.a.
IIC	6,103	7,004	7,414	N.A.	7,543
LIIC	6,106	7,006	7,420	N.A.	7,546
LRHC	6,245	7,146	7,550	N.A.	N.A.
FIII	6,204	7,104	7,508	7,950	7,640 LIII only)
FRIII	6,286	7,186	7,590	8,130 (89–gall)	n.a.

*Empty weight is the airframe and engine complete, but without fuel, oil, or ammunition

	IB(45)	IIC(46)	LIIC	FIII	LIII	HEIGHT
LEVEL SPEED (MPH)	295	280	316	304	331	Sea Level
			335		358	6,000ft
				352		11,500ft
		355	335			13,000ft
					350	15,000ft
	341	345	328	345	331	19,000ft
RATE OF CLIMB (FT/MIN)	2,700	2,250	3,300	2,500	2,650	Sea Level
NORMAL RATING			3,600		3,450	6,000ft
COMBAT RATING	3,620	3,100	4,380	3,650	4,160	Sea Level
			4,600		4,310	6,000ft
TIME TO HEIGHT (MINS)			1.7		1.9	5,000ft
		7.0	5.0	6.0	5.5	15,000ft
	8.0	1	8.0	8.0		20,000ft
USEFUL CEILING (FT = 1,000)	28	29.5	24	31.3	24	
RADIUS OF ACTION (STATUTE MILES)	125	120	140	140	140	(45g D/T)
					185	(89g D/T)
				200	200	(90g D/T)
PATROL ENDURANCE (HRS, MINS) – TIME ON STATION	1.55	1.50	2.05	2.05	2.05	(45g D/T)
				3.10	3.10	(90g D/T)

CARRIER TAKE-OFF RUN (FEET) WITH 45–GALLON DT RELATIVE WIND					
20 KNOTS	390	400	330	375	330
30 KNOTS	265	280	225	260	230
40 KNOTS	180	195	140	160	140

Appendix II

Former Students of New Plymouth Boys' High School Serving in Fleet Air Arm 1939–1945

Keith Adams
Maxwell H. Burn (prisoner of war 1941–45) died post war
John C. Casey – killed 13.09.39
G. Dennis Cook – killed 08.04.42
Fred J. Duncan
Peter Dixon
Terence C. R. Fenwick – killed 19.09.44
Francis J. Flannagan – killed 30.05.42
R. Stewart Fleming
Bernard L. Finch – died post war
Donald V. Fitzpatrick
Brian Huggett (prisoner of war 1941–45) died post war
John W. Johnston – died post war
E. Graeme King
Mervyn Kibby – died post war
Derek Lightbourne – died post war
Claude Leighton – died post war
Douglas V. Lunn – killed 10.08.43
Rex Griffiths
Alister S. MacLeod
Ian N. MacLeod – killed 13.01.45
A. Owen Masters
Ralph Mander
Donald Mander
Alan Meuli – died post war
Charles G. Patrick – died post war
Jack Pepperell – killed 01.05.42
Leslie J. Ryan
William Skeet

Darcy Self
John Sisely
William Squire – died post war
Michael F. Stringfield
Nelson Tollerton
Alex N. Thomson – killed 14.01.43

Total complement 35

2 prisoners of war 8 killed on active service

*John C. Casey was probably the first New Zealander killed in active service in the Second World War.

There would be few schools, if any, in Britain and the Commonwealth, which could claim as many volunteers to the Fleet Air Arm as the New Plymouth Boys' High School.

Slightly over 1000 New Zealanders joined the Fleet Air Arm 1939–1945.

Over 25% of pilots and observers in the British Pacific Fleet were New Zealanders

Appendix III

The Boys Who Were Killed

The following is the official Navy Office list of those New Zealanders in the Fleet Air Arm who died overseas –

ADAMS, David Winton, S/Lt. (A), 9.3.42.
ADAMS, Russel Byers, S/Lt. (A), 1.9.43.
ALEXANDER, James Douglas, Lt. (A), 30.7.45.
ANDERSON, Jasper Murray, S/Lt. (A), 14.4.44.
ANDREWS, Frederick Ernest, C.P.O. (A), 9.6.44.
APPLEBY, William Seddon, S/Lt. (A), 3.2.44.
ARCHIBALD, Arthur Herbert Percy, P.O. (A), 19.7.43.
BATTEN, Frederick Moncrieff, S/Lt. (A), 5.12.44.
BAXTER, Evan John, Lt. (A), 31.7.45.
BENNETT, Jock, S/Lt. (A), 10.2.42.
BISMAN, Royden Thomas, S/Lt. (A), 29.6.44.
BLACK, Gordon, S/Lt. (A), 11.11.41.
BLACK, John Ross, S/Lt. (A), 7.7.44.
BONIFACE, Douglas Philip Hurlstone, S/Lt. (A), 18.1.44.
BOWMAN, Colin Sutherland, Lt. (A), 23.3.44.
BREINGAN, Robert Ian, Lead/Air, 11.10.42.
BROWN, John Atkinson, S/Lt. (A), 10.8.43
BROWN, MacDonald Cody, S/Lt. (A), 27.3.44.
BROWNE, Barrie Hawtrey, P.O. (A), 8.7.45.
BUSH, Thomas Noel, Lt. (A), 5.12.42.
CAMERON, Stewart Ross, S/Lt. (A), 29.1.44.
CAMPBELL, Kenneth Neil, Lead/Air, 17.4.41.
CASEY, John Clutha, Midship (A) RN, 7.9.39.
CHETTLE, Richard John, S/Lt. (A), 20.6.43.
CHITTENDEN, John David, S/Lt. (A), 29.6.44.
CHURCHILL, Adrian Hugh, Lt. (A), 7.4.45.

COLBECK, Ralph Austin, S/Lt. (A), 11.11 43.
COOK, George Denys, Mid. (A), 8.4.42.
COSSILL, Royce Ivan, S/Lt. (A), 10.2.43.
COWPER, Valentine Henry George, S/Lt. (A), 15.11.42.
CRANWELL, Robert Arthur, S/Lt. (A), 8.5.44.
CULPAN, Desmond Keith, S/Lt. (A), 24.11.44.
CURD, Victor Selwyn, Lt. (A), 4.7.44.
DAVIES, Robert Usher, S/Lt. (A), 1.2.43.
DILLNER, Beverley Oscar, S/Lt. (A), 9.2.44.
DILLON, Donald Frederick, S/Lt. (A), 30.3.43.
DOUGLAS, John Mackenzie, S/Lt. (A), 11.12.42.
DOWELL, Avery David, S/Lt. (A), 14.3.43
DRAKE, James David, S/Lt. (A), 29.8.44.
EATON, Albert Neville, S/Lt. (A), 14.7.43.
EDNEY, Stanley William, Lt. (A), 17.5.44.
ELWOOD, Desmond Nelson, S/Lt. (A), 1.8.42.
FARRER, Mathew Cameron, Lt. (A), 27.8.45.
FENWICK, Terence Charles Robert, Lt. (A), 19.9.44.
FERGUSON, William George, Lead/Air, 4.3.44.
FLANNAGAN, Francis Patrick Joseph, S/Lt. (A), 30.5.42.
FLINTOFF, Robert Hayward, S/Lt. (A), 12.10.43.
FORBES, Robert Wilson Derrick, S/Lt. (A), 27.7.43.
GALL, Robert John, S/Lt. (A), 14.12.43.
GALLAGHER, Charles Anthony, Lead/Air, 25.2.42.
GAMBRILL, Edward Boys, S/Lt. (A), 4.7.45.
GOODFELLOW, Richard Maclaurin, Lt. (A), 19.10.44.
GRAHAM, David Neil, S/Lt. (A), 24.7.45.
HABERFIELD, John Kerle Tipaho, Lt. (A), 21.7.45.
HAMILTON, Brian Charles, Lead/Air, 25.8.41.
HARRIS, John Douglas Morton, S/Lt. (A), 24.5.43.
HARRISON, William, S/Lt. (A), 19.9.42.
HAWKER, Harold Tolmie, Lt. (A), 13.8.43.
HAYWARD, Leslie Frank, S/Lt. (A), 1.5.44.
HERROLD, John Dean, S/Lt. (A), 26.4.44.
HEWETSON, Edward De Aulton, S/Lt. (A), 11.7.44.
HOOSON, William Clive, S/Lt. (A), 2.1.42.
HORNBY, John Samuel, S/Lt. (A), 10.10.48.
HOSKIN, Redge Dennis, S/Lt. (A), 18.11.43.
HOUSTON, John David, S/Lt. (A), 25.10.42.
HOWDEN, David Anthony, S/Lt. (A), 13.3.42.
INGLE, Ewan Seymour, Lead/Air, 19.8.41.
JAMIESON, Raymond, S/Lt. (A), 15.11.43.

JENKINS, Donald Andrew Lt. (A), 26.5.44.
JOHNSON, Lloyd Harding, S/Lt. (A), 3.2.43.
KNOWLES, Pat Thomas , S/Lt. 16.11.44.
LATTER, Meliss Stuart, Lt. (A), 15.11.42.
LAWSON, Robert Arthur, S/Lt. (A), 15.6.43.
LEE, Allen Stephen, S/Lt. (A), 16.4.44.
LIBEAU, Clutha Campbell, S/Lt. (A), 21.8.45.
LUNN, Douglas Vernon, S/Lt. (A), 10.8.43.
McALEESE, Daniel, S/Lt. (A), 13.4.45.
McBRIDE, Robert Nesbitt, S/Lt. (A), 17.11.43.
McBRIDE, Thomas Chalmers Glen, S/Lt. (A), 10.8.45.
McCABE, Robert Douglas, S/Lt. (A), 25.5.44.
McCRACKEN, Alan Cairnhill, S/Lt. (A), 15.5.43.
McDONALD, James Ninian, S/Lt. (A), 14.6.43.
McKAY, Ian Alexander, S/Lt. (A), 22.11.43.
McLEAN, Dennis Beresford, S/Lt. (A), 11.8.42.
McLEOD, Gordon Edward, S/Lt. (A), 23.6.45.
McMILLAN, Rex, S/Lt. (A), 22.4.42.
MacKAY, Henry Alexander, Lt. (A), 24.6.44.
MacLEOD, Norman Ian, S/Lt. (A), 13.1.45.
MAFFEY, Leslie Walden Ellyett, Lt. (A), 22.2.45.
MARKS, Frank Ernest, S/Lt. (A), 23.1.45.
MARSHALL, John Esmond, S/Lt. (A), 13.2.44.
MARTIN, Alistair Edgar, S/Lt. (A), 5.5.44.
MEDHURST, Peter Thurston, Lt. (A), 1.10.42.
MEIKLEJOHN, Arnott Roy, S/Lt. (A), 6.5.42.
MITCHELL, Lawrence Edmund, S/Lt. (A), 10.12.41.
MORRISON, Hugh, Lt. (A), 4.5.45.
MORRISON, John Craig, Lt. (A), 28.5.44.
MURPHY, Duncan Bryce, Lead/Air, 20.9.43.
NURSE, John Hugh, S/Lt. (A), 19.11.43.
OLDS, David Leonard, S/Lt. (A), 21.8.44.
PARKER, Godfrey Hudson, S/Lt. (A), 5.7.44.
PATERSON, Gray Duncan, S/Lt. (A), 30.6.44.
PATERSON, Robert Murray, Lead/Air, 26.2.42.
PATTERSON, Brian Arthur, Lead/Air, 13.5.42.
PATTERSON, Jack Campbell, S/Lt. (A), 5.3.43.
PEARCE, Arthur Leslie, S/Lt. (A), 27.1.45.
PEERS, Richard George, S/Lt. (A), 15.12.44.
PENNINGTON, Frank Athol Joseph, Lt/Cdr. (A), 24.4.44.
PEPPERELL, Jack Radford, S/Lt. (A), 1.5.42.
PICKARD, John Allnutt, S/Lt. (A), 26.6.42.

PRATT, Ernest Frank, S/Lt. (A), 19.1.43.
RAINES, Andrew Todd, S/Lt. (A), 23.9.42.
REEVES, John Henry, S/Lt. (A), 1.5.43.
REID, Francis Graham, S/Lt. (A), 12.3.44.
RICHARDS, Owen Grawden, S/Lt. (A), 14.3.43.
RICHARDSON, Archibald, Lt/Cdr. (A), 24.8.44.
ROBERTS, Kenneth Sutherland, S/Lt. (A), 7.6.44.
RYALLS, Grant, Lead/Air, 26.7.41.
SANDILANDS, George Victor, Lt. (A), 8.5.46.
SHADBOLT, Frederick John, Lead/Air, 17.11.44.
SHARP, Alan, S/Lt. (A), 19.8.44.
SHAW, Raymond Martin, Lt. (A), 26.10.44.
SHERRIFF, Ernest Charles, S/Lt. (A), 15.3.45.
SIME, Bruce, Lt. (A), 25.3.45.
SIMMONDS, Douglas, S/Lt. (A), 25.9.41.
SMALL, William Henry Hagar, S/Lt. (A), 6.12.43.
SPENCER, Charles Douglas, S/Lt. (A), 11.10.44.
STARK, Winston Vernon, S/Lt. (A), 7.3.43.
STREET, Arthur Robert, Lt. (A), 27.6.43.
TAIT, Douglas Haig, S/Lt. (A), 10.10.42.
TAYLOR, John Charles, S/Lt. (A), 10.4.43.
TAYLOR, Stuart Crouch, S/Lt. (A), 18.9.44.
THOMPSON, Arthur George, S/Lt. (A), 14.1.43.
THOMSON, Alexander Neilson, S/Lt. (A), 22.4.42.
THOMSON, Percy Donald, S/Lt. (A), 7.6.44.
TUCKER, Donald, P.O. (A), 29.12.41.
URLICH, Joseph John, S/Lt. (A), 9.9.43.
VOYSEY, Russel Lawrence, S/Lt. (A), 7.11.45.
WALLACE, John David, S/Lt. (A), 1.12.43.
WARNER, Desmond Harold, S/Lt. (A), 1.2.43.
WARNER, William Francis, S/Lt. (A), 12.11.42.
WAUGH, James Alexander, S/Lt. (A), 11.6.44.
WEATHERALL, Louis Frank, S/Lt. (A), 26.4.44.
WEBB, Douglas, S/Lt. (A), 29.1.45.
WEBB, John Fenner, Lt. (A), 11.5.44.
WEBBER, Alexander David Richmond, S/Lt. (A), 15.11.42.
WILLIAMS, Maurice Walton, S/Lt. (A), 23.5.44.
WILSON, Ian Lewis Ruxton, S/Lt. (A), 1.5.44.
WILSON, Rex Samuel, S/Lt. (A), 2.8.45.
WIREN, Lonsdale Hollis, Lt. (A), 4.6.43.
WOODWARD, Clive Eustace, S/Lt. (A), 24.8.44.

Appendix IV

69 Mill Road,
NEW PLYMOUTH

NEW ZEALAND

11/10/76

The Secretary
German Fighter Pilots Association
Luftwaffe Headquarters
Berlin
WEST GERMANY

Dear Sir,

As I am at present engaged in some research into naval air operations in Italy in 1943 I wondered whether you could furnish me with some details relating to an incident which took place over the beachhead at Salerno on 9th September 1943.

Early in the morning of that date I was a member of a flight of four Seafires from 897 Squadron operating from the aircraft carrier HMS *Unicorn*. Our duty was a high cover patrol at 26,000 feet above the beachhead and to intercept any hostile aircraft approaching that area. In the latter part of our two-hour patrol a radio signal was received from HMS *Palomares*, the invasion force fighter direction ship, to intercept an unidentified aircraft, which was not showing IFF (Identification Friend or Foe) on the ship's radar screen. The height of the interception was 30,000–31,000 ft. about 30 miles south east of Capri. On approaching the target, however, we discovered that it was an American Lightning aircraft showing the appropriate national marking.

We closed in, formed up on either side and exchanged visual greetings with the pilot.

At the debriefing session after our return to the carrier we were informed by the ship's intelligence officer that unbeknown to us, this Lightning was, in all probability flown by a German reconnaisance pilot.

This supposition was given evidence as a result of a radio listening unit which was based in HMS *Palomares* for the purpose of monitoring all German radio-traffic. It was suspected that one or more German aircraft were in a position to report on the progress of the landing and the deployment of the naval units.

As no German reconnaisance aircraft had been intercepted and it was most unusual to encounter a lone Lightning aircraft, not showing IFF at high altitude it was concluded that this could be the source of the German radio reports.

I am the sole surviving member of the four Fleet Air Arm pilots on this sortie, so I am interested to ascertain the reality of this incident, and if possible to contact the pilot of the Lightning Aircraft, if, in fact, it was flown by a German pilot.

Any information which you may be able to give me would be most appreciated.

Yours sincerely.
A. O. Masters

Herrn
A.O. Masters
69 Mill Road
New Plymouth
Neu Seeland

Betr.: Identifizierung eines deutschen Aufklärers, Einsatz Italien 2. Weltkrieg

Bezug: Ihr Schreiben vom 11.10.1976, hierher abgegeben

Sehr geehrter Herr Masters!

Die Unterlagen der Luftflotte 2 sowie die der wenigen in Italien eingesetzten fliegenden Verbände sind leider zu 90% vernichtet worden, soda es unmöglich ist, den von Ihnen geschilderten Fall zu klären. Ich bitte um Ihr Verständnis.

Hochachtungsvoll
Im Auftrag
(Noack)

Embassy of the
Federal Republic of Germany
Wellington
RK 520 SE Masters

Wellington, March 7th, 1977
PO Box 1687
KB/Cr

Mr A. D. Masters
69 Mill Road
New Plymouth

Dear Mr Masters,
re: your letter of Feb. 28th, 1977,
This Embassy regrets to have to inform you that due to shortage of staff this office is not in a position to do any translation work. Please return to a translation service, such as

Wellington Chamber of Commerce
Translation Service
PO Box 1590
Wellington

or

Commercial Translations
PO Box 2768
Auckland

Your enclosure is returned herewith.

Yours faithfully
(K. D. Brock)

Courtesy translation: The 'Bundesarchiv' regret that they cannot answer your question, since more than 90% of the files on the Air Squadron 2 and the united in Italy have been destroyed.

Appendix V

EXECUTION BY JAPANESE OF FLEET AIR ARM OFFICERS

Sub-Lieutenant (A) J. K. Haberfield, RNZNVR, of HMS *Indomitable*, and Sub-Lieuteant (A) E. J. Baxter, RNZNVR, of HMS *Illustrious*, were shot down on 26 January 1945 during an attack on the oil refineries at Palembang, Sumatra. They were captured by the Japanese and, in February 1945, sent to Singapore where they were placed in Outram Road gaol. At the end of July 1945 they were executed, together with seven other Fleet Air Arm pilots.

Earlier reports said that the prisoners were missing after the transport in which they were being taken to Japan from Singapore had been sunk by Allied air bombing in the middle of March 1945.

Koh, a Chinese prisoner in Sumatra, said that after his release on 20 February 1945 it was town gossip that the photograph of a well-built, blindfolded pilot prisoner was shown for propaganda purposes at the premises of the Palembang *Sumboeng*, a local newspaper. From the description it tallied with that of Haberfield. Koh said that Haberfield was admitted to the Palembang Prison on or about 1 February 1945. When he was being interrogated, his requests for food and water were refused. On the seventh day of his confinement Haberfield was taken, blindfolded, to an unknown destination.

Lieutenant-Commander L. F. G. Pritchard, RNVR, who was responsible for the investigation of this atrocity, said that in September 1945 it was known that thirty-two pilots had been lost. A report was received that certain British prisoners had been executed and they were thought to be Fleet Air Arm pilots. Investigations were continued for a month and it was found that they were not Fleet Air Arm pilots. The inquiry then had to start afresh.

This time it was begun at Palembang, where it was learned that nine Fleet Air Arm pilots had been sent thence to Singapore. After many people in Singapore had been interrogated, Captain Toshio Kataoka was found; he said that the men had been shipped to Japan, but on their way the ship was sunk and all were presumed to have been drowned.

'We thought that was the truth, because as a rule in a big centre the Japanese did not execute prisoners of war without a court martial. After a few weeks General Atsuka, who was Chief of the Judicial Department of the 7th Area Army, Singapore, let the cat out of the bag. He did so because he thought we knew that these men had been executed without trial and he did not want his department to be blamed. He gave the rumours he had heard before the Japanese surrender. Within 24 hours we had the whole story, or a good part of it and sent out orders for the arrest of the culprits. They were warned at 6 p.m. that they would be going to Singapore next day and were not prepared to face the music and committed suicide on 26 December 1945. There were others who were believed to be implicated in the affair and it is possible that they may be brought to trial as accomplices.'

There was no trial before the execution of the prisoners. The two Japanese particularly concerned were Captain Toshio Kataoka, who was the senior officer, and a Captain Ikeda. These men committed suicide.

Kataoka, in a will made before his suicide, said:

> We took nine prisoners from Outram Road in a lorry to the beach at the northernmost end of Changi and executed them with Japanese swords. The bodies were put in a boat prepared beforehand and sunk in the sea with weights attached. Now that the responsibility must be borne out publicly, I hereby pay for my deeds with suicide.

It was not until 15th August 1992 47 years after the Japanese surrender that a memorial tablet was installed in the Changi Prison memorial to officially recognise the diabolical execution of these 9 gallant naval airmen.

Their names had not previously been included in the main Krangi war memorial at Singapore.

Appendix VI

Fleet Air Arm Songs

MR INSTRUCTOR

Oh, Mr Instructor – Oh, Mr Instructor,
Can you tell me how my flying's been assessed?
Though I spin out of control,
When I try a half flick roll,
A guy can do no better than his best.

Oh, Mr Pupil – Oh, Mr Pupil,
Say, your best is not quite good enough for me.
You'll enjoy much better health
In a thing that rolls itself.
    In a Martlet, Mr Instructor?
    In a corvette, Mr P.

Oh, Mr Instructor – Oh, Mr Instructor,
These precautionary landings are a bore.
For my technique is a treat,
Holding off at zero feet,
Can you tell me what this horn is sounding for?

Oh, Mr Pupil – Oh, Mr Pupil,
There's a lever on your left side, don't you see,
Its position you should check,
Or you'll land too close the deck.
    Three-pointer, Mr Instructor?
    On your belly, Mr P.

Oh, Mr Instructor – Or, Mr Instructor,

Hunting U-boats is quite easy they tell me.
Why it's just a piece of cake,
When you see a U-boat's wake,
You drop your bombs and buzz off home to tea.

Oh, Mr Pupil – Oh, Mr Pupil,
A Marine dive-bombed a U-boat out at sea,
But his aim was much too sound,
In ten minutes he came round.
In the water, Mr Instructor?
In the U-boat, Mr P.

THE BARRIER SONG
(Air: 'Elmer's Tune')

Why does Corbett get morbid and give a dirty look,
When he lands upon the deck and forgets about his hook,
What does Doolan start foolin' and give his bus the gun,
The Barrier, my son!

CHORUS

Barrier! Barrier!
It's the biggest bugbear in a Carrier,
Batsmen, crazy,
You feel helpless as you float,
And the Goofers stand and gloat.

Why is Regan just seekin' another place for lust,
Why is Henton just bent on a pilot he can trust,
Why does Mac get the sack from position number one,
The Barrier, my son!

CHORUS

Why is Johnson like a Ronson when he flickers in the gloom,
And he navigates his pilot, almost to his ruddy doom,
Why is Newton away shootin', guess the Monk must,
have his fun,
The Barrier, my son!

CHORUS

As for Buster, well he must'a done a lot of time – then some,
And apart from sundry minor faults is really not so dumb,
But if we hang on long enough the time is sure to come,
    The Barrier, my son!

CHORUS

THE AIR-SEA RESCUE
(Air: 'The Church's One Foundation')

We are the Air-Sea Rescue,
  No flaming use are we,
The only time you'll see us
  Is breakfast, lunch and tea
And when you're in your dinghy
  By day or in the night,
Per ardua ad astra,
  Up you, Jack, we're all right.

THANKS FOR THE MEMORY
(Air: 'Thanks for the Memory')

Thanks for the memory,
Of biplanes in the sky,
Of pilots who could fly,
Of four-hour trip, attacking ships,
Returning with a sigh,
How lovely it was.

Thanks for the memory,
Of large fixed undercarts,
Of Hatson playing darts.
Of Buster rushing around,
To fix old Digger for spare parts,
How lovely it was.

Many's the time we've pranged 'em,
On many an A.L.T.,

And many's the time we've slanged 'em:
No A.S.V.! No W/T!

So thanks for the memory,
Of drunken nights ashore,
Of love and life galore
Of gin and limes and flying times,
And popsies by the score,
How lovely it was.

Thanks for the memory,
Of pitching decks at night,
Of pilots full of fright,
Of taking off with little wind,
And dropping out of sight,
How lovely it was.

We said 'good-bye' to the carrier
We gave all our aircraft away,
And now we've no fear of the barrier,
For here we'll stay for many a day.

So thanks for the memory,
Of only one front gun,
With which to hack the Hun,
Of hangar toil and dripping oil,
And 'gen' that weighed a ton,
How lovely it was.

RUM AND COCA-COLA
(Air: 'Rum and Coca-Cola')

CHORUS

Drinking rum and coca-cola,
Drink whisky, play tombola,
Brandy's my consola,
Let's fill this ship with alcohola!

The British came to old Hongkong,
And found surrender going wrong,

Instead of signing on 'Indom'
The blighters chose the new 'Anson'!

CHORUS

Now the 'Anson' came from old U.K.,
She broke down three times on the way,
She never fired a shot in anger,
No kamikaze ever pranged 'er!

CHORUS

Now the 'Indom' lay off old Kai Tak,
We must admit she looked a wreck,
The 'Anson' gleaming in the sun,
Had never fired a ruddy gun!

CHORUS

When Kamikaze hit 'Indom',
Branch types sang this solemn song,
With enemy we'll come to grips,
Not like these ruddy battleships!

CHORUS

Day after day, day after day,
It seems that we are here to stay,
And lie rotting 'neath the sun,
With sampans, junks and B.S. One!

CHORUS

EASTERN FLEET SONG
(Air: 'Bless 'Em All')

They say that the Fleet came to Trincomalee,
  Early in 'forty-four,
Heavily laden with men with the gen,
  Bound for the Japanese war.

There's 'Vic' and 'Indom' and 'Illustrious', too,
  The 'Indefat' came for the ride.
You get no promotion in the Indian Ocean,
  We'd rather be back in the Clyde.

CHORUS

In the Clyde, in the Clyde,
  Where the runways are half a mile wide,
You get no promotion in the Indian Ocean,
We'd rather be back in the Clyde.

They say that the Racecourse is full of fine types,
  And Puttalam's pilots are swell,
The Wrens down at Katukurunda are nice,
  But Minnerya's climate is hell.
The Galle Face is galling, the Silver Fawn smells,
  And Kandy's got a helluva ride,
You get no promotion in the Indian Ocean,
We'd rather be back in the Clyde.

CHORUS

The booze is all rationed, the popsies are, too,
  The CO is getting the twitch,
I've had impetigo, foot-rot, prickly heat,
  And everyone's got Dhobie's itch.
There's Corsairs and Hellcats all over the sky,
  An Avenger's gone over the side,
You get no promotion in the Indian Ocean,
  We'd rather be back in the Clyde.

CHORUS

YOU CAN'T GO TO HEAVEN
(Old Negro Spiritual)

Oh! You can't go to heaven in a Barracuda Two,
'Cos a Barracuda Two won't see you through. (Repeat)

CHORUS

I ain't a-goin'a grieve my Lord no more,
I ain't a-goin'a grieve my Lord no more,
I ain't a-goin'a grieve my Lord no more.

Oh! You can't go to heaven in a Ford Coupé,
'Cos the Lord he got shares in Chevrolet. (Repeat)

CHORUS

Oh! You can't go to heaven in a T B F,
'Cos the Lord he ain't got not V II.F. (Repeat)

CHORUS

Oh! You can't go to heaven in a woman's arms,
'Cos the Lord he don't hold with da feminine charms. (Repeat)

CHORUS

Oh! You can't go to heaven on roller-skates,
You'll roll right past them pearly gates. (Repeat)

CHORUS

Oh! You can't go to heaven if you're CO,
'Cos all CO's go down below. (Repeat)

CHORUS

THE STRINGBAG SONG

(Air: 'My Bonnie Lies Over The Ocean')

My Stringbag flies over the ocean,
My Stringbag flies over the sea,
If it wasn't for King George's Swordfish,
Where the hell would the Royal Navy be?

CHORUS

Stringbag, Stringbag,
Oh, bring back my Stringbag to me, to me
Stringbag, Stringbag,
Oh, bring back my Stringbag to me.

At Taranto and chase of the Bismarck,
In the Battle of Cape Matapan,
'Twas the fish from the Swordfish that fixed 'em,
And those who could run, how they ran!

CHORUS

Now the science of dropping torpedoes
Is taught at RNAS Crail,
Where the instruction's so good that pupil
With the Swordfish aren't likely to fail.

CHORUS

No doubt when we get Barracudas,
The Swordfish's day will be done,
So remember, 'twas this kite that fixed 'em,
And gave them their place in the sun!

CHORUS

FORTRESS SONG

(Air: 'John Brown's Body')

We're flying flaming Fortresses,
At fifty thousand feet,
We're flying over Germany,
To give the Huns a treat.
We've bags of ammunition,
And a flaming little bomb,
And we drop the blighter from so high,
We don't know where's it gone.

CHORUS

What a flaming awful aircraft,
What a flaming awful aircraft,
What a flaming awful aircraft,
And we drop the blighter from so high,
We don't know where it's gone.

We're flying flaming Swordfish,
At fifty flaming feet,
We're flying out through rain and hail,
And snow and flaming sleet,
And when we think we're flying south
We find we're flying north,
And we make our flaming landfall
In the Firth of flaming Forth.

CHORUS

We're flying Barracudas,
And we're getting bags of twitch,
We sit up there a-thinking of
The time we've got to ditch,
Our job's to find the enemy
And sink him with a fish.
But to get back home to England,
Is our only flaming wish.

A.25

(Air: 'Charlotte the Harlot')

They say in the RAF that the landing's okay,
If the pilot gets out and can still walk away,
But in the Fleet Air Arm the prospect is grim
If the landing's p . . . poor and the pilot can't swim.

CHORUS

Cracking show! I'm alive!
But I've still got to render my A.25.

I fly for a living and not just for fun,
I'm not very anxious to hack down the Hun;
And as for deck-landings at night in the dark-
As I told Wings this morning, 'Damn that for a lark!'

CHORUS

When the batsman gives 'Lower'! I always go higher,
I drift o'er to starboard and prang a Seafire,
The boys in the Goofers all think that I'm green,
But I gets me commission from Supermarine.

CHORUS

I thought I was coming in low enough, but-
I was fifty feet up when the batsman gave 'Cut!'
Loud in my earholes the sweet angels sang,
'Float, float, float, float, float, float, float, float, float, PRANG!'

CHORUS

As I sat on the squirter awaiting the kick,
Amusing myself by rotating the stick,
Down went the blue flag, the thing gave a turn,
'Gor blimey,' said Wings, 'He's gone over the stern.'

CHORUS

They gave me a Seafire to beat up the fleet;
I polished off the 'Nelson' and 'Rodney' a treat,
Forgot all the masts that stick out from 'Formid'-
Now a seat in the Goofers is worth fifty quid!

CHORUS

When you come o'er the round down and see old Wings frown,
You can safely assume that your hook isn't down;
A ruddy great barrier looms up ahead,
There's a shout from old Wings, 'Let us pray for the dead.'

CHORUS

Now I come to the end of last ruddy verse,
And to all you sprog pilots I am really am terse,
Keep your eye on the Batsman, the Clock and the Deck,
And you'll carry on flying and not break your neck.

CHORUS

I DON'T WANT TO JOIN THE NAVY

I don't want to join the Navy,
  I don't want to go to sea,
I'd rather hang around Piccadilly and The Strand,
  And live upon the earnings of a high-born lady.
I don't want a bullet in my ear-hole,
  I don't want my necktie shot away,
No, I'd rather stay in England, in Merry, Merry England,
  And roger all my blooming life away!

BALLS UP
(Air: 'The Hut Zat Song')

CHORUS:
There's a balls-up on the Flight Deck,
And the Wavy Navy's done it.
There's a balls-up on the Gangway,
And they don't know who to blame.

The 'K.G.V's' ten miles astern,
  She should be twelve ahead,
'Cos every turn by a makee learn
  Reads blue instead of red.

CHORUS

Twelve Albacores were neatly ranged
  To bomb and blitz Bodo,
Commander 'F' was sold a pup,
  'Cos seven wouldn't go.

CHORUS

The Captain's walk is disturbed by the talk,
  Of the fishermen on the rail,
Discussing skirt and swapping dirt,
  From Hatson, Twatt and Crail.

CHORUS

There's reds galore from an Albacore,
  Hell diving for the drink,
Di-da, di-da comes from afar,
  As a Fulmar starts to sink.

CHORUS

A solitary straight 'A' stood and sighed,
  As the first one hit the barrier
'My God! These blighters may wear Wings,
  But they're no damn use on a Carrier.'

FURIOUS SONG
(Air: 'Lily of Laguna')

We are the 'Furious',
We're mighty strange and curious,
Here we lie at anchor all the day,
Waiting for a signal from the RAA,
We range up aircraft, we range up aircraft,
In the morning,
And then we strike down in the evening,
There'll be no flying for today.

ANY OLD IRON
(Adapted from original Fulmar Song-809 Squadron)

Any old iron! Any old iron! Any, any, any old iron!
Down at Lee you get them free,
Built by Fairey for a crew of three.
Not much use, no ruddy juice,

No nice bunk to lie on.
So you know what to do with your Barracuda Two,
  Old iron! Old iron!

Any old iron! Any old iron! Any, any, any old iron!
Tail up high pointing to the sky,
Nobody knows if the blighter will fly.
Your first flight, too much fright,
A kite you can't rely on,
So you know what to do with your Barracuda Two,
  Old iron! Old iron!

The Naval Version of Lili Marlene

Underneath the lantern
By the barrack gate,
Darling, I remember
The way you used to wait;
'Twas there that you whispered tenderly
That you loved me.
You'd always be
My Lili of the lamplight,
My own Lili Marlene.

Orders came for sailing
Somewhere over there,
All confined to barracks
Was more than I could bear;
I knew you were waiting in the street.
I heard your feet,
But could not meet:
My Lili of the lamplight,
My own Lili Marlene.

About October 1944 I formed the idea that I might be able to terminate my batting appointment by applying for 'foreign service leave' in New Zealand.

Hereunder is a copy of a signal from the Admiralty in London to RANASIO (Rear Admiral Naval Air Stations Indian Ocean) repeated to Royal Naval Air Station, Puttalam.

RANASIO

(R) RNAS PUTTALAM ADMIRALTY
SECRET – IMPORTANT

Your 3010382 October. Regret owing to shortage DLCO's no relief available at present for Sub-Lieut Masters.

T/D P/L TOO 181346A
1.2.3.4.23 November 44T.OR 200230 T.G.

Deck Landing Training School, Easthaven
Long Course – Part I.
DLCO Course completed
. . . 30.4.44

Assessed: *AVERAGE*

Date . . . (Sgd.) . . .

LIEUT-COMMANDER, RN

HMS Unicorn
S/Lt (A) A. Masters RNZNVR has completed four deck landings on Corsairs and is considered competent to deck land Corsairs by day.
Signed . . .
Assessment: Above Average Date: 24th Jan 1945

Glossary

Adrift (1) absent without leave
(2) to return late from leave
Akkers – cash
Andrew – the Royal Navy
Asdic – submarine detection equipment
Batsman – deck landing control officer
Belay – to stop
e.g. belay the pipe – means ignore the last instruction
Bible Bosun – the ship's padre
Bells & Smells – Malta
Blood Bucket – ship's lifeboat
Bought it – killed on operations
Bubbly – rum
Buffer – Chief Bosun's Mate
Bulk heads – walls within the ship
Bunting tosser – signalman
Carley float – a life raft
Cashed his chips – killed on operations
Cha – tea
Chippy – the ship's carpenter
Chokka – fed up, frustrated
Crash the swede – have a sleep
Cox'n – senior chief seaman petty officer
– the helmsman
Dhobying – washing laundry
Dipped – to fail a training course
Ditty box – a receptacle for personal effects
Dose – VD
Fo'c'sle – the forward part of the ship
Gash – rubbish, garbage
Golden rivet – a mythical installation at the bottom of the ship's hull

Gone for a burton – killed
God walloper – ship's padre
Gremlin – a mythical object that exists on surfaces of an aircraft and causes accidents
Guns – ship's gunnery officer
Heads – ship's toilet
Hooky – a killick
H.O.'s – hostilities only men
Jack – a term to describe all sailors
Jacob's ladder – a ladder over the ship's side
Jankers – punishment
Jaunty – the ship's master at arms
Jimmy – first lieutenant
Killick – a leading hand, the anchor badge worn by a leading hand
Knackers – testicles
Knockshop – brothel
Kye – cocoa
Lid – the sailor's cap – to lift your lid is to remove your cap
Make & mend – a ship's holiday
Matelot – French for all sailors
Nelson's Blood – navy rum. (After death Nelson was preserved in a barrel of navy rum.)
O.D. – an ordinary seaman – the lowest rating
Oggin – the sea
OOD – officer of the day
OOW – officer of the watch
Oppo – a friend
Ossifer – an officer
Pipe – an order of the ship's loudspeaker
Pipe down – time to go to sleep
Pipes out – the order to return to work
Pompey – Portsmouth Barracks
Pongo – a soldier
Pontius Pilate – a naval padre
Poodle-faker – a matelot who constantly chases females
Prang – an aircraft crash
Pusser – origin purser, the keeper of the purse
– ship's stores officer, hence pussers store,
– pusser issue
Prune – a useless RAF pilot
Quarter deck – officers' quarters at the after end of the ship
Rattle, in the rattle – under punishment

Rescrub – to be given a second chance to pass a course
Ringer – officers' ring
sub-lieutenant – one ringlieutenant – two rings
lieutenant commander – $2^1/_2$ rings
commander – 3 rings
captain – 4 rings
Rig 'o the day – dress of the day
also square rig and fore and aft rig
describing two types of uniforms, matelots and petty officers
Sick pay tiffy – sick berth attendant
Sippers – A share of one's daily tot of rum. The daily tot is supposed to be consumed on the spot, but sometimes 'sippers' can be saved and bottled for shore leave etc.
Scratcher – bed or hammock
Skurs – a matelot wearing a beard
derived from whiskers
Sky pilot – naval padre
Slops – clothing & bedding issued from Pussers Store
Snotty – a midshipman
Sparks – a wireless rating
Splice the mainbrace – a special issue of rum on special occasions
Stripey – a matelot who wore good conduct chevrons on his sleeve, usually with no other badge of rank
Subby – a sub-lieutenant
Swing the hook – to hide or be idle
Tally – the ship's name on the cap
Ticklers – duty free cigarettes
Tiddley – ship shape, good looking, well dressed
Tin fish – a torpedo
Toothey – dental officer
Wings – commander flying
Little Wings – lieutenant commander flying